Child Development in Social Context 3

Growing up in a Changing Society

Child Development in Social Context

Other volumes in the series:

Volume 1 Becoming a Person
Edited by Martin Woodhead, Ronnie Carr and Paul Light

Volume 2 Learning to Think
Edited by Paul Light, Sue Sheldon and Martin Woodhead

If you would like to study this course, please write to The Central Enquiries Office, The Open University, Walton Hall, Milton Keynes MK7 6AA for a prospectus and application form. For more specific information write to The Higher Degrees Office at the same address.

Child Development in Social Context 3

Growing up in a Changing Society

A Reader edited by
Martin Woodhead, Paul Light and
Ronnie Carr
at The Open University

London and New York
In association with The Open University

First published 1991
by Routledge
11 New Fetter Lane, London EC4P 4EE

Simultaneously published in the USA and Canada
by Routledge
a division of Routledge, Chapman and Hall, Inc.
29 West 35th Street, New York, NY 10001

Typeset by Witwell Ltd, Southport
Printed and bound in Great Britain by Mackays of Chatham PLC, Kent

British Library Cataloguing in Publication Data
Child development in social context.
  Vol. 3, Growing up in a changing society: areader
  1. Children. Development. Cultural factors
  I. Woodhead, Martin II. Light, Paul III. Carr, Ronnie
  IV. Open University
  155.4

  ISBN 0–415–05826–0
  ISBN 0–415–05827–9 pbk

Library of Congress Cataloguing in Publication Data
has been applied for

  ISBN 0–415–05826–0
  ISBN 0–415–05827–9 (pbk)

Contents

Figures and Tables

Preface

Child Development in Social Context is a module of the Open University's taught MA in Education. This is the third of three volumes of readings specially selected to serve as students' major source material. They should provide suitable reading for all psychology students, as well as teachers and others concerned with child development and education. These readings cover a range of topics from infancy through to the primary school years. They illustrate the increasing attention now being paid by developmental psychologists to social context and social relationships as fundamental in shaping the course of development, the processes of learning and thinking, and the construction of personal identity and educational achievement.

The emphasis on social context in developmental psychology is evident at various levels. In terms of methodology, there is growing dissatisfaction with artificial experimental procedures. Bronfenbrenner (1977) was prompted to remark: 'much of contemporary developmental psychology is the science of the strange behaviour of children in strange situations with strange adults for the briefest possible periods of time'. Whereas in the past developmental psychologists tended to model their work on the physical sciences, referring at conferences to 'research going on in my lab', many are now spending time squatting in the corners of sitting-rooms and classrooms making naturalistic observations of everyday life in families and schools. Of course there is still a place for controlled experiments, and modern research technologies have greatly amplified the power of the researcher's observations. This is especially true in the field of infancy, where frame-by-frame analysis of fleeting everyday encounters between young children and their parents has greatly enriched our understanding of interrelationships between the responsiveness of care-givers and the emerging competencies of children. This line of work is well illustrated by many of the articles in the first volume of the series, *Becoming a Person*.

Taking account of context is not only about adopting sensitive research methods. As Richards and Light (1986: 1) put it: 'social context is . . . intrinsic to the developmental process itself'. It is not just 'the icing on the cake, it is as much a part of its structure as the flour or eggs'. This is nowhere more clearly illustrated than in changing perspectives on cognitive development during the past decade. Piaget's theory has informed a popular image of the child as a solitary thinker struggling to construct a personal understanding of the mathematical and logical properties of the physical world. But this image is now giving way to a view of the child being initiated into shared cultural understandings through close relationships with parents and teachers, as well as siblings and peers. Viewing children's learning and thinking as embedded in social relationships owes much to the insights of Vygotsky. It is the major theme of the second volume of the series, *Learning to Think*.

The co-existence of these very different paradigms of child development is a reminder of psychology's ambivalent position as a science. While the psychologist may rightly keep one foot firmly in the exactitude of the laboratory, the other foot is entangled in more ephemeral cultural ideas about the nature and needs of children. Major psychological accounts of the child have not originated independently of social and educational practices, nor arguably should they. The problems arise when scientific statements become ethical imperatives, or when descriptive accounts became normative (Kessen 1979). This tendency is well illustrated by the role of psychological theory in reinforcing social attitudes to child care in and out of the family. This issue, along with studies of development in that more recent cultural invention, the school, is amongst the topics of this third volume in the series, *Growing up in a Changing Society*.

The underlying theme of all these volumes is that the study of the individual child, once taken to be the solid bedrock on which to build psychological knowledge, turns out to be a shifting sand. Children are physically distinct and separated off, but psychologically they are embedded in a particular society and culture. Clearly, in adopting this perspective, there are dangers of substituting for an untenable universalistic model of human development an extreme culturally relativistic model which, as Campbell has acknowledged, carries the risk of 'ontological nihilism' (cited in Edelstein 1983). In defence, there is no dispute that children inherit a distinctive human nature. However the expression of that nature depends on another distinctive inheritance, human society and culture.

In one sense the new emphasis on context in child development represents a long-overdue rapprochement between the individualism of psychology, the social structural concerns of sociology and the cultural descriptions of anthropology. The idea that individuals are shaped by the social order is of course the 'bread and butter' of introductory sociology courses. But just as psychology has remained myopic about the significance of social influences, so sociology has failed to look seriously beyond such favourite general concepts as 'socialization' and 'social reproduction', in search of a more thorough understanding of the process of interpenetration between the social and the individual. The problem has been characterized by Super and Harkness (1981) by analogy with the well-known perceptual conflict between figure and ground popularized by 'gestalt' psychologists. Hopefully the current shift towards a more context-sensitive psychology will restructure the gestalt sufficiently that we shall before long be able to hold figure and ground, individual and social context, simultaneously in perspective.

REFERENCES

Bronfenbrenner, U. (1977) 'Toward an experimental ecology of human development', *American Psychologist* 32: 513–31.

Edelstein, W. (1983) 'Cultural constraints on development and the vicissitudes of progress', in F.S. Kessel and A.W. Siegel (eds) *The Child and Other Cultural Inventions*, New York: Praeger.

Kessen, W. (1979) 'The American child and other cultural inventions', *American Psychologist*, 34: 815–20.

Richards, M. and Light, P. (1986) *Children of Social Worlds*, Cambridge: Polity Press.

Super, C.M. and Harkness S. (1981) 'Figure, ground and gestalt: the cultural context of the active individual', in R.M. Lerner and N.A. Busch-Nagel (eds) *Individuals as Producers of Their Own Development*, New York: Academic Press.

Part one

Concepts of childhood, concepts of parenthood

Introduction

The lesson of history and anthropology . . . [is] . . . that many varieties of development are possible, and that our notions of maturity, attachment, abilities, stages of development – even the notion of childhood itself – are very specific to our culture.

(Ingleby 1986: 301)

We consider ourselves a 'child-centred' society. Patterns of care, health provision, schooling and recreation are based on elaborate conceptions about the nature and needs of children at each stage from conception to maturity. Developmental psychology plays a major part in elaborating these conceptions through theory, systematic observation and controlled experimentation. It is this scientifically-informed concept of childhood that in large measure defines our expectations of parenthood, as well as the roles defined for those professionally assigned to promoting children's interests, notably their teachers. Unfortunately scientific descriptions all too readily become translated into cultural prescriptions, and theoretical conjectures into universal certainties. The first three chapters invite us to step back from this process and recognize various respects in which the concept of childhood, the tasks of parenthood and teaching, and even theories of child development may all be culturally located.

Levine and White (Chapter 1) offer a very broad historical/ anthropological perspective on the way late-twentieth century concepts of childhood are associated with urbanization, industrialization, declining birth and infant mortality rates, the growth of mass schooling and the rise of public interest in children. Whereas in agrarian societies children are an important economic asset, and are rapidly initiated into specific valued skills and social relationships, childhood is a period of protracted immaturity in western societies; children are valued for their capacity to reciprocate love and affection and the emphasis of their rearing is on broad-based play and learning in preparation for an uncertain future.

The increasing attention paid to psychological aspects of development is closely linked to the rapid growth of child psychology this century, especially in North America. In Chapter 2 Kessen suggests that not only is it our conceptions of childhood that should be recognized as a cultural invention, but also this ephemeral status extends to the supposedly scientific discipline of psychology itself. Even if psychologists choose to practise their trade in a laboratory setting, with all the apparent clinical control of white-coated technicians, the subjects they study, the research questions they ask and the concepts they apply to interpreting their data are necessarily imported from the culture-drenched outside world.

Later in the chapter Kessen makes the radical claim that the influence of dominant cultural values even extends to that most basic of assumptions – that the proper unit of analysis for child psychology is the child: 'Impulses are in the child; traits are in the child; thoughts are in the child; attachments are in the child'. To Kessen's list we might add that according to the culture of individualism, 'needs' are also believed to be within the child. The place of children's needs in psychology and social policy is the subject of a close study by Woodhead (Chapter 3). He argues that the device of identifying 'children's needs' has enabled professional, policy-makers and child care experts alike to make apparently objective statements about immutable laws of childhood, which in many cases represent little more than the projection on to children of a complex of cultural values and attitudes. The challenge in providing an adequate theory of childhood is to disentangle the scientific from the evaluative and the natural from the culture.

REFERENCE

Ingleby, D. (1986) 'Development in social context', in M. Richards and P. Light (eds) *Children of Social Worlds*, Cambridge: Polity Press.

1   Revolution in parenthood

Robert A. Levine and Merry I. White
Source: R. A. Levine and M. I. White (1986) *Human
Conditions: The Cultural Basis of Educational Development,*
London: Routledge & Kegan Paul, ch. 3.

During the past 200 years, the conditions of child development in
much of the world have changed more drastically than they had in
millennia – perhaps since the spread of agrarian conditions after 7000
BC. The history of this recent change can be traced numerically, with
school enrollments rising and infant mortality rates falling; when
countries industrialized, populations moved to the city and families
reduced their fertility. It can be told as a moral tale, with the
elimination of child labor and illiteracy, when parents and public
policy-makers alike recognized the rights and expanded the
opportunities of children. It can be, and often is, looked upon as a
struggle for the welfare of children which is not yet won, particularly
since many of the conditions abolished in the industrial countries, e.g.
high infant mortality, illiteracy and child labor, still exist in the Third
World.

However one regards this shift, it represents a fundamental change
not only in the means by which children are raised but also in the
reasons for which they are brought into the world and the goals which
they pursue during their lives. It is a change we are only beginning to
understand in terms of its history, its causes and its contemporary
directions. This chapter provides an overview of its major elements,
particularly in the West, and considers its implications for the
comparative analysis of parenthood and child development.

The social changes we review have undermined the agrarian
conceptions of the life span [. . .] particularly the centrality of fertility
and filial loyalty in the social identities of men and women. This shift
has occurred in the industrial countries of the West, Eastern Europe
and Japan. It has been occurring, and continues, in certain countries
of the Third World, though not uniformly within those countries. That
the shift deserves to be called 'revolutionary' can hardly be disputed;

the question is whether it should be thought of as one revolution or many. Are all the socio-economic, demographic, educational and ideological changes involved but different aspects of one comprehensive process of social transformation (e.g. 'modernization') or separable processes that happen to be linked in particular historical cases? Are the sequences and outcomes of recent change – particularly in Japan and the Third World – replicating those of the past, particularly of nineteenth-century Europe and the United States?

This question, even in specific regard to family life, has concerned sociologists for a long time, but many of them chose to resolve it by positing a unitary process, driving history in a single direction – in advance of strong empirical evidence. In retrospect, theories of global modernization, like the classical Marxist stages of history, seem examples of what Hirschman (1979) has called 'paradigms as a hindrance to understanding': they prevented taking diversity seriously enough, until evidence of diversity overwhelmed the very theories that had denied their importance. Fortunately, social scientists have brought a wealth of new evidence to bear on questions of historical change in family life and the conditions of child development in social and cultural settings throughout the world. This evidence points to a history of the family changing in response to specific local conditions rather than moving in one preordained direction.

The abandonment of unilinear evolution as a conceptual framework for analyzing social change in family life does not mean the denial of recurrent trends that can be documented and are clearly significant. On the contrary, those broad trends must be the starting-point for our inquiry. We begin with a brief consideration of the radically diverse perspectives from which children are viewed in the contemporary world, both in the private contexts of family life and the public contexts of national and international policy. Then we ask: How did it come to be this way? How did human societies develop such differing perspectives on children? In our view, this amounts to asking how – given a world with primarily agrarian perspectives only two centuries ago – did some societies move so far from these perspectives? [. . .]

THE MEANINGS OF CHILDREN: DIFFERENCES AND SIMILARITIES IN THE CONTEMPORARY WORLD

In contrast with agrarian values, the cultures of industrialized countries, particularly their middle-class subcultures, tend to value parent–child relationships which provide unilateral support – economic, emotional and social – from parents to their children, with parents not

Table 1.1 Advantages of having children: per cent mentioning economic utility

	Urban middle class	Rural
Japan	2	11
Taiwan	3	36
Philippines	30	60

Source: Arnold *et al.* 1975: Table 4.4

expected to receive anything tangible in return. The period of such support in Western societies has been lengthening, from childhood through adolescence into adulthood, and the proportion of family resources devoted to children increasing.

The current state of the evidence has been summarized by Hoffman and Manis (1979):

> [The] economic value of children is particularly salient among rural parents and in countries where the economy is primarily rural. In addition, children are often seen as important for security in old age. Children are valued for this function, particularly where there is no official, trusted, and acceptable provision for the care of the aged and disabled.
>
> In a highly industrialized country like the United States, however, with a government-sponsored social security system, children are less likely to have economic utility. Even their utility in rural areas might be lessened because of rural mechanization and the greater availability of hired help. And, since the cost of raising children is higher in the more urban and industrially advanced countries, children are not likely to be seen as an economic asset.
> (Hoffman and Manis 1979: 590)

When a national sample of Americans was asked about the advantages of having children, only 3.1 per cent of the white mothers with more than twelve years of schooling gave answers involving economic utility (Hoffman and Manis 1979: 585). The rest of that sub-sample mentioned a variety of social, emotional and moral benefits. The responses of East Asian mothers to this question help to place the American figure in a global context [Table 1.1].

In the industrial countries, Japan and Taiwan, the proportion of urban middle-class respondents mentioning the economic utility of children is virtually identical to the more educated white mothers in the United States, despite differences in culture. In the Philippines, a largely agrarian country, the proportion of the urban middle class perceiving economic benefits in children is ten times higher. Within each of the three Asian countries, with national policies of old-age assistance held constant, the rural proportion is at least twice as high as that of the urban middle class. While such figures from one limited question are only suggestive, they show the magnitude of the differences in attitudes and their powerful association with agrarian life both within and between contemporary countries.

The fact that the majority of middle-class parents in industrial countries expect no tangible return from children is paradoxical, not only from the perspective of utilitarian economics, which assumes that substantial investment must be motivated by the expectation of material return, but also from the viewpoint of agrarian cultures, in which reciprocity between the generations is a basic principle of social life. It does not seem paradoxical to most Westerners, who take it for granted that the parent–child relationship is exempted from ideas of material return and long-term reciprocation.

Indeed, the Western notion that the welfare of children should represent the highest priority for society as well as parents and that children should be unstintingly supported without calculation of reward – a revolutionary idea in world history – has established itself as an unchallengeable principle of international morality. The most fervent support for the idea, however, continues to come from northwestern Europe and the United States, where the public defense of children is an established cultural tradition, religious and secular, generating symbols used to arouse intense emotions, mobilize voluntary activity and subsidize programs of action.

What is most remarkable about this basically Western ideology that has been accepted in international forums as a universal moral code is that it entails a passionate concern with the welfare of *other people's children*. In other words, it presumes that the current well-being and future development of children are the concern and responsibility not only of their parents but also of a community – local, national and international – that is not based on kinship. Westerners are proud, for example, of the long and ultimately successful campaign against child labor waged by reformers in their own countries, but their ideology requires that such benefits be extended to all children everywhere. In some Western countries such as Sweden, the Netherlands and Canada, there is more concern with, and activity on behalf of, poor children in Third World societies than there is among the privileged segments of the latter societies. This gap in cultural values belies the apparent consensus embodied in UN declarations and points to the radical disagreement about practices such as child labor that would emerge if Western reformers tried harder to implement their ideals as global programs of action. How did the West acquire its contemporary cultural ideals concerning parent–child relationships and other people's children? That is the question to be explored in this chapter, in terms of four topics: (a) the shift from agrarian to urban-industrial institutions, (b) the demographic transition, (c) mass schooling, and (d) the rise of a public interest in children.

THE SHIFT FROM AGRARIAN TO URBAN-INDUSTRIAL INSTITUTIONS

The industrialization of Europe and North America made its primary impact on the family through the rise of wage labor and bureaucratic employment as alternatives to agricultural and craft production, the consequent separation of the workplace from the home and of occupational from kin-based roles and relationships, the migration from rural villages to concentrated settlements where jobs were available, and the penetration of labor market values into parental decisions regarding the future of children. Each of these channels needs to be analyzed in terms of how it operated to alter the assumptions on which agrarian parents had based their conceptions of childhood.

The rise of wage labor and bureaucratic employment meant in the first instance that an increasing number of children would make their future living through jobs that were unfamiliar to their parents and which the latter therefore could not teach them. This was in itself a break with the agrarian tradition in which the work roles of one generation largely replicated those of its forebears: if parents had not mastered the skills their child would live by, they had kin, neighbors or friends who had. Under the new conditions, however, increasing numbers of parents would have to acknowledge that they lacked not only the specific competencies required by their children for future work, but also the social connections with others who had the skills.

This decline in the parental capacity to provide training for subsistence was accompanied by a loss of supervisory control, as children and adults worked in factories, shops and offices under other supervisors. The dual role of the agrarian parents as nurturers and supervisors of their immature and adult children working at home – a role they could transfer to foster parents through apprenticeship in domestically organized craft workshops – was not possible when employers and foremen had no social ties with the parents of their laborers. This set the stage for the abuse of child labor that led ultimately to its abolition.

Equally significant, however, was the 'liberation' of adult workers from parental supervision in domestic production, even as they were exploited by industrial employers. Industrialism in the West cast off the kinship model of relationships that had prevailed in craft production in favor of a rationalistic and contractual model of work relationships we now think of as 'bureaucratic'. Industrial paternalism was not unknown, but the polarization of work *v.* family roles and relationships rose with increasing mass production, labor migration and the creation of a heterogeneous work force that lacked pre-existing social ties or common origins. The workplace required of employees not only skills but also conformity to a new code of social behavior not foreshadowed in the domestic group; it re-socialized workers and gave them new identities distinct from those of birth and marriage. But since work for a particular firm was often not permanent, identification with it as an object of loyalty and idealization was the exception rather than the rule. Industrial employment was contractual, and the social identities of workers came to incorporate this sense of contractual distance from the firm. Sprung loose from the permanence of agrarian kin and community affiliations and from the parental control involved in domestic production, the more mobile industrial workers found new identities in religious sects, nationalism, voluntary associations – and in the ideals of organizations like trade unions and professional associations that were organized by occupation but offered membership more permanent than employment with any firm was likely to be. Whether one views this trend as facilitating personal autonomy or promoting anomie and social disintegration, it meant the greater salience of models of behavior that were not based on domestic relationships. It meant also a decline in parental control as an expectable concomitant of work roles.

Large-scale industrialization draws people from the countryside into concentrated settlements, either large cities with many functions or specialized industrial communities such as mining and mill towns, and this relocation is likely to have a great impact on the family. This does not meant the break-up of family and kin networks, for social historians and anthropologists have shown how resourceful rural migrants were and are in preserving these ties after moving to the city. But urbanization eroded many of the premises on which agrarian family values rested. The availability of residential housing, wild game and assistance from neighbors, for example, was taken for granted in many rural areas, but the migrant to the city found such resources to be commodities that had to be purchased, and at a steep price. Many more consumer goods were available in urban centers, and material aspirations quickly rose, but migrants had to develop a new awareness of what things cost in relation to their limited incomes. Thus urbanization encouraged families to examine the choices in their lives in explicitly economic terms.

The family's recognition of having moved from country to city in order to better its economic position through employment is another important factor. In the rural areas it was possible to see one's residence, occupation and social position as simply inherited together from the past and therefore fixed, but the knowledge of having moved to where the jobs were inevitably gave subjective priority to occupation and earnings as the source of the family's position, and it encouraged the younger generation to think of improving their lives through maximizing their incomes.

In the cities and increasingly even outside them, the influence of the labor market on parental thinking and family decision-making grew. Childhood was seen as a time for acquiring whatever skills would enhance their future employability in a competitive labor market where workers outnumbered jobs. The uncertainties inherent in this situation brought new anxieties to parents. In the agrarian past, the future position and livelihood of a son was pre-ordained through inheritance of land and an inherited role in domestic production, that of a daughter through marriage. Parents helped their children marry and start a household but (except where primogeniture was the rule) did not have to find occupations for their sons. The rise of industrial employment eroded the predictability inherent in this agrarian situation, forced parents to concern themselves more broadly with what would become of their children once they grew up, and offered hope for success in the future labor market only through adequate preparation in childhood. The domestic group, once the setting for the entire life in its productive as well as relational dimensions, became a temporary nest for the nurturance of fledglings who would leave to wrest a living from an uncertain and competitive outside world. Parent–child relations, once conceived as a lifelong structure of reciprocity, were increasingly thought of as existing between adults and their immature offspring, leaving the future ambiguous.

By moving to cities, European families in the nineteenth century were moving closer to expanding urban school systems and enhancing the likelihood that their children would become enrolled. As the population of each country became more concentrated through urbanization, the difficulties of distributing formal eduction were reduced and literacy grew. Urban populations were generally more exposed than rural ones to the laws and programs of increasingly active and bureaucratized national governments, and schooling provided children contact with the symbols and doctrines of the national state.

Urbanization became a mass phenomenon in the nineteenth century as European villagers migrated to cities and towns in Europe, North and South America. Australia and New Zealand – and have continued to do so throughout the present century. In 1800, 7.3 per cent of the population of all these regions (in South America, only Argentina, Chile and Uruguay) lived in settlements of at least 5,000 people; by 1900, it was 26.1 per cent and in 1980 70.2 per cent. Western Europe urbanized earliest and most heavily. Great Britain had by 1850 become the first major country with more than half of its population residing in cities; by 1900, 77 per cent of the British were urban residents and by 1980, 91 per cent. The major industrial cities of England and Germany grew to ten times their size and those of France grew by five times, in the course of the nineteenth century alone (United Nations 1980). These figures suggest that massive increase in the proportion of the population affected by the impact of industrial employment on family life. Urban migrants did not necessarily lose their kin ties nor the significance of kinship in their lives, but their livelihoods and those of their children depended on the labor market. This was an irreversible change, and it reached out into the countryside, commercializing work relationships in agriculture and inducing even rural parents to regard wage labor as a major alternative path of life for their children.

Thus industrialization and urbanization changed the economic basis of family life (i.e. the role of the family as a productive unit) and replaced the local age–sex hierarchy of rural communities with new social identities and sources of motivation centered on the urban occupational structure. This trend has long been known in general terms, but it is only in recent decades that social historians have investigated whether and how particular Western countries fit in the general picture. Did they all start at the same place? Did they change in the same ways in terms of sequence and intensity? Did they arrive at the same outcomes in terms of resultant patterns of family life and child development? While the evidence is far from complete, the answer to all these questions is 'No'.

It has been shown, for example, that contractualism in property relations within and outside the family, as well as the independence of adolescent and pre-adolescent children from their parents, has a much longer history in England than on the Continent, and MacFarlane (1977) argues that these patterns antedate even England's pre-industrial economic development, representing a cultural tradition that sets England off from the rest of Europe. While his cultural argument is subject to controversy, there is no dispute concerning English primacy in industrial development and urbanization and in the utilitarian ideology of market relationships that social scientists have seen as an integral part of the urban-industrial transformation. In other words, England, along with its American colonies and the Calvinist communities of the Netherlands, Geneva and Scotland, may in the seventeenth century have had many of the social and psychological characteristics that the rest of Europe did not acquire until the urban-industrial transformation of the mid-nineteenth century.

Similarly the pre-industrial family structures of the Western countries were far from identical, and some of them can plausibly be seen as preparing rural families for urban life under industrial conditions. Wherever the rules of inheritance did not permit the division of family land, for example, the 'stem family' in rural populations assured only heirs of a future on the parental land and created for the other sons something closer to the uncertainty of the industrial labor market. This situation in Sweden and Ireland was a factor in early (i.e. pre-nineteenth century) migration of rural labor to urban markets at home and abroad. The United States, with its lack of a feudal tradition and expanding rural as well as urban settlements, provided more opportunities for migration into newly established communities less dominated by inherited kinship and status relationships. Thus the Western countries, far from being homogeneous in culture and family structure before major industrial and urban development, were significantly varied in ways that bore directly on how they would enter and experience that historical transition.

It is equally clear that the processes of industrial and urban development were not the same throughout the West. France, for example, never became urbanized to the extent that England did. A much larger proportion of Frenchmen remained in rural villages participating in agriculture. In Italy and the United States, urban growth and industrialization were heavily concentrated in their northern regions, leaving the south rural and 'underdeveloped' down to the present, but this was not the case in smaller and more densely populated countries like the Netherlands. Thus the suddenness of the shift from agrarian to urban-industrial conditions, the proportions of the population who were uprooted from rural areas and absorbed in the urban labor force, the continuity of urban centers with a pre-industrial culture – all of these and many other factors were variable among (and within) the Western countries and are highly relevant to family life and the raising of children.

Do such historical variations make a difference in terms of late-twentieth-century outcomes? Not if outcomes are measured only by economic indicators such as gross national product per capita and demographic indicators such as birth and death rates for all the countries of the contemporary world. In these comparisons the Western countries stand out (with Japan) at the high end economically and the low end demographically – particularly in contrast with the Third World. There are major differences among the Western countries, however, in the results of industrial and urban development, especially in regard to the quality of life and the options and ligatures of Dahrendorf's framework. Indeed, he sees Britain and Germany as contrasting sharply in these terms.

The contrast between the United States and virtually all of Europe in residential mobility, for example, is enormous and of great significance in how occupational identities and local ties affect childhood and adult experience. Divorce, female participation in the work force and the extent of government welfare entitlements are other widely varying quantitative factors that affect both life chances and the family life among the Western countries. On the qualitative side, the salience of social class divisions, trade union affiliations and religious participation represent other variables that create differing contexts for life experience in the several countries of the West.

It is clear, then, on the basis of available evidence that industrial and urban development has not simply homogenized Western countries as social environments for the development of children. They did not enter the transition from agrarian life at the same places, they did not undergo quite the same historical experiences, and they did not arrive at identical destinations in terms of the conditions of family life and childhood. Their similarities in the urban-industrial transition are well established, particularly in comparison with other parts of the world, but neither the process nor the outcome of the transition should be considered uniform.

THE DEMOGRAPHIC TRANSITION

Between the late eighteenth and mid-twentieth centuries, Western birth and death rates declined drastically, eliminating the agrarian expectations of natural fertility and a relatively short life as normal features of the human condition. The impact on family life was as great as that of the more or less concomitant decline in domestic production and child labor. So many conditions affecting the family were changing during that time, however, that the connections between socio-economic and demographic change are matters of theoretical controversy rather than straightforward fact. 'Demographic transition theory' (Caldwell 1982: 117–33) includes all historical formulations that assume the inevitability and irreversibility of declining birth and death rates and the coupling of those declines to each other and to other socio-economic trends, regardless of which factors they claim to be driving the change. From our perspective, demographic transition theory is interesting not only because it attempts to make sense of secular trends affecting parents but also because it explicitly proposes parallels between nineteenth-century Europe and the contemporary Third World. Recent research in historical demography enables us to make comparisons between what happened in the West and Japan and what is now happening in the rest of the world.

The basic facts have been succinctly summarized by van de Walle and Knodel (1980):

> In the first half of the 19th century, there were two general levels of birth rates in Europe. West of an imaginary line running from the Adriatic to the Baltic Sea, birth rates were under 40 per 1,000 persons per year – the result of late marriage and widespread celibacy – and death rates were in the 20s. East of the line, universal and early marriage made for birth rates above 40 per 1,000 – not unlike those in much of Asia and Africa today – while death rates were in the 30s. Now, at the end of the transition, most birth rates are under 15 per 1,000 in Western Europe and only a little higher in Eastern Europe. And death rates on both sides of the line are down to about 10 per 1,000.
> (van de Walle and Knodel 1980: 5)

The magnitude of these shifts, particularly if one considers them irreversible, deserves to be emphasized: contemporary Europeans bear only one-third as many children and have a death rate only half as high as Europeans in the early nineteenth century. The decline in infant mortality was even more precipitous, from early-nineteenth-century rates of about 200 infant deaths of every 1,000 births to about ten at present; contemporary Europeans thus lose only 1/20th as many infants as their forebears in 1800. Similar changes occurred at roughly the same time in North America and Australia.

The timing, sequence and socio-economic concomitants of these shifts are important to an understanding of how they might have affected, and been affected by, parental attitudes. Crude death rates, though not infant mortality, dropped moderately and gradually throughout the nineteenth century, then more steeply after 1900. The onset of mortality decline, probably in the late eighteenth century, was well in advance of improvements in medicine and has been attributed by McKeown (1976) to the greater availability of potatoes and maize, which improved the diet of ordinary people and made them more resistant to infection. Fertility, having increased in the late eighteenth century, began to decline around 1880 (much earlier in France, Switzerland and the United States), had dropped substantially by 1920, and continued its decline in the mid-twentieth century. Infant mortality declined little in the nineteenth century, except in Sweden, but dropped precipitously between 1900 and 1920, probably due to the pasteurization of milk, continuing its decline thereafter.

When European parents started to limit the number of their children, they had not yet experienced the enhanced probability of infant survival that came with the twentieth century. Thus the *onset* of fertility decline cannot be attributed to the greater parental confidence in child survival that follows reduced infant mortality. Whatever their reasons for limiting births (which are still a matter of speculation), they accomplished it through abstinence and withdrawal – methods theoretically available to all humans – rather than through advances in contraceptive technology. Parents in the nineteenth century were healthier on the average and lived longer than their forebears and they had large families that were less likely to be disrupted by the death of a parent during the reproductive years. The drop in infant mortality that followed the onset of fertility decline probably strengthened the trend but could not have instigated it.

Deliberate birth limitation on the scale that occurred in Europe and North America in the late nineteenth century and early twentieth centuries was unprecedented in human history and seems to have marked a turning point in concepts and conditions of child development. The small-family ideal that emerged represented a departure from agrarian values toward a view of parent–child relations attuned to an urban-industrial economy, one in which each child signified increased costs and reduced contributions.

The relations of fertility decline to the urban-industrial transition and the spread of schooling are discussed below. At this point it should be noted that each of the major demographic trends of the nineteenth and twentieth centuries seems to have been instigated by changes in socio-economic conditions and subsequently amplified by

. use of new medical technologies rather than the other way round. Thus the decline in crude death rates around 1800 may have resulted from improved nutrition due to the more abundant food supply of early capitalistic economies, though the trend was certainly strengthened later on by better medical care. Fertility decline began because married couples decided to limit births and used existing techniques, though their efforts were later facilitated by the availability of contraceptive technology. Infant mortality may have begun to decline after fertility due to better parental care for each of fewer children, though the trend was powerfully strengthened by the pasteurization of milk, immunization and more effective drugs. In other words, demographic transition should not be seen as the simple result of changes in biotechnology but rather as the outcome of parental responses to changing socio-economic conditions.

The West, Eastern Europe and Japan arrived at roughly the same demographic destination by the last quarter of the twentieth century, with only a few exceptions. Their birth and death rates are low and vary within a narrow range. They did not begin the demographic transition at the same place, however, and did not move along identical pathways to their present positions. In other words, it would be a mistake to conclude that their current similarities in comparison with Third World societies are the outcomes of the same historical process or represent a shared historical background. This is particularly important to bear in mind when attempting to generalize from their past patterns of change in order to forecast what is possible and probable for the Third World.

As historical demography is pursued in greater depth, more country-specific patterns – including features of the pre-transitional social order – are identified as having been crucial to the process of demographic transition. Wrigley (1983), for example, argues that household formation in England from the seventeenth century was sensitive to the cost of living. Couples postponed marriage – and therefore child-bearing – when prices were high, thus reducing the birth rate. The customary practices by which families regulated the establishment of reproductive unions in response to economic conditions constitute a type of influence on fertility prior to the industrial revolution that might have facilitated the English fertility transition at a later date.

In France and the United States, the secular decline in birth rates began before 1800 – perhaps a century before the rest of Europe – and probably for different reasons. In both countries, however, the decline was initiated before industrialization and urbanization. This is particularly noteworthy because both France and the United States did not become as urban in the proportions of their populations living in cities as England and some of the other industrial countries. In other words, the forefront of fertility decline in the nineteenth century occurred in settings characterized by agrarian, or at least predominantly agricultural, conditions. This should provide a note of caution for those who see contemporary fertility decline as inexorably linked to urbanization.

A recent comparison of fertility decline in Japan and Sweden also emphasizes the influence of country-specific pre-transitional characteristics, in this case the patriarchal stem family, which is shared by those two countries but not by others in their respective regions (Mosk 1983). Here again the evidence points to the conclusion that the demographic transition encompasses varied trajectories to the same destinations.

MASS SCHOOLING

There were schools in Europe from ancient times, but until the nineteenth century a relatively small proportion of children attended them. In the fifty years between 1840 and 1890 primary school attendance was enormously broadened and became compulsory in Western Europe, North America and Australia. This marks one of the most radical shifts in the parent–child relationship in human history. Mass schooling must be seen as both a reflection of powerful antecedent trends in social, political and economic conditions and a determinant of subsequent changes in reproduction and family life. The extension of schooling in the individual life span and its expansion across the globe have proved to be irresistible and apparently irreversible tendencies, fundamentally altering the way we think about children.

How did mass schooling affect the parent–child relationship? First, it kept children out of full-time productive work and minimized their economic contributions to the family. It furthermore established in a public and unavoidable way that childhood was dedicated to preparation for an uncertain future. It gave children a certain kind of power *vis à vis* their parents, either because the latter saw their better educated children as bearers of potentially higher social status or because the children themselves, having gained access to a new world of valuable skills and information, asserted themselves more within the family. Assertive, school-going children cost more than compliant children who work under parental supervision in domestic production;

they required a larger share of family resources for their clothes, for space in which to study and for the satisfaction of the consumer tastes they acquired outside the home. Their demands, implicit and actual, were strongly supported by the wider society, particularly after compulsory school legislation, which had the effect of informing parents that the State had officially determined how their offspring should spend their time during childhood.

The parental response to this revolutionary change was first to minimize its impact, then to devise strategies to maximize the advantages it offered. At first, children enrolled in school were frequently kept home when their work was needed, as daily attendance figures show. In 1869–70, for example, although 57 per cent of the United States population aged 5 to 17 was enrolled in school, only 35 per cent attended daily (Fine 1983). Even those children who did attend daily were probably required to perform chores at home and to 'make themselves useful' to their parents. Caldwell (1982: 117–31) has argued that so long as this was the case, parents could realistically consider numerous offspring advantageous even though they were not directly involved in domestic production. Eventually, however, the advantages of children in performing household chores must have been outweighed by their rising costs to the family, particularly if parents could not count on sharing their future wages, thus creating an economic incentive for birth control. According to Caldwell's theory, however, this shifting cost–contribution ratio was subjectively experienced in terms of parental ideology rather than economic calculation.

A new model of parenthood arose, with the goal of optimizing life chances for each of a few children through extended education and a measure of adult attention that had formerly been reserved for heirs to the throne. Thus did 'quality' replace 'quantity' as the focus of child-rearing efforts, first in the middle classes but with a rapid spread into other classes.

The new model was effective as a strategy for optimizing the competitive position of offspring in a labor market that increasingly favored more education and personal autonomy, but what did it do for parents? Not very much in material terms, for economic 'returns' to parents were usually unfavorable. The code of filial reciprocity which had prevailed in agrarian communities was no longer binding on adult children, at least to a dependable degree. But something happened which cannot be accounted for in strictly economic terms, that is parents came to identify with the children in whom they had invested so much of themselves as well as their resources, and they were able to derive subjective satisfaction from the economic and reproductive careers of their children even in the absence of material support. The ideological sources of this subjective satisfaction are considered in the following section.

The history of schooling in the West varied from one country to another. Before 1800, schooling (often limited to literacy acquisition) was widespread in England, Scotland, the United States, the Netherlands and Prussia. In these countries, at least half of the entire male population attended school, if only for a few years, and became literate. In the rest of Europe, smaller proportions ever attended school or became literate (Craig 1981: 70). Thus the nineteenth century opened with major differences in educational development among the countries of Europe.

Policies of mass schooling were implemented through diverse forms of organization. Prussia pioneered the development of a governmentally planned and hierarchically organized school system, and France also built a centrally controlled national network of schools. England, on the other hand, had a wide and unregulated variety of religious and private schools, many of them of poor quality, until late in the nineteenth century, and never imposed the bureaucratic controls found in France. In the United States, schools were built and managed under state and local control (and financing), with a degree of decentralization unknown in Europe. These institutional variations affected long-range outcomes, for variability in school quality by social class in England and by locality (which is correlated with social class) in the United States have remained strong into present times. Hence the relations of schools to the central government and to the national system of social status have varied widely across Western countries.

THE RISE OF PUBLIC INTEREST IN CHILDREN

There can be no doubt that European attitudes toward children changed radically during the nineteenth century, but the changes had so many expressions and concomitants that they are not simple to describe or explain. Furthermore, ideas spread more quickly from one country to another than economic, demographic and institutional patterns and are harder to isolate for analysis. Most of the revolutionary ideas of the nineteenth century had been formulated in earlier centuries, and questions remain as to when their impact was fully felt. Stone (1977) and Plumb (1980) trace some of these ideas to the second half of the seventeenth century in England. On the Continent, the ideas formulated by Rousseau in *Emile* early in the eighteenth century were basic to the changing concepts of child development and education a century and more later. Pestalozzi, the eighteenth-century Swiss educator, spread these concepts to Prussia before 1800.

This complex intellectual and social history is still being investigated by historians and remains an area of controversy. From a comparative perspective, however, its outlines are clear. Western conceptions of childhood after 1500 reflected a growing and changing debate over freedom, individualism and authority. At first this debate was conducted in religious terms and was associated with the rise of Protestant Christianity. Calvinism conceptualized the child as born with a will of its own, but viewed this as symptomatic of original sin, to be subdued by parental authority in the interests of moral virtue and divinely sanctioned moral order. Later, philosophers such as Locke and Rousseau proposed the natural goodness of the child and an acceptance of the child's playful impulses as beneficial for educational and individual development. Such ideas grew in influence during the eighteenth century, particularly in the arts (e.g. the poetry of William Blake) and in philosophical discourse on education (e.g. Pestalozzi). During the same period liberal political theory – emphasizing individual freedom rather than obedience to authority – not only developed but also was dramatically implemented in the American and French revolutions. In the nineteenth century, literary and artistic romanticism established an emotional climate on which the struggle for children's rights as a form of political liberation could draw. It was during the nineteenth century, then, that the sentimental idealization of childhood combined with the liberal notion that children had rights to be publicly enforced, in such cultural phenomena as the novels of Charles Dickens and the legislative struggle against child labor.

Much of the complexity of this history derives from the fact that the debate over freedom *v.* constraint in childhood has not led to a final resolution but continues even today, in issues specific to contemporary contexts. Furthermore, the Western countries represent a variety of experiences with this debate in terms of the particular sequences of intellectual discourse, public policy and effects on family life. What distinguishes the Western ideology as a whole from that of many non-Western cultures is not so much the preference for freedom, even for children, as the definition of freedom as liberation from authority – a polarity that pits options against ligatures in the struggle for a better life. This struggle, this morality play on behalf of children, provided the basic terms in which the modern European conceptions of the child emerged during the nineteenth century.

The new ideas were hostile to agrarian models of obedience and, reciprocity. Focusing on childhood as a distinct and valuable phase of life, they emphasized autonomy, children's development as separate and equal human beings, supported and protected by loving parents as they developed their capacities to make free and intelligent choices. In philosophy, literature and the arts, these ideas were advanced and elaborated. In psychology and child study they were justified on scientific grounds. In politics they inspired legislation to defend children against exploitation in factories and to restrict parental control. And in the family they inspired an emotional commitment that knew no precedent except in the rearing of royal princes.

The relation of these ideas to the socio-economic trends reviewed above and to the larger cultural ideologies from which they were derived deserves more intensive research. It is clear that these ideas were important in forming the emotional attitudes of parents and policy-makers alike and thus had an important impact. It also seems true, however, that the emotional component, and particularly the sense of struggle for children against those who do them harm, was stronger in some countries than in others. In some European countries, then, the cause of children gained a political constituency of reformers, crusading against evil, while in others reforms were enacted, perhaps somewhat later, as the necessary steps required of a civilized society but without overt conflict.

All of these trends focused more public and private attention on childhood and the development of children than had previously been the case in European societies and in agrarian societies generally. Children were as never before depicted as valuable, lovable, innocent but intelligent individuals, to be cherished, protected, defended and developed. Public and private poles of this general tendency might seem to have been in conflict, for the public laws prohibiting child labor and compelling school attendance embodied the assumption that the citizenry bore a collective responsibility for other people's children in addition to their own offspring, while romantic sentimentalism promoted an intensification of the parent–offspring bond in the most private and exclusive terms. Both poles, however, were based on the notion that every individual child was uniquely valuable, to his or her own parents *and* to the wider society – an idea compatible with Western traditions but newly applied to children in the context of a secular national state.

The ideological complementarity of these two poles can be seen in the presumption that parents who cherished their own children would be able to support the public cause of all children through a process of identification, i.e. by imagining how they would feel if their own children were the victims of neglect or exploitation. Similarly the argument that the development of children represented a national resource for public investment was expected to evoke in parents a complementary 'investment' in the educational and occupational aspirations of their own offspring. In the larger cultural ideology that emerged, then, the potential conflict between public and private interests in children was not only conceptually reconciled but also embedded in the idea of their convergence to the benefit of children.

CONCLUSIONS

All of the trends reviewed above favor the bearing of *fewer* children receiving *more* attention (and other resources) over a *longer* period of their lives than was typical in agrarian societies. Changing economic, demographic and structural conditions led Western parents in the late nineteenth century to perceive the allocation of greater resources to each child as enhancing the future advantage of the child in an increasingly competitive environment. Changing ideological conditions motivated their willingness to commit resources to each child without expecting a material return. Similar trends have been observed in Japan and in some Third World countries as they have moved from agrarian to urban-industrial conditions.

This brief overview has also indicated differences among Western countries in the conditions of family life and child development before 1800, in the processes and sequences of change during the nineteenth and twentieth centuries and in the outcomes as of the present time. European countries were not homogeneous to begin with and are not homogeneous today, however much they contrast with other countries in the world. Moreover, their advances in formal education and the regulation of birth and death were not achieved by taking the same steps in the same order but through various pathways reflecting the diversity of their socio-economic and cultural conditions. This historical record as we now know it suggests that family change will continue to reflect the diversity of settings in which it occurs. Those who formulate policy will have to pay close attention to the unique resources and limits of each setting rather than assuming a universal series of prerequisites for replicating progress.

In attempting to explain how the West was transformed from its agrarian condition, it is not only diversity in local settings that must be taken into account but also temporal diversity in the circumstances under which each major change occurred in a given country. Each secular trend showed at least two surges, often 80 or 100 years apart.

Fertility began its major decline in the nineteenth century, but fell sharply after the First World War. Infant mortality dropped after 1900 but continued to decline thereafter until it reached present levels. The spread of primary schooling was a nineteenth-century phenomenon, but secondary schooling as a mass process did not occur until the twentieth century. New concepts of the child and education arose between the mid-seventeenth and early nineteenth centuries but did not have their major institutional impact until a good deal later. In each case the socio-economic and ideological conditions affecting the consciousness of parents were different by the time the later surge occurred, and different social forces were mobilized to advance the trend. This makes it possible for largely economic factors to have determined the first surge and largely ideological factors the second, or vice versa. It means that secular trends cannot be treated as single historical events and that the telescoping of historical process that seems to occur in 'late developing countries' cannot be treated as replicating a trend that took centuries in Europe.

REFERENCES

Arnold, F., Bulato, R., Burikpakdi, C., Chung, B., Fawcett, J., Iritani, T., Lee, S. and Wu, T. (1975) *The Value of Children: vol. 1, Introduction and Comparative Analysis*, Honolulu: East-West Population Institute.

Caldwell, J. 1982) *Theory of Fertility Decline*, New York: Academic Press.

Craig, J.E. (1981) 'The expansion of education', *Review of Research in Education* 9: 151–213.

Fine, E. (1983) 'The rise of universal education in the 19th century', *Project on Human Potential*, May.

Hirschman, A., *et al.* (1979). *Towards a New Strategy for Development: A Rothko Chapel Colloquium*, New York: Pergamon Press.

Hoffman, L. and Manis, J. (1979) 'The value of children in the United States: a new approach to the study of fertility', *Journal of Marriage and the Family* 41: 583–96.

MacFarlane, A. (1977) *The Origins of English Individualism*, Cambridge: Cambridge University Press.

McKeown, T. (1976) *The Modern Rise of Population*, New York: Academic Press.

Mosk, C. (1983) *Patriarchy and Fertility: Japan and Sweden, 1880–1960*, New York: Academic Press.

Plumb, J. (1980) 'The new world of children in eighteenth century England', in V. Fox and M. Quitt (eds) *Loving, Parenting and Dying*, New York: Psychohistory Press.

Stone, L. (1977) *The Family, Sex and Marriage in England, 1500–1800*. New York: Harper & Row.

United Nations, Department of International Economic and Social Affairs

(1980) *Patterns of Urban and Rural Population Growth*, New York: United Nations.

van de Walle, E. and Knodel, J. (1980) 'Europe's fertility transition: new evidence and lessons for today's developing world', *Population Bulletin* 34 (6).

Wrigley, E. (1983) 'The growth of population in eighteenth century England: a conundrum resolved', *Past and Present*, 98: 121–50.

2 The American child and other cultural inventions

William Kessen
Source: *American Psychologist* (1979) 34 (10): 815–20

The theme of the child as a cultural invention can be recognized in several intellectual and social occasions. Ariès' (1962) commentary on the discovery and transformation of childhood has become common knowledge; there is an agitated sense that American children are being redefined by the present times (Lasch 1978); there is a renewed appreciation of the complexity of all our children (Keniston 1977); and ethnographic and journalistic reports tell us of the marvelous departures from our own ways of seeing children that exist in other lands (Kessen 1975). In simple fact, we have recently seen a shower of books on childish variety across cultures and across the hierarchies of class and race.

We could have just as readily discovered commanding evidence of the shifting nature of childhood by a close look at our own history. Consider just three messages drawn haphazardly from the American past. To the parents of the late eighteenth century:

> The first duties of Children are in great measure mechanical: an obedient Child makes a Bow, comes and goes, speaks, or is silent, just as he is bid, before he knows any other Reason for so doing than that he is bid.
>
> (Nelson 1753)

Or to our parents and grandparents:

> The rule that parents should not play with their children may seem hard but it is without doubt a safe one.
>
> (West 1914)

Or hear a parent of the 1970s speak of her 6-year-old:

> LuAnn liked the school in California best – the only rules were no chemical additives in the food and no balling in the hallways.
>
> (Rothchild and Wolf 1976)

And we cannot escape the implications of an unstable portrait of the child by moving from folk psychology to the professional sort. On the contrary, a clear-eyed study of what experts have said about the young – from Locke to Skinner, from Rousseau to Piaget, from Comenius to Erikson – will expose as bewildering a taxonomy as the one provided by preachers, parents and poets. No other animal species has been cataloged by responsible scholars in so many wildly discrepant forms, forms that a perceptive extraterrestrial could never see as reflecting the same beast.

To be sure, most expert students of children continue to assert the truth of the positivistic dream – that we have not yet found the underlying structural simplicities that will reveal the child entire, that we have not yet cut nature at the joints – but it may be wise for us child psychologists [. . .] to peer into the abyss of the positivistic nightmare – that the child is essentially and eternally a cultural invention and that the variety of the child's definition is not the removable error of an incomplete science. For not only are American *children* shaped and marked by the larger cultural forces of political maneuverings, practical economics, and implicit ideological commitments (a new enough recognition), *child psychology* is itself a peculiar cultural invention that moves with the tidal sweeps of the larger culture in ways that we understand at best dimly and often ignore.

To accept the ambiguity of our task – to give up debates about the fundamental nature of the child – is not, however, a defeatist or unscientific move. Rather, when we seriously confront the proposition that we, like the children we study, are cultural inventions, we can go on to ask questions about the sources of our diversity and, perhaps more tellingly, about the sources of our agreements. It is surely remarkable that against the background of disarray in our definition of the child, a number of ideas are so widely shared that few scholars question their provenance and warrant. Paradoxically the unexamined communalities of our commitment may turn out to be more revealing than our disagreements. Within the compass of the next several pages, I point toward disagreements that were present at the beginnings of systematic child study, and then turn in more detail to the pervasive and shared themes of American childhood in our time, themes that may require a more critical review than we have usually given them.

PRESENT AT THE BIRTH

When child psychology was born, in a longish parturition that ran roughly from Hall's first questionary studies of 1880 (Hall 1883) to Binet's test of construction of 1905 (Binet and Simon 1916), there were five determining spirits present. Four of them are familiar to us all; the fifth and least visible spirit may turn out to be the most significant. One of the familiars was in the line of Locke and Bain, and it appeared later for Americans as John Broadus Watson; the line has, then and now, represented behavior, restraint, clarity, simplicity and good news. Paired in philosophical and theoretical opposition was the spirit that derived from Rousseau, Nietzsche and Freud, the line that represented mind, impulse, ambiguity, complexity and bad news. The great duel between the two lines has occupied students of children for just under 300 years.

The third magus at the beginning was the most fully American; William James can stand as the representative of the psychologists whose central concern was with sensation, perception, language, thought and will – the solid, sensible folk who hid out in the years between the World Wars but who have returned in glory. It is of at least passing interest to note that the cognitivists participated lightly in the early development of child study; James and, even more, Munsterberg and, past all measure, Titchener found results from the study of children too messy for the precision they wanted from their methods.

The godfather of child psychology, the solidest spirit of them all, was Charles Darwin, foreshadowing his advocates and his exaggerators. His contemporary stand-in, G. Stanley Hall, was the first in a long and continuing line that has preached from animal analogues, has called attention to the biological in the child, and has produced a remarkably diverse progeny that includes Galton, Gesell and the ethologists.

I rehearse (and oversimplify) the story of our professional beginnings to call attention to how persistent the lines have been, how little they have interpenetrated and modified one another, and how much their contributions to our understanding of the child rest on a network of largely implicit and undefended assumptions about the basis of human knowledge, social structures and ethical ascriptions. The lines of the onlooking spirits are themselves historical and cultural constructions that grew, in ways that have rarely been studied analytically or biographically, from the matrix of the larger contemporaneous culture.

And so to the fifth circumnatal spirit, the one that knew no technical psychology. In the middle fifty years of the nineteenth century, the years that prepared the United States for child psychology, dramatic and persistent changes took place in American society. I could sing the familiar litany of urbanization, industrialization, the arrival of the first millions of European immigrants (another strand of diversity among children that requires a closer look). We know that the Civil War transformed the lives of most American families, white and black (although we still know remarkably little about the daily lives of children during and after the war). The United States developed, and *developed* is the word of choice, from an isolated agricultural dependency to an aggressive and powerful state. Technology and science joined the industrial entrepreneurs to persuade the new Americans, from abroad and from the farm, that poverty was an escapable condition if one worked hard enough and was aggressively independent. But there were other changes that bore more immediately on the lives of American children; let me, as an example of cultural influences on children and child psychology rather than as a worked-through demonstration of my thesis, extract three interwoven strands of the changes that touched children.

The first, and the earliest, was the evolving separation of the domain of work from the domain of home. When women left or were excluded from the industrial work force in the 1830s and 1840s, the boundary marked by the walls of home became less and less penetrable. First for the white, the urban, the middle-class, the northeastern American, but enlisting other parts of the community as time went on, work (or *real work* as contrasted with *homework*, the activity of women and schoolchildren) was carried on in specialized spaces by specialized people, and home became the place where one (i.e. men) did not work (Cott 1977; Lasch 1977).

The second and entailed change was the radical separation of what a man was from what a woman was. Colonial and early Federal society, like all other cultures, had stable and divergent visions of the proper sphere of male and female. But in the half century under our present consideration, something of a moral metamorphosis occurred in the United States (and in large measure, in England, too) and one of modern history's most eccentric arrangements of human beings was put in place. The public world of men was seen as ugly, aggressive, corrupting, chaotic, sinful (not an altogether regretted characteristic) and irreligious. The increasingly private world of women was, in inevitable antithesis, sweet, chaste, calm, cultured, loving, protective and godly. The muscular Christianity of the Mathers and Edwardses became the feminized Christianity of matrons and pastors; the caretaking of culture became the task of women's groups (Douglas 1978). So dramatic a statement of the contrast is hardly an exaggeration of the facts. And the full story remains to be told; historians of medical practice, for example, are just beginning to reveal the systematic attempt to desex American and British women in the nineteenth century with methods that ranged from sermons to surgery (Barker-Benfield 1977).

The third change in American life that set the cultural context for child psychology followed on the first two. Children continued to be cared for by women at home, and in consequence, they took on the coloration of mother, hearth and heaven. The early American child, who was told 'consider that you may perish as young as you are; there are small Chips as well as great Logs, in the Fire of Hell' (eighteenth century primer, quoted by Johnson 1904), became Little Eva, Huckleberry Finn and eventually Peter Pan. The sentimentalization of children – caught for tombstones and psychology books best by Wordsworth's 'Heaven lies about us in our infancy!' – had implications for family structure, education and the definition of the child in expert writings that we have not yet, nearing the end of the twentieth century, fully understood or confronted.

Thus it was that American child psychology began not only under the conflicting attention of Locke, Rousseau, James and Darwin, but also with the progressivist, sexist and sentimental expectation of the larger culture standing by.

THE COMMON THEMES OF AMERICAN CHILD PSYCHOLOGY

Are we now free of our origins? It would be both unhistorical and undevelopmental to believe so, in spite of all we have learned about research and about children over the last 100 years. The positivist promise of pure objectivity and eternal science has been withdrawn. Therefore, it may be methodologically therapeutic to glance, however briefly, at several common themes of our field that seem dependent, in the usually complicated way of human history, on the story I have sketched thus far. All of the themes may be ready for a thoughtful new evaluation.

The commitment to science and technology

The notable success of the physical sciences in the nineteenth century, the elation that followed on the Darwinian revolution, and the culture's high hopes for a technological utopia joined at the end of the nineteenth century to define child psychology as scientific and ratio-nal. The vagaries of casual stories about children, the eccentricities of folk knowledge and the superstitions of grandmothers were all to be cleansed by the mighty brush of scientific method (Jacoby 1914; Watson 1928). The conviction that we are scientists remains one of the heart beliefs of child psychology, and in its humane and sensible forms, the commitment to a systematic analytic examination of the lives of children and their worlds is still the unique and continuing contribution of child psychology to American culture.

But some less obvious and perhaps less defensible consequences of the rational scientific commitment were pulled along into child psychology by the high hopes of its founders. Perhaps the one that we have had the most difficulty in handling as a profession is the implication *in all theories of the child* that lay folk, particularly parents, are in need of expert guidance. Critical examination and study of parental practices and child behavior almost inevitably slipped subtly over to advice about parental practices and child behavior. The scientific statement became an ethical imperative, the descriptive account became normative. And along the way, there have been unsettling occasions in which scraps of knowledge, gathered by whatever procedures were held to be proper science at the time, were given inordinate weight against poor old defenseless folk knowledge. Rigorously scheduled feedings of infants, separation of new mothers from their babies, and Mrs West's injunction against playing with children can stand as examples of scientism that are far enough away not to embarrass us enlightened moderns.

More, I risk the guess that the sentimental view of the child that prevailed at the beginnings of child psychology – a vision which, let it be said, made possible humane and appropriate reforms in the treatment of children – was strongly influential in what can only be called a salvationist view of children. Child psychologists, again whatever their theoretical stripe, have taken the Romantic notion of childish innocence and openness a long way toward the several forms of 'If only we could make matters right with the child, the world would be a better place.' The child became the carrier of political pro-gressivism and the optimism of reformers. From agitation for child labor reform in the 1890s to Head Start, American children have been saviors of the nation. The romantic inheritance of purity and perfectibility may, in fact, have misled us about the proper unit of developmental study and about the major forces influencing human growth and change. I shall return to the consideration of our unit of study shortly.

There has often also been a socially hierarchical message in our scientific-normative interactions with the larger culture. Tolstoy said that there is no proletarian literature; there has been no proletarian child psychology either, and the ethically imperative forms of chid psychology, our messages to practice, have ranged from pleas for equitable treatment of all children to recipes for forced assimilation to the expected forms of child behavior. Once a descriptive norm has been established, it is an antique cultural principle to urge adherence to it.

Finally, for some eras of child study, there has been an enthusiastic anticipation that all problems are reducible by the science of the moment; intellectual technology can succeed (and imitate) the nineteenth century's commercial and industrial technology in the progressive and ultimate betterment of humankind. The optimism of the founders of child study and their immediate successors is dimmer today – 'The sky's the limit' may be replaced by 'You win a few, you lose a few' — and serious questions have been posed even for the basic assumptions underlying the scientific analysis of human behavior (Barrett 1978). Child psychology may soon have to face anew the question of whether or not a scientific account of human development can be given without bringing in its wake the false claims of scientism and the arrogance of an ethic based on current findings.

The importance of mothers, early experience, and personal responsibility

Strangely at odds with the theme of rational scientific inquiry has been the persistence of the commitment to home and mother in otherwise varying portraits of the child. Some child psychologists have been less than laudatory about the effectiveness of particular mothering procedures (Watson dedicated his directive book on child rearing to the first mother who raises a child successfully), but critics and praisers alike have rarely doubted the basic principle that children need home and mother to grow as they should grow (again, the normative injunction enters). I do not mean to dispute the assumption here; I want only to suggest its connection with the mid-nineteenth-century ideology that long preceded systematic child psychology,and to point out several riders on the assumption that have, in the past, been less vividly visible.

Two riders on the home-and-mother position are under active debate and study nowadays – the irrelevance of fathers and the critical role of early experience. The cases represent with the starkness of a line-drawing the influence of contemporaneous cultural forces on the definition of psychology's child. It would be difficult to defend the proposition that the recent interest in the place of fathers or the possibilities of out-of-home child rearing grew either from a new theory of development or from striking new empirical discoveries. Rather, for reasons too elaborate to explore here, fewer and fewer American women have been willing or able to devote all of their work time to the rearing of children. It will be instructive to see how much the tasks assigned fathers and day-care centers reflect the old ascriptions to essential maternity. Psychology follows culture, but often at a discreet distance.

The blending of new social requirements into old ideology is precisely demonstrated by the incorporation of fathers and day-care workers into the premise that what happens to the child in the first hours, weeks, months of life holds an especially determining position in human development. Proclaimed on epistemological grounds by Locke, gathered into the American ethos in part because it so well fits the perfectionist argument, elevated to scientific status by evolutionary theory, the doctrine of the primacy of early experience has been an uncontested part of American culture and American child psychology throughout the history of both. Only in the last several years has the premise been called seriously into question (Kagan *et al.* 1978) and, even then, at a time when ever more extravagant claims are being made about the practical necessity of safeguarding the child's first hours (Klaus and Kennell 1976).

The assumption of essential maternity and the assumption of the determining role of early experience join to support yet another underdebated postulate of child psychology. If something goes wrong in the course of a child's development, it is the primary responsibility of the mother (or whoever behaves as mother), and once more in echo of the salvationist view, if a social problem is not repaired by modification of the child's first years, the problem is beyond repair. The working of the postulate has produced ways of blaming mothers that appear in all theoretical shapes and, more generally, ways of blaming other victims of social injustice because they are not readily transformed by the ministrations of the professionals (Ryan 1971).

The tendency to assign personal responsibility for the successes and failures of development is an amalgam of the positivistic search for causes, of the older Western tradition of personal moral responsibility, and of the conviction that personal mastery and consequent personal responsibility are first among the goals of child-rearing. It is difficult to imagine an American child psychology without a core commitment to the proposition that *someone* is responsible for what happens in the course of development.

The belief in the individual and self-contained child

Hovering over each of the traditional beliefs mentioned thus far is the most general and, in my view, the most fundamental entanglement of technical child psychology with the implicit commitments of American culture. The child – like the Pilgrim, the cowboy and the detective on television – is invariably seen as a free-standing isolable being who moves through development as a self-contained and complete individual. Other similarly self-contained people – parents and teachers – may influence the development of children, to be sure, but the proper unit of cultural analysis and the proper unit of developmental study is the child alone. The ubiquity of such radical individualism in our lives makes the consideration of alternative images of childhood extraordinarily difficult. We have never taken fully seriously the notion that development is, in large measure, a social construction, the child a modulated and modulating component in a shifting network of influences (Berger and Luckmann 1966). The seminal thinkers about children over the past century have, in fact, been almost undeviating in their postulation of the child as container of self and of psychology. Impulses are in the child; traits are in the child; thoughts are in the child; attachments are in the child. In short, almost every major theory of development accepts the premises of individualism and takes the child as the basic unit of study, with all consequences the choice has for decisions that range from selecting a method of research to selecting a therapeutic maneuver.

Uniform agreement on the isolable child as the proper measure of development led to the research paradigms that have dominated child psychology during most of its history; basically we have observed those parts of development that the child could readily transport to our laboratories or to our testing sites. The use of isolated preparations for the study of development has, happily, been productive of remarkable advances in our knowledge of children, but with the usual cost of uniform dogma, the commitment to the isolable child has occasionally led child psychology into exaggerations and significant omissions.

There are signals now aloft that the dogma of individualism, both in its claim of lifelong stability of personality and in its claim that human action can be understood without consideration of context or history, is under severe stress. The story that Vygotsky (1978) told fifty years ago, the story of the embeddedness of the developing mind in society, has finally been heard. The image of the child as an epigenetic and continuous creation of social and biological contexts is far more ambiguous and more difficult to paint than the relative simplicities of the traditional and culturally justified self-contained child; it may also illuminate our understanding of children and of our science.

THE PRESENT MOMENT

The cultural epigenesis that created the American child of the late twentieth century continues, and so does the epigenesis that created child psychology. Necessarily, there is no end of the road, no equilibrium. Rather, the transformations of the past 100 years in both children and child psychology are a startling reminder of the eternal call on us to be scrupulous observers and imaginative researchers; they may also serve to force our self-critical recognition that we are both creators and performers in the cultural invention of the child.

REFERENCES

Ariès, P. (1962) *Centuries of Childhood: A Social History of Family Life* (R. Baldick, trans.), New York: Knopf.

Barker-Benfield, G.J. (1977) *Horrors of the Half-Known Life*, New York: Harper and Row.

Barrett, W. (1978) *The Illusion of Technique*, Garden City, NY: Doubleday.

Berger, P.L. and Luckmann, T. (1966) *The Social Construction of Reality: A Treatise in the Sociology of Knowledge*, Garden City, NY: Doubleday.

Binet, A. and Simon, T. (1916) 'Upon the necessity of establishing a scientific diagnosis of inferior states of intelligence' (E.S. Kite, trans.), in A. Binet and T. Simon, *The Development of Intelligence in Children*, Baltimore, Md: Williams & Wilkins (originally published 1905).

Cott, N.F. (1977) *Bonds of Womanhood: Women's Sphere in New England, 1780-1835*, New Haven, Conn.: Yale University Press.

Douglas, A. (1978) *The Feminization of American Culture*, New York: Avon Books.

Hall, G.S. (1883) 'The contents of children's minds', *Princeton Review* 11: 249-72.

Jacoby, G.W. (1914) *Child Training as an Exact Science: A Treatise Based upon the Principles of Modern Psychology, Normal and Abnormal*, New York: Funk & Wagnalls.

Johnson, C. (1904) *Old-Time Schools and School-Books*, New York: Macmillan.

Kagan, J., Kearsley, R.B. and Zelazo, P.R. (1978) (With the assistance of

C. Minton) *Infancy: Its Place in Human Development*, Cambridge, Mass.: Harvard University Press.

Keniston, K. and Carnegie Council on Children (1977) *All our Children: The American Family under Pressure*, New York: Harcourt Brace Jovanovich.

Kessen, W. (ed.) (1975) *Childhood in China*, New Haven, Conn.: Yale University Press.

Klaus, M.H. and Kennell, J.H. (1976) *Maternal–Infant Bonding*, Saint Louis: Mosby.

Lasch, C. (1977) *Haven in a Heartless World: The Family Besieged*, New York: Basic Books.

Lasch, C. (1978) *The Culture of Narcissism: American Life in an Age of Diminishing Expectations*, New York: Norton.

Nelson, J. (1753) *An Essay on the Government of Children under Three General Heads: Viz., Health, Manners, and Education*, London: (no publisher).

Rothchild, J. and Wolf, S.B. (1976) *The Children of the Counter-Culture*, Garden City, NY: Doubleday.

Ryan, W. (1971) *Blaming the Victim*, New York: Random House.

Vygotsky, L.S. (1978) *Mind in Society: The Development of Higher Psychological Processes* (M. Cole, V. John-Steiner, S. Scribner and E. Souberman, eds), Cambridge, Mass.: Harvard University Press.

Watson, J.B. (1928) *Psychological Care of Infant and Child*, New York: Norton.

West, M. (1914) *Infant Care* (Publication no. 8), Washington DC: US Children's Bureau.

3 Psychology and the cultural construction of 'children's needs'

Martin Woodhead

Source: A. James and A. Prout (eds) (forthcoming) *Constructing and Reconstructing Childhood*, Lewes: Falmer Press.

Children's psychological 'needs' are at the heart of contemporary public concern, part of the everyday vocabulary of countless numbers of social welfare workers and teachers, policy-makers and parents. Conceptualizing childhood in terms of 'needs' reflects the distinctive status accorded to young humanity in twentieth-century Western societies. It is widely regarded as a progressive and enlightened framework for working with children. It gives priority to protecting and promoting their psychological welfare, by contrast with former times and other societies, where adult priorities have centred more on children's economic utility, their duties and obligations, rather than their needs (Newson and Newson 1974; Hoffman 1987).

So it may seem somewhat presumptuous to challenge the ubiquity of this way of thinking about children, but by systematically analysing the concept of 'need', I hope to show that this seemingly innocuous and benign four-letter word conceals in practice a complex of latent assumptions and judgements about children. Once revealed, these tell us as much about the cultural location and personal values of the user as about the nature of childhood. My conclusion, provocatively, is that our understanding and respect for childhood might be better served if 'children's needs' were outlawed from future professional discourse, policy recommendations and popular psychology.

This chapter is a by-product of nearly two decades spent exploring the borderlands between child psychology, education and social welfare, especially relating to children under 5. I have encountered numerous statements about children's needs on the way, a small selection of which are reproduced below.

The first is taken from a policy document on nursery education which stated that:

There is now considerable evidence pointing to the importance of the years before five in a child's education – and to the most effective ways of providing for the *needs*, and potential, which children display at this age . . . most *needs* could be met by part-time nursery education.

(DES 1972: para. 16, my emphasis)

Social work professionals have framed their recommendations in similar terms:

It is the responsibility of the worker to be aware of the *needs* of the child – *needs* appropriate to his age (para. 2.6). . . . One of the most essential *needs* of the young child is that of continuity in his experience of being cared for.

(British Association of Social Workers, undated: para. 4.12, my emphasis)

Evidently both education and social work professionals are in little doubt about the existence of 'children's needs'; indeed, in many cases they are the foundation on which policies and practices are built. A clear example is in the debate about day care for the children of working parents. One prominent child-care expert has taken up a very firm position:

My ideal society has no day nurseries, residential nurseries or crèches in it. None at all. Babies and very small children each *need* a 'special' and continuous person or people and they *need* to have their daily lives based on somewhere they know as 'home'.

(Leach 1979: 161, my emphasis)

One of the clearest examples of framing statements about children's welfare in terms of an understanding of their needs can be found in the writings of the former Director of the National Children's Bureau, Mia Kellmer-Pringle. She argued against full-time day care as follows:

Full-time mothering is unique in the sense that the mother has the time, and hence the patience, to develop sensitivity to her baby. This enables her to recognize and adapt to his very special, individual *needs*. . . . The *need* for love and security is met by the child experiencing from birth onwards a stable, continuous, loving and mutually enjoyable relationship with his mother or mother figure. . . . The same applies to her ability to meet the second *need*, for new experiences. These are essential for the mind as food is for the body. . . . It is very difficult to meet this *need* either in a day nursery or by child minders, essentially because they provide a group setting whereas this learning and simulation is *needed* on a one-to-one basis.

(Kellmer-Pringle 1976: 97–8, my emphasis)

These needs, along with two further 'basic needs' (for praise and recognition and for responsibility), have been elaborated in detail (Kellmer-Pringle 1975; 1980).

All the examples so far have been from British sources. But the concept of 'children's needs' is much more extensively used than this. It even found a place in the United Nations Declaration of the Rights of the Child, Principle 6, which begins:

The child, for the full and harmonious development of his personality, *needs* love and understanding. He shall, wherever possible, grow up in the care and under the responsibility of his parents, and in any case in an atmosphere of affection and moral and material security; a child of tender years shall not, save in exceptional circumstances, be separated from his mother.

(United Nations 1959, my emphasis)

Finally, the specification of children's needs is a perennial activity. This is illustrated by my final example, which returns to the topic of nursery education, but was prepared over fifteen years after the first:

A variety of *needs* . . . were drawn to our attention. . . . Young children *need* to be with adults who are interested and interesting, and with other children to whom they may relate. They *need* to have natural objects and artefacts to handle and explore. They *need* opportunity to communicate through music and imaginative play. . . . These *needs* can only be met if an appropriate environment is provided with adults who understand something of child development and are ready and able to listen, encourage and stimulate.

(House of Commons 1988: para. 5.1, my emphasis)

Clearly, in each of these cases, it is possible to view the concept of 'need' merely as shorthand, an economical way of conveying the author's conclusions about the requirements of childhood. There are certainly virtues in condensed prose! But arguably such expressions may also be serving as a very credible veil for uncertainty and even disagreement about what is 'in the best interests of children'. Philosophers have frequently drawn attention to complexities in the concept of 'need' that are rarely recognized in everyday use (e.g. Taylor 1959). Its use in social welfare policy has been analysed by Walton (1969), G. Smith (1971) and Bradshaw (1972). Applications in educational thinking have been considered by Hirst and Peters (1970), Dearden (1972), Wilson (1973) and Wringe (1981).

One way of beginning to understand the latent meaning in 'need' statements is by substituting other expressions for 'need'. Thus while 'want' would convey the idea of a child's demands, 'should have' implies that an observer is judging what is desirable for the child. But 'need' is endowed with a more complex meaning structure. And it also makes a more powerful impact on the reader than either 'want' or 'should have'.

In part this is because the extracts quoted earlier appear to be describing qualities of childhood which are timeless and universal. Identification of needs appears to be a matter of empirical study by the psychologist, or close observation by professional or parent. This apparently 'factual' basis of needs is signalled in the extracts themselves. Caring adults are described as able 'to *recognise* and *adapt to*' the child's needs, or become '*aware of* the needs of the child', or respond to the needs 'which children *display* at this age'. In each case there is a strong implication that, provided the adult is sufficiently astute, needs can be identified mainly or solely through observing children themselves.

But the authority of 'need' statements does not come only from their apparently straightforward descriptive quality. They also convey considerable emotive force, inducing a sense of responsibility, and even feelings of guilt if they are not heeded. This power comes partly from the connotation of helplessness and passivity of any individual who is 'in need', and partly from the implication that dire consequences will follow if the need is not met through appropriate intervention. This combination of descriptive and imperative authority provides a persuasive basis for defining policy. But are 'need' statements quite so robust as they seem? To find out, we need to look more closely at their formal structure.

THE CONCEPT OF CHILDREN'S NEEDS

Statements of the form '*X* needs *Y*' generally make an assumption about the goal of meeting the need as well as the consequence of failing to do so. They are in effect an abbreviation of '*X* needs *Y*, for *Z* to follow'. Indeed the significance of the relationship between *X* and *Y* gains its strength only when *Z* is known. So it is important to note that *Z* is rarely made explicit. Usually it is unstated, or incompletely stated, presumed as a shared understanding between author and reader. There is one exception in the extracts cited above (the United Nations

Declaration of the Rights of the Child) which helps clarify the formal structure of statement about children's needs, as follows:

The child (*X*), for the full and harmonious development of his personality (*Z*), needs love and understanding (*Y*).

This example can be understood as making a factual statement (or hypothesis) about the relationship between *X*, *Y* and *Z*, in which *Y* is seen as a prerequisite for *Z*. In other words it could be restated more simply in the form:

Children that are not given love will grow up emotionally unstable.

So the first step in evaluating a 'need' statement is to identify the outcome *Z* and test the descriptive claim that *Y* is a necessary condition to achieve it. But this gets us only part of the way towards appreciating the power in claims about children's needs.

The examples cited at the beginning of this chapter suggest much more than just an empirical relationship between *X*, *Y* and *Z*. They also imply a desirable relationship, that *Z* is a desirable goal for *X*, and *Y* is the way to achieve it. In other words, statements about children's needs convey an element of judgement about what is good for them and how this can be achieved. It is this aspect of such statements that imbues them with emotive force, implying an imperative for action.

To take a more straightforward example, if an amateur gardener receives the expert advice 'Your plants need water', it is most likely intended to do more than just inform about the factual relationship between plants (*X*), water (*Y*), and the unstated outcome, growth (*Z*). Not unreasonably it also implies that where plants are concerned, growth is desirable. The gardener would be expected to fill up the watering can without delay; after all the survival of the plants is at stake. In other words, the expert's statement presumes a totally uncontroversial value judgement about what is good for plants. The same applies to the statement 'Children need love'. The desirability of emotional stability is so generally accepted that we hardly recognize there to be an unstated goal; the existence of an implicit value judgement is not at all self-evident.

To summarize the analysis so far, I have argued that concealed beneath the apparent simplicity and directness of 'need' statements is a highly condensed combination of both empirical and evaluative claims. They are often not fully specified, but depend on a consensus of knowledge and values between author and reader, horticultural adviser and gardener, social-worker and client, policy-maker and community, etc. A more explicit statement of the sentiment 'A child needs love' might read:

> It is desirable for a child to grow up emotionally secure. A child who is not given love will not grow up emotionally secure. Therefore a child should be given love.

Besides economy of words, what is the significance of condensing this set of ideas into such a short and compelling phrase as 'Children need love' with all the power and connotations discussed earlier? Why is this construction so much more frequently used than, for example, 'Parents should give love to their children' or 'Society should make sure children are loved'? These alternatives are not so bizarre as they seem at first sight. After all, judgements about what is desirable for children and how to achieve it are made by parents, by teachers, by policy-makers, by society – not by the children themselves! Unless, that is, we are attributing to children themselves a sense of the prospect of emotional security that lies ahead, and an understanding of the kinds of experience that will promote it. I shall consider this possibility in a moment. But from the analysis so far I think it should already be clear why statements of policy are so frequently framed in terms of 'children's needs'.

A statement which appears to describe qualities of children's nature as young humanity has a very different status to a judgement by parents, teachers, experts or politicians about what is good for them. Identification of 'need' with children themselves has the effect of reducing the task to an empirical one, of better understanding the natural course of development, rather than a matter of cultural or personal values, of deciding what is good for them. If needs can be identified with children's nature, with universal qualities of their biological and psychological make-up, then the evidence of scientific inquiry can provide the basis of social and educational policy and practice. But if, on the other hand, needs have to be seen as a cultural construction, superimposed on children 'in their best interests' as future adult members of society, personal values and cultural ideologies have a much bigger part to play and the politician's or practitioner's authority is substantially diminished. To put it bluntly, the one appears mainly a matter of establishing 'the facts', and the other appears as also a matter for personal choice and political discussion.

I have set these up as extremes – between 'needs' as intrinsic to children, part of their make-up, and 'needs' as a cultural construction.

But in the rest of the chapter I shall argue that the picture is more complex than that. I want to suggest that there are at least four distinct bases for establishing children's needs. In trying to unravel them, I shall be guided by a deceptively simple question: When we speak of children as having needs, where exactly are their needs?

WHERE ARE 'CHILDREN'S NEEDS?'

Needs in children's nature

As noted above, much of the authority of statements about children's needs comes from assuming that the needs are a property of children themselves, something that they possess, endowed by nature, and detectable in their behaviour. Needs are most literally identified with children's nature when used in the noun form, 'X has a need for Y'.

Kellmer-Pringle's four basic needs (for love and security, for new experiences, for praise and recognition, and for responsibility) come into this category. They are identified with the biological/psychological make-up of young humanity – their instincts, drives, motives and wants. This is clear from the analogy (in the quotation cited at the outset) between the need for new experiences and the need for food, which seems to imply that there are regulatory processes within the organism for monitoring the level of need and initiating behaviour, in accordance with basic homeostatic principles (Mace 1953).

On this model, 'need' is complementary to 'want', provided we can assume that the organism's actions are congruent with its needs. Where children are concerned we can as a rule say that the need for food *is* an intrinsic drive signalled in infancy by rooting for the breast, as well as a distinctive pattern of crying, which is differentiated by care-givers from other types of cries (Thoman 1975).

But what of the need for love, new experiences, praise and recognition, and responsibility? Can these be literally identified with the psychological make-up of the individual such that in some sense (to follow the formal proposition given earlier) X has a drive to seek out Y in order to achieve the state of Z? To focus on the 'need for love and security', the most influential theorist, John Bowlby, was careful to avoid referring to 'needs' or 'drives'. But he did view children's attachment behaviour as closely analogous to patterns of *imprinting* observed in non-human species (Bowlby 1969: 224, 272-3). It is certainly true that young infants are predisposed to pay attention to the human face and seek proximity, comfort and nutrition from care-givers (Schaffer 1984). They also protest vigorously if they are separated from attachment figures, at least after about 7–8 months of age (Schaffer and Emerson 1964) and this is not greatly modified by the cultural setting in which they have been brought up (Kagan *et al.* 1978).

On this evidence, it seems reasonable to conclude that a general predisposition to seek out enduring human relationships is a feature of the infant. But it is much less clear to what degree this is linked to specific features of early nurturing environments, as in 'a stable, continuous, loving and mutually enjoyable relationship with his mother or mother figure' (Kellmer-Pringle); or 'a "special" and continuous person or people and [. . .] daily lives based on somewhere they know as "home" ' (Leach 1979). Specification of these particularities of 'need' and ways in which they can be met seem to have a rather different kind of knowledge base. They are for the most part based on an inference from beliefs and evidence about the undesirable consequences of deprivations.

Needs and psychological health

Whereas in the first model the need *Y* is identified as lying within the child, the emphasis of the second model is on the outcome *Z*, as a universal quality of psychological well-being in children. Giving children sufficient of *Y* is seen as a prerequisite for *Z*, but without presuming that they have any intrinsic drive to achieve it. This is a pathological approach to defining children's needs, analogous to a doctor diagnosing that a child needs a heart operation. The diagnosis is based on a judgement about the desirability of a particular outcome i.e. physical health, and a prescription of how to achieve it. There is no sense in which the doctor's diagnosis is referring to the drive structure of the child. This is essentially a teleological basis for defining need, which in this case is most commonly associated with pathological models of children's welfare. Particular experiences in early childhood are being judged according to their consistency with later mental health, and projected onto children as their 'needs'.

This model has been widely applied in child welfare work, again very largely through the influence of John Bowlby. Indeed, several of the extracts quoted at the beginning of this chapter are derivative from his famous statement about maternal deprivation:

What is believed to be essential for mental health is that an infant and young child should experience a warm, intimate, and continuous relationship with his mother (or permanent mother substitute

– one person who steadily 'mothers' him) in which both find satisfaction and enjoyment.

(Bowlby 1953: 13)

'Need' here does not presume qualities that are intrinsic to children; it is an inference from the relationship between certain qualities of mothering and a valued consequence for children. In many respects this is a powerful basis for prescribing for childhood, which acknowledges the relative helplessness and dependency of the infant and the important role of care-givers who (whether by native instinct, social learning or parent education courses) have the disposition to give love and affection.

Much research has centred on the validity of the claim that particular qualities in early relationships have repercussions for mental health. Studies have focused on the numbers of adults that fulfil a caring role, the patterns of care, and the reversibility of early deprivations. For example Tizard (Tizard and Rees 1974; Tizard and Hodges 1978) conducted a long-term follow-up study of children who had spent much of their infancy (up to four and a half years) in institutions and were then placed either with adoptive parents, or with their natural parents, or remained in an institution. Despite the very different life experiences of these children, and the evidence that in some respects the effects of early deprivation were reversible, consistent long-term effects of institutionalization were found right through to the age of 16 (Hodges and Tizard 1989a; 1989b). Some of the most consistent results were based on teachers' reports of behaviour problems. Reporting on the data when children were 8 years old, Tizard concluded:

it seemed to us possible that all the children's problems at school stemmed not from a conduct disorder of the usual kind, but from two basic characteristics, both concerned with their social behaviour – an almost insatiable desire for adult attention, and a difficulty in forming good relationships with their peer group, although often they got along much better with younger and older children.

(Tizard and Hodges 1978: 114)

It is an easy step to infer from such evidence that children 'need' the loving care of which these institutional children are deprived. After all, such statements have a sound foundation in systematic research. The problem is that global inferences neglect the cultural context of particular child-care arrangements in which the children's development was embedded, and the cultural definitions of mental health and psychological adjustment that the research presumed. These can be variable even within one social setting, as cross-generational research has shown. For example, Wadsworth (1986) has argued that differences in cultural attitudes toward the consequence of divorce during different epochs may modify the impact of that trauma on children. Wadsworth cites evidence from a 1946 cohort for which an association was found between the experience of parental separation or divorce during children's first five years and the incidence of criminal convictions among boys by the age of 21. He postulates a series of transmission pathways that might account for this relationship, including the social stigma associated with divorce at that time, which may have altered the relationship of children to significant adults with whom they came into contact. Most important, he recognizes that the effect of this transmission pathway might be specific to the era in which these children grew up, during which professionals were encouraged to hold strong expectations that children would be severely adversely affected by the experience.

Psychologists are only beginning to tease out the complex social processes that can modify, amplify or alleviate the impact of early childhood experiences (e.g. Woodhead 1988; Rutter 1989). But the inadequacy of making simplistic inferences about children's needs from such complex and often context-specific processes is already abundantly clear.

Needs and social adjustment

Despite the utility as well as persuasive power of applying a pathological paradigm to child welfare judgements, normative relationships are all too readily interpreted as if they were universally valid prescriptions for childhood. The clearest example concerns the number of adults who take care of children. On the evidence available to him at the time Bowlby (1953) argued that children have a predisposition to become attached to one major figure (the theory of 'monotropism'). This is reflected in the claims quoted earlier. Monotropism has certainly been the normal pattern in Western society although it does underestimate the role of fathers and other members of the family as primary care-givers (Osborn *et al.* 1984). Monotropism is also adaptive in a society which emphasizes maternal care in a nuclear family. But for other cultures other patterns are equally adaptive, and so, in their terms, equally consistent with mental health. For example, on the basis of cross-cultural evidence, one reviewer concluded that infants generally seem able to form strong and secure relationships with up to five, possibly ten, 'caretakers' (P.K. Smith 1979: 504; 1980). And Weisner and Gallimore (1977) have described the special place of sibling care in traditional African societies. Clearly multiple caretaking may orient children to patterns of relationships in adult life other than monotropism (Zukow 1989). But there is little justification for translating the observation that normative patterns of early rearing are culturally adaptive into a judgement that these patterns are necessary prerequisites of mental health.

The point has been made most clearly by analogy with two species of monkey (Schaffer 1977). Bonnets are gregarious creatures, and share care of infants widely within the group. By contrast, pigtails live in closely knit family units and are exclusive in their patterns of care. Each pattern is in its own terms adaptive, though an individual brought up in one pattern might find it difficult to adapt to the other:

> A bonnet-reared child is unlikely to become an effective pigtail parent; any particular cultural tradition rests on continuity between child rearing, personality development, and social setting. Yet that is very different from equating any one such tradition with mental health and all other traditions with ill health.
>
> (Schaffer 1977: 110)

Of course, there is no direct parallel within the cultural complexities of human society. But the general perspective certainly applies (e.g. Super and Harkness 1983).

Within this perspective, models of children's welfare based on a concept of need could still have some validity, but they would be relative, not absolute. Thus within a particular cultural framework, X_1 might be said to need Y_1 for Z_1 to follow. But within another cultural framework a different need might be equally vociferously argued for; hence X_2 might be said to need Y_2 for Z_2 to follow; X_3 need Y_3 for Z_3, and so on. This is similar to a pathological model, but it recognizes that determination of need depends as much on appreciation of the particular constellation of relationships in the social environment (past, present and future) as it does on knowledge of universal qualities of human nature. So when it comes to making statements of policy or offering professional advice, personal and cultural values are much more strongly implied. A statement about children's needs would depend on value-judgements, stated or implied, about which patterns of early relationship are considered desirable, what the child should grow up to become, and indeed what makes for the 'good society'.

By way of illustration, consider Kellmer-Pringle's fourth basic children's need – for responsibility. This is a highly valued attribute amongst Western nations where individualism, independent thinking, flexibility and assertiveness are the routes to personal achievement. Thus in a cross-national study of parents' attitudes to children Hoffman (1987) found that parents in the USA laid stress on the importance of a child 'becoming a good person', being 'independent and self-reliant'. By contrast, in countries (such as Turkey, the Philippines and Indonesia) where children's economic contribution is highly valued, parents placed much greater stress on 'deference to elders' and 'obedience'. Presumably parents in the two societies would view their children's 'needs' quite differently.

In short, while in certain very general respects, 'need' statements may have universal validity, detailed prescriptions about children's needs are normative, and depend on a judgement about processes of cultural adaptation and social adjustment. This conclusion could have important implications for any inter-cultural generalizations. For instance, it could be argued that the emphasis in the United Nations Declaration (quoted at the outset) on the need for maternal care, which was informed by Western family arrangements and research, risks being ethnocentric.

Needs and cultural prescriptions

There is one other common usage of the concept of children's needs which is even further removed from an understanding of children's nature, their mental health, or their social adjustment. It is most clearly illustrated by the policy statements on early education quoted at the outset. Take the conclusions of the House of Commons Select Committee in 1988. In what sense do children 'need to be with adults who are interested and interesting, . . . need to have natural objects . . . to handle, need . . . to communicate through music and imaginative play'? Such educational needs are largely a cultural construction. They are illustrated in even more extreme form by such claims as 'children need to learn physics, pottery and parent craft'. These needs are certainly not a part of the psychological make-up of individual children, nor even a prerequisite for their psychological well-being, either in absolute or relative terms. There is a weak sense in which children in Western society deprived of educational opportunities may be culturally maladapted, but there is plenty of room for argument about the appropriate criteria for judging that.

To understand the ubiquity of such 'need' statements we have to consider the relationship between experts who make such authoritative pronouncements (in this case educators) and clients who receive them (usually parents on behalf of their children). Framing professional judgements in terms of 'children's needs' serves to direct attention away from the particular adult value-position from which they are made. Projected onto children themselves, they acquire spurious objectivity. In this way, cultural prescriptions for childhood are presented as if they were intrinsic qualities of children's own psychological make-up.

CONCLUSION: HUMAN NATURE OR CULTURAL CONSTRUCTION?

When policy recommendations and professional advice are expressed in terms of children's needs, they give an impression of universal objectivity. It is tempting to accept them at face value as authoritative statements of fact. But beneath the veneer of certainty I have argued there lies a complicated array of personal and cultural values alongside empirical claims about childhood.

Framing prescriptions in terms of children's needs may serve important functions for those who make them, notably the greater authority that comes from projecting their decision-making criteria onto the child. But as a consequence they fail to differentiate several quite distinct bases for making prescriptions about what is in the best interests of children. Four categories of usage have been distinguished: 'need' as a description of children's psychological nature; 'need' as an inference from what is known about the pathological consequences of particular childhood experiences; 'need' as a judgement about which childhood experiences are most culturally adaptive; and 'need' as a prescription about which childhood experiences are most highly valued in society. These are not just matters of emphasis. The different usages have quite different statuses, which become merged and confused when rendered into apparently unproblematic generalizations about children's needs.

In a homogeneous society, where the findings of psychological research derive from and feed back into a shared normative framework of cultural values and practices, these distinctions might not seem too important. But when the reference point is a culturally diverse society like Britain, and especially when it is a group of societies as diverse as the United Nations, simple generalizations about children's needs are much more problematic. In these circumstances, it becomes imperative to disentangle the scientific from the evaluative, the natural from the cultural.

How much better it might be to abandon this problematic way of construing childhood altogether? This would help break down the mystifications that are locked in much professional language, forcing those who make judgements about what is and is not in children's interests to make explicit and justify their decision-criteria, and unveil their assumptions for external scrutiny.

In drawing this conclusion, I want to emphasize that I am not suggesting that judgements about the adequacy of children's care, education and welfare are to be avoided. On the contrary. Despite the diversity of cultural arrangements for child-rearing, it is clearly imperative to establish consensus on the boundaries of minimal adequacy, although even this task may be problematic, as comparative studies of child abuse have discovered (Korbin 1981). Neither am I arguing that the perspectives on childhood that inform these judgements are a purely cultural construction. Children inherit a distinctively human nature as well as being brought up in a particular culture. Their dependency on others to protect their interests during the long period of human immaturity known as childhood means that judgements must continually be made by those responsible for them, although the length of their dependency and the cultural articulation of what is in their best interests will vary from society to society and from time to time.

The challenge is not to shy away from developing a perspective on childhood, but to recognize the plurality of pathways to maturity within that perspective. This is all the more important at a time when the influence of child psychology is extending well beyond the societies (notably North America and Europe) from which dominant theories and research data have been derived. For example a *Handbook of Asian Child Development and Child Rearing Practices* has been prepared by mainly Thai child development experts explicitly to assimilate Western child development theory into Third World contexts. The following brief extract vividly illustrates the profound but largely unacknowledged issues that are raised by the enterprise:

Asian parents have a long history of well developed cultures behind them. They are mostly agriculturalists who are submissive to the earth's physical nature. Thus many of their traditional beliefs and practices prevent them from seeking and using the new *scientific* knowledge in child rearing.

The *Handbook of Child Rearing* may require parents to change many of their beliefs, attitudes, values, habits and behaviours. Therefore, many necessary changes will be met with some resistance. For example, giving the child more of the independence the child *needs* and making less use of power and authority during adolescence will shake the very roots of those Asian families where authoritarian attitudes and practice are emphasized.

(Suvannathat *et al.* 1985: 4–5, my emphasis)

Cross-cultural research has always held a respectable, albeit marginal, role in psychological work (e.g. Warren 1980). But it is only in the last ten years or so that consideration of cultural and social context have begun to occupy centre-stage as an integral element in mainstream theory and research (e.g. in the USA, Bronfenbrenner 1979; Kessen 1979; Kessel and Siegel 1983 and in the UK, Richards 1974; Richards and Light 1986). Whether the emerging 'cultural constructivist' perspective on child development will make sufficient impact to modify the assumptions in the extract (above) remains to be seen. If it does not, as seems likely, and Western culture and values continue to be promoted in the guise of science, then a gradual process of homogenization of child-rearing patterns seems inevitable. In the long term, such trends could have important implications for the concept of 'children's needs'. The arguments in this chapter in favour of a more explicit, culturally sensitive, perspective on childhood will lose much of their force. Children's needs will become universal.

REFERENCES

Bowlby, J. (1953) *Child Care and the Growth of Love*, Harmondsworth: Penguin.

Bowlby, J. (1969) *Attachment and Loss, Volume 1: Attachment*, Harmondsworth: Penguin.

Bradshaw, J. (1972) 'The concept of social need', *New Society* 30 March.

British Association of Social Workers (undated) *Children Under Five* (mimeo).

Bronfenbrenner, U. (1979) *The Ecology of Human Development*, Cambridge, Mass.: Harvard University Press.

Dearden, R.F. (1972) 'Needs in education', in R.F. Dearden, P.H. Hirst, and R.S. Peters (eds) *A Critique of Current Educational Aims*, London: Routledge & Kegan Paul.

DES (1972) *Education: A Framework for Expansion*, Cmnd 5174 (White Paper), London: HMSO.

Hirst, P.H. and Peters, R.S. (1970) *The Logic of Education*, London: Routledge & Kegan Paul.

Hodges J. and Tizard, B. (1989a) 'IQ and behavioural adjustment of ex-institutional adolescents', *Journal of Child Psychology and Psychiatry* 30(1): 53–76.

Hodges, J. and Tizard, B. (1989b) 'Social and family relationships of ex-institutional adolescents', *Journal of Child Psychology and Psychiatry* 30(1): 77–98.

Hoffman, L.W (1987) 'The value of children to parents and child-rearing patterns', in C. Kagitcibasi (ed.) *Growth and Progress in Cross-Cultural Psychology*, Berwyne, Swets North America Inc.

House of Commons (1988) 'Educational provision for the under-fives', *First Report of the Education, Science and Arts Committee*, vol. 1, London: HMSO.

Kagan, J., Kearsley, R.B. and Zeloza, P.R. (1978) *Infancy: Its Place in Human Development*, London: Harvard University Press.

Kellmer-Pringle, M. (1975; 2nd edn 1980) *The Needs of Children*, London: Hutchinson.

Kellmer-Pringle, M. (1976) 'A policy for young children', in S. Reedy and M. Woodhead (eds) (1981) *Family, Work and Education*, London: Hodder & Stoughton.

Kessel, F.S. and Siegel, A.W. (eds) (1983) *The Child and Other Cultural Inventions*, New York: Praeger.

Kessen, W. (1979) 'The American child and other cultural inventions', *American Psychologist* 34: 815–20.

Korbin, J.E. (ed.) (1981) *Child Abuse and Neglect*, Berkeley, Calif.: University of California Press.

Leach, P. (1979) *Who Cares?*, Harmondsworth: Penguin.

Mace, C.A (1953) 'Homeostasis, needs and values', *British Journal of Psychology* August: 201–8.

Newson, J. and Newson, E. (1974) 'Cultural aspects of child-rearing in the English-speaking world', in M.P.M. Richards (ed.) *The Integration of a Child into a Social World*, Cambridge: Cambridge University Press.

Osborn, A.F., Butler, N.R. and Morris, T.C. (1984) *The Social Life of Britain's Five Year Olds*, London: Routledge & Kegan Paul.

Richards, M.P.M. (ed.) (1974) *The Integration of a Child into a Social World*, Cambridge: Cambridge University Press.

Richards, M.P.M. and Light, P. (eds) (1986) *Children of Social Worlds*, Cambridge: Polity Press.

Rutter, M. (1989) 'Pathways from childhood to adult life', *Journal of Child Psychology and Psychiatry* 30(1): 23–52.

Schaffer, H.R. (1977) *Mothering*, London: Open Books.

Schaffer, H.R. (1984) *The Child's Entry into a Social World*, London: Academic Press.

Schaffer, H.R. and Emerson, P.E. (1964) 'The development of social attachments in infancy', *Monograph of the Society for Research in Child Development* 29:94.

Smith, G. (1971) 'Some research implications of the Seebohm Report', *British Journal of Sociology* 22: 295–310.

Smith, P.K. (1979) 'How many people can a young child feel secure with?', *New Society* 31 May.

Smith, P.K. (1980) 'Shared care of young children: alternative models to monotropism', *Merrill-Palmer Quarterly* 6(4): 371–89.

Super, C. and Harkness, S. (1983) 'The cultural construction of child development: a framework for the socialization of effect' *Ethos* 11: 221–31.

Suvannathat, C., Bhanthumnavin, D., Bhaupirom, L. and Keats, D.M. (eds) (1985) *Handbook of Asian Child Development and Child Rearing Practices*, Bangkok, Thailand: Srinakharinwirot University, Behavioural Science Research Institute.

Taylor, P.W. (1959) ' "Need" statements', *Analysis* 19(5): 106–11.

Thoman, E.B. (1975) 'Sleep and wake behaviours in neonates: consistencies and consequences', *Merrill-Palmer Quarterly* 21(4): 295–314.

Tizard, B. and Hodges, J. (1978) 'The effect of early institutional rearing on the development of eight year old children', *Journal of Child Psychology and Psychiatry* 19: 99–118.

Tizard, B. and Rees, J. (1974) 'A comparison of the effects of adoption, restoration to the natural mother, and continued institutionalisation on the cognitive development of four year old children', *Child Development* 45: 92–9.

United Nations (1959) Declaration of the Rights of the Child, in *Resolution 1386 (XIV)* of 20 November 1959, *Yearbook of the United Nations*, p. 198, New York: United Nations.

Wadsworth, M. (1986) 'Evidence from three birth cohort studies for long-term and cross-generational effects on the development of children', in M.P.M. Richards and P. Light (eds) *Children of Social Worlds*, Cambridge: Polity Press.

Walton, R. (1969) 'Need: a central concept', *Social Service Quarterly* 43: 1.

Warren, N. (ed.) (1980) *Studies in Cross-Cultural Psychology* vol. 2, London: Academic Press.

Weisner, T. and Gallimore, R. (1977) 'My brother's keeper: child and sibling caretaking', *Current Anthropology* 18: 2.

Wilson, P.S. (1973) 'What is an educational need?', *Forward Trends* 17(2): 52–8.

Woodhead, M. (1988) 'When psychology informs public policy: the case of early childhood intervention', *American Psychologist* 43(6): 443–54.

Wringe, C.A. (1981) *Children's Rights: A Philosophical Study*, London: Routledge & Kegan Paul.

Zukow, P.G. (ed.) (1989) *Sibling Interaction Across Cultures: Theoretical and Methodological Issues*, New York: Springer-Verlag.

Part two
Frameworks for child care

Introduction

The twentieth century has . . . seen the emergence of prescriptive childcare philosophies which take little account of the reality of socio-economic circumstances. . . . ideological pressure for women to fulfil their 'natural' destiny has built up within idealized definitions of what a 'good mother' should be.

(Duxbury 1987: 16)

The chapters in Part II take the analysis of interrelationships between cultural influences and psychological ideas one stage further by concentrating on the issue of child care. Tizard (Chapter 4) introduces Bowlby's theory of maternal deprivation, explains its pervasive influence on post-war social policy and maternal practices, and then re-evaluates it from the perspective of cultural trends and research evidence at the end of the 1980s. Bowlby's ideas played a powerful role in reforming and improving child-care regimes, especially in children's homes. At the same time, however, his emphasis on the fundamental importance of continuous care by the child's principal attachment figure (generally the mother) reinforced the postwar social climate of domestic constraint and imposed guilt on those mothers who went out to work, whether through necessity or choice. Tizard draws on a wide range of recent studies to argue that the psychological significance of separation in the early years has been overstated and that day care in particular need not be damaging and in some respects may be beneficial.

Controversy about day care still rages in the academic literature, especially in respect of the issue of possible effects on the infant–mother attachment relationship. The so-called 'Strange Situation' has become the standard measure of variations in attachment, and there is now some evidence that infants whose mothers work full time are more likely to measure as insecurely attached. Clarke-Stewart (Chapter 5) cites the work of those who argue that this is a worrying indication that full day care from infancy may indeed be harmful, but goes on to offer a very different interpretation, suggesting that the experimental procedure may not be psychologically equivalent for day-care and home-based children. For the latter the experience of separation is a daily event; they are used to relating to a wider range of adults. Clarke-Stewart also reports conflicting evidence on children's social development, and argues that whether effects on children's behaviour are interpreted as harmful or benign depends as much on competing cultural definitions of what is desirable as on scientific evidence.

One of the curious features about this debate is that it is carried on within such a narrow framework of assumptions about patterns of care. Historically particular cultural arrangements in Western societies this century have been generalized as the norm for child-rearing and even as a necessary condition for mental health. Yet a survey of anthropological literature by Weisner and Gallimore (1977) indicated that mothers were the primary care-givers in only 46 per cent of sampled societies: in many cases siblings and other children carried a major burden of responsibility. Older siblings were important care-givers in our own society until the introduction of compulsory education took them away from the home for the major part of the day. Even so, most young children inhabit a wide network of relationships from birth, which have been neglected by psychologists, with a few notable exceptions (e.g. Dunn 1988). In Chapter 6 Hill describes the networks of care for children under 3 in an Edinburgh sample, concentrating not on formal day-care arrangements, which were rare in this sample, but on the very many relationships with relatives, friends and neighbours which young children established and, for the most part, enjoyed.

In Chapter 7 Hetherington reminds us that child-care arrangements outside the family are not the only area of social concern. Young children also commonly have to cope with disturbed, distorted, disrupted and reconstructed relationships associated with their parents' marital discord, separation, divorce and frequently also remarriage to another partner. Hetherington summarizes the findings of her longitudinal study in the United States to show that there is no simple pattern of long-term effects. Whether children of divorce become winners, losers or survivors depends on their personal characteristics, and the events that follow breakdown of their parents' relationship. It also depends on children being able to turn to a wider network of other social relationships that can buffer the trauma and support their adjustment. In such situations, overly exclusive patterns of parental care might not turn out to be in children's best interests at all.

REFERENCES

Dunn, J. (1988) *The Beginnings of Social Understanding*, Oxford: Basil Blackwell.

Duxbury, S. (1987) 'Childcare ideologies and resistance', in A. Pollard (ed.) *Children and their Primary Schools*, Lewes: Falmer Press.

Weisner, T.S. and Gallimore, R. (1977) 'My brother's keeper: child and sibling caretaking', *Current Anthropology* 18(2): 169–90.

4 Working mothers and the care of young children

Barbara Tizard

Source: E. Lloyd, A. Phoenix and A. Woollett (eds) (forthcoming, January 1991) *Social Construction of Motherhood*, London: Sage.
Used by permission of Sage Publications Ltd, London.

ATTACHMENT AND THE EMPLOYED MOTHER

After the ending of the Second World War a powerful opposition to the employment of mothers developed, based on the threat of supposed long-lasting psychological damage to their children. Earlier opposition to maternal employment had tended to dwell on the dangers of physical and moral neglect, but the new threat was much more potent. The principal theoretician of this movement was John Bowlby, a medically qualified psychoanalyst. Bowlby came from the heart of the British Establishment, the son of a baronet, educated at the Royal Naval College, Dartmouth, and Trinity College, Cambridge. Like all psychoanalysts, he believes that the root of personality development lies in the child's early relationships with the mother. But while Freud believed that a baby becomes attached to its mother because she gratifies its instinctual hunger and oral drives, Bowlby believes that attachment itself is instinctual. Further, while Freud believed that the Oedipal crisis and its resolution is the key to later development, Bowlby believes that it is the quality of the mother–child attachment in the first three years which shapes the child's later personality development.

Bowlby originally developed his theory to explain his finding that young delinquents who were 'affectionless', that is incapable of love, had experienced prolonged separation from their mothers in the first few years of life. In his most famous book, *Maternal Care and Mental Health* (1951), Bowlby put forward the concept of 'maternal deprivation', a state of affairs in which the young child does not experience an essential need, that is a 'warm, intimate and continuous relationship with his mother'. He argued on the basis not only of his study of young thieves, but also of research by others in orphanages and hospitals, that maternal deprivation 'may entirely cripple the capacity to make relationships with other people'. He concludes that the damage is likely to be permanent, unless the situation can be reversed in the first few years of life.

For Bowlby, the age at which separation occurs is critical. Below the age of about 6 or 7 months babies do not appear to be disturbed by separation. After the age of 3, children gradually become less vulnerable to separation because of their growing capacity to understand explanations and to conceive of a future when their mother will return. But between about 7 months and 3 years young children are likely to show intense distress when separated from their mothers. Studies in residential nurseries and hospitals showed that they pass through a regular sequence of behaviour, in which distress is initially accompanied by protest, and then followed by despair and eventually by emotional detachment from the mother, resulting, Bowlby believes, from repression of the child's feelings of anger and anxiety. After reunion the detachment may persist for a while, to be succeeded by ambivalence to the mother, clinging, anxiety and hostility. Repeated or prolonged episodes of this kind, he believes, permanently scar development.

Why should the experience of separation be so traumatic to young children? Bowlby believes that this can be understood only in relationship to the attachment to the mother that develops some time between the ages of about 7 and 12 months, and remains intense until about the age of 3. Attachment is the tendency for the child to show a marked preference for a specific person, to derive security from being near her, especially when frightened, tired or ill, and to protest if she goes out of sight. Bowlby believes that attachment is a biologically adaptive mechanism which, by keeping the young close to their mothers, enables them to survive. He pointed out that the same tendency for the young to cling to or be 'imprinted on' their mothers can be seen in many other animal species, where it clearly functions to protect them from predators. It is because separation is potentially life-threatening that it is such a frightening and traumatic experience for the young child. The attachment bond serves other important developmental functions, enabling children to learn from their mothers and providing a secure basis from which to explore and play. (The reader will note that Bowlby's views on separation and attachment antedate and are different from the recent theory that if separation occurs in the period after delivery, the mother may fail to establish a bond with her baby: e.g. Klaus and Kennell 1976). According to Bowlby, all children are biologically biased to form an attachment to the person looking after them, and will do so even if abused. It is only rarely, after repeated experiences of separation, that children become permanently emotionally detached and incapable of giving love. However, attachments vary in quality, and children with no confidence that their mother will be accessible and responsive to them may be 'insecurely' attached.

To explain the long-lasting influence of this early attachment relationship, Bowlby (1973) postulates that children form internal working models of themselves and others, and that these persist, relatively unchanged, throughout life. Children in a warm, loving relationship with their mother will develop a model of themselves as loveable, and of others as trustworthy. Children who had an insecure early attachment are likely to see others as untrustworthy, or rejecting, and to believe themselves incapable of being loved.

The concept of insecure attachment was further elaborated by Bowlby's colleague, Ainsworth, on the basis of experimental work with children of 12–24 months in the 'Strange Situation' (Ainsworth *et al.* 1978). Briefly the experiment involves taking mother and child to a strange room, and observing the child's responses to a series of increasingly stressful events, including the introduction of a stranger, the mother's departure, leaving the child alone with the stranger, and reunion with the mother. Securely attached children explore freely when their mother is present, and use her as a secure base when a stranger appears. They greet her warmly on reunion, and are readily comforted by her. Children who do not behave in this way are said to be insecurely attached. When reunited with their mother they may be ambivalent or angry, or they may avoid or ignore her. Their attachment to her is real, but it does not provide them with security.

Although they saw separation from the mother as an important cause of insecure attachment, Bowlby and Ainsworth state that insecure attachment more commonly occurs in babies who have never been separated from their mothers, but who have been inadequately mothered. Ainsworth *et al.* (1978) found that those babies who were securely attached at the age of 12 months had mothers who, at an earlier age, had been observed by researchers to be more affectionate to them, more effective at soothing them, and more often engaged in face-to-face behaviour and physical contact with them than other mothers. The mothers of ambivalently attached, clinging babies tended to be insensitive to their signals and inept in handling them, while the mothers of avoidant babies had been more rejecting than other mothers. Several follow-up studies by other authors (e.g. Sroufe 1984) have shown that security of attachment in infancy is a good predictor of later emotional and social adjustment. At age 3 to 6 years those children who had been classified as securely attached at 12 or 18 months were functioning better in nursery school, in terms of such qualities as social competence, independence and high self-esteem, than those who had been insecurely attached.

An important aspect of attachment for both Bowlby and Ainsworth is that it is 'monotropic'. This term was defined by Bowlby (1969) as 'a strong bias for attachment behaviour to become directed towards one particular person and for a child to become strongly possessive of that person'. Bowlby (1958) believes that the bond formed with the mother is different in kind from all others: 'The integrating function of the unique mother-figure is one the importance of which I believe can hardly be exaggerated'. It is this relationship which he believes is essential for the child's security, and it is disturbances in this relationship which he believes lead to psychological disorder. Hence his insistence that mothering cannot in any real sense be shared, although an adoptive mother or a permanent nanny may substitute for the biological mother. He did not consider the possibility that 'mothering' may be provided by a man.

IMPLICATIONS OF BOWLBY'S THEORIES FOR THE CARE OF CHILDREN

Bowlby (1951) was in no doubt as to the importance of his demonstration of the role of mothering in mental health, which he described as 'a discovery comparable in magnitude to that of the role of vitamins in physical health'. In evaluating this claim it is important to set Bowlby's contribution in an historical context. He was writing at a time when many children's homes and residential nurseries were grossly under-staffed and when, even if this was not the case, care was dominated by considerations of hygiene rather than psychological need. Babies in institutions often received only essential physical care; children were shifted at frequent intervals from one foster home to another, and hospitalized for long periods without family contact. There is no doubt that the humanization of these practices owes much to Bowlby.

At this stage, Bowlby was almost entirely concerned with the welfare of children who come into long-term care. Others, however, immediately seized on the implications of his writings for the employment of women. A WHO report (1951) stated that the use of day nurseries would inevitably cause 'permanent damage to the emotional health of a future generation', a dictum that was quickly to become very influential.

In his later writings Bowlby concentrated on the development of attachment theory, and made only scattered references to the implications of his theories for the care of children. However, he did express the view that 'to start nursery school much before the third birthday is for most children an undesirably stressful experience' (Bowlby 1973). In his view, a mother with a young child should 'give him as much of her presence as he seems to want [so that] he can satisfactorily regulate his own intake [of mothering]. Only after he reaches school years may there be occasion for gentle discouragement' (Bowlby 1969).

It became accepted wisdom amongst doctors, teachers and social workers that women with children under the age of 3, or even 5, put them at serious risk by going out to work, that day care or nursery schooling is harmful for children under the age of 3, and that even over this age it should only be part-time. Few people now realize that British nursery schools until the 1950s took children from the age of 2, and that full-day school was seen as important to allow for the valuable social experiences of communal meals, rest and a balanced day.

Since the effect of Bowlby's advice is to impose severe constraints on the activities of the mothers of young children it is worth considering why a whole generation of British and American mothers followed it, or felt intense guilt if they did not. One reason is, no doubt, that the prevailing post-Second World War ideology, quite independently of Bowlby's beliefs, was to discourage women from entering the labour market. But it is too simplistic to see this as the whole story. In the first place, much that Bowlby had to say rang true. Mothers know that young children pass through a stage of clinging to them, that they are likely to be distressed if left with strangers, and may be disturbed on their return home. If an important psychologist had apparently shown that this distress leaves lasting effects, many women were prepared to believe him. This was probably especially true of those who to some extent and at some level had absorbed a psychoanalytic approach.

A further reason for accepting Bowlby's views was that he challenged the inhumane approach of orthodox doctors at that time. By stressing the reality and importance of children's distress on separation their protests could no longer be dismissed as trivial, or as bad behaviour resulting from mothers' hysteria or past spoiling. In consequence, children's emotional needs began to be seen as at least as important as their physical needs, and as matters to be taken into account by doctors and administrators. Bowlby thus provided prestige and theoretical back-up for a more humane attitude to the care of children in hospitals and nurseries.

But along with this humanity went an insistence on the enormous importance for children's development of their relationship with one particular person, their mother. His earlier requirement that mothers of young children must be more or less constantly available to them was demanding enough. But the message of his later work, and that of Ainsworth, that children's future mental health depends entirely on the sensitivity of the mothering they receive in the first years of life, imposed an even heavier burden. While in principle it is simple, although in practice it may be difficult, to avoid separations, the obligation to be continuously and appropriately responsive is much more difficult and onerous. More generally, any theory that attributes the origin of adult neurosis to inadequate mothering in the early years may be said to champion children at the expense of imposing guilt on their mothers.

A CRITIQUE OF BOWLBY'S THEORY

Separation does not in itself cause harmful effects

Research since Bowlby's early studies has shown that delinquency and an inability to care for others does not result from early separation *per se*, but may develop in association with a variety of adverse factors. Separation *per se*, whether it lasts a month, a year, or is permanent, has not been found to have any direct long-term effects on development. It seems rather that any apparent adverse effects on the child are due to the train of adverse experiences that may follow separation, e.g. being taken into care, or the pattern of chronic adverse experiences that may have preceded it, e.g. abuse or marital discord (Rutter 1981).

Bowlby's claim that even transient separations of a day or a week are in themselves inevitably distressing and damaging has also not been substantiated. Of course, these separations may cause intense distress, but the evidence suggests that this is only the case when separation from the mother occurs in combination with one or more of the following adverse factors: the absence of other people to whom the child is attached; the child is in a strange environment; the child is passed from one person to another, and no one person takes over the 'mothering' role, that is gives particular attention, comfort and affection to the child (Robertson and Robertson 1971). When these conditions prevail, distress is likely to follow, and repeated total separations, as when a child has frequent changes of foster homes, may well be damaging, although research evidence on this point is limited. There is certainly reason to believe that familiarity and continuity play an important role in early development (Tizard 1986).

Day care is not in itself psychologically damaging

One of the most widely known aspects of Bowlby's thinking is his opposition to day care, and hence to the employment of women with young children. This attitude arises, of course, from his belief that even transient separations, especially if repeated daily, damage the security of children's attachment to their mother, and hence their personality development.

Viewed historically and cross-culturally, the belief lacks plausibility. In agricultural and peasant communities grandmothers and older children have always played an important role in child-rearing; wealthy women in all societies have employed nannies. Weisner and Gallimore (1977) found that of 186 contemporary non-industrial societies there were only 5 where the child was almost exclusively looked after by the mother. Of course, it does not follow that because a practice is nearly universal it is necessarily beneficial. Nevertheless, strong evidence would be required to prove the contrary. So far as current Western society is concerned, there is no convincing evidence of the detrimental effect of day care. At whatever age children enter day care, they develop attachments to both their mothers and to their care-giver, and their attachment to their mother is much the stronger (Clarke-Stewart and Fein 1983).

However, Ainsworth and her colleagues have argued that these attachments are likely to be insecure. Most recently Belsky (1988), in reviewing US studies, has concluded that 'more than 20 hours a week of non-parental day care during the first year of life' puts infants at risk of developing insecure attachments. These studies certainly show a difference between the babies of employed mothers and non-employed mothers (though the sample sizes are small), but the interpretation of this difference is disputed. Clarke-Stewart (1988) has pointed out that the 'Strange Situation' (see p. 63), which is used to assess the security of attachment, may not be very stressful for the children of working mothers, who are more used to being left with strangers in a strange room. Hence the finding that they are more likely to ignore their mothers on reunion may therefore simply reflect their greater familiarity with situations of this kind, and their consequent greater independence from their mothers.

This interpretation is supported by the findings of European studies of slightly older children of working mothers. Although some research, both in the USA and Britain, has found a high rate of behaviour problems amongst children in nurseries, these appear to be studies involving families with many problems. In Britain, for example, priority in admission to day nurseries is given to families with serious psychosocial problems, so it is not surprising that day nursery children tend to show behaviour difficulties (McGuire and Richman 1986). But when the children studied come from families without any particular problems, pre-school children who have been in day care as infants seem to do as well on general measures of intelligence, personality, self-confidence and emotional adjustment as other children. A recent study from the Thomas Coram Research Unit in London, for example, followed a large sample of children whose mothers returned to full-time employment, mostly to professional and managerial jobs, after maternity leave. The children were cared for by child-minders, relations or in private nurseries. At age 3 the only difference between these children and those who had been cared for by their mothers was that the children of employed mothers tended to be less timid and more sociable towards unfamiliar people, and more willing to share with other children. This was especially true of the children cared for in nurseries. There were no differences in 'problem' behaviour or aggressiveness between mother-reared and other children (Melhuish 1990).

The early years are not decisive for development

Bowlby's claims about the long-term effects of the security or otherwise of early attachment on adult personality and relationships remain speculative. No one as yet has assessed the security of attachments in infancy, and followed the children into adolescence or adult life. But there is mounting evidence that theories of the permanent effects of early experience are too simplistic.

Methodologically the issue is extremely difficult to study, since for the great majority of children the environment, the people caring for them, and the child's own temperament remain fairly constant. It may be this constancy, rather than the influence of early experiences, which accounts for continuities in the child's behaviour. Thus the finding that securely attached 1-year-olds, as assessed in the Strange Situation, tend to become co-operative, mature 3-year-olds may be due in part or in whole to continuities in family circumstances, rather than solely to the quality of mothering in the first twelve months. There is, in fact, evidence that major changes in family circumstances, e.g. the father's unemployment or parents' divorce, are associated with changes in the security of attachment (Campos *et al.* 1983).

Opportunities to isolate the long-term effects of early experience arise only in unusual circumstances. The classic example is when a drastic change of environment occurs after infancy, so that it is possible to see whether the effects of early adverse – or beneficial – experience are reversed. Most studies of such changes suggest that a large amount of reversibility can occur, and that children are often extraordinarily resilient.

Resilience was certainly evident in a small group of children who were studied after they had survived German concentration camps, and later interviewed in middle age (Moskovitz 1985). They had all been orphaned in the first few months of life, and thereafter had been given only basic physical care by a succession of camp inmates. They had been subjected to many terrifying experiences, including being present at camp hangings. On release, at the age of 3, all were severely malnourished, their language was delayed, and they were aggressive and hostile to adults, although closely attached to each other. In middle age, four of the six were interviewed by a psychologist familiar with their earlier behaviour and history. Two of the four were described as happily married, successful and effective in their work, with charming and warm personalities. A third felt very insecure and was subject to depression, while the fourth was still preoccupied with the insecurities and privations of his childhood.

Another dramatic example was the case of Czech twins who were reared in virtual isolation in cupboards and cellars from the age of 1½ to 7 years. When rescued they were severely retarded and disturbed, had almost no speech, and could hardly walk. However, a strong emotional bond between them was evident. After foster placement they become devoted to their foster mother. By the age of 14 their IQ scores were average and they were described as agile, gay, and popular at school (Koluchova 1976). It seems most unlikely that their early suffering had no long-term effects on the twins. However, the extent of their recovery, and that of some at least of the camp orphans, throws serious doubt on the theory that even very severe adverse experiences necessarily have a devastating influence on development, if the children's situation markedly changes. In both these examples it seems likely that the strong attachments between the children served as an important protective factor.

Less dramatic but well-documented evidence about the long-term effects of lack of early mothering comes from my own follow-up study of children who were adopted from residential nurseries between the ages of 2 and 10. Before this time the children were looked after by a large number of constantly changing nurses – on average fifty by the time they were 4½ – who were encouraged to relate to them in a detached, 'professional' manner. In other respects the care of the children was good, and their intellectual development was average. By the age of 4½, 70 per cent of the children still in institutions were said by the staff 'not to care deeply about anyone'. It was notable that they had not formed attachments to other children (Tizard 1977).

Nevertheless, after adoption most of the children quickly formed deep, reciprocated attachments to their new parents. At age 16 their relations with their adoptive parents in most cases continued to be good. But many, though by no means all, still had more problems relating to their peers than did the control children, and they also tended to be more anxious (Hodges and Tizard 1989).

A characteristic of this and other follow-up studies of children who have suffered adverse early experiences is that a sizeable proportion of children seem to escape without any ill effects, even when they remain in an adverse environment throughout childhood. Thus Quinton and Rutter (1985) followed up women who had spent their childhood in care from a very early age. As adults, 30 per cent had marked psychosocial problems, and 40 per cent were rated poor parents. But 20 per cent were said to have no psychosocial problems, and 31 per cent were rated as good parents. The parenting difficulties that were found rarely amounted to neglect or abuse, and the ex-care women were as affectionate with, and involved in, their children as the controls.

Bowlby and Ainsworth argue that the resilience of some individuals does not invalidate their hypothesis about the effects of early maternal deprivation, any more than the fact that some children do not succumb to the polio virus invalidates the hypothesis that the virus causes polio. However, the evidence seems better explained by a 'transactional' model, which can account for both the continuities and discontinuities in development. According to this model, individuals and their environments have a reciprocal influence on each other. Whether early experience determines later development depends on later events, which can maintain, amplify or counteract the influence of early experience. Quinton and Rutter (1985) were able to show that whether or not the women referred to above had current personality and parenting difficulties could be related to events occurring after early childhood, starting with whether their experiences at school had been positive, and extending to the supportiveness or otherwise of their husbands and the number of socioeconomic stresses under which they were currently living. It was not the case that the later events had been inexorably set in motion by events in the early years.

These and similar findings suggest that although early adverse experience often does have a marked influence on development, positive experiences occurring at least as late as early adulthood can lead to improvements in functioning. Equally such evidence as there is suggests that unfortunately a secure early' childhood is not an insurance against later psychological damage. Loss of a parent during adolescence, for example, or loss of a spouse as an adult, seems to predispose towards depression, irrespective of the early circumstances (Brown and Harris 1978).

Is the early mother–child relationship of unique importance?

It has already been pointed out that attachment theory is especially threatening to women because of its message that the child's entire future can be permanently damaged by 'inadequate' mothering in the first year of life. But women do not always dote on their babies. They may be under a variety of pressures which lower their sensitivity, e.g. poverty, poor housing, the care of a large number of other children, illness in the family, or marital discord, or they may have ambivalent feelings towards their child. The effects of psychosocial stresses of these kinds on relationships have rarely been studied, but most mothers will have experienced their reality at times. It has already been argued that insensitive mothering is unlikely to have long-term significance for the child if the mother's circumstances improve. However, there is another reason for doubting whether a less than perfect relationship is of crucial significance – that is, the important contributions to the child's development which are undoubtedly made by a variety of other people. Ainsworth (forthcoming) argues that attachment to the mother differs from other affectionate relationships the child may have, in that it provides a unique experience of security and comfort. However, as the studies below show, there is ample evidence that people other than the mother can provide children with a sense of security. Of these, the most obvious is the child's father.

Until the late 1970s there were virtually no studies of father–infant relationships, and there seemed to be implicit agreement amongst psychologists with Bowlby's view that fathers are of little significance in the early years. For example, no one commented on the fact that the child separated from her mother in a hospital or nursery was also separated from her father and the rest of her family. Yet it now seems very obvious that considering the mother–child dyad in isolation is artificial – even in a small nuclear family other family members play key roles in the child's life, as may friends and neighbours. So far as fathers are concerned, it is well established that they are important attachment figures for most young children, and may be the child's most preferred person, despite the fact that fathers generally spend much less time than mothers with the infant (Kotelchuk 1976). In the 'Strange Situation', some babies have been found to be securely attached to their fathers, but not to their mothers. The intensity of the infant's attachment to his or her father seems to depend on a complex of factors, including the father's sensitivity to the baby's signals, his playfulness with the baby, and the amount of time he spends in face-to-face interaction with the baby (Chibucos and Kail 1981). At a later age, research has shown that if one parent is emotionally unstable, the presence of a stable parent seems to a large extent to 'buffer' the children from adverse effects (Rutter 1979).

The fact that children are likely to be attached to both parents does not mean that their relationships with them are identical. Most researchers have found consistent and striking differences between the patterns of mother–child and father–child interaction. Mothers tend to hold their children more, smile at them more, display more affection to them, and carry out more routine physical care of them than fathers do, while fathers tend to be more involved in play, especially physically stimulating and exciting play (Lamb 1977). This traditional differentiation of parental roles may change when both parents work; one study found that working mothers stimulated and played with their babies more than mothers at home did (Pedersen *et al*. 1982). On the other hand, a Swedish study of fathers who looked after the child while the mother worked found that the fathers tended to interact with the children in a 'fatherly' way, rather than switching to a 'motherly' style (Lamb *et al* 1982).

As to sibling relationships, in the past they have mainly been viewed in a negative light by psychologists, if they were considered at all. Some earlier psychologists, such as Adler, believed that sibling rivalry was a major influence on development. But throughout what might be called the Bowlby period, sibling relationships received even less attention from psychologists than father–child relationships. It is only since the 1980s that detailed studies of how young siblings interact have appeared, most of them based on observations made in the children's homes. One of the major contributors has been a British psychologist, Judy Dunn (1983). The studies suggest that siblings play a complex and important role in each other's development, a role in which rivalry is only one component amongst many.

One of the first findings to be documented was the very large amount of sibling interaction that takes place. Throughout the first year of life interactions between infant and older sibling become increasingly frequent. In two-child homes in London 12-month-old children have been found to spend almost as much time interacting with their older siblings as with their mothers, and far more time than with their fathers (Lawson and Ingleby 1974). These interactions are an important learning resource for the infant. For example, by 14 months children will play chasing games with older sibs, co-operating with and anticipating their actions in a remarkably mature manner (Dunn and Kendrick 1982). Advanced imaginative play has been observed between 2-year-olds and their older siblings, in which the 2-year-olds appropriately enact a role in the game, a level of play never seen at this age with peers (Dunn 1983).

Dunn points out that the special feature of sibling relationships is the variety of roles that they encompass. Older siblings are at different times teachers, familiar playmates, aggressors, comforters and protectors. Like parent–child relationships, sibling relationships tend to be highly charged with emotion, and siblings tend to be markedly ambivalent to each other. Yet several researchers who have observed in the home have found that unfriendly and hostile encounters between siblings tend to be considerably outnumbered at all ages by friendly and affectionate behaviour (Abramovitch *et al.* 1979).

There is no doubt that siblings are usually attached to each other, and display the same attachment behaviour, although at a lower intensity, that they do to their parents. This attachment develops during the first year of life: infants as young as 8 months may cry when their older siblings leave the room, and greet their return with pleasure. By the age of 14 months, many children go to their older sibling for comfort, and from the age of 2½ an older sibling can comfort a younger effectively, and be used by them as a 'secure base' (Dunn and Kendrick 1982).

As to peers, until recently many psychologists believed that children under the age of 2 or 3 have little to contribute to each other. Yet as early as 6 months, babies will smile and vocalize at another infant, especially when they are well acquainted. After crawling develops, they may follow another child around, poking and touching [. . .], although sustained interactions are usually beyond the capacity of children in the first year of life (Vandell and Mueller 1980). During the second year of life the frequency and complexity of social acts with peers increases. By the age of 2, well-acquainted children may interact more with each other than with adults. Interactions with peers in the second year of life are not only more frequent and complex than in the first year, but also less often emotionally neutral. Conflicts, especially struggles for possession of an object, become common, but so does friendly behaviour. Between 18 months and 24 months children will hug and pat each other, share toys, and display sympathy and helpfulness to peers, as well as to parents and sibs. By the age of 2, many children will attempt to comfort another child in distress, protect a victim, and seek help for them (Zahn-Waxler and Radke-Yarrow 1980). Familiar 2-year-olds can also provide each other with emotional support. One research project showed that pairs of 2-year-olds from the same nursery group were able to take in their stride the situation of being left alone in a strange room, which distressed children on their own, or those paired with an unfamiliar child (Ispa 1981).

In the complete absence of parents, or parent-substitutes, very familiar peers will in some respects act as parents to each other. The six children kept together as a group in a German concentration camp (referred to on p. 69) were found when released to have the same kind of intense attachment to each other that children normally have for their parents, and an absence of the jealousy and rivalry towards each other usually found in sibs. They refused to be separated, even for a moment, and were extremely considerate and generous to each other. Towards adults they reacted with cold indifference or hostility.

The social network of children includes many people to whom they may in varying degrees be attached – aunts, uncles, neighbours, grandparents, child-minders, friendly shopkeepers, older and younger children. It seems likely that because of the different kinds of relationships they form with the child, each plays a distinctive role in the child's development. These relationships do not develop out of children's relationships with their mothers; rather, they seem to develop concurrently. However, they have been very little researched, although one study has shown that a close relationship with an adult other than the parents, most often a grandparent, tended to protect children from the ill-effects of a disharmonious marriage (Jenkins and Smith, forthcoming).

Implications

The evidence briefly summarized here suggests that young children are unlikely to suffer psychological damage if their mothers go out to work, although they may suffer initial distress. Indeed, they will benefit from the greater variety of social contacts outside the family. Young children can and do become attached to those who look after them, as well as to other children. These attachments are not likely to weaken their attachment to their mothers, but can provide additional sources of comfort and security. Further, if the child's relationship with her mother is less than good, other long-standing relationships, for example with her father, siblings and grandparents, may serve as an important protective factor. In addition, all these people, because of their different personalities, skills and relationship to the child, contribute something different to her enjoyment and enrich her development. Further, Bowlby's belief that any separation from the mother in the early years is in itself likely to inflict permanent damage on the child's development is not supported by the evidence. This does not of course imply that the quality of day care (an issue which there is no space to discuss here) is unimportant, or that it does not matter who cares for children, or how many changes of care or adverse experiences they may have. Children may be resilient, but some environments stimulate development more than others, and they need the security of attachment to familiar people, who are responsive to their needs. But even if the child's relationship with her mother is insecure, or broken by separation, at one stage in her development, there is little evidence that this will necessarily inflict permanent damage, provided that she is part of a social network which provides her with alternative sources of security.

REFERENCES

Abramovitch, R., Corter, C. and Lando, B. (1979) 'Sibling interaction in the home', *Child Development* 50: 997–1003.

Ainsworth, M.D.S. (forthcoming) 'Attachments and other affectional bonds across the life cycle', in C.M. Parkes and J. Stevenson-Hinde (eds) *Attachment Across the Life Cycle*, New York: Routledge.

Ainsworth, M.D.S., Blehar, M., Waters, E. and Wall, S.L. (1978) *Patterns of Attachment*, Hillsdale, NJ: Erlbaum.

Belsky, J. (1988) 'Infant day care and socioemotional development', *Journal of Child Psychology and Psychiatry* 29: 397–406.

Bowlby, J. (1951) *Maternal Care and Mental Health*, Geneva: World Health Organisation; this was rewritten for the general public under the title *Child Care and the Growth of Love* (1953) Harmondsworth: Penguin.

Bowlby, J. (1958) 'The nature of the child's tie to his mother', *Journal of Psychoanalysis* 39: 350–73.

Bowlby, J. (1969) *Attachment and Loss: Volume 1, Attachment*, London: Hogarth Press.

Bowlby, J . (1973) *Attachment and Loss: Volume 2, Separation, Anxiety and Anger*, London: Hogarth Press.

Brown, G.W. and Harris, T. (1978) *Social Origins of Depression: A Study of Psychiatric Disorders in Women*, London: Tavistock.

Campos, J.J., Barrett, K.C., Lamb, M.E., Goldsmith, H.H., Steinberg, C.

(1983) 'Socioemotional development', in P. Mussen (ed.) *Handbook of Child Psychology, Vol. 2*, New York: Wiley.

Chibucos, T. and Kail, P. (1981) 'Longitudinal examination of father–infant interaction and infant–father interaction', *Merrill-Palmer Quarterly* 27: 81–96.

Clarke-Stewart, K.A. (1988) 'The "effects" of infant day care reconsidered', *Early Childhood Research Quarterly* 3: 293–318.

Clarke-Stewart, K.A. and Fein, G.G. (1983) 'Early childhood programs', in M.M. Haith and J.J. Campos (eds) *Handbook of Child Psychology, Vol. 2*, New York: Wiley.

Dunn, J. (1983) 'Sibling relationships in early childhood', *Child Development* 54: 787–811.

Dunn, J. and Kendrick, C. (1982) *Siblings*, London: Grant McIntyre.

Hodges, J. and Tizard, B. (1989) 'Social and family relationships of ex-institutional adolescents', *Journal of Child Psychology and Psychiatry* 30: 77–97.

Ispa, J. (1981) 'Peer support among Soviet day care toddlers', *International Journal of Behaviour Development* 4: 255–69.

Jenkins, J. and Smith, M. (forthcoming) 'Factors protecting children living in disharmonious homes', *American Academy of Child and Adolescent Psychiatry*.

Klaus, M. and Kennell, J. (1976) *Maternal–Infant Bonding*, St Louis: C.V. Mosby.

Koluchova, J. (1976) 'The further development of twins after severe and prolonged deprivation: a second report', *Journal of Child Psychology and Psychiatry* 17: 181–8.

Kotelchuk, M. (1976) 'The infant's relationship to the father: experimental evidence', in M.E. Lamb (ed.) *The Role of the Father in Child Development*, New York: Wiley.

Lamb, M.E. (1977) 'Father–infant and mother–infant interaction in the first year of life', *Child Development* 48: 167–81.

Lamb, M.E., Frodi, A.M., Hevang, C.P., Frodi, M. and Steinberg, J. (1982) 'Mother- and father–infant interaction involving play and holding in traditional and non-traditional Swedish families', *Developmental Psychology* 18: 215–21.

Lawson, A. and Ingleby, J.D. (1974) 'Daily routines of preschool children', *Psychological Medicine* 4: 399–415.

McGuire, J. and Richman, N. (1986) 'The prevalence of behaviour problems in three types of preschool groups', *Journal of Child Psychology and Psychiatry* 27: 455–72.

Melhuish, E.C. (1990) 'Research on day care for young children in the United Kingdom', in E.C. Melhuish and P. Moss (eds) *Day Care for Young Children: International Perspectives*, London: Routledge.

Moskovitz, S. (1985) 'Longitudinal follow-up of child survivors of the Holocaust', *Journal of the American Academy of Child Psychiatry* 22(4): 401–7.

Parkes, C.M., Stevenson-Hinde, J. and Marris, P. (eds) (forthcoming) *Attachment Across the Life Cycle*, London: Routledge.

Pedersen, F.A., Cairn, R. and Zaslow, M. (1982) 'Variation in infant experience associated with alternative family roles', in L. Laosa and L. Sigel (eds) *The Family as a Learning Environment*, New York: Plenum Press.

Quinton, D. and Rutter, M. (1985) 'Parenting behaviour of mothers raised "in care" ', in A.R. Nichol (ed.) *Longitudinal Studies in Child Care and Child Psychiatry*, Chichester: Wiley.

Robertson, J. and Robertson, J. (1971) 'Young children in brief separation: a fresh look', *Psychoanalytic Study of the Child* 26: 264–315.

Rutter, M. (1979) 'Protective factors in children's response to stress and disadvantage' in M.W. Kent and J.E. Rolf (eds) *Primary Prevention of Psychopathology, Vol. 3: Social Competence in Children*, Boston, Mass.: University Press of New England.

Rutter, M. (1981) *Maternal Deprivation Re-assessed*, 2nd edn, Harmondsworth: Penguin.

Sroufe, L.A. (1984) 'Individual patterns of adaptation from infancy to pre-school', in M. Perlmutter (ed.) *Minnesota Symposium on Child Psychology, 16*, Hillsdale, NJ: Erlbaum.

Tizard, B. (1977) *Adoption: A Second Chance*, London: Open Books.

Tizard, B. (1986) *The Care of Young Children: Implications of Recent Research*, Thomas Coram Research Unit Working and Occasional Paper no. 1, Institute of Education, University of London.

Vandell, D.L. and Mueller, E.C. (1980) 'Peer play and friendships during the first two years', in H.C. Foot, A.J. Chapman, and J.R. Smith (eds) *Friendship and Social Relations in Children*, New York: Wiley.

Weisner, T.S. and Gallimore, R. (1977) 'My brother's keeper: child and sibling caretaking', *Current Anthropology* 18: 169–90.

WHO Expert Committee on Mental Health (1951) *Report on the Second Session, 1951*, Geneva: World Health Organization.

Zahn-Waxler, C. and Radke-Yarrow, M. (1980) 'The development of altruism', in N. Eisenberg-Berg (ed.) *The Development of Pro-Social Behavior*, New York: Academic Press.

5 Infant day care: maligned or malignant?

K. Alison Clarke-Stewart
Source: American Psychologist (1989) 44(2): 266–73.

[. . .]

One of the most striking social changes in [the United States] over the past decade has been the dramatic increase in the number of mothers going back to work within the first few months after their babies are born. What was rare in the 1960s and unusual in the 1970s is now common. Half the infants in the United States today have employed mothers, twice the proportion that there were in 1970. Mothers of young infants are the fastest growing segment of the labor market (US Bureau of the Census 1986).

Not surprisingly, this social change has been greeted by concerned questions. What are the effects on these infants of repeated separations from their mothers? What will be the long-term outcomes for these children of spending so many hours with paid professionals instead of with their loving parents? What will happen to society when these children themselves become parents? These are important questions, but when they have been put to developmental psychologists, the answers have been inconsistent. The results of studies addressed to the issue of short- and long-term effects of infant day care have been unclear enough to allow varied interpretations. Thus some (e.g. Barglow *et al* 1987; Belsky 1988a), interpreting the available data, have claimed that full-time maternal employment puts infants at risk for developing emotional insecurities and becoming socially maladjusted. Others (e.g. Clarke-Stewart 1988; Phillips *et al*. 1987b), evaluating the same studies, have concluded that there is insufficient evidence to support this claim. What is the empirical evidence concerning the effects of infant day care, and how has the controversy over interpreting this evidence arisen? Is day care truly bad for babies, or has it been undeservedly maligned?

OUTCOMES OF INFANT DAY CARE

Does day care result in emotional insecurity?

The major source of controversy has been the research assessing infants' relationships with their mothers. The infant–mother relationship has been central in theories of development from Freud onward and has been shown to be an important index of infants' overall emotional well-being. It is also a likely candidate for disturbance when infants are separated from their mothers for eight to ten hours a day. Although research consistently has shown that infants of working mothers do form attachments to their mothers and prefer their mothers to their substitute caregivers (Clarke-Stewart and Fein 1983), the question is whether the *quality* of their attachments is as good, as emotionally secure, as the attachments of infants who are being raised exclusively by their parents.

As a first step in answering this question, one can tabulate data from all studies that have included the current standard assessment of children's attachment to their mothers, Ainsworth's 'Strange Situation' [see also p. 63] (Ainsworth *et al.* 1978), studies by Ainslie and Anderson (1984); Barglow *et al.* (1987); Beckwith (1987): Belsky and Rovine (1988); Benn (1986); Burchinal and Bryant (1988); Chase-Lansdale and Owen (1987); Easterbrooks and Goldberg (1985); Easterbrooks and Harmon (1987); Goossens (1987); Jacobson and Wille (1984); Lipsitt and LaGasse (1987); Owen and Cox (1988); Owen *et al.* (1984); Rodning (1987); Thompson *et al.* (1982); and Vaughn *et al.* (1980). Tabulation of these data show that infants whose mothers are employed full time, compared with infants whose mothers do not work or who work part time, are disproportionately likely to be classified as insecurely attached. Of the infants of full-time working mothers, 36 per cent have been classified as insecure; of the infants of non-employed or part-time working mothers, only 29 per cent have been so classified. Although differences in individual studies often are not statistically significant, this overall difference, with a sample size of 1,247, certainly is ($\chi^2 = 6.21$, $p<.01$).

There is no disagreement that this difference exists and that it merits examination. The question is: What does the difference mean? Does it mean, as Barglow *et al.* (1987) and Belsky (1988a) have suggested, that infants of working mothers are at risk for emotional insecurity because they interpret their mothers' absence as rejection, or because repeated separations have disturbed their emerging attachment relationship, making them doubt their mothers' availability and responsiveness and leading them to develop a coping style that masks this anger? These interpretations, extrapolated from knowledge of the correlates of insecure attachment in children raised exclusively by their parents, may be correct. However, at present, they are highly speculative. They are not based on data, and indeed alternative explanations have some empirical support.

At the heart of the problem is the fact that the observed difference between infants of working and non-working mothers is based on behavior observed in a single assessment procedure. Although having a common assessment method is invaluable for combining subjects from different studies, having only one assessment method raises problems. The Strange Situation has turned out in past research to be a reliable and useful measure of the mother–infant relationship and a predictor of later behavior problems in home-reared children (Ainsworth *et al.* 1978). But it is important to validate the behavior patterns observed in the Strange Situation for infants whose mothers work using other – ecologically valid – assessment procedures.

This is important, for one thing, because the Strange Situation may not be psychologically equivalent for infants of working and non-working mothers. The validity of the Strange Situation procedure depends on creating a situation in which infants feel moderately stressed and therefore display proximity-seeking behavior to the object of their attachment. The Strange Situation may not be equally stressful for the infants of working and non-working mothers. Consider the features that make up the Strange Situation – the infant plays with someone else's toys in a room that is not his or her own; the infant is left by his or her mother with a woman who is a stranger; the infant plays with and is comforted by that women in the mother's absence; the mother returns to pick the infant up. Although at least some infants of non-working mothers undoubtedly have had experiences like these before their assessment in the Strange Situation, infants of working mothers are more likely to have had them regularly and routinely and, therefore, to be more accustomed to them.

Any of these elements of familiarity could affect infants' behavior in the Strange Situation. Although strong evidence that infants whose mothers work find the Strange Situation less stressful has not yet been collected, there are hints that this may be the case. Researchers have found that in the Strange Situation, infants who have been in day care, compared with infants who have not, are less wary initially. They are less likely to resist contact with the stranger and less likely to seek proximity and contact with the mother [Hock, 1980]; are less disturbed by the mother's absence (they are less likely to search for the mother and more likely to play comfortably with the toys after the mother has left the room) [Doyle and Somers 1978; Jacobson and Wille 1984]; and are less likely to seek proximity and contact with the mother on her return [Goossens 1987].

Clearly we need to assess infants' attachment using procedures that are not biased by differential familiarity and potentially differential stressfulness. Several recent attempts to do this by using a Q-sort assessment technique in which mothers, teachers or observers rate infants' attachment behavior in daily situations have not revealed differences between infants of working and non-working mothers (Belsky 1988b; Howes *et al.* in press; Strayer *et al.* in press; Weinraub *et al.* in press). But, of course, these studies do not settle the issue. It may be that with a larger data set of Q-sort ratings differences between infants of working and non-working mothers would be revealed; in Belsky's data, for example, the Q-sort results, although not significant, were in the same direction as the Strange Situation results. More research using more clinically sensitive assessments is needed.

A second issue of importance for interpreting the observed difference in attachment between the infants of working and non-working mothers is the question of how large the difference is. The difference may be statistically significant, but in practical terms how significant is it? Is it large enough to conclude that infants are in danger if their mothers work? There are several ways of presenting the differences observed between infants of working and non-working mothers in the studies using the Strange Situation. The most extremely negative way (in terms of the dangers for infants) is to select only the low-risk subjects from the data set and to use the small percentage of insecure at-home infants as the base, saying that for the 'average' infant there is a 39 per cent increased risk of an insecure attachment when the mother works full time (11% ÷ 28%). Less extreme would be the parallel statement, based on the entire data set, that for a 'wide range' of infants there is a 24 per cent increased risk of insecurity when the mother works (7% ÷ 29%). These same data could be used to make a statement that reduces the apparent difference substantially, however, by using as the base the percentage of secure children in maternal care. Then the statement would be that the probability that an infant will be securely attached is only 10 per cent less if the mother works (7% ÷ 71%). Finally, the most positive statement of the differences would be the statement that for infants from high-risk families there is a 19 per cent lower likelihood that an infant will be insecure if the mother works (9% ÷ 47%). Thus one can pick one's statement to emphasize or minimize the extent of the difference.

Moving beyond this semantic sleight of tongue, in an effort to evaluate the risk of insecure attachment for infants of working mothers, one might use the strategy of comparing the distribution of attachment categories for the infants of working mothers in this data set with a broader sampling of studies, including those in other countries. As it turns out, the observed distribution of insecure infants of working mothers in the United States (22% type As and 14% type Cs) is virtually identical to the global distribution reported by van IJzendoorn and Kroonenberg (1988) for studies around the world (21% type As and 14% type Cs). This seems to suggest that the observed likelihood of insecurity in infants of working mothers, even if it is somewhat elevated (more or less depending on the sample and the form of the statement one chooses) is within the normal population range.

Yet another way of looking at how different the infants of working and non-working mothers are is to examine the size of the mean difference between the groups on the scale of insecure (avoidant) attachment behavior. When this is done for the combined samples from the studies reporting these data (Barglow *et al.* 1987; Belsky and Rovine 1988; Schwartz 1983), the average avoidance score for infants of working mothers is 5.0 (n = 129; SD = 2.9), and for the infants of non-working or part-time working mothers it is 3.8 (n = 198; SD = 2.0). This difference of about 1 point on a 7-point scale, similarly, suggests that although day-care infants are more avoidant of their mothers they are not extremely so.

A third issue in interpreting the difference between infants of working and non-working mothers in the Strange Situation concerns the meaning of attachment itself. In theory, an attachment is a relationship; it is not a global personality trait. If the children of working mothers are more insecure with them, this does not necessarily mean that these children are emotionally insecure in general. Before labeling the infants of working mothers emotionally insecure, we need to assess their emotional health in a range of situations and with a variety of partners. On other measures of security, self-confidence and emotional adjustment, children who were in day care as infants have been observed to do as well as children who were not (Andersson 1987; Golden *et al.* 1978; Ramey *et al.* 1983; Rubenstein *et al.* 1981; Vandell and Corasaniti 1988). In the one study in which children who had been in infant day care were rated as more anxious by their teachers (McCartney *et al.* 1982), these children were still well within the normal range and, in fact, were rated by their parents as less anxious. As further evidence that day-care infants are not emotionally disturbed in general, it might also be noted that the infants of working mothers who were coded as insecure in the Strange Situation have been found to perform better than the infants of non-working mothers on a variety of other tasks (Strayer and Moss 1987; Vaughn *et al.* 1985). Taken together, these findings seem to suggest that day-care infants are not more anxious, insecure, or emotionally disturbed overall.

The final and perhaps most significant difficulty in interpreting the data showing that infants of working mothers are more likely to be insecurely attached to their mothers is the problem of self-selection. Mothers who work (and their infants) differ in many ways from those who do not (e.g. Hock *et al.* 1980; McBride and Belsky 1985). These differences may lead to the disproportionate number of children classified as insecure among the infants of working mothers. In sum, there are a number of major obstacles to our interpretation of the observed difference in attachment between infants of working and nonworking mothers. At the present time, in my view, it is not appropriate to interpret the difference as suggesting that these children are emotionally insecure.

Does day care result in social maladjustment?

One reason that psychologists have interpreted the difference in infants' attachments as reflecting emotional insecurity is that they have put this difference together with another provocative finding. In a number of studies, children who spent their first year in day care later were observed to be more aggressive with their peers and less compliant with their parents (Barton and Schwarz 1981; Haskins 1985; McCartney *et al.* 1982; Rubenstein and Howes 1983; Schwarz *et al.* 1974; Vandell and Corasaniti 1988; Vaughn *et al.* 1985). Unfortunately it is impossible to combine data from these studies as was done for attachment to get an overall estimate of the likelihood of aggression and non-compliance among children who were in infant day care because no common measure of these behaviors was used in these studies. One can only point out that although these studies do provide strong evidence of greater aggression and non-compliance in day-care children, no such evidence has been obtained in other studies using similar measures (Braun and Caldwell 1973; Golden *et al.* 1978; Gottfried *et al.* 1988; Howes 1988; Kagan *et al.* 1978), or in the same studies using other measures (McCartney *et al.* 1982, aggression to peers; Rubenstein and Howes 1983, behavior problems; Vaughn *et al.* 1985; compliance and aggression to mother) or assessing the children at later ages (McCartney *et al.* 1982; Schwarz *et al.* 1974).

Even accepting the possibility that a meta-analysis would reveal a trend for children who had been in day care as infants to be more aggressive and less compliant, however, one might question whether these behaviors should themselves be interpreted as evidence of maladjustment. It is possible that the pattern of aggression and non-compliance observed in these studies to some extent reflects greater independence rather than disturbed behavior. One notes that children who had been in day care as infants in these and other studies did as well as or better than children who had not on measures of advanced development – sociability, social competence, language, persistence, achievement, self-confidence and problem-solving (Andersson 1987; Golden *et al.* 1978; Haskins 1985; Lay and Meyer 1972; Macrae and Herbert-Jackson 1976; McCartney *et al* 1982; Ramey *et al.* 1983; Rubenstein and Howes 1983; Rubenstein *et al.* 1981; Schwartz 1983; Schwarz *et al.* 1973; Strayer and Moss 1987). Another argument against viewing children who were in infant day care as maladjusted is the argument that this same pattern of negative behavior and advanced development appears in children who start full-time day care after infancy, as toddlers or pre-schoolers (Clarke-Stewart and Fein 1983).

What this pattern of behavior may suggest, then, is not that children who have been in day care beginning in infancy or later are socially maladjusted, but that they think for themselves and that they want their own way. They are not willing to comply with adults' arbitrary rules. In one study (Siegal and Storey 1985), for example, pre-schoolers who had been in day care thought that moral transgressions (like hitting or stealing) were worse than social transgressions (like not putting toys away), but children who were just starting day care thought that it was just as bad to break the social rules. Children who have spent time in day care, then, may be more demanding and independent, more disobedient and aggressive, more bossy and bratty than children who stay at home because they want their own way and do not have the skills to achieve it smoothly, rather than because they are maladjusted. To find out whether maladjustment is a consequence of infant day care, what is called for, again, are more clinically sensitive assessments.

Does day care result in intellectual precocity?

The third finding in the literature on infant day care is that children who have been in infant day care are, on the average, advanced in their intellectual development. Quite consistently, researchers have found that when children are given intelligence tests any time between 18 months and 5 years, those who had been in day care as infants score higher than those who had not (Clarke-Stewart and Fein 1983).

What does this difference in intellectual functioning mean? Is day care giving infants an intellectual head start, increasing their level of intelligence or pushing them too fast? Longitudinal studies of children suggest that the difference is a temporary acceleration of children's intellectual development, not a permanent enhancement of abilities. As home-care children enter day care, pre-school, kindergarten or elementary school, they too make intellectual gains and quickly catch up to the children with early day-care experience (Clarke-Stewart and Fein 1983). Infancy does not appear to be a critical period for accelerating intellectual development. There is also no evidence that infant day care pushes infants too fast; when home-care children catch up, they do not surpass day-care children. In brief, day care does appear to give infants an intellectual head start – but a shortlived one.

MODERATORS AND MEDIATORS OF INFANT DAY-CARE EFFECTS

Not all the children who are in day care as infants are insecurely attached, aggressive, non-compliant or intellectually advanced. There are individual differences in development for infants in day care just as there are for infants at home. What factors contribute to these developmental outcomes in day-care children and tip the balance to produce group differences between day-care and home-care infants?

Mediators of emotional insecurity

Day-care factors

It has been suggested that the emotional security of individual infants in day care may be related to the type, stability or quality of day care experienced by the infants. To date, however, very limited support for this suggestion has been found. Insecure attachments have been observed in a wide range of day-care programs – in sitter care (Barglow *et al.* 1987; Schwartz 1983) as well as centers (Belsky and Rovine 1988), and in stable arrangements (Barglow *et al.* 1987) as well as unstable ones (Vaughn *et al.* 1985). Deliberate efforts to link insecure attachment to the quality of day care generally have not been successful (Belsky and Rovine 1988; Benn 1986; Burchinal and Bryant 1986; Howes *et al.* in press; Thompson *et al.* 1982), although in one of these studies (Howes *et al.*) insecurity of attachment to mother was more likely for children in centers with poor adult–child ratios. Perhaps it, is not surprising that the quality of day care is not closely related to the development of infants' attachments to their mothers. Poor day care might affect the attachment relationship because it would affect the child's general emotional well-being, but it does not follow that good day care would enhance the infant–mother relationship or ensure its security.

Child factors

It is somewhat more likely that moderating factors would be found in the characteristics of the children themselves. It has been suggested (Belsky 1988a), for example, that boys whose mothers work are more likely to develop insecure attachments than are girls. In a meta-analysis of studies of attachment in day-care children, however, the child's sex did not turn out to be a significant moderator of day-care effects (McCartney and Phillips 1988). It has also been suggested that the child's constitutional vulnerability might moderate the effects of day care. So far, only data from one study (Belsky and Rovine 1988) are available to examine this issue. This study did reveal that among infants of working mothers those who were insecurely attached had more difficult temperaments. More interesting, though, was the finding in this study that it was not the objective assessment of infants' behavior that was linked to insecure attachment, but rather mothers' perceptions of their infants' temperaments – suggesting that mothers' perceptions, attitudes and actions may be more important than child characteristics for determining who is vulnerable and who is at risk.

Family factors

There are several kinds of working mothers who might promote their children's insecure attachments. One kind undoubtedly is the mother whose rejection of contact with the infant has been linked to insecurity in home-reared children. Perhaps there is even an increased likelihood of this kind of rejection among working mothers. This could occur through self-selection: mothers who like babies stay home; mothers who don't, go to work. In a study by Hock *et al.* (1985), for example, mothers who intended to stay home when their babies were born but who ended up going to work in the baby's first year did so after experiencing a decline in their positive attitude toward motherhood and expressed a strong aversion to infant fussiness. It could also occur through the increased stress of handling two full-time jobs – work and motherhood – which would lead to more rejection of every additional burden, including the baby. Other mothers might foster insecure attachments in their infants because of their lack of availability, not only because they are away all day at work, but also because they have to do chores and tasks that compete with the infant when they *are* together. Yet other mothers might be psychologically inaccessible. Many working mothers feel overworked and tired; they feel life is hard; they are rushed and harried. It is not unreasonable that these mothers would be less accessible to their infants. The reason their infants might be insecurely attached, in other words, is not that forty hours of day care is hard on infants but that forty hours of work is hard on mothers. Yet another kind of mother whose infant might be insecurely attached is the insensitive mother, whose insensitivity could be increased by spending less time with the infant and so knowing the infant's needs and signals less well. Finally, employed mothers might value and deliberately encourage their infants' independence more than non-working mothers, and so their infants would not appear to be as securely attached.

What then is the empirical evidence that working mothers' attitudes and behavior are sources of infants' insecure development? Unfortunately there have been only a few studies in which links between working mothers' behavior and their infants' development have been explored. Farber and Egeland (1982) found that working mothers whose infants were insecure expressed less desire for motherhood even before their infants were born. Benn (1986) and Belsky and Rovine (1988) observed that working mothers whose infants were insecure were less competent, sensitive, integrated, empathic and happily married. In Owen and Cox's (1988) study, mothers who had to work long hours (more than forty hours a week) were more dissatisfied and anxious; anxious mothers were less sensitive, animated and reciprocal in their interactions with their infants; and their infants were more likely to develop insecure attachments. These studies suggest that there are links between mothers' behavior and attitudes and infants' development in families with working mothers, just as there are in families with non-working mothers. We need more research to identify and clarify these links.

Mediators of sociability and aggressiveness

Day-care factors

The positive side of the social behavior pattern observed in day-care children – advanced sociability, social competence and self-confidence – has been associated with characteristics of day care in a straight-forward and reasonable way. Children who are most socially competent are found in day-care programs, in which they interact with a variety of peers, including some who are older and more socially skilled, under the close supervision and guidance of caregivers who are educated, responsive, nurturant and positive, who offer children choices and suggestions and encourage their activities (Clarke-Stewart 1987; Golden *et al* 1978; Hamilton and Gordon 1978; Rubenstein and Howes 1979).

More surprising is the fact that the dark side of children's social behavior – aggression and non-compliance – also has been linked to participation in such 'good' programs (Haskins 1985; McCartney *et al* 1982; Schwarz *et al* 1974). The responsive style of teaching in such programs, which contrasts with the more authoritarian style of mothers (Clarke-Stewart 1984; Hess *et al.* 1981; Rubenstein and Howes 1979), could easily be seen as permitting or even promoting children's assertiveness, non-compliance and even aggression. It is a style fostered by training in child development and an academic orientation. Teachers with child development training and an academic orientation are more likely to have attitudes and behaviors that encourage children's independence, not their obedience (Arnett 1987; Berk 1985; Howes 1983), that foster social and cognitive knowledge, but neglect social skills (Clarke-Stewart 1984; Finkelstein 1982).

Of course increased non-compliance and aggression are not just the province of good day care. Low social competence and aggression have also been observed in children who are in poor day care, that is day-care settings in which children spend most of their time playing with peers rather than interacting with the caregiver because there are too many children for the caregiver to give close attention to everyone and because the caregiver has no training in child development (Clarke-Stewart 1987; Howes 1988; Phillips *et al.* 1987a; Vandell and Corasaniti 1988; Vaughn *et al.* 1985). This is especially true if the poor-quality day care begins in infancy and continues through the pre-school years (Howes 1988). In good or poor day-care programs, it seems, children do not learn to follow social rules or to resolve social conflicts without resorting to aggression unless special efforts are made by their caregivers. If children are given direct training in social skills, however, they are more socially competent and less likely to exhibit aggression (e.g. Finkelstein 1982; Iannotti 1978; Orlick 1981; Smith *et al.* 1983).

Child factors

Although there is some suggestion that boys may be more susceptible to day-care influences on negative social behavior and girls to day-care influences on positive social behavior (e.g. Vandell and Corasaniti 1988), sex differences are not always found, and the data are still insufficient to make strong claims that sex – or other child characteristics – acts as moderator of day-care effects on social adjustment or behavior.

Family factors

The data are also insufficient to determine whether parents moderate the effects of day care on their children's social behavior. The pattern of obnoxious behavior and advanced social competence we have described has been observed in both rich and poor families, although more of the latter have been studied. There is only the slightest hint that the effect on negative behavior may be stronger for children in lower-class families (e.g. Vandell and Corasaniti 1988); we have no reason to make strong claims that families moderate these day-care effects. More likely, families reinforce their children's experiences in day care. Children in high-quality day-care programs, for instance, have been found to have parallel experiences at home: their mothers are more nurturant and responsive and less restrictive and authoritarian than other mothers (e.g. Edwards *et al.* 1987; Howes and Stewart 1987).

Mediators of intellectual gains

Day-care factors

Many attempts have been made to identify aspects of day care that predict intellectual gains in toddlers and pre-school children. There have been fewer attempts to identify qualities of infant care that predict later intellectual levels. Golden *et al.* (1978) did observe that more stimulating, positive and affectionate care was related to infants' language development; other researchers (Burchinal *et al.* 1986; McCartney *et al.* 1985) report that children who had been in cognitively-oriented model programs as infants did better than children in community day-care programs. The problem is that measurable differences in children's IQs do not show up until past infancy, and by then infants who were in high-quality infant care have also received high-quality toddler and pre-school care, confounding the quality of infant care with the quality of later care (which we know also contributes to intellectual gains). We need research in which the quality of later experience is controlled, before we can establish the qualities of infant care that are linked to intellectual gains.

Child factors

Once again, the literature contains only hints about whether individual differences between infants moderate the effects of day care on intellectual development. Perhaps most interesting is Ramey *et al.*'s (1982) finding that easy infants gained more on IQ tests if they were in a day-care center than if they were at home, whereas difficult infants did better at home. This makes intuitive sense, but requires further study.

Family factors

Day-care-linked IQ gains have been observed for infants from a range of socioeconomic levels; the size of the gain has not been found to be systematically related to socioeconomic status (Fowler and Khan 1974; Kagan *et al.* 1978). Thus there is no evidence that families moderate day-care effects on children's intellectual development, but do parents contribute to the IQ gains observed in day-care infants? Parents of children in good day care have been observed to be less authoritarian and more stimulating and playful than parents of children who are not in these day-care programs (Edwards *et al.* 1987; Garber and Heber 1980; Ramey *et al.* 1983; Rubenstein *et al.* 1981). One might question, therefore, whether parents are mediating the apparent day-care effect on children's intellectual development. Because samples in the studies showing this difference between parents include subjects who were randomly assigned to day care as well as subjects who chose the better programs themselves, and because the changes in parents' behavior seem to be at least to some extent responses to changes in children's behavior rather than initiated by the parents, it seems more likely that parents are augmenting the day-care effect than that they are causing it.

CONCLUSION

As should be clear from even this brief review, we have much to learn about the effects of day care on infants' development. We know that there is a somewhat elevated likelihood that infants in day care will avoid their mothers after a brief separation and that children who were in day care as infants are more likely to disobey their mothers and bully their peers. We also know that infants and children in day care gain knowledge and self-confidence from their experience. We know less of whether these patterns have any short- or long-term benefits or disadvantages for individuals or society and of the factors that moderate and mediate these effects. The consequences of infant day care need continued monitoring by patient, painstaking researchers, who carry out longitudinal studies of infants' development in the context of their family characteristics and their early and later experiences in day care. In the meantime, infant day care policy must proceed from reality. Maternal employment is a reality. The issue today, therefore, is not whether infants should be in day care but how to make their experiences there and at home supportive of their development and of their parents' peace of mind.

REFERENCES

Ainslie, R.D. and Anderson, C.W. (1984) 'Day care children's relationships to their mothers and caregivers: an inquiry into the conditions for the development of attachment' in R.C. Ainslie (ed.) *The Child and the Day Care Setting*, New York: Praeger.

Ainsworth, M.D.S., Blehar, M., Waters, E. and Wall, S. (1978) *Patterns of Attachment: Observations in the Strange Situation and at Home*, Hillsdale, NJ: Erlbaum.,

Andersson, B.-E. (1987) 'The importance of public day-care for preschool children's later development', paper presented at the biennial meetings of the Society for Research in Child Development, Baltimore, Md, April.

Arnett, J. (1987) 'Training for caregivers in day care centers' paper presented at the biennial meetings of the Society for Research in Child Development, Baltimore, Md, April.

Barglow, P., Vaughn, B.E. and Molitor, N. (1987) 'Effects of maternal absence due to employment on the quality of infant–mother attachment in a low-risk sample', *Child Development* 58: 945–54.

Barton, M. and Schwarz, J. (1981) 'Day care in the middle class: effects in elementary school', paper presented at the annual meeting of the American Psychological Association, Los Angeles, August.

Bayley, N. (1969) *The Bayley Scales of Mental Development*, New York: Psychological Corporation.

Beckwith, L. (1987) [Longitudinal study at UCLA of high-risk preterm infants]. Work in progress.

Belsky, J. (1988a) [Unpublished data]. Data from Belsky and Rovine's (1988) study.

Belsky, J. (1988b) 'The "effects" of infant day care reconsidered', *Early*

Childhood Research Quarterly 3: 235-72.

Belsky, J. and Rovine, M. (1988) 'Nonmaternal care in the first year of life and infant–parent attachment security', *Child Development* 59: 157-67.

Benn, R.K. (1986) 'Factors promoting secure attachment relationships between employed mothers and their sons', *Child Development* 57: 1,224-31.

Berk, L. (1985) 'Relationship of educational attainment, child oriented attitudes, job satisfaction, and career commitment to caregiver behavior toward children', *Child Care Quarterly* 14: 103-29.

Braun, S.J. and Caldwell, B.T. (1973) 'Emotional adjustment of children in day care who enrolled prior to or after age of three', *Early Child Development and Care* 2: 13-21.

Burchinal, M. and Bryant, D.M. (1986) 'Does day care affect infant–mother attachment level?' paper presented at the annual meeting of the American Psychological Association, Washington, DC, August.

Burchinal, M. and Bryant, D.M. (1988) [Longitudinal study at the Frank Porter Graham Center, University of North Carolina, of a mixed SES sample]. Work in progress.

Burchinal, M., Lee, M.W. and Ramey, C.T. (1986) 'Day-care effects on preschool intellectual development in poverty children', paper presented at the annual meeting of the American Psychological Association, Washington DC, August.

Chase-Lansdale, P.L. and Owen, M.T. (1987) 'Maternal employment in a family context: effects on infant–mother and infant–father attachments', *Child Development* 58: 1,505-12.

Clarke-Stewart, K.A. (1984) 'Day care: a new context for research and development', in M. Perlmutter (ed.) *Parent–child Interaction and Parent–Child Relations in Child Development. The Minnesota Symposia on Child Psychology* (vol. 17, pp. 61-100), Hillsdale, NJ: Erlbaum.

Clarke-Stewart, K.A. (1987) 'Predicting child development from day-care forms and features: the Chicago study', in D.A. Phillips (ed.) *Quality in Child Care: What does Research Tell us? Research Monographs of the National Association for the Education of Young Children* (Vol. 1, pp. 21-42), Washington, DC: National Association for the Education of Young Children.

Clarke-Stewart, K.A. (1988) 'The "effects" of infant day care reconsidered' reconsidered: risks for parents, children and researchers', *Early Childhood Research Quarterly* 3: 293-318.

Clarke-Stewart, K.A. and Fein, G.G. (1983) 'Early childhood programs', in P.H. Mussen (ed.) *Handbook of Child Psychology: Vol. 2. Infancy and Developmental Psychobiology*, New York: Wiley.

Doyle A. and Somers, K. (1978) 'The effects of group and family day care on infant attachment behaviours', *Canadian Journal of Behavioural Science* 10: 38-45.

Easterbrooks, M.A. and Goldberg, W. (1985) 'Effects of early maternal employment on toddlers, mothers, and fathers', *Developmental Psychology* 21: 774-83.

Easterbrooks, M.A. and Harmon, R.J. (1987) [Longitudinal study at the

University of Colorado of preterm and full-term infants from middle-class, two-parent families]. Work in progress.

Edwards, C.P., Logue, M.E., Loehr, S.R. and Roth, S.B. (1987) 'The effects of day care participation on parent–infant interaction at home', *American Journal of Orthopsychiatry* 57: 116–19.

Farber, E.A. and Egeland, B. (1982) 'Developmental consequences of out-of-home care for infants in a low-income population', in E.F. Zigler and E.W. Gordon (eds) *Day Care: Scientific and Social Policy Issues*, Boston, Mass.: Auburn House.

Finkelstein, N.W. (1982) 'Aggression: is it stimulated by day care?' *Young Children* 37: 3–12.

Fowler, W. and Khan, N. (1974) *The Later Effects of Infant Group Care: A Follow-Up Study*, Toronto: Ontario Institute for Studies in Education.

Garber, H. and Heber, R. (1980) 'Modification of predicted cognitive development in high-risk children through early intervention', paper presented at the annual meeting of the American Educational Research Association, Boston, Mass., April.

Golden, M., Rosenbluth, L., Grossi, M.T., Policare, H.J., Freeman, H., Jr., and Brownlee, E.M. (1978) *The New York City Infant Day Care Study*, New York: Medical and Health Research Association of New York City.

Goossens, F.A. (1987) 'Maternal employment and day care: effects on attachment', in L.W.C. Tavecchio and M.H. van IJzendoorn (eds) *Attachment in Social Networks*, Amsterdam: North-Holland.

Gottfried, A.E., Gottfried, A.W. and Bathurst, K. (1988) 'Maternal employment, family environment and children's development: infancy through the school years', in A.E. Gottfried and A.W. Gottfried (eds) *Maternal Employment and Children's Development: Longitudinal Research*, New York: Plenum.

Hamilton, V.J. and Gordon, D.A. (1978) 'Teacher–child interactions in preschool and task persistence', *American Educational Research Journal* 15: 459–66.

Haskins, R. (1985) 'Public school aggression among children with varying day-care experience', *Child Development* 56: 689–703.

Hess, R.D., Price, G.G., Dickson, W.P. and Conroy, M. (1981) 'Different roles for mothers and teachers: contrasting styles of child care', in S. Kilmer (ed.) *Advances in Early Education and Day Care* (Vol. 2, pp. 1–28), Greenwich, Conn.: JAI Press.

Hock, E. (1980) 'Working and nonworking mothers and their infants: a comparative study of maternal caregiving characteristics and infant social behavior', *Merrill Palmer Quarterly* 26: 79–102.

Hock, E., Christman, K. and Hock, M. (1980) 'Factors associated with decisions about return to work in mothers of infants', *Developmental Psychology* 16: 535–6.

Hock, E., Morgan, K.C. and Hock, M.D. (1985) 'Employment decisions made by mothers of infants', *Psychology of Women Quarterly* 9: 383–402.

Howes, C. (1983) Caregiver behavior in center and family day care', *Journal of Applied Developmental Psychology* 4: 99–107.

Howes, C. (1988) 'Can the age of entry and quality of infant care predict behaviors in kindergarten?' paper presented at the International Conference on Infancy Studies, Washington, DC, April.

Howes, C. and Stewart, P. (1987) 'Child's play with adults, toys, and peers: an examination of family and child-care influences', *Developmental Psychology* 23: 423-30.

Howes, C., Rodning, C., Galluzzo, D.C. and Myers, L. (in press) 'Attachment and child care: relationships with mother and caregiver', *Early Childhood Research Quarterly*.

Iannotti, R.J. (1978) 'Effect of role-taking experiences on role taking, empathy, altruism, and aggression', *Developmental Psychology* 14: 119-24.

Jacobson, J.L., and Wille, D.E. (1984) 'Influence of attachment and separation experience on separation distress at 18 months', *Developmental Psychology* 20: 477-84.

Kagan, J., Kearsley, R.B. and Zelazo, P.R. (1978) *Infancy: Its Place in Human Development*, Cambridge, Mass.: Harvard University Press.

Lay, M.Z. and Meyer, W.J. (1972) *Effects of Early Day Care Experience on Subsequent Observed Program Behaviors* (Final report to the Office of Education, Subcontract 70-007), Syracuse, NY: Syracuse University.

Lipsitt, L. and LaGasse, L. (1987) [Longitudinal study at Brown University of normal full-term infants]. Work in progress.

McBride, S.L. and Belsky, J. (1985) 'Maternal work plans, actual employment and infant temperament', paper presented at the biennial meetings of the Society for Research in Child Development, Toronto, April.

McCartney, K. and Phillips, D. (1988) 'Motherhood and child care', in B. Birns and D. Hayes (eds) *Different Faces of Motherhood*, New York: Plenum.

McCartney, K., Scarr, S., Phillips, D., Grajek, S. and Schwarz, J.C. (1982) 'Environmental differences among day care centers and their effects on children's development', in E.F. Zigler and E.W. Gordon (eds) *Day Care: Scientific and Social Policy Issues*, Boston, Mass.: Auburn House.

McCartney, K., Scarr, S., Phillips, D., and Grajek, S. (1985) 'Day care as intervention: comparisons of varying quality programs', *Journal of Applied Developmental Psychology* 6: 247-60.

Macrae, J.W. and Herbert-Jackson, E. (1976) 'Are behavioral effects of infant day care program specific?', *Developmental Psychology* 12: 269-70.

Orlick, T.D. (1981) 'Positive socialization via cooperative games', *Developmental Psychology* 17: 426-9.

Owen, M. and Cox, M. (1988) 'Maternal employment and the transition to parenthood', in A.E. Gottfried and A.W. Gottfried (eds) *Maternal Employment and Children's Development: Longitudinal Research*, New York: Plenum.

Owen, M.T., Easterbrooks, M.A., Chase-Lansdale, L. and Goldberg, W.A. (1984) 'The relation between maternal employment status and the stability of attachments to mother and to father', *Child Development* 55: 1894-901.

Phillips, D.A., McCartney, K. and Scarr, S. (1987a) 'Child-care quality and children's social development', *Developmental Psychology* 23: 537-43.

Phillips, D.A., McCartney, K., Scarr, S. and Howes, C. (1987b) 'Selective review of infant day care research: a cause for concern', *Zero to Three* 7(3): 18-21.

Ramey, C.T., MacPhee, D., and Yeates, K.O. (1982) 'Preventing developmental retardation: a general systems model', in L. Bond and J. Joffe (eds) *Facilitating Infant and Early Childhood Development*, Hanover, NH: University Press of New England.

Ramey, C.T., Dorval, B. and Baker-Ward, L. (1983) 'Group day care and socially disadvantaged families: effects on the child and the family', in S. Kilmer (ed.) *Advances in Early Education and Day Care* (Vol. 3, pp. 69-106), Greenwich, Conn.: JAI Press.

Rodning, C. (1987) [Longitudinal study at UCLA of infants in middle-class, two-parent families.] Work in progress.

Rubenstein, J.L. and Howes, C. (1979) 'Caregiving and infant behavior in day care and in homes', *Developmental Psychology* 15: 1-24.

Rubenstein, J.L. and Howes, C. (1983) 'Social-emotional development of toddlers in day care: the role of peers and of individual differences', in S. Kilmer (ed.) *Early Education and Day Care* (Vol. 3, pp. 21-45), Greenwich, Conn.: JAI Press.

Rubenstein, J.L. Howes, C. and Boyle, P. (1981) 'A two year follow-up of infants in community based infant day care', *Journal of Child Psychology and Psychiatry* 22: 209-18.

Schwartz, P. (1983) 'Length of day-care attendance and attachment behavior in eighteen-month-old infants', *Child Development* 54: 1073-8.

Schwarz, J.C., Krolick, G., and Strickland, G. (1973) 'Effects of early day care experience on adjustment to a new environment', *American Journal of Orthopsychiatry* 43: 340-6.

Schwarz, J.C., Strickland, R.G. and Krolick, G. (1974) 'Infant day care: behavioral effects at pre-school age', *Developmental Psychology* 10: 502-6.

Siegal, M. and Storey, R.M. (1985) 'Day care and children's conceptions of moral and social rules', *Child Development* 56: 1001-8.

Smith, C.L., Leinbach, M.D., Stewart, B.J. and Blackwell, J.M. (1983) 'Affective perspective taking exhortations, and children's prosocial behavior' in D.L. Bridgeman (ed.) *The Nature of Prosocial Development*, New York: Academic Press.

Strayer, F.F. and Moss, E. (1987) 'Social constraints on information exchange during mother–child interaction', paper presented at the biennial meeting of the Society for Research in Child Development, Baltimore, Md, April.

Strayer, F.F., Moss, E. and Blicharski, T. (in press) 'Biosocial bases of representational activity during early childhood' in L.T. Winegar (ed.) *Social Interaction and the Development of Children's Understanding*, Norwood, NJ: Ablex.

Thompson, R.A., Lamb, M.E. and Estes, D. (1982) 'Stability of infant-other attachment and its relationship to changing life circumstances in an unselected middle-class sample', *Child Development* 53: 144-8.

US Bureau of the Census (1986) *Estimates of the Population of the U.S. by Age, Sex, and Race, 1980–1985* (Current Population Reports. Series P-25, No. 985). Washington, DC: US Government Printing Office.

Vandell, D.L. and Corasaniti, M.A. (1988) 'Variations in Early Child Care: do they predict subsequent social, emotional and cognitive differences?' unpublished manuscript, University of Texas at Dallas.

van IJzendoorn, M.H. and Kroonenberg, P.M. (1988) 'Cross-cultural patterns of attachment: a meta-analysis of the Strange Situation', *Child Development* 59: 147-56.

Vaughn, B.E., Gove, F.L. and Egeland, B. (1980) 'The relationship between out-of-home care and the quality of infant–mother attachment in an economically disadvantaged population', *Child Development* 51: 1203-14.

Vaughn, B.E., Deane, K.E. and Waters, E. (1985) 'The impact of out-of-home care on child–mother attachment quality: another look at some enduring questions', *Monographs of the Society for Research in Child Development*, 50 (1-2, Serial No. 209), 110-35.

Weinraub, M., Jaeger, E. and Hoffman, L.W. (in press) 'Predicting infant outcomes in families of employed and non-employed mothers', *Early Childhood Research Quarterly*.

6 The role of social networks in the care of young children

Malcolm Hill
Source: *Children and Society* (1989) 3(3): 195–211.

INTRODUCTION

Nearly all children in Britain over the age of 5 spend a considerable proportion of each weekday away from their parents, in order to fulfil legal requirements concerning their education. Before then, however, there is a widespread presumption that they should spend their time largely with their parents, and especially their mothers, except perhaps for part-time playgroup or nursery school arrangements from about 3 years onwards. Although there is a growing body of dissent, many people still believe that it is harmful in some way for children to be away from their parents for more than a few hours, particularly before they are 3. As a result, the great bulk of research about care arrangements for young children has been devoted to detailed analysis of mother–child interactions and of major deviations from what is regarded as 'normal' maternal care, as in nurseries or by child-minders. It is only quite recently that fathers, brothers and sisters have been brought into the picture (Dunn 1985; Lewis 1986).

Yet we know from our own experiences that most parents do share the care of their young children with other people for all manner of reasons. Grannies, aunts, uncles, friends, neighbours and babysitters may all be called on to look after children so that parents may work, get on with domestic chores, go out socially, and so on. There is very little systematic knowledge available concerning such arrangements within families, social networks, or about their social, emotional and other consequences (Long 1983; Tizard 1986). It seems plausible, however, that the extent of children's experience with different kinds of care by relatives, non-relatives and strangers will have significant effects on them. These effects may be direct or indirect, positive or negative (Cochran and Brassard 1979; Crittenden 1985). Greater understanding of the care functions of social networks should be of general interest as regards childhood socialization processes and family lifestyles. It may also be of crucial importance for professionals involved with families in difficulties (Packman *et al.* 1986; Cooper and Ball 1987).

This chapter describes some of the findings from a study of the care arrangements made by parents for their 3-year-old children since birth. Interviews were carried out with both parents in seventy-three two-parent households in Edinburgh (see Hill 1987 for further details). Supplementary information was obtained from two-week diaries of the children's movements, carers and activities. About half the sample families were middle class and half working class, according to a combination of criteria which included both partners' occupations, educational levels and self-classifications. No claims are made for the representativeness of the sample, which lacked ethnic diversity and excluded single parents. However, the broad picture that emerged was consistent with that found in other areas (Allan 1985; Hill *et al.* 1985; Willmott 1987). Although the study examined use of formal group care as well as use of networks, it is the latter which is the focus of the present paper.

REASONS FOR SHARING CARE

It was seldom stated explicitly, but the consistent background factor when children were looked after outside the nuclear family was the father's absence at work, which went largely unquestioned. In this sample, mothers had always looked after the children more than fathers had, usually much more. Indeed, the diaries indicated that *on average* (and there was great variation), children spent as much time with network carers away from their mothers as they did with their fathers alone. It also seems that even when men are unemployed, they usually still tend to resist taking over primary child-care responsibilities (Binns and Mars 1984; Fagin and Little 1984; Burgoyne 1987).

As might be expected, the longest periods children spent apart from their parents were due to hospitalization (of the mother or child) or to both parents' wish to work at the same time. However, this affected only a minority of the children. For two-thirds of them, no care arrangement had been made for these purposes over the three years.

Daytime care had none the less occurred for all the sample. This had usually taken place for 'adult-oriented' reasons, of which the most typical was to make it easier for the mothers to go shopping or keep a medical or dental appointment. Virtually everyone saw this as a legitimate reason to share care. However, there was much greater variability in relation to the other kinds of circumstances which might be seen as requiring children to stay with someone else. What one person depicted as a quite normal and legitimate 'need' to share care was seen by someone else as unacceptable, so that the activity in question ought to be avoided or adapted to fit in with parental care. This applied, for example, to mothers engaging in leisure or sporting activities, or simply having a 'break'. Only some mothers felt all right about being apart from their children for these reasons, while others averred that they did not need or were not entitled to such separations. A small number of parents admitted to needing crisis relief from the stress of looking after demanding children or infants who woke and cried consistently at night.

There were also two types of 'child-oriented' care arrangements. The first type happened in order to promote relationships between children and close relatives (especially grandparents) or more rarely good friends. Some parents liked to do this with young babies, while others thought it was necessary to wait until later when they considered the child was ready to handle separations. The second kind of child-oriented care occurred mainly from toddlerhood onwards. It involved children going to play with others of the same age, while just one of their mothers kept an eye on them or organized more structured activities. As they grew older, many children asked to go and play. Indeed, over half the children were said to have requested staying with a relative or other carer before they were 3. Play-based care was much more common amongst middle-class families. They tended to have strong values about helping children to mix and learn through play *before* they went to formal preschool groups. Working-class parents usually did not appear to see this as something they should deliberately organize themselves. Many were also reluctant to trust 'untrained' other mothers with their children. In any case, their accommodation and access to outdoor playspace were normally not well suited to entertaining groups of children. Consequently, they thought peer contact was best arranged through official groups.

Evening care was mainly fixed up so that parents could go out together, but sometimes one went to an evening class or social engagement at the same time as the other was working.

Overnight care had occurred for half of the sample, excluding the five who had had to stay in hospital overnight without a parent present. For a number of working-class families, regular overnight care acted as an extension of evening babysitting and/or was part of 'child-oriented' care by relatives. Fewer middle-class parents had left their children overnight, especially before the age of 2. Then they did so mainly in order to have a weekend away or to go on holiday.

FREQUENCY OF SHARING CARE

The number of times children had stayed with other people varied enormously. A few had apparently been apart from their mothers on only a handful of occasions over the three years, while some dual worker families had shared care daily. However, it was clear that sharing care amongst social networks was a normal process, in spite of the strong norm of maternal responsibility in our society (Barry and Paxson 1971; Smith 1980). Between the ages of 2 and 3, half the sample had stayed with someone else in the daytime at least once a week (excluding formal groups) and a similar proportion of families used an evening babysitter at least monthly.

Most parents reported an increase in the frequency of sharing care as the child grew older. Many began weekly or fortnightly arrangements during the second year. Interestingly this is the period when children are supposed to be most vulnerable to separation distress, compared with both before and after (Schaffer 1977). Evidently this may not apply within the familiar context of personal social networks.

There were many things which influenced parents' propensity to share care. Work patterns clearly played a part, but less than might be expected, because a number of mothers worked part time in the evenings or at weekends, so that their husbands could look after the children while they were away. Parents' values about their responsibilities were important. Many had acquired from their own upbringing strong wishes to minimize sharing, while some mothers in particular had to overcome strong guilt before feeling comfortable about leaving their children. The language used to describe non-parental care often portrayed it as unfeeling or rejecting behaviour by the parents, whereas it may be seen as affording positive opportunities for the child. Such terms as 'dumped', 'farmed out', 'got rid of' and 'palmed off' were used by some respondents to disparage what other people did, while a few employed such phrases apologetically or ironically to describe their own arrangements. This negative presumption was applied by different people to working mothers, early use of group care or simply any babysitting which was not seen as 'necessary' or unavoidable according to the person's views about what circumstances justified children being in the care of someone else. Both men and women frequently spoke about 'parental responsibility' in this context, even though in practical terms the onus primarily rested on mothers.

Beliefs about the nature of children contributed to parents' willingness or unwillingness to share care, too. Some saw children as easily upset and needing to establish a secure base over the first three years of life before they would feel comfortable elsewhere. This may be termed an attachment ideology. Others thought children were more resilient. They expected that their youngsters would learn to cope with separation or indeed enjoy it as an additional experience and not a deprivation (a social learning ideology). Similarly parents appeared to have predispositions to see a child's upset during the transfer to a carer either as a brief protest rapidly overcome or as major distress to be avoided if at all possible.

Attitudes were sometimes modified by experience. Many had become more willing to let their children stay elsewhere as time went by. Some came to see that it did little harm, contrary to their earlier fears. Others realized that their children's unfamiliarity with separation became a disadvantage once they started at playgroup or nursery school. In addition, some families who lived in streets where mutual babysitting was the norm became gradually socialized to join in, perhaps after initial reluctance. Thus there was commonly a greater preparedness to share care with second and later born children. It was also thought that brothers and sisters together helped each other cope with separations (cf. Stewart 1983). Less often, parents became more apprehensive about sharing care. This was typically explained by citing a 'crucial incident' when a child was very upset on being left with someone else.

THE CARERS

The number of carers used regularly by each family ranged from one to a dozen or so. Normally a child's 'set' of carers increased as they grew older. Sometimes carers were more or less interchangeable, as in the case of certain relatives or of local friends with children of a similar age. There could also be a hierarchy of carers (first, second and third choice) or specialization according to the purpose, timing or location of care. For instance, one girl had been looked after by her grandmother when her parents were working, by two mothers along the street for play and by members of a babysitting group in the evenings.

Nearly all the network care arrangements were made by the women and so were very much influenced by the nature of their own relationships and by their attitudes to the various kinds of potential carer. Often choices were not consciously made, because in different families it seemed almost automatic that it should be 'my Mum' or 'Jill next door' or 'Mary who minded his older sister'. When asked to explain their choices, hardly anyone mentioned gender, since it was taken for granted that it would be mainly women who were available, willing and suitable. In fact, over 90 per cent of the children's main daytime carers were women, but in a few cases an uncle or grandfather was important. It is not surprising that secondary care of children outside the nuclear family is, like primary care, chiefly a female activity. On the other hand, two-thirds of the children had been looked after by a male carer on his own at some point, though only six children frequently.

The main other factors taken into account in the choice of carers were

1 kinship
2 friendship
3 familiarity with the child
4 competence and trustworthiness
5 presence of similarly aged children
6 availability and willingness.

There was wide variation in the comparative significance of these. Many did not question the primacy of 'family', while others considered friends with young children preferable even if relatives were available. A small number believed it was best to pay previously unknown carers in order to ensure quality of care and control of the care arrangement. Not many could afford that option, of course.

RELATIVES

Although the demise of extended kinship networks has been repeatedly feared, they appeared to be alive and well for the great majority of this sample. The main carers for half the children were relatives and the proportion had been greater during infancy. Most overnight care had been with relatives. Whereas nearly all other carers lived close by, kin from other parts of the city or even some distance outside were still important carers for many of the children. Even relatives who lived many miles away had looked after the children during visits or holidays. Furthermore, a fair number of people who relied on non-kin carers indicated that this was only because their relatives lived too far away.

With a few exceptions, care by kin was restricted to members of the parents' original nuclear families – the children's grandparents, aunts and uncles. Choices within these categories depended on a number of considerations, such as distance, health, age and interest in children, but in the sample as a whole there were biases towards grandparents, maternal kin and female kin.

Grandparents were the principal carers for one-third of the children and the second carers for a further third. Just under half the children had stayed with grandparents overnight without their parents. When mothers went into hospital, arrangements for the children nearly always centred on fathers and grandparents, perhaps aided by a neighbour or aunt. So obvious was the choice of grandparents (or at least grandmothers) to some people, that they were puzzled to be asked 'Why?'. Reasons given included their familiarity to the child, strong desire to be with the children and a shared expectation that this was their role, even their entitlement. One father described babysitting as 'a privilege of grandparents, and we benefit'. There was also no need for any kind of 'payment' in cash or kind, although this sometimes caused discomfort so that parents showed their appreciation symbolically or indirectly (for example by giving presents or doing odd jobs). Cunningham-Burley (1983) has noted how grandparents seek contact with their grandchildren, yet are reluctant to interfere. Helping the parents by babysitting provides an ideal way of reconciling that tension.

Not everyone favoured grandparental care, however, and some were rueful about problems which resulted. Rivalry, intrusiveness and disputes about handling the children were all mentioned. There was also the added difficulty involved if parents wanted to stipulate or modify what their own parents did with the children, since this would reverse the normal direction of authority and by implication question their own upbringing. The most common area of contention related to spoiling. A number of respondents were unhappy about grandparents giving sweets and letting children do as they please. On the other hand, some accepted or welcomed such indulgence, for example: 'She does get spoilt, but what are grannies for?', 'I think it's a grandmother's privilege to spoil their grandchildren'.

Unwillingness by grandparents to act as carers at all was rare and seen as abnormal, though of course many were glad to limit the extent of their care-giving commitments. Restricted use of grandparents was primarily explained in terms of age, health and location, though these may sometimes have been convenient excuses. Even considerable distance did not preclude grandparental care as it did with virtually all other kinds of carer, but merely altered the nature of care, so that it was, for example, confined to babysitting during mutual visits. Age did not seem to become a significant influence by itself, until the late 70s. Although the parents in the sample ranged in age from 22 to 52, half were in their early 30s and the majority of grandparents under 70. In only one case were all four grandparents dead and three-quarters of the children had both grandmothers still living. When poor health meant that grandparents could not look after their grandchildren, usually other relatives substituted.

Other relatives were important in many cases, especially if grandparents lived far away, were infirm or had commitments to other grandchildren. In contrast to grandparents, by whom and towards whom there were typically strong expectations of a babysitting role, aunts and uncles were more often self-selecting, with just one or two from several available taking a particular pleasure in the care of the children. Quite a few single uncles were also popular carers. Whereas families of all social statuses normally shared care with grandparents if it was practicable, care by other relatives was much more prominent amongst working-class families. Some of these had a traditional pattern of intergenerational caring, whereby an older sister looked after a younger one, who later on babysat for *her* nephews and nieces, who might in turn grow up to be carers for their aunt's children.

FRIENDS AND NEIGHBOURS

The distinction between neighbours and friends is not a clear-cut one. The word 'neighbour' may be restricted to the person next door, applied to anyone in the block or street or used more widely to refer to people in nearby streets. Quite often neighbours who interact frequently come to regard each other as friends, although some people require much more intimacy than others before they class a person as a friend (Duck and Perlman 1985). In this study, care by old friends or ex-neighbours living at some distance was occasionally important, but on the whole care by non-relatives on a non-paying basis was carried out by other parents (mainly mothers) living in the vicinity or by immediate neighbours. People next door or on the same stair who acted as carers ranged from teenagers to pensioners, but otherwise there was a strong tendency for sharing care to take the form of exchanges between families at a similar stage in the life-course. For the families involved, reciprocal child-care arrangements were often intimately linked with the development of social relationships for both the adults and children concerned.

The two-week diaries revealed marked differences in the children's involvements with other local families. There were significant class contrasts. Twice as many middle-class as working-class children spent some time with four or more neighbours or friends during the fortnight. There were thirteen children, nearly all working class, who had not visited the home of a friend or neighbour at all. Some of these had had frequent contact with relatives, but a few were evidently quite isolated. Even more strikingly, three-quarters of the middle-class children had stayed with local friends without their parents, but this was true for only four of the working-class children (one-seventh).

These class differences appeared to be linked to different broader patterns of social relationships, although of course there were exceptions to the generalizations. The interviews suggested that working-class parents had as many close friends as middle-class parents, but they were less likely to visit their homes with the children and only a few families shared care with friends. This was partly because most felt little need to look outside their kin network, but there was also a common view that it would be an imposition to ask friends to 'watch' your children when they had commitments to their own families. By contrast, many middle-class parents saw other families in the same position as child-care resources with similar needs. In part, this was because more of the middle-class families lived far from close relatives, but even those with kin nearby usually also shared care with local friends. Correspondingly a much higher proportion regarded people in their street as friendly than was the case for the working-class families. Many of the working-class mothers had not made new friends since having children, but remained involved socially with relatives and perhaps old friends. Most of the middle-class mothers on the other hand had made acquaintanceships or friendships through their children, whether by meeting at playgroups, clinics or school, or simply from developing casual encounters. They seemed more inclined to extend relationships from one setting or purpose to another, as Allan (1979) has also noted. Most working-class parents expressed their desire that relationships with people round about should be basically private, ideally accompanied by the absence of trouble and a preparedness to help in emergencies. Other commented on difficulties they had in furthering their relationships with other mothers they met at school or nursery school.

One reason why it was easier for middle-class mothers to become involved with other families locally was the existence of social institutions which made contacts easier even for diffident women. Playgroups are more available in middle-class areas (Osborn and Milbank 1987; Cohen 1988). They encourage participation with the groups and, even though not all mothers want that, it does facilitate getting to know other families at the same life-stage. Just as important, many of the mothers in the present study went to coffee mornings in each other's houses to which newcomers were readily invited. There was a common expectation, too, that new people in the area should be asked to come round for tea or coffee, or for the children to play, which hardly any of the working-class mothers had experienced.

The key characteristic of shared care by non-relatives was that it nearly always involved some kind of exchange. Occasionally this did not apply to older or single next-door neighbours, for whom symbolic 'repayments' were made as with respect to kin. Otherwise, sharing care in local networks was normally based on reciprocity. People looked after each other's children on different occasions and care arrangements were made precisely because there was a mutual need and a capacity to repay on a non-cash basis. This took two forms – pair swopping and generalized exchange.

Half the sample were engaged in some kind of twinning with another local family with young children and one in six had swop care arrangements on a regular basis. This occurred amongst families of both broad social classes. However, many of the middle-class families were also involved in wider care networks embracing several families. Children could be left with whichever of the other mothers was available or with the person who was most 'indebted' as a result of previous use of the network. Moreover, some networks had developed their own 'mini-groups' referred to earlier, whereby a number of children from different families met in each other's homes in turn. Often these were set up initially or ostensibly to enable the children to play together with all the mothers present, but it soon became possible for them to take it in turns to slip away or plan other activities.

Such daytime arrangements often became routinized in manner and timing, but expectations about getting return care services from other members of the network were normally flexible. In the evenings, some families used the same or similar setups, but more commonly they took part in more formalized babysitting circles. In this study, use of babysitting groups was confined to middle-class families and all of them were familiar with the concept, while as many as one-half of the working-class parents did not understand what such groups entail. Some middle-class families preferred not to join a circle, as they did not wish to give up the time or felt no need, but most working-class parents were actively hostile to the very idea, because it was based on care by 'strangers', a concept which will be explored further below.

Babysitting circles are based on the principle of generalized exchange (Ekeh 1974; McCormack 1976), whereby the repayment of the (child-care) service is not due to the particular provider of the service but to any member of the network, on the understanding that each member's giving and receiving of the service will be in rough balance overall. In effect, families exchange time, so that on separate occasions they gain free time from their own children for leisure pursuits in return for giving up time on another occasion to look after someone else's children. A mechanism is required to ensure approximate equivalence. Two such mechanisms were present in the study area – first, use of a book or periodic list and second, employment of an exchange medium (tokens or beans).

The book system involved one person in rotation keeping a record of how many hours of babysitting members gave and received. Usually choice of the babysitter was determined centrally by the book-holder depending on which families were in 'credit' or 'debit'. Such accounting terms were used by the families themselves. In the second type of group, exchangeable items substituted for written records as measures of time periods. One bean or token represented a unit of time which the parties exchanged at each session. Often there was a system for 'weighting' unsocial hours, so that periods before 6 p.m. or after midnight might require twice as many tokens, for example. By contrast with the book groups, choice of carers for particular occasions rested with individual members.

The book systems were confined to smaller groups of up to twenty families, probably because the work involved in co-ordination became excessive beyond a certain point. Exchange medium circles were larger (up to fifty members) and some spread over a wide area, as people who moved away liked to keep up their membership.

Some informal evening networks and circles were restricted to women, but others included men. Quite a lot of the fathers did not want to be involved, seeing it as a woman's affair or feeling ill-equipped for the task. Some women, too, preferred to leave the husbands out of it or had not even considered the possibility. However, a number of couples appeared to accept readily that either partner could or indeed should babysit. Circles often had social as well as child-care functions. They had developed regular meetings, outings and clubs. These were, as usual, mainly organized by the women, but sometimes men were involved too.

PAID CARERS

Normally cash payment was seen as inappropriate for care by relatives or friends. One woman paid her own mother for looking after the children while she worked, but the grandmother reasserted her own altruistic role by spending the money on toys and clothes for the grandchildren. Another mother had wanted to pay her mother but 'she more or less told me to get lost'. The main exception to the non-cash rule involved teenage carers, whether they were relatives or the older children of friends and neighbours.

One-quarter of the families had paid a non-relative to look after the children in the daytime. Only people in well-paid jobs can afford to pay for children to be looked after in their own homes (Scarr and Dunn 1987). Six families had used a daily help for child care, while four had employed *au pairs*. All were middle class. Mostly the parents were well pleased with the arrangement, because the carers soon got to know the children very well and there was little disruption of the child's routine. Only four families had used a child-minder to look after their children outside the home. This small number was to be expected since, on a national basis, only a low proportion of families are using child-minders at any one time (Clarke-Stewart 1982; Moss 1987). In the present study, two children seemed to have gained very much from a close relationship with virtually an additional set of parents and to have become close friends with the minders' children. The remaining two instances exemplified some of the problems of turnover and poor care reported in other studies (Jackson and Jackson, 1979; Mayall and Petrie 1983). However, there is evidence that much child-minding is satisfactory, particularly if inappropriate value-judgements are avoided (Shinman 1981; Poland 1988).

STRANGERS

For obvious reasons, most parents are much more wary about leaving their children with someone they do not know well than with a relative or friend. Concern is perhaps now greater than ever, given the wide recent publicity about abductions and child abuse, though the evidence is that more children suffer ill-treatment from people they know well than from complete strangers (LaFontaine 1988; Stone 1989). Some respondents were particularly conscious of tragedies reported in the media. One man said: 'Look at the things you read. These people get a babysitter they ken for 15 years and the next thing you know the bairn is burnt'.

Parents varied not only in their views about care by strangers, but even in their ideas of what was meant by a stranger. In middle-class families, a stranger was normally taken to be a person unknown to the child or parents, but a number of working-class parents included acquaintances and even friends as strangers. Several indicated that, as regards care of the children, people counted as strangers if they were not family or very close friends. A characteristic distinction was as follows: 'I wouldna have any sort of stranger watching them, only a relative that I know very well.' Interestingly many of the comments about strangers were made by the men, as if in the role of family protector. Similarly whereas middle-class concerns about care by strangers were mainly couched in terms of the child's separation anxiety, working-class fears derived from worries about physical harm to the child or about theft.

As a result, many working-class families drew quite rigid and restricted boundaries about the kinds of people they would trust their children with. Middle-class parents not only were usually more willing to contemplate a wider circle of potential carers, but also extended their boundaries quite readily, either to local parents they hardly knew or, less commonly, to paid carers they had not met before. Their apparent greater willingness to trust people was related to assumptions that residential segregation processes ought to ensure that 'unsuitable' people were unlikely to come within their ambit. Members of babysitting circles believed that access to the group was controlled, yet several admitted that any incomer to the area with children was asked to join, evidently without knowledge of their history and trustworthiness.

THE IMPLICATIONS OF SHARED CARE PATTERNS

The preoccupations of most writers in the day-care field has been to establish, refute or just test out presumed emotional effects on the children. There has also been an interest in possible cognitive implications, but the issue of whether children benefit more from preschool groups or from home-based care remains an open question (Tizard and Hughes 1984; Osborn and Milbank 1987). Probably the main conclusion that can be drawn is that good care helps children whether it is provided by the biological family, another family, group-care or a combination of these, whereas unstimulating, unresponsive or highly changeable care is likely to be deleterious. In other words, it is the characteristics of the care rather than the form of the care which appear most important (Hill 1987).

The current study did not set out to ascertain the effects on the children using standard 'objective' measures, but parents were asked to describe how the children responded. Even including the transition to playgroups and nursery schooling, which most had experienced, over half were said never to have been troubled by staying with other people. Many had thoroughly enjoyed it. Undoubtedly this had much to do with the careful selection of carers and preparations for care by parents, but it seems that none the less sharing care within social networks at the very least does children no harm, by contrast with the frequent perception of it as an abdication of responsibility. There was indeed evidence that the children who were most shy and anxious were those with least experience of shared care, although the relationship is not necessarily causal.

When reactions to toddler groups, crèches, playgroups and nursery schools were all taken account of, it was fairly common for children to have been upset by one care episode but not others. Apparently distress shown at a certain age or in response to a specific situation often does not generalize to other circumstances. About one in eight of the children had apparently been persistently difficult to leave. Several of the descriptions indicated that this was a temperamental trait evident from an early age (Thomas and Chess 1977).

Care arrangements in networks are important not only because of children's emotional development. They are closely intertwined with the development of social relationships, not only of the adults as we have seen, but also of the children. There were many variants, but children immersed in kin networks tended to have more contacts and attachments with men and older children (notably cousins), while those integrated in local street caring and play networks usually had more friends of their own age. Children not involved in either were often isolated, although in a few instances significant contacts with other adults and children resulted from their child-minder's networks.

The class differences in care patterns outlined earlier were associated with contrasts in relationship patterns, although naturally not every family fitted in with the general patterns. In brief, more middle-class children had frequent peer contacts, while working-class children were more likely to have close relationships with men and with older children (who were usually relatives). Thus 70 per cent of the working-class children were said to be fond of a man besides their father, but only 25 per cent of the middle-class children. During the diary fortnight, half of the working-class children saw a cousin or other related child, but only three middle-class children. Conversely all but four of the middle-class sample met four or more other unrelated children during the two weeks (outside of pre-school groups), but this was true for only half of the working-class children. Eighty per cent of the former spent time with another 3-year-old (again ignoring group attendance) during the diary fortnight compared with 40 per cent of the latter. Correspondingly the middle-class children had *on average* twice as many peer friends (i.e. within two years of their own age) as did the working-class children. A good many middle-class children were already imitating some of their mothers' social skills in initiating plans for friends to come to tea or for parties. On the other hand, the working-class children were benefiting from more mixed age contacts of the kind which is more common elsewhere in the world (Konner 1975; Weisner and Gallimore 1977). One-third of them were said to have an older cousin as their 'best friend'.

Care by members of families' social networks was not normally a substitute for official care arrangements, but mainly performed separate or preparatory functions. For that reason, virtually the whole sample of parents were in favour of their children attending pre-school groups. Much of the information parents had about pre-school facilities came from relatives and friends, who also were the main sources of advice and evaluation concerning particular establishments. Those children with very little experience of non-parental care were less likely to adjust well when starting at playgroup or nursery school, although a few did settle happily. Many more of the middle-class children began their pre-school group already knowing others who were attending, which reflected their generally more extensive peer contacts.

Evidently children's life experiences are very much affected by relationships outside the nuclear family, but so also are parents' functioning and well-being closely related to network contacts and their ability to sustain supportive relationships (Brown *et al.* 1986; Titterton 1989). We know that the very people who professionals think need better support are often those least able to use their own networks effectively (Timms 1983; van der Eycken 1982). By and large the present study comprised families who *were* coping effectively. Most acknowledged that parenthood brought considerable stresses and a few recognized the thin line between themselves and child abuse. Both regular support and sympathetic offers of care in a 'crisis' had helped prevent pressures get out of hand. A standard measure (the Malaise Inventory) showed that more 'low sharing' parents were anxious than others, although there are several directions of causation which could account for this.

The majority of families were *interactive*, that is actively involved socially and open to new relationships, though some were *satiated* (exclusively engaged with their existing network) or *autonomous* (with little apparent need for external relationships). Those who expressed dissatisfaction had *insufficient* network contacts, because there were few or no relatives living close by and they found it hard to develop friendships. Both individual and neighbourhood factors affected this latter phenomenon. A lack of skills and confidence was important, especially for women who had lost touch with friends when they stopped work to have children. This was compounded if they lived surrounded by people at different life-stages or who individually or collectively were not interactive. It could be overcome when there were local norms of making friends through children or facilitation of social contacts by organized children's pre-school facilities.

CONCLUSIONS

Within limits and provided there is a basic family attachment, children seem to cope with and benefit from a wide range of care arrangements within their families' personal social networks. Indeed a number of parents come to regret their earlier restrictive attitudes about this. The patterns of shared care are affected by many material, environmental and social factors. Income, accommodation, housing layout and the local 'density' of young children play a part. Besides these influences, sharing care is also intimately bound up with norms concerning children's needs and socialization, the nature of kinship and friendship ties, and the perceived rights and responsibilities of mothers and fathers. These in turn influence the demand for and responses to public services. Both critics and defenders of welfare provision should recognize that children's lives are not merely the result of actions by parents and the state, but are embedded within a more complex web of relationships. We need a deeper understanding of how such relationships operate, not only with respect to 'intact families' (as in the present study) but also non-conventional family forms and ethnic minorities.

REFERENCES

Allan, G. (1979) *The Sociology of Friendship and Kinship*, London: George Allen & Unwin.
Allan, G. (1985) *Family Life*, Oxford: Basil Blackwell.
Barry, H. and Paxson, L.M. (1971) 'Infancy and early childhood', *Ethnology* 10: 466–508.
Binns, D. and Mars, G. (1984) 'Family, community and unemployment', *Sociological Review* 32: 662–95.

Brown, G.W., Andrews, B., Harris, T., Adler, Z. and Bridge, L. (1986) 'Social support, self-esteem and depression', *Psychological Medicine* 16: 813–31.

Burgoyne, J. (1987) 'Change, gender and the life course', in G. Cohen (ed.) *Social Change and the Life Course*, London: Tavistock.

Clarke-Stewart, A. (1982) *Day Care*, Glasgow: Fontana.

Cochran, M.M. and Brassard, J.A. (1979) 'Child development and personal social networks', *Child Development* 50: 601–16.

Cohen, B. (1988) *Caring for Children*, London: Commission of the European Communities.

Cooper, D. and Ball, D. (1987) *Social Work and Child Abuse*, London: Macmillan.

Crittenden, P.M. (1985) 'Social networks, quality of child rearing and child development', *Child Development*, 56: 1299–313.

Cunningam-Burley, S.J. (1983) 'The meaning and significance of grandparenthood', PhD thesis, Aberdeen.

Duck, S. and Perlman, D. (eds) (1985) *Understanding Personal Relationships*, London: Sage.

Dunn, J. (1985) *Sisters and Brothers*, Glasgow: Fontana.

Ekeh, P. (1974) *Social Exchange Theory – The Two Traditions*, London: Heinemann.

Fagin, L. and Little, M. (1984) *The Forsaken Families*, Harmondsworth: Penguin.

Hill, M. (1987) *Sharing Child Care in Early Parenthood*, London: Routledge & Kegan Paul.

Hill, M., Triseliotis, J. and Buist, M. (1985) *Adoption Allowances – For Love and Money*, Edinburgh: Department of Social Administration and Social Work.

Jackson, B. and Jackson, S. (1979) *Childminder: A Study in Action Research*, London: Routledge & Kegan Paul.

Konner, M. (1975) 'Relations among infants and juveniles in comparative perspective', in M. Lewis and L. Rosenblum (eds) *Friendship and Peer Relations*, New York: Wiley.

LaFontaine, J. (1988) *Child Sexual Abuse*, London: ESRC.

Lewis, C. (1986) *Becoming a Father*, Milton Keynes: Open University Press.

Long, F. (1983) 'Social support networks in day care and early child development', in J.K. Whitaker and J. Garbarino (eds) *Social Support Networks*, New York: Aldine.

McCormack, G. (1976) 'Reciprocity', *Man* 11: 89–103.

Mayall, B. and Petrie, P. (1983) *Childminding and Day Nurseries: What Kind of Care*, London: Heinemann.

Moss, P. (1987) *A Review of Childminding Research*, London: Thomas Coram Research Unit.

Osborn, A. and Milbank, J. (1987) *The Effects of Early Education*, Oxford: Oxford University Press.

Packman, J., Randall, J. and Jacques, N. (1986) *Who Needs Care?*, Oxford: Basil Blackwell.

Poland, F. (1988) 'Some dilemmas of in-house social services research: problems in evaluating services to childminders', *Research, Policy and Planning* 6: 7–14.

Scarr, S. and Dunn, J. (1987) *Mother Care/Other Care*, Harmondsworth: Penguin.

Schaffer, H.R. (1977) *Mothering*, London: Open Books.

Shinman, S.M. (1981) *A Chance for Every Child?*, London: Tavistock.

Smith, P.K. (1980) 'Shared care of young children: alternative methods to monotropism', *Merrill-Palmer Quarterly* 26: 371–87.

Stewart, R.B. (1983) 'Sibling attachment relationships: child infant interactions in the strange situation', *Developmental Psychology* 19: 192–9.

Stone, F. (ed.) (1989) *Child Abuse: The Scottish Experience*, London: BAAF.

Thomas, A. and Chess, S. (1977) *Temperament and Development*, New York: Brunner/Mazel.

Timms, E. (1983) 'On the relevance of informal social networks to social work intervention', *British Journal of Social Work* 13: 405–15.

Titterton, M. (1989) *The Management of Personal Welfare*, London: Report for the ESRC.

Tizard, B. (1986) *The Care of Young Children*, London: Thomas Coram Research Unit.

Tizard, B. and Hughes, M. (1984) *Young Children Learning*, Glasgow: Fontana.

Van der Eycken, (1982) *Home-Start*, Leicester: Home-Start Consultancy.

Weisner, T.S. and Gallimore, R. (1977) 'My brother's keeper: child and sibling caretaking', *Current Anthropology* 18: 169–90.

Willmott, P. (1987) *Friendship Networks and Social Support*, London: Policy Studies Institute.

7 Coping with family transitions: winners, losers and survivors

E. Mavis Hetherington
Source: *Child Development* (1989) 60: 1–14.
Reprinted by permission of The Society for Research in
Child Development.

[. . .]
One of the things that is notable in studies of family transitions is the
great diversity in the response of parents and children to divorce and
remarriage. Most family members undergo an initial period of
emotional distress and disrupted functioning following divorce but
recover within a two to three-year period if the divorce is not
compounded by continued stress and adversity. Some parents and
children show intense and enduring deleterious outcomes. Others
show delayed effects, appearing to adapt well in the early stages of
family reorganization but having problems or developmental disruptions that emerge at a later time. Finally, a substantial minority of
adults and children are able to cope constructively with the challenges
of divorce and remarriage and emerge as psychologically enhanced
and exceptionally competent and fulfilled individuals. In this chapter I
shall examine some of the long-term outcomes of divorce and
remarriage as well as the factors that contribute to children being
survivors, winners or losers following these family transitions.

One difficulty in attempting to assess the long-term effects of
divorce on parents and children and the factors that may mediate these
outcomes is that sequences of family reorganizations and family
experiences following divorce vary widely, and the timing of these
events may be critical in predicting the long-term adjustment of family
members. For most parents and children, divorce is only one in a
series of family transitions that follow separation. Life in a single-
parent household following divorce is usually a temporary condition
since 80 per cent of men and 75 per cent of women will remarry. About
25 per cent of children will spend some time in a stepparent family
before they are young adults. Moreover, since the divorce rate is
higher in subsequent marriages than in first marriages, some parents

and children encounter a series of divorces, periods in a one-parent household, and remarriages.

VULNERABILITY AND PROTECTIVE FACTORS

Garmezy (1983) and Rutter (1983) have underscored the importance of vulnerability and protective factors that modulate responses to stress. Rutter (1983) has advanced a chemical analogy, saying that these factors are largely inert on their own but serve as catalysts in combination with stressful events. When such variables increase the effect of stressors they may be viewed as vulnerability factors; when they diminish the effects of stressors they can be seen as protective factors. After reviewing the literature on the stressors of childhood, Garmezy (1983) concluded that a triad of protective factors repeatedly emerges. The first of these is positive personality dispositions, the second a supportive family milieu, and the third external societal agencies that function as support systems for reinforcing and strengthening children's coping efforts. The effects of this triad of protective factors are not automatic, for as Rutter (1987) has emphasized, protection does not lie in the availability of potentially supportive resources but in the use made of them. As we shall see, some children are less able or willing than others to seek out or use available resources when coping with the marital transitions of their parents.

Different protective or vulnerability factors may shape the adaptation of individuals to different family transitions at different times. In addition, adaptation to family transitions may depend on the experiences that have preceded these changes. For example, it should be kept in mind that, in remarriage, the challenge for the child is coping with the changes triggered by the addition rather than the loss of a family member as it was in divorce. Moreover, remarriage follows a period of time in a one-parent household. The response to divorce will be influenced by pre-divorce family relationships, and adjustment and roles and relations in the one-parent household will shape the child's subsequent response to the addition of a stepparent. It seems reasonable to assume that as the salient vulnerability and protective factors shift in different phases following a marital transition, some discontinuities in the coping and adjustment of individuals in response to these family reorganizations will occur.

THE VIRGINIA LONGITUDINAL STUDY OF DIVORCE AND REMARRIAGE

In order to examine vulnerability and protective factors that contribute to children's long-term adjustment to divorce and remarriage, I am going to discuss a six-year follow-up of a longitudinal study of divorce and remarriage that I began in collaboration with Martha and Roger Cox (Hetherington *et al.* 1982). The sample in the original study was composed of 144 well-educated, middle-class white parents and their children. Half of the children were from divorced, mother-custody families, and the other half were from non-divorced families. Within each group, half were boys and half were girls. A target child who was 4 years of age at the beginning of the study and his or her parents were studied at two months, one year, two years, and six years following divorce.

In the six-year follow-up, the subjects were residential parents and their children in 124 of the original 144 families who were available and willing to continue to participate in the study. A new group of families matched on demographic characteristics with the original sample was added in order to expand the size of the groups to thirty sons and thirty daughters in each of the three groups – a remarried mother/stepfather group; a non-remarried, mother-custody group, and a non-divorced group – a total of 180 families. For some analyses, the remarried group was broken down into those who were remarried less than two years and those remarried longer than two years. The cross-sectional analyses of families six years after divorce for the most part were based on the expanded sample, the longitudinal analyses on the original sample.

ADJUSTMENT IN THE TWO YEARS FOLLOWING DIVORCE

During the first two years following divorce, most children and many parents experienced emotional distress; psychological, health and behavior problems; disruptions in family functioning; and problems in adjusting to new roles, relationships and life changes associated with the altered family situation. However, as is reported in other studies, by two years following divorce, the majority of parents and children were adapting reasonably well and certainly were showing great improvement since the time of the divorce. Some continuing problems were found in the adjustment of boys and in relationships between divorced custodial mothers and their sons. Boys from divorced families, in comparison to boys in non-divorced families, showed more anti-social, acting-out, coercive, non-compliant behaviors in the home and in the school and exhibited difficulties in peer relationships and school achievement. In contrast, girls from divorced families in which remarriages had not occurred were functioning well and had positive relationships with their custodial mothers.

In considering these results, two things must be kept in mind. First, this study involves only mother-custody families, and there is evidence that children adjust better in the custody of a parent of the same sex (Camara and Resnick 1988; Santrock and Warshak 1986; Zill 1988). Second, age of the child may be an important factor in sex differences in children's responses to divorce and remarriage. The children were 4 years of age at the beginning of this study, on average, 6 at the two-year assessment, and 10 at the time of the six-year assessment. Reports of the more severe and long-lasting disruption of behavior in boys than girls following their parents' divorce have tended to come from studies of pre-adolescent children. Our children, however, were just entering adolescence at the time of the six-year follow-up, and this is a time when behavior problems in girls and conflicts in the interactions between daughters and mothers in divorced mother-custody families may emerge (Hetherington 1972; Wallerstein *et al.* 1988).

The six-year follow-up had not been planned as part of the original study. We initiated the six-year follow-up because we were concerned that at two years after divorce we had not followed these families long enough to see a restabilizing in the mother–son relationship and a final readjustment of the sons. Moreover, it was apparent that the effects of divorce alone could not be considered in appraising the long-term adjustment of the children since remarriages were presenting new adaptive challenges to many of our parents and children. Let us turn now to the triad of individual, familial and extrafamilial factors that protect the child or that put the child at risk for long-term adverse consequences following marital transitions (see Hetherington 1987; 1988; in press).

TEMPERAMENT AND PERSONALITY

Although many individual characteristics protected children or made them vulnerable to long-term adverse effects following their parents' marital transitions, I shall focus only on the child's temperament. Temperament will be used to illustrate the complexity of interactions of such individual characteristics with risk and protective factors in determining long-term adjustment. However, it should be noted that other individual characteristics, such as intelligence, age and sex, were important, with more intelligent children being more resilient, older children being more affected than younger children by extrafamilial factors, and younger children coping more readily than late pre-adolescent or early adolescent children with their parent's remarriage. Finally, marked sex differences were found in response to divorce and remarriage: boys were more adversely affected than girls by divorce and life in a mother-custody one-parent household, and girls had more long-term difficulty than boys in adjusting to the introduction of a stepfather (Hetherington *et al* 1985).

Temperamentally difficult children have been found to be less adaptable to change and more vulnerable to adversity than are temperamentally easy children. However, the research literature on the relation between early temperament and later adjustment is confused and inconsistent, and the discussion about to ensue is a good example of the complexities involved.

One of the problems in this area is that much of the work on infant temperament relies on parents' reports – often retrospective ones. In this study, retrospective parental ratings of children's temperament as infants and current parent and observer ratings of temperament were available at each of four times. However, in assessing the role of children's temperament in their adaptation to divorce, it seemed desirable to obtain a measure of temperament before the divorce had occurred and one that might be less biased than parental ratings. We were fortunate in being able to have temperament ratings made by nurses based on pediatric records of well-baby visits during the first two years of life on a large subset of our sample. These included ratings of irritability, soothability, fearfulness, activity, sociability and irregularity or difficulty in basic biological functions such as sleep, feeding and elimination. The nurses' ratings of infant temperament better predicted later child behaviors than did mothers' ratings of infant temperament, and the mothers' ratings of infant temperament better predicted their own later behavior toward the child, although they also were significantly but modestly correlated with the child's behavior. Nurses' ratings of infant temperament in the first 6 months of life did not predict later behavior; therefore, only ratings in the 6-month to 2-year period were included. Fathers' ratings of early infant temperament did not seem to be related to anything.

Although individual differences in temperament may be biologically based, Rutter (1987) has noted that the increased risk of the temperamentally difficult child is, in part, attributable to transactions with the parent. He proposes that the difficult child is more likely to be both the elicitor and the target of aversive responses by the parent, while in times of stress the temperamentally easy child is not only less likely to be the recipient of criticism and displaced anger and anxiety but also more able to cope with adversity when it hits. We found some support for this position in our six-year follow-up data, but these interactions were modified by the personality problems of the parent (a composite index of depression, irritability and anxiety), parental stress (a composite index of negative stressful life events occurring in the last year and daily hassles recorded six times in the past month), and parental support systems. Under conditions of a stable maternal personality and low stress there were no differences in the conditional probabilities of mothers responding more negatively to difficult, as compared with easy, children, although difficult children emitted more aversive behavior. Thus, unless temperamental difficulty was compounded by other risk factors, there was no difference in the conditional probability of aversive maternal responses. However, the presence of either personality problems in the mother or high levels of stress increased the probability of negative behaviors in mothers. Furthermore the co-occurrence of these risk factors significantly increased maternal aversive responses over the level found with either stress or personality problems alone. These effects occurred more often with temperamentally difficult children, with sons, and with divorced non-remarried mothers.

These effects were moderated in a somewhat unexpected way by the availability of social supports. Under conditions of low stress and few maternal personality problems, the availability of supports had no effect on the aversive behaviors of mothers in dealing with either easy or difficult children. Surprisingly, the availability of supports also had no effects in situations involving a combination of maternal personality problems, high stress and a difficult child. Apparently, then, there were not enough deleterious factors under low stress conditions to need support. Under high stress conditions, however, the compounding of deleterious factors was so great that it overwhelmed the effects of these resources. Furthermore, the data suggest that, even when supports were available, multiply-stressed mothers did not use them effectively. Supportive resources had their greatest effect in moderating maternal responses toward difficult children when only maternal personality problems or only life stresses were present.

The effects of personality problems and/or stress in the responses of fathers and stepfathers to difficult and easy children were similar to the pattern found in mothers. However, fathers who had been remarried longer than two years, in contrast to those remarried for a shorter time and to non-divorced fathers, were more likely to target girls than boys with aversive responses. Fathers were also not able to use extrafamilial supports to moderate their aversive responses when they were under duress. This inability of fathers in contrast to mothers to solicit or utilize emotional support from friends and family was frequently found. For many men their wives were the only persons to whom they would disclose their feelings or turn for solace. When there was an alienated or discordant marriage, or a divorce, their one source of support was gone. Mothers, on the other hand, sought emotional support and confided in a wide network of friends and family. We found similar sex differences in the ability to self-disclose and to obtain emotional support in boys and girls, and these differences increased with age.

Overall, the data are consistent with Rutter's proposal that temperamentally difficult children are likely to be the target of their parents' aversive responses; moreover, we have identified some of the conditions under which this occurs. Let us turn now to his second proposal, that is that temperamentally difficult children are less able than temperamentally easy children to cope with this abusive behavior from parents when it occurs. To do this, we examined the relation between temperament, an index of family stress, a composite index of support available to the child, and an index of the child's adaptability at age 10.

No differences in the adaptive ability of easy and difficult children were observed under conditions of low stress and high support. Under conditions in which supports were not readily available, increased frequency of family stressors led to less adaptive behavior among both easy and difficult children, although easy children were more adaptable than difficult ones. Under conditions of high availability of protective factors, however, a very different pattern emerged. For difficult children, a linear relation between stress and adaptive behavior was obtained. Increased stress was associated with less adaptability. For the temperamentally easy children, a curvilinear relation emerged: under supportive conditions, these children actually developed more adaptive skills when stress levels were moderate than when either extremely low or high. For temperamentally easy children, then, some practice in solving stressful problems under supportive conditions enhanced their later abilities to delay gratification, to persist on difficult tasks, and to be flexible and adaptive on problem-solving tasks and in social relations. In addition, if stresses did not occur simultaneously but were distributed across time, these children could cope with them more easily. The simultaneous occurrence of multiple stressors or a series of unresolved stresses with no available protective resources had the most deleterious outcomes for children's long-term adjustment. As Rutter has stated, 'Inoculation against stress may be best provided by controlled exposure to stress in circumstances favorable to successful coping or adaptation' (Rutter 1987: 326). However, when stressful life events outweigh available protective factors, even the most resilient child can develop problems (Werner 1988). These differences were more marked in children from divorced and remarried families than in children from non-divorced families, and the effects of temperament and family type were greater for boys than for girls.

Our analysis is relatively gross, grouping together diverse family stressors and diverse protective factors. As will be seen, different stressors and resources are salient for children in different families. Familial factors are especially potent for young children, and extrafamilial experiences, stresses and resources in the school and the peer group become increasingly important as children grow older. In addition, goodness of fit between stressors and protective factors is critical. For example, a close relationship with one parent is the best protection against the adverse consequences of rejection or emotional disturbance in the other parent; and, among older children, good peer relationships or a close relationship with one good friend can buffer against acrimonious relations with a sibling. Let us turn now to family relationships that make children vulnerable or protect them from long-term adverse consequences following divorce and remarriage.

FAMILY RELATIONSHIPS

How do family relationships buffer or exacerbate children's long-term adjustment to divorce and remarriage? Remember that our divorced-mother-custody families are what we might call 'stabilized' divorced families since they have been divorced for an average of six years and are well beyond the initial crisis. We separated our stepfamilies into those remarried more or less than two years, making the tenuous assumption that the crisis period and the period needed for stabilization following remarriage would be about the same as that in divorce. Family interactions in our different types of families will be described first, and then the association of these interactions with the long-term adjustment of the children will be discussed.

The findings indicate that the mother–son relationships in the divorced non-remarried families and parent–child relationships in newly remarried families, particularly with stepdaughters, were problematic. Divorced non-remarried mothers continued to exhibit many of the behaviors with their sons six years after divorce that were seen two years after divorce. More differences in punishment and control than in warmth and affection distinguished divorced mothers from mothers in the other family types. Divorced mothers were ineffectual in their control attempts and gave many instructions with little follow-through. They tended to nag, natter and complain and were often involved in angry, escalating coercive cycles with their sons. Spontaneous negative 'start-ups', that is negative behavior initiated following neutral or positive behavior by the other person, were twice as likely to occur between mothers and sons in divorced families as in non-divorced families. Moreover, once these negative interchanges between divorced mothers and sons occurred, they were likely to continue longer than in any other dyad in any family type. The probability of continuance of a negative response was higher in the divorced mother–son dyads than in any other parent–child dyad, with the exception of daughter and stepfathers in the early stages of remarriage. In spite of these conflicts, however, it might be best to view the relationship of custodial mothers and their early adolescent sons as intense and ambivalent rather than as purely hostile and rejecting since warm feelings were also expressed in many of these dyads.

Both sons and daughters in divorced families were allowed more responsibility, independence and power in decision-making than were children in non-divorced families. In the words of Robert Weiss (1979), 'these children grow up faster'. They successfully interrupted their divorced mothers, and their mothers yielded to their demands more often than in other families. In some cases this greater power and independence resulted in an egalitarian, mutually supportive relationship. In other cases, especially when the emotional demands or responsibilities required by the mother were inappropriate, were beyond the child's capabilities, or interfered with the child's normal activities, resentment, rebellion or behavior problems often followed.

Finally, divorced mothers monitored their children less closely than did mothers in non-divorced families. They knew less about where their children were, who they were with, and what they were doing than did mothers in two-parent households. In addition, children in one-parent households were less likely than those in the two-parent households to have adult supervision in parental absence. Both Weiss (1979) and Wallerstein and Kelly (1980) report that one way children cope with their parents' divorce is by becoming disengaged from the family. We found, too, that boys from divorced families were spending significantly less time in the home with their parents or other adults and more time alone or with peers than were any of the other children. Stepsons were also significantly more disengaged than were sons in non-divorced families.

In contrast to the situation with divorced mothers and sons, few differences were observed in the relationship between divorced mothers and their daughters and those of mother and daughters in non-divorced families. In fact, mothers and daughters in mother-headed families express considerable satisfaction with their relationship six years after divorce. One exception to this happy picture, however, is found among divorced mothers with early-maturing daughters. Family conflict was higher in all three family situations for early-maturing girls versus late-maturing girls, but it was most marked between mothers and daughters in single-parent households. Early maturity in girls was associated with premature weakening of the mother–child bond, increased parent–child conflict and greater involvement with older peers. Past research suggests that divorced mothers and daughters may experience problems as daughters become pubescent and involved in heterosexual activities (Hetherington 1972). Thus, the difficulties in interactions between these early-maturing girls and their divorced mothers may be precursors of more intense problems yet to come.

It is important to distinguish between those stepfamilies in the early stages of remarriage, when they are still adapting to their new situation, and those in later stages, when family roles and relationships should have been worked through and established. The early stage of remarriage may be a honeymoon period when the parents, if not the children, want to make the family relationship successful. Neither mothers nor stepfathers were successful in controlling and monitoring their children's behavior in stepfamilies, although controls were more successful in mothers who had been remarried for more than two years. In the first two years following remarriage, conflict between mothers and daughters was high. These daughters also exhibited more demandingness, hostility, coercion and less warmth toward both parents than did girls in divorced or non-divorced families. Their behavior improved over the course of remarriage, but even two years after remarriage, these girls were still more antagonistic and disruptive with their parents than were girls in the other two family types.

The behavior of stepsons with their mothers and stepfathers was very different than that of stepdaughters. Although mothers and stepfathers initially viewed sons as extremely difficult, the sons' behavior improved over time. Boys whose mothers had been remarried for over two years were showing no more aggressive, non-compliant behavior in the home or in the school than were boys in non-divorced families (Hetherington *et al.* 1985). It should be noted that this improvement may be found only when the remarriage has occurred before adolescence. In another study (Hetherington and Clingempeel 1988), we found that even two years following their mother's remarriage, both early adolescent boys and girls were exhibiting many behavior problems. In this study, although stepfathers continued to view stepchildren, especially stepdaughters, as having more problems than non-divorced fathers saw in their children, they reported greater improvement among stepsons and greater warmth and involvement with them than with stepdaughters. In fact, stepsons in longer remarried families frequently reported being close to their stepfathers, enjoying their company, and seeking their advice and support.

What might explain these differences in responses to their mother's remarriage by sons and daughters? Some answers are found in the different patterns of correlations between marital satisfaction and children's responses in non-divorced and remarried families. Among non-divorced couples, closeness of the marital relationships and support by the spouse for participation in child-rearing were positively related to parental warmth and involvement with the child and negatively to parent–child conflict. Among the stepfamilies, however, there occurred what might appear to be an anomalous finding. As in other studies (Brand *et al.* 1988; Bray 1987), among remarried families, closeness in the marital relationship and active involvement in parenting by the stepfather were associated with high levels of conflict between the child and both the mother and the stepfather. These conditions were also associated with high rates of behavior problems, especially when the stepchild was a girl. For sons, these relations were significant in the early but not the later stages of remarriage.

How can we explain these unexpected results? It seems likely that, in the early stages of remarriage, new stepfathers are viewed as intruders or competitors for the mother's affection. Since boys in divorced families often have been involved in coercive or ambivalent relationships with their mothers, in the long run, they may have little to lose and something to gain from the remarriage. In contrast, daughters in one-parent families have played more responsible, powerful roles than girls in non-divorced families and have had more positive relationships with their divorced mothers than have sons. They may see both their independence and their relationship with the mother as threatened by a new stepfather, and therefore resent the mother for remarrying. This was reflected in sulky, resistant, ignoring, critical behavior by daughters towards their remarried mothers and stepfathers. Furthermore, it is notable that positive behavior of stepfathers toward stepdaughters did not correlate with the girls' acceptance of their stepfathers in the early stages of remarriage. No matter how hard stepfathers tried, their stepdaughters rejected them.

Early adolescence may be a particularly difficult age in which to gain acceptance of stepparents by stepchildren. The adolescent's increased striving for independence from the family and their concerns about their awakening sexuality may make them especially resistant to the introduction of a stepfather. Most adolescents do not like to think of their parents as sexual objects, and it is difficult, when parents remarry, not to recognize them as such. Stepchildren often distort reasonable displays of affection by the newly married couple into something inappropriate or unacceptable. Moreover, the lack of biological relatedness between the stepfather and the pubescent daughter may heighten concerns about what constitute appropriate forms of affection between them. As it turns out, early adolescent children (i.e. from approximately 9 to 15 years of age) are more resistant to the introduction of a stepparent than are either older or younger children (Hetherington and Anderson 1987). Most younger children in supportive homes with 'normal' levels of conflict eventually accept a warm and involved stepfather. Older adolescents are future-oriented and are anticipating leaving the home. For them, the presence of a stepfather to some extent relieves their own responsibilities for the economic and emotional well-being of the mother.

It has been said that there is considerable ambiguity in the role of a stepparent (Cherlin 1981). How does the stepfather deal with this ambiguity, particularly in the face of ambivalence or active antagonism from his stepchildren? In the first two years following remarriage, stepfathers reported themselves to be relatively low in felt affection for their stepchildren, but they reported spending time with them attempting to establish relationships. In fact, although they expressed less strong positive affect during this period, they also showed fewer negative, critical responses than did the non-divorced fathers: they resembled polite strangers. Biological fathers, on the other hand, were freer in expressing affection and in criticizing their children for poor personal grooming, for not doing their homework, not cleaning up their rooms, and for fighting with their siblings. However, they also were more involved and interested in the activities of their children. Stepfathers were far less supportive initially of their stepsons than their stepdaughters, managing to remain relatively pleasant in spite of the aversive behavior they encountered from their stepdaughters. Two years after remarriage, however, they were more impatient than earlier, and intensely hostile exchanges sometimes ensued between stepfathers and stepdaughters, especially concerning parental authority and respect for the mother.

Although stepfamilies change over time, stepfathers remained much less authoritative and much more disengaged than were fathers in non-divorced families (Hetherington 1987). Many stepfathers wanted to minimize the amount of time, effort and interference with their own needs and their marital relationships that child-rearing entailed. A frequently heard complaint was 'I married her, not her kids', or on confronting disruptive behavior on the part of stepchildren, 'That's their mother's problem, not mine'. Indeed, a sequence analysis of observed family interactions in our study indicated that a pattern of 'mother command/child non-comply/father intervene' was found significantly less in the remarried than in the non-divorced families. Although the number of authoritative stepfathers increased modestly over time for boys, authoritative behavior by stepfathers with daughters decreased; disengagement doubled as the remarriage went on. In addition, even for boys after two years of remarriage, dis-engagement remained the predominant parenting style of stepfathers. Even in longer remarriages, many stepfathers and stepchildren did not mention each other when asked to identify the members of their families.

How does parental behavior protect the child or put the child at risk for developing problem behaviors? As Diana Baumrind (1973) has been telling us for many years, authoritarian, disengaged and permissive parenting styles are more likely than authoritative parenting to be associated with the development of behavior problems and low social and cognitive competence in children. Generally we found the same thing, although the effects varied somewhat with sex of the child and sex of the parent.

Authoritative parenting was associated with high social competence and low rates of behavior problems, especially with low externalizing problems, and especially among boys. Authoritative parenting involving warmth and firm but responsive control was particularly important in divorced and remarried custodial parents in protecting children from the adverse effects of marital transitions. Thus, in coping with stressful life events, a supportive, structured, predictable parent–child relationship plays a critical protective role.

An exception to this positive relation between authoritative parenting and child outcomes was found, however, among stepfathers and stepchildren. Both authoritative and authoritarian parenting in stepfathers were related to high rates of behavior problems in both stepdaughters and in stepsons in the first two years of remarriage. These two parenting styles both involve high levels of control, although the former involves warm, responsive control while the latter is punitive, coercive and rigid. Apparently any kind of active control by the stepfather is initially aversive to the stepchild. After two years, though, authoritative parenting by stepfathers was related to fewer behavior problems and greater acceptance of the stepfather by stepsons than before, but was not, even at this time, significantly related to stepdaughters' behavior. The best strategy of the stepfather in gaining acceptance of the stepchildren thus seems to be one where there is no active attempt initially to take over, shape and control the child's behavior. Instead, a period of time is needed, first to work at establishing a relationship and to support the mother in her parenting, followed, later, by more active authoritative parenting. Such a strategy leads to constructive long-term outcomes, at least for boys.

By the time these children were 10, maternal behaviors had more impact on the antisocial and prosocial behavior as well as the self-esteem of girls than of boys in all family types. In contrast, biological fathers in non-divorced families had more impact on such behaviors in boys. In families remarried for over two years, stepfathers also played a significant role in modifying prosocial and problem behaviors in stepsons. Moreover, although only one-quarter of our non-custodial fathers were seeing their children once a week or more, those who were warm, involved and reasonably competent played a positive role in their son's development when there was also low conflict between the divorced spouses. Over all, the salience of the same-sexed parent increased markedly from the pre-school years to age 10.

SIBLING RELATIONSHIPS

Although considerable research has been done on parent–child relationships in divorced and remarried families, there is little work on the role siblings may play in exacerbating or buffering the effects of marital transitions (Hetherington and Clingempeel 1988; Wallerstein *et al.* 1988). Two alternative hypotheses might be offered about siblings and the marital transitions of their parents. One would be that siblings become increasingly rivalrous and hostile as they compete for scarce resources of parental love and attention following their parents' divorce or remarriage. Alternatively, siblings in families that have gone through marital transitions may view relationships with adults as unstable, untrustworthy and painful and turn to each other for solace, support and alliance.

Four main findings were apparent in our data. First, siblings in stepfamilies and boys in divorced families had more problematic relationships than siblings in non-divorced families or girls in divorced families. They were more aggressive, avoidant and rivalrous and were less warm and involved than other siblings. Negative start-ups, reciprocated aggression and long chains of aggressive, coercive behaviors with siblings were more common among stepchildren than among children in non-divorced families but were most frequently found among sons in divorced families. These behaviors were more frequent if the target child was interacting with a male sibling. Second, sibling relationships in stepfamilies improved over time but remained more disturbed than those in non-divorced or divorced families. Disengagement and avoidance of female children toward their siblings remained more common in stepfamilies than other families, even two years after remarriage. Third, any sibling dyad involving a boy was more troubled than those involving only girls. Not only were boys seen as exhibiting more aversive behaviors than girls, but also girls behaved in a less congenial fashion when interacting with brothers than sisters. Both sons and daughters in stepfamilies and daughters in divorced families were less likely to initiate conversations or activities and more likely to refuse or ignore overtures on the part of a male than a female sibling. Brothers were not getting much support from their female siblings in these families. Fourth, older girls in divorced families often played a supportive, nurturing role in relationships with younger female siblings. Daughters in divorced families were more involved in teaching, play and caretaking activities with their younger sisters than were other children. Usually this was associated with positive outcomes (e.g. higher rates of prosocial behavior, lower externalizing and better peer relationships) in both the female sibling care-giver and the recipient of the care. Sometimes the close relationship found between female siblings became too enmeshed, however, and was associated with adverse outcomes.

We used cluster analysis to identify four styles of sibling relation-ships (Hetherington 1988). One of these was a small cluster that included fewer than 10 per cent of our children and that was characterized by very high warmth, involvement and communication, along with very low rivalry and aggression. These children spent little time playing with other children, most of their time with each other, were dependent on one another, and fiercely protective of each other. Although they were nurturant and empathetic with each other, they showed little sensitivity or concern with the feelings of adults or peers. They scored moderately high on internalizing, sometimes got into problems with parents and teachers, and were usually neglected rather than rejected on peer nominations. These relationships seemed to be pathologically intense, enmeshed, symbiotic and restrictive. These siblings were most likely to be girls and to be found in divorced or remarried families and in families where the child had no regular contact or involvement with an affectionate, involved adult. This enmeshment, then, tends to occur under stressful life conditions without available adult support.

To our initial question, whether marital transitions promote productive alliances or competition between siblings, the answer is clear in our study: ambivalent or hostile, alienated relationships were more common in siblings in remarried families and in boys in divorced families than among siblings in non-divorced families. Companionate, caring relationships, on the other hand, were more common in non-divorced families and in female siblings in divorced families. Furthermore, sibling rivalry, aggression and disengagement played a more important role in increasing externalizing, antisocial behavior and in decreasing prosocial behavior in divorced and remarried families than did warmth, support and involvement in protecting siblings from adverse developmental consequences. Positive sibling relationships, however, played a more important buffering role among older than among younger children and in the advanced rather than the earlier stages of marital transitions. In the early stages of divorce and remarriage the effects of parent–child relationships were so powerful that sibling relationships could do little to moderate them.

GRANDPARENTS

Grandparents offer support not only to their divorced and remarried children but also to their grandchildren. Studies of black families have found that children in homes in which there is a mother and grandmother are better adjusted than those in which the mother is alone (Kellam *et al.* 1982; Kellam *et al.* 1977). At six years following divorce, about half of our grandparents and stepgrandparents lived within 100 miles of their divorced children; only a few mothers who were unemployed or had not remarried were living with their parents. In our white, middle-class families, the divorced custodial mothers appreciated the emotional, economic and child-care support offered by grandparents, but, when they were economically independent, they preferred to live alone and have grandparents accessible. When divorced women lived with their parents, they often reported feeling infantilized and not treated as adults by their parents. Loss of independence, shared control over their children, conflicts about discipline and the divorced mother's social life were frequent areas of disagreement. Relationships between divorced mothers and residential grandmothers were frequently ambivalent, although this ambivalence was not as frequently found with residential grandfathers.

For both parents of the custodial and the non-custodial parent, frequency of contact with grandchildren was related to proximity. In our divorced families, amount of contact by children with the parents of the non-custodial parent was directly related to the amount of contact maintained by the non-custodial parent (see also Furstenberg 1988). Since for most children contact with the non-custodial father decreased over time – especially if he remarried – so did contact with those grandparents. However, six years after divorce, half of our parents of non-custodial fathers reported that they had as much or more contact with their grandchildren as before the divorce.

When divorced parents remarried, the complexity of the child's social network increased dramatically. Involvement of stepgrandparents with stepchildren was related to age of the child at the time of remarriage and whether the stepfather had children from a previous marriage. When there were no biological grandchildren and when stepgrandchildren were young at the time of the remarriage, stepgrandparents became more actively involved.

But contact is one thing, influence another. What role do grandparents play in increasing or buffering risks for children in divorced and remarried families? Our findings are congruent with those of Cherlin and Furstenberg (1986). In most cases, there was little evidence that grandparents play a potent role in the social, emotional and cognitive development of their grandchildren unless they live in the home. In fact, there was a low positive correlation between the number of behavior problems in grandchildren and the amount of contact with grandparents. The more problems, the more contact. Grandparents were called in to help with difficult children, especially in families headed by a divorced non-remarried mother. Grandparents are thus the parent's reserves when things go wrong. Cherlin and Furstenberg (1986: 183) have said, 'Grandparents in America are like volunteer firefighters: they are required to be on the scene when needed but otherwise keep their assistance in reserve'. Even so, one exception should be noted to the finding that grandparents have a negligible influence on the adjustment of their grandchildren. Involved grandfathers may have salutary effects on the social behavior and achievement of boys in divorced-mother-custody families, and increased conflict between divorced mothers and residential grand-mothers increases externalizing behavior in boys. In general, however, the relationship with non-residential grandparents had little direct influence on the long-term adjustment of grandchildren. The effects of support by the grandparents were mediated by changed maternal behavior in response to such support.

SCHOOLS AND PEERS

As the children become older, schools and peers played an increasingly salient role in their adjustment to divorce and remarriage. We had found earlier that, even in the pre-school period, the social and cognitive development of young children from divorced families was enhanced if children were in schools with explicitly defined schedules, rules and regulations and with consistent, warm discipline and expectations for mature behavior. Just as authoritative parents played a protective function for children going through family transitions, authoritative schools play a buffering role for children undergoing stress. Under stress, children gained security in a structured, safe, predictable environment. I had earlier predicted that this effect might be most marked in young children under high stress since they may not be able to exert internal control and may require more external controls than either less stressed or more mature children. Even at age 10, though, we found that authoritative teachers and school environ-ments attenuated adverse outcomes for children in divorced and remarried families and in non-divorced families with high conflict. This protective effect of authoritative schools is most marked for boys, for children with difficult temperaments, and for children exposed to multiple stressful life events.

Attainments in school also modified adverse or salutary outcomes for children from divorced and remarried families. Academic achieve-ment and, for boys only, athletic achievement were associated with fewer behavior problems than those found in their less academically successful peers among children in divorced and remarried families.

Peer relationships did not play roles as protective or vulnerability factors in pre-school children but became more influential with age. Children who were actively rejected by their peer group or who did not have one close friend showed increased long-term problems in adjust-ment. Moreover, it did not take a high level of general popularity to enhance development. A supportive relationship with a single friend could moderate the adverse consequences of marital transitions and could modify the effects of rejection by other children.

About one-third of adolescent children became disengaged from the family following divorce and remarriage. They become involved in school activities and the peer group or, if they are fortunate, they attach themselves to a responsive adult or to the family of a friend. Whether these are desirable coping mechanisms depends on the child's family situation and on the particular activities and type of associates with which the child becomes involved. If they are socially constructive activities and the child's associates are well adjusted, this move can be advantageous. Undesirable activities and an antisocial or delinquent peer group, on the other hand, usually have disastrous consequences. When disengagement from the family occurs, however, contact with an interested, supportive adult plays a particularly important role in buffering the child against the development of behavior problems.

WINNERS, LOSERS AND SURVIVORS

Which children are the winners, losers and survivors six years after divorce? Cluster analyses of observational, interview and standardized tests were done on the measures of current adjustment for all children in our sample, and for boys and girls separately. These analyses included the children in all family groups, that is with non-divorced parents, with divorced non-remarried custodial mothers, and with remarried mothers. The clusters were fairly similar for boys and girls, although some sex differences will be noted. Although five clusters of children emerged, children from divorced or remarried families were over-represented in only three; these are discussed in this chapter. The first cluster was clearly maladaptive, and the last two involved more successful coping.

One cluster involved *aggressive, insecure* children. These children manifested multiple problems in multiple settings. They were noncompliant, impulsive and aggressive in the home, with their parents and siblings, in the school, and in the peer group. These children were prone both to impulsive, irritable outbursts and to sullen, brooding periods of withdrawal. They were unpopular with peers; in fact, 70 per cent of the children in this group did not have a close friend. Moreover, they had difficulties in school: placement in special classes, poor grades, referrals for disciplinary problems, and retention in grade were more common in this group than in any other group of children. These children had few or no areas of satisfaction and attainment, and this was reflected in their exceptionally low levels of self-esteem. In short, these were lonely, unhappy, angry, anxious, insecure children.

What kinds of attributes, experiences and family relationships were associated with this pattern of adjustment? First, there were three times as many boys as girls in this group, although girls from remarried families and boys with divorced, non-remarried mothers and recently remarried mothers were over-represented. The homes of these children were characterized by high levels of negative affect, conflict and unsatisfactory conflict-resolution styles in parents involving verbal or physical attacks, power assertion or withdrawal rather than compromise. Authoritative parenting was rarely found with these children. They were more likely to be exposed to disengaged, neglecting or ineffectually authoritarian parenting styles. Boys in this group had been temperamentally difficult children early in life, and their behavior problems seem to have been exacerbated by family conflict or divorce. In these late pre-adolescent or early adolescent children, the relationship with the same-sexed parent was especially significant for the development of behavior problems or competence. Boys in this aggressive, insecure cluster tended to have no close relationship with an adult male. Many of these boys had unavailable fathers or fathers or stepfathers who actively rejected them. However, the behavior of divorced custodial mothers was also important for sons. Boys in this cluster with divorced mothers also had conflicted or alienated relations with their mothers. Their mothers also tended to work full time. In this study, full-time maternal employment in divorced mothers was associated with adverse outcomes for boys but positive outcomes for girls. In contrast to parental relationships with boys, girls in this cluster in all types of families had poor relationships with their mothers and were unaffected by their relationships with their fathers.

Children in two other clusters can be labeled *opportunistic-competent* and *caring-competent* children; individuals in both clusters appeared to be adapting exceptionally well. Children in both clusters were high in self-esteem, popular with their peers and teachers, and low in behavior problems. In addition, they were performing at an average or above average level academically. Both groups of children were described by others as curious, energetic, assertive, self-sufficient and as having wide-ranging interests and skills in interpersonal relations. In addition, children in both groups were unusually competent, flexible and persistent in dealing with demanding or stressful situations. A manipulative, opportunistic quality was apparent, however, among the opportunistic-competent children and not among the caring-competent children. Nearly equal numbers of girls and boys were in the opportunistic-competent group, and they were more frequently found in divorced and remarried families and in non-divorced families with high conflict than in non-divorced families with low conflict. The family-conflict level in these families was higher for girls than for boys. Parents reported that these children, even when they were young, had attempted to use disagreements and conflicts between parents for their own gains. They often played parents off against one another, thereby exacerbating the parents' acrimony. Although these children had close, supportive relationships with at least one parent – usually a parent of the same sex – they often had one parent who rejected or neglected them and/or who had problems in personal adjustment.

The egocentric, manipulative quality in these opportunistic-competent children was frequently remarked on by interviewers and observers. These children were oriented toward people in power, such as parents and teachers and even peers with high status or resources. Their attempts to ingratiate themselves with such powerful people were often done with considerable grace, charm and humor and were usually successful. The friendships of these children, however, were often shortlived. Children in this group seldom had the same best friends from one testing session to another. Finally, almost all of the girls in this group had working mothers and had been encouraged by their mothers to be autonomous and independent. These maternal characteristics were found in this cluster for girls but not for boys.

Children in the caring-competent cluster were similar to those in the opportunistic cluster in many ways. In social relations, however, they were less manipulative. They got along well with adults and peers, but they were less concerned about prestige and power in their relationships. Although they were co-operative, there was less striving to gain the attention and approbation of adults. Friendships were more stable and less likely to be focused on high-status peers. In fact, caring-competent children often befriended children who were neglected or even rejected by the peer group. There was a notable difference, however, in prosocial behavior: the children in this group were higher in helping and sharing than children in any other group.

Can we identify differences in the experiential factors that might differentiate between the opportunistic-competent and caring-competent children? The most striking factor is that the caring-competent cluster is comprised almost totally of girls. Only five of the twenty-three children in this cluster were boys, and none of these boys had divorced, non-remarried mothers. In contrast, over half of the girls in this cluster were daughters of divorced, non-remarried mothers with whom they had a close relationship. Experiences in a one-parent, mother-headed family seemed to have a positive effect for these girls. Like the girls in the opportunistic-competent cluster, these girls had working mothers who encouraged their children in mature indepen-dent behavior. They had mothers who usually were warm and supportive but not always available. A salient characteristic in the backgrounds of both the opportunistic-competent and caring-com-petent children was contact with a caring adult, whether a parent, other relative, teacher or neighbor. However, the most notable experience in the background of caring-competent girls, but not the opportunistic-competent children, was that they had assumed responsibility for the care of others even at this young age. This usually involved the care and nurturance of younger siblings; in seven cases, however, it involved supporting a physically ill, lonely, alcoholic or depressed mother, and in three cases it involved helping to care for an aged or physically feeble grandparent. This early required helpful-ness was the most powerful factor in predicting later membership in the caring-competent cluster. These responsibilities, clearly associated with what Weiss (1979) has called 'growing up faster' in divorced one-parent households, seem to have enhancing effects for girls but not for boys. The adverse experiences, for boys, of living in a one-parent, mother-headed household seem to counteract any possible salutary effects of early caretaking responsibilities.

CONCLUSION

What can be said in response to the frequent query, What enduring effects do divorce and remarriage have on children? When I began to study children in divorced families, I had a pathogenic model of divorce. However, after more than two decades of research on marital transitions, I would have to respond: depending on the characteristics of the child, particularly the age and gender of the child, available resources, subsequent life experiences, and especially interpersonal relationships, children in the long run may be survivors, losers or winners of their parents' divorce or remarriage.

REFERENCES

Baumrind, D. (1973) 'The development of instrumental competence through socialization', in A.D. Pick (ed.) *Minnesota Symposia on Child Psycho-logy*, vol. 7, Minneapolis: University of Minnesota Press.
Brand, E., Clingempeel, W.E. and Bowen-Woodward, K. (1988) 'Family relationships and children's psychological adjustment in stepmother and

stepfather families: findings and conclusions from the Philadelphia Stepfamily Research Project', in E.M. Hetherington and J.D. Arasteh (eds) *Impact of Divorce, Single Parenting, Stepparenting on Children*, Hillsdale, NJ: Erlbaum.

Bray, J.H. (1987) *Becoming a Stepfamily*, symposium presented at the meeting of the American Psychological Association, New York, August.

Camara, K.A., and Resnick, G. (1988) 'Interparental conflict and cooperation: factors moderating children's post-divorce adjustment', in E.M. Hetherington and J.D. Arasteh (eds) *Impact of Divorce, Single Parenting, and Stepparenting on Children*, Hillsdale, NJ: Erlbaum.

Cherlin, A. (1981) *Marriage, Divorce, Remarriage: Changing Patterns in the Postwar United States*, Cambridge, Mass.: Harvard University Press.

Cherlin, A. and Furstenberg, F.F., Jr. (1986) *The New American Grandparent: A Place in the Family, a Life Apart*, New York: Basic Books.

Furstenberg, F.F. (1988) 'Child care after divorce and remarriage', in E.M. Hetherington and J.D. Arasteh (eds) *Impact of Divorce, Single-Parenting, and Stepparenting on Children*, Hillsdale, NJ: Erlbaum.

Garmezy, N. (1983) 'Stressors of childhood', in N. Garmezy and M. Rutter (eds) *Stress, Coping and Development in Children*, New York: McGraw-Hill.

Hetherington, E.M. (1972) 'Effects of fathers' absence on personality development in adolescent daughters', *Developmental Psychology* 7: 313–26.

Hetherington, E.M. (1987) 'Family relations six years after divorce', in K. Pasley and M. Ihinger-Tollman (eds) *Remarriage and Stepparenting Today: Current Research and Theory*, New York: Guilford.

Hetherington, E.M. (1988) 'Parents, children and siblings six years after divorce', in R. Hinde and J. Stevenson-Hinde (eds) *Relationships within Families*, Cambridge: Cambridge University Press.

Hetherington, E.M. (in press) 'The role of individual differences and family relations in coping with divorce and remarriage', in P. Cowan and E.M. Hetherington (eds) *Advances in Family Research: Vol. 2. Family Transitions*, Hillsdale, NJ: Erlbaum.

Hetherington, E.M. and Anderson, E.R. (1987) 'The effects of divorce and remarriage on early adolescents and their families', in M.D. Levine and E.R. McArney (eds) *Early Adolescent Transitions*, Lexington, Mass.: Heath.

Hetherington, E.M. and Clingempeel, W.G. (1988) *Coping with Remarriage: The First Two Years*, symposium presented at the Southeastern Conference on Human Development, Charleston, SC, March.

Hetherington, E.M., Cox, M. and Cox, R. (1982) 'Effects of divorce on parents and children' in M. Lamb (ed.) *Nontraditional Families*, Hillsdale, NJ: Erlbaum.

Hetherington, E.M., Cox, M. and Cox, R. (1985) 'Long-term effects of divorce and remarriage on the adjustment of children', *Journal of American Academy of Psychiatry* 24: 518–830.

Kellam, S.G., Adams, R.G., Brown, C.H. and Ensminger, M.A. (1982) 'The long-term evolution of the family structure of teenage and older mothers', *Journal of Marriage and the Family* 4: 539–54.

Kellam, S.G., Ensminger, M.E. and Turner, R.J. (1977) 'Family structure and the mental health of children: concurrent and longitudinal community-wide studies', *Archives of General Psychiatry* 34: 1012–22.

Rutter, M. (1983) 'Stress, coping and development: some issues and some questions', in N. Garmezy and M. Rutter (eds) *Stress, Coping, and Development in Children*, New York: McGraw-Hill.

Rutter, M. (1987) 'Psychosocial resilience and protective mechanisms', *American Journal of Orthopsychiatry* 57: 316–31.

Santrock, J.W. and Warshak, R.A. (1986) 'Development of father custody relationships and legal/clinical considerations in father-custody families', in M.E. Lamb (ed.) *The Father's Role: Applied Perspectives*, New York: Wiley.

Wallerstein, J.S. and Kelly, J.B. (1980) *Surviving the Breakup: How Children and Parents Cope with Divorce*, New York: Basic Books.

Wallerstein, J.S., Corbin, S.B. and Lewis, J.M. (1988) 'Children of divorce: a ten-year study', in E.M. Hetherington and J. Arasteh (eds) *Impact of Divorce, Single-Parenting and Stepparenting on Children*, Hillsdale, NJ: Erlbaum.

Weiss, R.S. (1979) 'Growing up a little faster: the experience of growing up in a single-parent household', *Journal of Social Issues* 35: 97–111.

Werner, E.E. (1988) 'Individual differences, universal needs: a 30-year study of resilient high risk infants', *Zero to Three Bulletin of National Center for Clinical Infant Programs* 8: 1–5.

Zill, N. (1988) 'Behavior, achievement, and health problems among children in stepfamilies: findings from a national survey of child health', in E.M. Hetherington and J.D. Arasteh (eds) *Impact of Divorce, Single-Parenting and Stepparenting on Children*, Hillsdale, NJ: Erlbaum.

Part three
Expectations in early education

Introduction

> The social stratification of knowledge and ignorance . . . impinges on the child in his earliest encounters with formal institutional mechanisms . . . Within the school social control is maintained through the initiation of pupils, teachers and parents into appropriate attitudes and modes of action.
>
> (Sharp and Green 1975: 221–2)

One feature of childhood that now unites virtually all the world's children is the experience of going to school. As Bruner has pointed out, in evolutionary terms planned instruction is a relatively recent cultural invention (see Volume 1, Chapter 12). Its extension to the great mass of children in British society is little more than a century old. Yet as we approach the end of the twentieth century, the schoolhouse has become a significant part of even the most remote Third World village community. Resources may be sparse and teaching rudimentary, but few children now go through childhood without some initiation into reciting tables and deciphering text. Despite the recency of the phenomenon, the necessity for schools and their function in children's development is largely taken for granted. Chapters 8 to 11 explore the impact of children's first contact with schooling on their social development, identity and achievement.

The school is a very specialized context for child development, quite different from the home, the playground and the park. Teachers approach their task with clear expectations about what kinds of child behaviour and learning constitute a well-functioning classroom. Teachers consistently report between 13 and 15 per cent of children to have difficulties adjusting to the demands of school (Hughes *et al.* 1979). It is tempting to interpret such statistics in pathological terms, as evidence of behavioural disturbance, family inadequacies or both.

Chapter 8 cautions against this conclusion by demonstrating the way 'adjustment' is defined in teachers' minds in terms of the social context and demand characteristics of school life. Klein and Ballantine's research has its origins in American studies of individual differences in temperament as these affect the way children adjust to features of their social environment. They show that amongst the wide range of temperamental characteristics found in children starting school, teachers have a very clear idea of the ideal combination, and this is closely linked to their judgements about which children in their class are in fact well-adjusted. Such research prompts an inversion of the conventional question to enquire: 'Are schools well-adjusted to their children?'

Teachers are not alone in making judgements about children's aptitude for learning. Children themselves soon learn to make judgements about their competencies and their ignorance, especially in comparison with other children. Although in family settings children may gain an early awareness of areas of strength and weakness, these are writ large in the age-segregated social environment of the classroom, even when teachers are at pains to avoid the more public signs of ability grading (notably the once ubiquitous coloured stars). Crocker and Cheeseman illustrate the point in their simple but elegant study (Chapter 9), which demonstrates that after only a few terms in school, children are able to judge their position in the class 'pecking order' of abilities, a judgement that closely coincides with that of their peers and their teachers.

Children's attempts to understand the social order of the classroom and their place within it can combine with teachers' own judgements to generate a cycle of expectations which may become 'self-fulfilling'. Rogers (Chapter 10) summarizes the evidence, arguing that expectancy effects arising from the process of interaction (e.g. amount of personal attention, praise and encouragement) may be less important than those based on administrative decisions (e.g. about grouping children, level of work to introduce, etc.). One of Rogers's conclusions is that the processes shaping children's perceptions of their abilities and their attributions of success and failure need to be understood in long-term perspective.

This theme is developed further by Woodhead in Chapter 11. His starting-point is the evidence that programmes of educational intervention can have long-term effects on the life chances of socially disadvantaged children. Woodhead rejects simplistic causal accounts which assume that long-term effects on children's competencies are directly due to the pre-school programme. He discusses the implications of a transactional model which recognizes that effects are embedded in the child's relationship to the social context of school and community.

REFERENCES

Hughes, M., Pinkerton, G. and Plewis, I. (1979) 'Children's difficulties on starting infant school', *Journal of Child Psychology* 20(3): 187–96.

Sharp, R. and Green, A. (1975) *Education and Social Control*, London: Routledge & Kegan Paul.

8 The relationship of temperament to adjustment in British infant schools

Helen Altman Klein and Jeanne H. Ballantine
Source: Journal of Social Psychology (1988) 128(5): 585–95.

[. . .]

A goodness-of-fit model has been proposed by several researchers (e.g. Gordon 1981; Keogh and Pullis 1980; Lerner and Lerner 1982; Thomas and Chess 1977) to describe the impact of setting on the relationship between the individual temperament characteristic of a child and that child's adjustment. According to the model, each setting has features, demands and values. If the features, demands and values are compatible with the characteristics of an individual child, then that child is perceived as well adjusted. The child whose individual characteristics do not show a good fit with the demands and features of the setting is viewed as poorly adjusted.

Longitudinal studies of development support the goodness-of-fit model. The New York Longitudinal Study group (e.g. Thomas and Chess 1977; Thomas *et al.* 1968; Thomas *et al.* 1963) observed temperament characteristics of individual children and related these characteristics to adjustment over time. Parental and home features, demands and values, considered together with individual temperament characteristics, were shown to be useful in understanding the fit or adjustment for normal children as well as for children with behavioral disorders (Thomas and Chess 1984).

Research in group-care settings has supported the goodness-of-fit model. In studies of early childhood group care (Klein 1980; 1982), high activity was a powerful predictor of adjustment difficulty in task-oriented programs. Activity was not a predictor of adjustment in open, unstructured settings where the opportunity for free, large-muscle activity was available. Setting has also affected the relationship between persistence and adjustment. Carey *et al.* (1977) and Klein (1982) reported that high persistence was related to adjustment in well-defined but not in loosely defined programs.

Cross-cultural studies have also supported the goodness-of-fit model. Cultures and societies differ with respect to the environmental features, demands and values that impinge on children. Both Super and Harkness (1981) and Thomas and Chess (1977) reported distinctive standards and values held by parents and teachers for children in different societies. Klein (1987) compared temperament and adjustment relationships in American and Israeli children. Not only did the two groups of care-givers differ in their evaluations of temperament characteristics, but also the children within the groups differed in the relationship between temperament and adjustment. This cross-cultural comparison allowed an exploration of environmental features that impact on fit. It left open the question of comparability, however, because research tools for the Israeli sample had to be translated into Hebrew.

The present research focused on the British infant school as a setting to which children are expected to adjust. British children were expected to provide relevant data for a cross-cultural study of temperament and adjustment because the research tools are identical to those used on American children, requiring no translation, whereas the settings differ in features, values and demands. Much has been written about the distinctive qualities of the British infant schools (Ballantine 1983). These schools have an open, unstructured, educational approach that involves students in the learning process by facilitation, interaction, individual and group work, and an informal classroom atmosphere. At the same time, the schools have well-defined overall goals.

Within the British infant school setting, the present research assessed adult perceptions of the temperament characteristics of an ideal child. It was hypothesized, within the goodness-of-fit model, that the British infant school setting would generate a distinctive pattern of temperament-adjustment relationships. To evaluate this hypothesis, teachers provided information on ideal temperament characteristics as reflected by responses to the Teacher Temperament Questionnaire (Keogh *et al.* 1982). They then provided adjustment rankings for children in three areas: peer relationships, program adjustment and adult interactions. Finally, the Teacher Temperament Questionnaire (Keogh *et al.* 1982) was used to assess actual temperaments of children.

METHOD

Setting

The study was undertaken in twelve state-run British infant schools in two locations: Reading and Cambridge. Each participating school grouped children of heterogenous abilities into classes by ages. British infant schools enroll children between the ages of 5 and 8 years. The programs and classroom arrangements were very similar in all schools. Teaching material is selected from a common core of material approved for state schools. Overall, the standardized infant school curriculum as well as the standardized curriculum and training for British infant school teachers provides considerable consistency across schools.

There were, however, a broad range of schools represented in this study. Some were considered to be better schools: the families were of a higher social class, and the parents were actively involved in their children's progress and in fund-raising efforts for extra equipment and facilities. Other schools faced problems of language training for immigrant students as well as of parent and child indifference. Some of the schools were built recently and served newer housing developments or council (government-subsidized) housing, whereas others were in city centers. Two were Church of England schools.

Subjects

Participants were thirty British infant school teachers, all women. Each teacher had been with her class for at least the first six months of the academic year and so was familiar with the children in her care.

Materials

The short form of the Teacher Temperament Questionnaire (Keogh *et al.* 1982) was used to assess both ideal and actual temperament ratings. The Teacher Temperament Questionnaire is based on the dimensions of the New York Longitudinal Studies (e.g. Thomas and Chess 1977; Thomas *et al.* 1968; Thomas *et al.* 1963). The twenty-three item questionnaire was scored on eight dimensions: activity level, adaptability, approach/withdrawal, distractability, intensity, persistence, mood and threshold of responsiveness. Each of the items described a behavior such as 'child sits still when a story is being told or read'. The participant was asked to indicate whether the item was *very descriptive of the child* (6), *not at all descriptive* (1), or descriptive at one of the four intermediate levels between these extremes. The direction of the statements was varied to prevent response bias. A complete description of the development and psychometric analysis of the scale is given by Keogh *et al.* (1982).

An Adjustment Ranking scale was used to assess adjustment rank on three dimensions. The scale listed the names of ten children in the class. The first dimension was peer adjustment: forming healthy, age-appropriate relationships with other children. The second was adjustment to the program: fitting in appropriately to the curriculum, routines and schedules. The third was adjustment to adults: forming healthy, age-appropriate relationships with teachers and other staff members in the school environment. The participants provided a rank of 1 through 10 for each child for each dimension.

Procedure

Initial contact for this research was made through the Local Education Authority and with the head teacher of the individual infant schools. The investigators visited each school at a time convenient to the teachers. At each site, between one and six teachers participated. They were told about the overall goals of the project and about their involvement.

Each teacher, working independently, completed three types of research scales: the Teacher Temperament Questionnaire for ideal temperament, the Adjustment Ranking scale, and the Teacher Temperament Questionnaire for the actual temperaments of six children. The first step of the procedure was the administration of the Teacher Temperament Questionnaire for the ideal child. Each teacher was asked to think of the temperament characteristics of a hypothetical child who would be ideal in her classroom. This meant the kind of child whom she believed would make the best possible adjustment to her classroom, taking into account peer relationships, program adjustment and adult interactions within the infant school setting. She was asked to keep this hypothetical child in mind as she completed a scale for Ideal Temperament Judgment.

The second step of this procedure was the adjustment rankings. Ten children were randomly selected from the class list with several constraints. Any child who was judged to have severe emotional or psychological problems, any child who had not spent six months in the class, and any child who could not speak English was excluded. The final list included five boys and five girls. Each teacher was asked to provide professional assessments of the adjustment of these ten children using the Adjustment Ranking scale for peer, program and adult adjustment. For adjustment to peers, the child on the list believed to have made the best possible adjustment to other children was to be assigned a ranking of 10, whereas the child who had made the worst adjustment was to be assigned 1. Using forced choice, each child was assigned a different rank from 2 to 9. In the same way, the teachers then ranked the children on adjustment to the program and adjustment to adults.

The last aspect of the procedure was the actual temperament assessments. The Teacher Temperament Questionnaire was used by teachers to rate the actual temperament characteristics of six children whose names had appeared among the ten names on the adjustment scale. The six were selected to include three boys and three girls and to balance the distribution over adjustment rankings. Overall, there were 180 children with temperament ratings and adjustment rankings.

The research procedure was completed with each teacher or group of teachers in 1- to 1½-hour sessions. In most locations the researchers also observed in classrooms and playgrounds. At the conclusion of the study, after teachers were given a description of the research question and were told about previous research in this program, their questions were answered.

RESULTS

Relationship between ideal and actual temperament scores

Each teacher provided temperament scores for the hypothetical ideal child and for six actual children in her classroom. Table 8.1 presents the means for all temperament dimensions on the Teacher Temperament Questionnaire for both the ideal ratings (N=30) and the actual ratings (N=180), along with F values of the differences. This analysis was performed by using the General Linear Model program from SAS (1985). The average teacher ratings for the actual children were significantly higher than for those of the ideal child on the dimensions of activity, distractibility and intensity. Actual children were rated significantly lower than the ideal on positive mood, persistence, approach/withdrawal and adaptability.

Relationship between temperament and adjustment

A main concern of the study was the relationship between temperament and adjustment within the British infant school setting. This

Table 8.1 Ideal and actual temperament ratings (means and *F* values) by British infant school teachers

Temperament	Ideals (N = 30)	Actual (N = 180)	F
Activity	5.456	3.96	25.57**
Mood	5.056	4.15	24.99**
Persistence	4.944	3.60	20.17**
Distractibility	5.089	3.19	43.50**
Approach/withdrawal	4.567	3.88	6.13*
Adaptability	4.944	3.98	15.48**
Intensity	4.000	3.23	11.57**
Threshold	3.783	4.20	3.58

Note: *$p < 0.05$. **$p < 0.01$.

Table 8.2 Correlations between temperament and adjustment for British infant school children

Temperament	Peer adjustment	Program adjustment	Adjustment to adults
Activity	0.513*	0.641*	0.488*
Mood	0.563*	0.496*	0.457*
Persistence	0.538*	0.667*	0.541*
Distractibility	0.500*	0.647*	0.519*
Approach/withdrawal	0.339*	0.275*	0.354*
Adaptability	0.435*	0.340*	0.422*
Intensity	0.362*	0.340*	0.282*
Threshold	0.039	0.014	−0.028

Note: *$p < 0.01$

analysis was undertaken by using the CORR program from SAS (1982). Table 8.2 shows the correlations between the temperament of the children as measured by the Teacher Temperament Questionnaire and the three adjustment ratings. Seven of the eight temperament dimensions showed significant correlations ($p < 0.01$) with the adjustment measures. Only threshold of responsiveness was not significantly correlated. The children judged to be higher in adjustment were also judged higher in positive mood, persistence, approach and adaptability and lower in activity, distractibility and intensity.

A multiple regression analysis of temperament predictors of adjustment was performed using the STEPWISE procedure of SAS (1985). Table 8.3 presents the results of the multiple regression analysis. For this stepwise analysis, the value of the probability to enter test was

Table 8.3 Temperament dimensions as predictors of adjustment for British infant school children: stepwise regression analysis

Adjustment area	Partial R^2	Model R^2	β	F
Peer				
Mood	0.3168	0.3168	0.7715	82.5363**
Persistence	0.0875	0.4043	0.2978	25.9940**
Adaptability	0.0312	0.4355	0.3534	9.7356**
Activity	0.0125	0.4480	0.4013	3.9597**
Approach/withdrawal	0.0076	0.4556	0.2310	2.4172
Program				
Persistence	0.4451	0.4451	0.6247	142.8005**
Activity	0.0383	0.4835	0.7034	13.1402**
Approach/withdrawal	0.0397	0.5232	0.3772	14.6612**
Threshold	0.0124	0.5356	0.2964	4.6792*
Adults				
Peristence	0.2927	0.2927	0.4369	73.6740**
Adaptability	0.0697	0.3624	0.3829	19.3361**
Activity	0.0188	0.3812	0.4754	5.3467*
Approach/withdrawal	0.0212	0.4029	0.3823	6.3701*

Note: *$p < 0.05$. **$p < 0.01$.

0.15. Adjustment to peers was best predicted by mood, persistence, adaptability, activity and approach/withdrawal, in that order, with no other variable meeting criteria. Adjustment to the program was best predicted by persistence, activity, approach/withdrawal and threshold. The inclusion of threshold here, when it did not correlate significantly with adjustment to program, suggests a repressor variable. Finally, adjustment to teachers and adults within the program was best predicted by persistence, adaptability, activity and approach/ withdrawal.

Gender differences in judged temperament and adjustment

An analysis of gender differences was performed by using the analysis of variance (ANOVA) program from SAS (1985). Table 8.4 presents the means of judged temperament and adjustment scores for boys and for girls along with F values of differences. The comparisons of temperament scores showed that four of the eight dimensions differed significantly by gender. The British infant school teachers rated the boys as higher in activity level, intensity and distractibility. They saw them as less positive in mood. The teachers also rated girls significantly higher in adjustment to peers and adjustment to the program.

Table 8.4 Actual temperament and adjustment ratings (means and F values) by gender for British infant school children

Rating	Boys	Girls	F
Temperament			
Activity	3.665	4.256	6.58*
Mood	3.842	4.448	19.58**
Persistence	3.393	3.793	2.79
Distractibility	2.953	3.425	4.34*
Approach/withdrawal	3.809	3.951	0.42
Adaptability	3.878	4.077	1.08
Intensity	3.000	3.456	7.00**
Threshold	4.309	4.088	1.77
Adjustment			
Peers	5.213	6.121	4.51*
Program	5.000	5.868	4.12*
Adults	5.079	5.868	3.45

Note: *p <0.05. **p <0.01.

DISCUSSION

This research was concerned with the relationship between temperament and adjustment within the British infant school setting. British infant school teachers provided both ideal patterns of temperament for the hypothetical child as well as actual temperament and adjustment judgments for individual children. Overall, the temperament ideal held by the predominantly middle-class British participants was one of a child who is low key (low in activity and intensity), flexible (positive mood, approaching and adaptable) and task oriented (low in distractibility and high in persistence). This pattern of the British ideal fitted that of the *easy* temperament pattern as outlined by the work of the New York Longitudinal Study (i.e. Thomas and Chess 1977; Thomas *et al.* 1963).

The ideals held by adults within a culture are part of the standard those adults use to judge adjustment. The goodness-of-fit model (Gordon 1981; Keogh and Pullis 1980; Lerner and Lerner 1982; Thomas and Chess 1984) conceptualized adjustment as a match between cultural expectations and actual temperament. It would be expected that those children whose traits were closest to those of the temperament ideal would be scored as highest in adjustment. In examining the best predictors of adjustment, some temperaments emerged repeatedly. High persistence, low activity and positive approach were temperaments predictive of adjustment in all three areas: peers, program and adults. Adaptability was a significant predictor for both peer adjustment and adjustment to adults. Mood was significant for peer adjustment, and high threshold was significant for program adjustment.

At first glance, the predictive value of persistence and low activity appears to conflict with the open, unstructured philosophy of the British infant school. Why would schools designed for openness show the best fit with low-activity and high-persistence children? Classroom observation suggested that, although the structure of the classroom was relatively open, the tasks to be accomplished and standards of appropriate behavior were not. The teachers had a clear agenda. The openness of the classroom distracted the child who was high in activity and low in persistence. When the child failed to meet the teachers' goals and standards, he or she appeared less well-adjusted. The low key, flexible and task-oriented child was not distracted by the open environment and was judged as making a positive adjustment.

The analysis of gender differences probably reflected cultural expectations for gender. British boys and girls (and men and women) are expected to show differences in behavior (Meigan 1986). The results of the present study demonstrated that teachers judged girls to be lower in activity, intensity and distractibility although more positive in mood than were boys. Observations of playground activity choices and behaviors also reflected these differences. These temperament dimensions were the ones associated with a better match to the ideal in this sample. Consistent with these actual and ideal ratings, the teachers saw the girls as better adjusted to peers and to the program. Several explanations are possible. First, gender differences may well be the end product of earlier socialization. Second, British teachers may expect and elicit the temperament characteristics by their own interactive behaviors and through the specific physical, temporal, and social environment provided. The importance of teacher expectations and environmental features is consistent with an interactive approach to behavior (Bell 1968; Belsky and Tolan 1981). Finally, gender differences in temperament may have their root in genetic differences.

This research together with parallel research on Israeli and American children (Klein 1987) and Japanese children (Klein and Ballantine 1985) supports the goodness-of-fit model. The relationship between temperament and adjustment varied among countries emphasizing the importance of features, demands and expectations for understanding the adjustment of individual children. A better understanding of the contribution of features of the setting to individual adjustment may provide a basis for maximizing the adjustment of individual children.

REFERENCES

Ballantine, J.H. (1983) *The Sociology of Education: A Systematic Approach*, Englewood Cliffs, NJ: Prentice-Hall.

Bell, R.Q. (1968) 'A reinterpretation of the direction of effects on studies of socialization', *Psychological Review* 75: 81–95.

Belsky, J. and Tolan, W.J. (1981) 'Infants as producers of their own development: an ecological analysis', in R.M. Lerner and N.A. Busch-Rossnagel (eds) *Individuals as Producers of their Own Development*, New York: Academic.

Carey, W.B., Fox, M. and McDevitt, S.C. (1977) 'Temperament as a factor in early school adjustment', *Pediatrics* 60: 621–6.

Gordon, B.N. (1981) 'Child temperament and adult behavior: an exploration of "goodness of fit" ', *Child Psychiatry and Human Development* 11: 167–78.

Keogh, B.K. and Pullis, M.E. (1980) 'Temperament influences on exceptionality', in B.K. Keogh (ed.) *Advances in Special Education: Vol. 1. Basic Constructs and Theoretical Orientations*, Greenwich, Conn.: JAI Press.

Keogh, B.K., Pullis, M.E., and Cadwell, J. (1982) 'A short form of the Teachers Temperament Questionnaire', *Journal of Educational Measurement* 19: 323–9.

Klein, H.A. (1980) 'Early childhood group care: predicting adjustment from individual temperament', *Journal of Genetic Psychology* 11: 125–31.

Klein, H.A. (1982) 'The relationship between children's temperament and adjustment to kindergarten and Head Start settings', *Journal of Psychology* 112: 259–68.

Klein, H.A. (1987) 'Temperament and childhood group care adjustment: a cross-cultural comparison', unpublished manuscript.

Klein, H.A. and Ballantine, J.H. (1985) 'Japanese temperament ideals: a preliminary investigation', unpublished manuscript.

Lerner, J.V. and Lerner, R.M. (1982) 'Temperament and adaptability across life: theoretical and empirical issues', in P.B. Baltes and O.G. Brim, Jr. (eds) *Lifespan Development and Behavior* vol. 5, New York: Academic.

Meigan, R. (1986) *A Sociology of Education*, 2nd edn, London: Holt Rinehart & Winston.

SAS Institute Inc. (1982) *User's Guide: Basics, 1982 Edition.*, Cary, NC: Author.

SAS Institute Inc. (1985) *SAS User's Guide: Statistics, Version 5 Edition*, Cary, NC: Author.

Super, C.M. and Harkness, S. (1981) 'Figure, ground and gestalt: the cultural context of the active individual', in R.M. Lerner and H.A. Busch-Rossnagel (eds) *Individuals as Producers of their Own Development: A Life-Span Perspective*, New York: Academic.

Thomas, A. and Chess, S. (1977) *Temperament and Development*, New York: Bruner/Mazel.

Thomas, A. and Chess, S. (1984) 'Genesis and evolution of behavior disorders: from infancy to early childhood', *American Journal of*

Psychiatry 141: 1–9.

Thomas, A., Chess, S., Birch, H., Hertzog, N. and Korn, S. (1963) *Behavioral Individuality in Early Childhood*, New York: New York University.

Thomas, A., Chess, S. and Birch, H. (1968) *Temperament and Behavior Disorders in Children*, New York: New York University Press.

9 The ability of young children to rank themselves for academic ability

Tony Crocker and Rosemary Cheeseman
Source: *Educational Studies* (1988) 14(1): 105-10.

[. . .]

Children acquire an awareness of 'self' through interaction with others; via their attitudes and values, rewards and punishments, examples and teachings to name just a few of the variables involved. As Cooley (1902) pointed out over 80 years ago, our understanding of self is defined and developed by our experience. Initially this occurs in the family, and gradually expands to include friends, neighbours, school fellows and later, colleagues at work. If the majority of these approve of us then we will tend to learn that we are worthy persons.

Allport (1961), in looking at the development of personality, concluded that the child's concept of 'self' is still far from complete by the age of 6. Doubts at this age may be heightened by newly acquired school friends who are quick to spot – and point out – differences that they deprecate. The teacher too, in her position of unique relative importance, has a powerful role to play in the child's acquisition of a 'self-image'. The child is able to observe and feel not only the way in which the teacher interacts with him or her but also the way in which the teacher interacts with all of the other children in the class. Nash (1973) found that children are able to accurately assess their teacher's perception of themselves and also their classmates. Furthermore they then behave according to that perception.

Brophy has shown that the development of a favourable self-concept in children is dependent upon being successful and *perceiving* themselves as successful. Often this depends upon the way in which the child interprets the teacher's reaction to his performances. One of the authors of this article well remembers, [. . .] when visiting a class of 6-year-olds, asking one child if she was pleased to have 'good' written on her work. 'Oh that doesn't mean anything,' she replied, 'He puts that on for everybody every time.' That child had already learned to discount that piece of teacher behaviour as having any relevance with respect to her concept of the worth of her work. Even young children are observant, and able to interpret the actions of others with considerable skill.

The ability to ingest the beliefs others have as to our academic ability has been shown by Brookover *et al.* (1967), and Jackson and Strattner (1964) to be related to how well children subsequently perform in their school work. Nash (1973) concluded that schools are extremely successful at teaching hierarchical levels of personal worth. It seems unlikely that the schools do more than strengthen the learnings that children acquire in the greater world outside the classroom door. In our society we are constantly ranking ourselves and others for job-status, strength, health, sun-tan, ability to acquire girl-friends, etc. Those we judge to be better than us we put on a pedestal and aspire to join them, those we judge to be our inferiors we either ignore, sneer at, lord it over or show how nice we are by proclaiming that differences don't matter. They may not, but we have made the evaluation. In school Nash had shown that children knew how they rated for ability to do 'sums' while other workers such as Harter (1975), and Settles and Ham (1973), have shown that the children's concept of academic worth usually matched that of the teacher.

This study set out to extend our knowledge of children's ability to assess the academic worth of self and others down the age range to those in their earliest years of schooling. Is the ability to rate self and peers in school dependent upon maturity or does the earlier commencement of school in Britain mean that British children acquire this competence a year ahead of American children because it is dependent upon experience rather than age? In particular the study set out to ask the following:

1 Can children in their first years at school assess their own academic rank relative to their peers?
2 What level of match exists between self-estimate, peer-estimate and teacher-estimate of academic rank?
3 What criteria do these children use when making these judgements?

DESIGN

Three schools in the Midlands were willing to be the focuses of the study. The chosen age range was from 5 to 7 years. Head teachers in the three schools had nominated class teachers of this age range who were willing to participate in the study and to allow regular visits by an observer into their classrooms. 141 children in five classes formed the sample. Observations occurred on 20 half-day visits to each class, making a total of 100 in all. An anthropological approach was adopted so that the observer was able to interact with individual children without having to withdraw them from the classroom, or needing to maintain an aloof distance. In all the classes the observer was introduced to the children by the teacher and told that there would be regular visits so they should carry on with their normal work unless the visitor wanted to talk to them. Initial visits were made without any attempt to record anything, in order that the observer could become familiar with classroom practice and so that both children and teachers could become desensitized. Observations were made from any convenient place in the classroom or hall, playground or television room. All notes were kept in a school exercise book of the type used in that particular school in order to minimize its intrusion into the children's awareness. They were not told that notes were being kept of their interactions. For the same reason, audio recordings were not kept. During each half day the observer deliberately withdrew for half an hour in order to provide the teacher and the children with time to themselves. The teacher was aware that this would happen as deliberate policy.

In discussions with the children wherever possible their language was used rather than 'correct' English if it appeared that this meant the meaning was clearer. For example, many described relative academic performance as being 'Gooder than me at work'. If it seemed that this was an unambiguous way of describing relative position then the observer would use it as an alternative that made sense to the children.

Each child was given pieces of paper with the names of everyone in the class on and asked to put them in two piles – those who the child thought were better than self at school work and those who the child thought were not as good as self. Many established a third pile of peers that they said were 'as good as me'. This pile was subsequently re-examined with the observer asking the child of each name whether he or she was perhaps just a bit better or just a bit poorer than self. All of the children were able to resolve the other children into the two piles when given this further stimulus. No child suggested that the task was one which he or she couldn't do. No child placed *all* the children in his or her class above self, or even placed themselves with only one peer below self. Only one girl placed herself above all other children in her class, a position that the teacher also allocated but from which her peers deviated slightly. In almost every other class the child who was

Table 9.1 Class 1*: the percentage any child was perceived to be 'better than' the nominating children

Sarah	was seen as	'better than me' by	75%	of the class
Ian	"	"	75%	"
Simon T.	"	"	75%	"
Glenn	"	"	71%	"
Charlotte	"	"	64%	"
Stephenie	"	"	64%	"
Andrea	"	"	61%	"
Trevor	"	"	61%	"
Scott	"	"	61%	"
Simon R.	"	"	61%	"
Fiona	"	"	57%	"
Craig	"	"	57%	"
Natalie	"	"	54%	"
Stephen	"	"	54%	"
Carol	"	"	46%	"
Marc	"	"	43%	"
Sally	"	"	39%	"
Stuart B.	"	"	36%	"
David	"	"	29%	"
Jeremy	"	"	25%	"
James	"	"	25%	"
Ben S.	"	"	21%	"
Joanne	"	"	21%	"
Rachel	"	"	21%	"
Ben M.	"	"	21%	"
Brian	"	"	18%	"
Stuart C.	"	"	14%	"
Lisa	"	"	14%	"
Tracy	"	"	14%	"

Note: *One class from the five that carried out the self-peer rating exercise.

placed top by both the teacher and all of the other children placed himself or herself in second place. These relative self rankings were converted to a percentage of children seen to be 'better than me' in each class (see Table 9.1).

TEACHER ESTIMATES

Each teacher was asked to rank all the children in her class, without recourse to any form of standardized test. One teacher would only group her children into three broad bands. All of the five said they found the task to be difficult. Spearman's rank order correlations were calculated between self–teacher, self–peer and peer–teacher rankings. The impact of tied rankings was felt to be negligible following the 1943

Table 9.2 Correlations between the various estimates of academic rank

Class	Self–peer	Self–teacher	Peer–teacher
1	0.68	0.62	0.82
2	0.72	0.74	0.80
3	0.59	0.55	0.86
4	0.83	0.59	0.65
5	0.70	0.68	0.82

Note: All correlations are significant beyond the 0.01 level.

evaluation by Kendall of this potential problem with Spearman's technique.

[. . .]

There was a high degree of agreement between self estimates of rank position, peer estimate and teacher estimate (Table 9.2). These correlations seem to support the findings of Brophy and Good (1970), Barker-Lunn (1970) and Nash (1973), all of whom found broad agreement between self, peer and teacher ratings.

Once the children had rated their classmates relative to themselves they were asked to explain why they thought that other children were either better or worse than they were. The replies were analysed to see if such things as favouring own sex, or for that matter the opposite sex, had influenced their decision. It did not appear to be a variable that had affected them as a group. Similarly there was no evidence that friendship bonds had influenced the children. One noticeable difference was that children who rated themselves high tended to comment on only a few other children, while children who rated themselves as near the bottom of the class tended to make comments on rather more of their classmates.

Not all of the reasons for rating a person as better or worse than the rater were academic reasons. Among a wide range, such reasons as reading ability, mathematical ability, writing ability, always working and works hard were amongst the more common but sits up straight, is very tidy, waits her turn, has lots of girl friends were also listed by many of the children. In those classes where the teacher grouped the children for level of work being tackled the children all knew the significance of the groupings and at times used this as an explanation of the reasons for deciding someone was above themselves, etc., 'She's in the top group for sums'. A few comments were non-specific such as: 'She's better than me at everything'. Although the criteria used were not always academic, all of the children, including the reception class, ranked their peers and four of the five classes gave reasons for their

Table 9.3 Academic and non-academic comments

Class	Number of academic comments	Number of non-academic comments
2	330	72
3	379	69
4	437	125
Total	1,146	266
Reception class	146	295

rankings. Only the reception children gave more non-academic reasons for their decisions. For both groups the value for chi square was significant beyond the 0.01 level for a two-tailed test. [Table 9.3]

CONCLUSIONS

It would appear that the youngest children in our schools quickly acquire a knowledge of those academic criteria that teachers use to evaluate the pupils in their classrooms. In this study it appeared that there was always a high degree of agreement between self, peers and teacher as to the rank order of children in any particular classroom. Only the youngest appeared to use non-academic measures to any great extent and this had largely disappeared by the time the children were 6 years old.

REFERENCES

Allport, G.W. (1961) *Pattern and Growth in Personality*, New York: Holt, Rinehart & Winston.

Barker-Lunn, J. (1970) *Streaming in the Primary School*, research report, Windsor: NFER.

Brookover, W.B. *et al.* (1967) *Self-Concept of Ability of School Performance. III Final Report*, Michigan State University.

Brophy, J.E. and Good, T.L. (1970) 'Teachers' communication of differential expectations for children's classroom performances', *Journal of Educational Psychology* 61: 365–74.

Cheeseman, R.G. (1986) 'Pupil and teacher perceptions of pupils' academic rankings', MPhil thesis, The Polytechnic, Wolverhampton.

Cooley, C.H. (1902) *Human Nature and Social Order*, New York: Scribner.

Crocker, A.C. (1983) *Statistics for the Teacher*, 3rd edn, Windsor: NFER/ Nelson.

Harter, S. (1975) 'Developmental differences in the manifestation of mastery motivation in problem solving tasks', *Child Development* 46: 370–8.

Jackson, P.W. and Strattner, N. (1964) 'Meaningful learning and retention: noncognitive variables', *Review of Educational Research Association* 513–23.

Kendall, M.G. (1943) 'The treatment of ties in ranking problems', *Biometrica* 43.

Nash, R. (1973) *Classrooms Observed: The Teacher's Perception and the Pupil's Performance*, London: Routledge & Kegan Paul.

Settles, D. and Ham, N. (1973) 'Effectiveness of social and correctness reinforcers with different aged children', *Psychological Reports* 33: 787–92.

10 Early admission: early labelling

Colin Rogers
Source: C.W. Desforges (1989) 'Early childhood education',
British Journal of Educational Psychology, Monograph 4,
Edinburgh: Scottish Academic Press.

Increasingly children are being exposed to some form of institutionalized education prior to the age of 5 (DES 1988). This development brings with it both new opportunities and new problems. [. . .]

Folk wisdom has it that the young child is particularly vulnerable. The obvious lack of physical, emotional and intellectual maturity that young children bring to school leaves them open to both the positive and the negative influences awaiting.

One of these influences involves the expectations that people have for the child, particularly those held by the child's teachers. Since the publication of Rosenthal and Jacobson's (1968) *Pygmalion in the Classroom*, educational researchers have been able to point to evidence to support the view not only that the expectations held by teachers for their pupils will correlate with the performance levels (or other outcome variables) of those pupils, but also that the teachers' expectations will have causal effects. The claim made then and since (Rosenthal 1985; Harris and Rosenthal 1986) by Rosenthal is that the expectations held by teachers will initiate a series of events which will culminate in the pupil outcome coming to match more closely the initial expectation. In the original Pygmalion study (and in numerous others that have followed) this was held to be the case even though the initial expectation had no factual basis.

This demonstration of the self-fulfilling prophecy in educational contexts will be familiar to many readers. The purpose of this chapter is to discuss the research and theorizing that has followed since *Pygmalion* in order to see if there is a case for assuming that the young child is any more likely to be susceptible to the teacher expectancy effect than his or her older counterparts. This is not intended to be a comprehensive review of the teacher expectancy literature. The interested reader can find more detail in a number of other sources (e.g. Rogers 1982; Dusek 1985; Harris and Rosenthal 1986; Cooper and Good 1983). Instead the intention is to focus upon the issue of the supposed vulnerability of the young child and to discuss the processes that might be involved in this. Calls for a stronger developmental emphasis in research into the teacher expectancy effect (Rogers 1982) have been only partially heeded and there are still many gaps in our understanding. Nevertheless, researchers have more often than not focused their attention upon pupils in the primary school age range. In itself, this imbalance in the ages that have been studied is interesting. It presumably represents a common assumption among researchers that this is the point in the educational system where expectancy effects are more likely to be found, although the assumption is generally implicit. It also has the effect of making it very difficult to compare the supposed susceptibility of younger and older pupils, as research relating to the latter is rare. In effect then, while our understanding of the role of development with respect to the teacher expectancy effect is limited, there are a number of studies demonstrating the effect with young children.

Indeed, some of the best known and most frequently cited studies fall into this category. Rosenthal and Jacobson (1968) themselves claimed that their results showed that the expectancy effect was greatest for the youngest children in their study (first and second grade children aged 6 and 7). (In fact, one of the many technical criticisms levelled at this study, e.g. Elashoff and Snow 1971, has been that the general effect claimed by the researchers is in fact only a specific one limited to this age group.) Rist (1970) in his classic study of ghetto schooling claims to have shown that decisions made by a kindergarten teacher during the first few days of children's schooling led to a pattern of teacher–pupil interaction and classroom organization that created a caste system that effectively guaranteed educational success for some and failure for others. Rist claims that this effect continued beyond the year for which the original teacher had responsibility. Palardy (1969) in another frequently cited study, showed that the progress made in reading during the first year of schooling was related to the expectations of teachers. Those teachers that expected girls to make better progress than boys had classes that produced such differences while those that assumed equal progress for each sex did not. In both cases the progress made was assessed relative to a measure of initial reading readiness. While the Palardy study shows the effect of the subject being taught as well as the age of the pupil – Good and Brophy (1987) argue that subjects where assessment of pupil performance is more subjective, such as reading, are more likely to produce expectancy effects than those, such as mathematics, where more objective criteria can be applied – all three studies seem to add weight to the claimed vulnerability of the young child.

The rest of this chapter will first of all present a brief summary of the findings of research into the teacher expectancy effect and then discuss some of the major models that have been put forward to account for its operation. In the process of doing this the point will be made that the younger child is generally assumed by reviewers and researchers to be more vulnerable. The models of the teacher expectancy effect will then be used as a basis for exploring those parts of the process that are more likely to be relevant to the application of the process to the young child.

Summaries of the now extensive research associated with the teacher expectancy effect need to be examined with care. According to Harris and Rosenthal (1985) over 400 studies have now been reported and the majority of these indicate the existence of the effect. Other reviewers (e.g. Rogers 1982) have also stated that the evidence shows quite clearly that the effect takes place. However, different researchers have examined different things. Raudenbusch (1984) draws attention to the finding that it has proved easier to demonstrate the effects of teachers' expectations upon pupil achievement and upon the level and type of teacher–pupil interaction, than it has to demonstrate the effect with respect to the child's IQ. The original Rosenthal and Jacobson study claimed that the IQ of pupils involved had actually increased as a result of positive teacher expectations.

Leaving these difficulties aside it is clear that teachers' expectations can and do have a causal effect upon various classroom outcomes. The effect has been demonstrated by a variety of procedures including studies that involved teachers' naturally occurring expectations as well as those that have been induced by the researchers, and under carefully controlled laboratory conditions as well as in the more complex but more ecologically valid environment of the classroom (see Rogers 1982 for a fuller discussion of these different research strategies).

Researchers concerned with the issue have increasingly turned their attention to model building in an attempt to mark out the process by which teacher expectations are translated into classroom-based outcomes as the research has confirmed the existence of not only the effect, but also its variability. One reviewer concluded that 'The self-fulfilling prophecy in all its several forms is not omnipresent in the classroom; what is omnipresent is its *potential* omnipresence' (Leigh 1977: 323).

A detailed review of each of the models is beyond the scope of this chapter. Major models have been presented by Rosenthal 1973; Brophy and Good 1974; Braun 1976; Cooper 1979; Rogers 1982; Blease 1983; Cooper and Good 1983; Harris and Rosenthal 1985. There are some common elements in these and an aggregate model, which would be a fairly crude thing actually to work with but which serves a useful illustrative purpose, would include the following stages.

First, the teacher has to form an expectation for the pupil. A large variety of types of information can be and are used at this stage – see Dusek and Joseph (1983) for a meta-analysis and discussion of these – not all of which will lead to accurate expectations. Second, the teacher's expectation is translated into differential behaviour towards pupils as a function of the expectations held for them. Good and Brophy (1987) have reviewed research into this aspect of the process and have produced a list of seventeen different aspects of teacher behaviour towards pupils that have been shown to vary as a function of teacher expectation. Some of these will be discussed again below.

Third, the pupil will need to notice, at some level of psychological functioning, these differences in teacher behaviour. Fourth, having noticed the differences the pupil will need to respond to them. Most models assume that this response will be concerned with some form of internalization of the attitude that the pupil infers the teacher to hold from the behaviour displayed. These internalizations will have an effect upon the pupil's self-concept. More recently (Rogers 1982; Weinstein 1985; Peterson and Barger 1985) motivational processes have also been held to be important at this stage.

Fifth, the pupil now makes a behavioural response to the expectation, as mediated by the pupil's perception of the teacher behaviour and the pupil's own psychological response to that perception. This behavioural response gives rise to the sixth stage consisting of effects on the pupil's academic performance or classroom conduct that are more in line with the teacher's original expectation. These effects provide the basis for the seventh and final stage consisting of feedback to the teacher, who finds that the expectation is apparently confirmed. With the expectation now strengthened a cyclic process is established and can be repeated.

This basic framework clearly assumes that the process by which teacher expectations are translated into matching pupil behaviour is one that centrally involves processes of interaction between the teacher and pupil. It is worth pointing out at this stage that such assumptions lead in turn to the further assumption that the younger child will be more vulnerable to the effect. Typically the young child experiences a school organization that puts him/her into prolonged contact with a single teacher. Stable patterns of interaction are more likely to develop and to have effects under these circumstances than in the later years of schooling when pupils typically spend shorter periods of time with each of a larger number of teachers. It is interesting to note that Cooper (1985) has suggested that graduate students may be at risk from expectation effects to a greater degree than pupils in the later stages of schooling. Graduate students also tend to be exposed to a limited number of tutors.

However, it is not the case that processes of interaction are in themselves the only means by which expectations may come to have self-fulfilling effects. Rogers (1982) draws attention to the distinction between expectancy effects arising from the process of interaction and those that arise from the consequences of administrative decisions taken by the teacher (possibly in conjunction with colleagues) in such a way as to ensure that the expectations are confirmed. For instance, one of the surest ways of confirming a low expectation regarding a pupil's prospects in a public examination is to refuse to enter the pupil for the examination. No entry – no pass. Whether these administrative effects are more likely to affect the older or the younger pupil has much more to do with matters of the organization of education than they do with the social psychology of teacher–pupil interaction. At present, it is probably safe to assume that the older pupil is more likely to be vulnerable to the effects of administrative expectations than is the younger but that neither will be immune. In some cases administrative and interactive effects will combine. The study of Rist (1970) already referred to above illustrates this well. The teacher studied by Rist made an early decision to group the children in her kindergarten class according to her view of their academic potential. Rist's account of what then followed over the rest of the school year shows that patterns of interaction between teacher and pupil (and in time between pupils) varied substantially depending upon the pupil's group membership. The administrative decision to group the pupils physically by seating them at separate tables clearly seems to have helped to determine and sustain the nature of the interaction patterns.

Cooper (1985) draws attention to an important distinction between self-fulfilling prophecies and sustaining expectations. The self-fulfilling prophecy occurs when an initially inaccurate expectation has the effect of influencing the behaviour of its subject in such a way as to make the expectation eventually come true. A sustaining expectation is based on an initially accurate assessment and has the effect of maintaining the status quo against outside influences. Cooper asserts that the sustaining variety is likely to be more common in education although he also points out that it is the harder of the two to demonstrate empirically. According to the list of teacher behaviours associated with expectation differences produced by Good and Brophy (1987), the pupil who has already enjoyed success is, for example, more likely to be given further opportunities to answer an initially incorrectly answered question than is the pupil with the weaker track record. Change in performance level is therefore made less likely.

Cooper himself is of the view that self-fulfilling prophecies are more likely to occur with children in the earlier years of schooling and sustaining effects are correspondingly more likely to take place in the later years. Rogers (1982) arrived at a similar conclusion with respect to the role of self-concept, arguing that the child was more likely to be influenced by school effects in the early years and that the self-concept would develop a sustaining role in the later years. Cooper argues that the essential difference between sustaining effects and self-fulfilling prophecies lies in the accuracy of the teacher's initial expectation. Younger pupils, or those new to a school or a new part of the school system (Raudenbusch 1984) bring less of a history with them and the teacher is therefore more likely to accept information that is inaccurate as a basis for an expectation.

Further distinctions between different types of expectation have also been suggested. Crano and Mellon (1978; but see Mitman and Snow 1985 for comment on the technique used) provide evidence showing that the expectations formed by teachers with respect to their pupils' social characteristics might be a more powerful factor in producing self-fulfilling prophecies than are expectations formed on the basis of their pupils' academic qualities (as perceived). The younger the child the less information the teacher will have available about academic qualities and the greater will be the role played by social expectations. Crano and Mellon also report stronger expectancy effects in the younger age groups (6- and 7-year-olds). The use of longitudinal data here adds some substance to this claim in spite of the concerns expressed by Mitman and Snow. Murphy (1974) provides related evidence in showing that his sample of teachers operated on the assumption that they were more likely to be able to change pupil social characteristics than they were academic/ intellectual ones. At a later stage in this chapter, when motivational processes can be discussed in a little more detail, it will begin to become clear that these social effects can have important longer-term consequences for the child's academic development.

As was pointed out above, more research has been conducted with younger than with older children. There has been little in the way of attempts to empirically demonstrate the greater vulnerability of younger children directly. There would be substantial methodological difficulties involved in trying to do this, as one would be looking to contrast situations in which all relevant factors are equal apart from the age of the child. As Eccles *et al.* (1984) argue in a paper concerned with the development of motivational style, the organization of schooling itself changes substantially with the age of the child and this in turn brings with it a myriad of possibilities regarding effects upon the child's development. In the absence of such evidence it is necessary to examine the processes implicated by theories of the expectancy effect with a view to determining what role the age of the pupil might play.

It would be possible to examine each of the seven stages of the aggregate model outlined above in order to determine the likelihood of young children being more or less susceptible to the expectancy effect. The degree to which this is possible will depend on the availability of appropriate data and some parts of the process have been more thoroughly investigated than others.

For example, there is still a clear need for detailed investigations of the ways in which teachers form expectations for pupils and the ways in which these processes might vary as a function of the age of the pupil and the precise responsibilities of the teacher. Teachers of younger children may well vary from teachers of older children on a number of personality dimensions. Research into impression formation has long since indicated that the personality of the perceiver plays a critical role in the process. The job demands of the reception class teacher clearly differ from those of the teacher at junior or secondary level, and again there is good reason to suppose that such differences can influence the process of impression formation. The review by Raudenbusch (1984) referred to above shows that studies that have attempted to induce expectation effects by supplying the teacher with random, and therefore possibly false, information are more likely to be effective if the teacher has had less than two weeks' contact with the pupil. Again reception class teachers are more likely to be in this position than any other of their colleagues.

These and other differences relate to the nature of the teacher or the circumstances under which the teacher will be required to operate. In line with the Eccles *et al.* (1984) analysis already referred to, such differences are likely to influence the degree to which the teacher expectancy effect will take place. The model of the expectancy process outlined above indicates that the pupil also has an important role to play. In recent years researchers have been turning their attention increasingly to factors that are relevant to the role of the pupil and it is the detail of some of this work that the rest of this chapter will seek to address.

The general model of the expectancy process outlined above indicates that in order for the teacher expectancy effect to operate it will be necessary for the pupil not only to notice the expectancy related behaviour of the teacher but also to respond to this. Researchers concerned with the teacher-expectancy effect have generally assumed that pupil self-concept plays an important part at this stage of the process. Models of a general pupil self-concept have however remained rather nebulous and poorly defined (see Burns 1979; 1982) and the nature of the associated dynamics and causal pathways continue to be obscure. For this and other reasons, researchers have been turning attention to the more specific models that have been developed by those concerned with motivational processes.

Again a full review of this work is well beyond the scope of the present chapter (for good introductions see Ames and Ames, vols 1 and 2, 1984, 1985; Deci and Ryan 1985). However, there are some common features of the various models currently being employed that are relevant to the issue of concern here. There is an emphasis upon the qualitative aspects of motivation (Ames 1986). Motivational differences are not simply described in terms of observable differences such as time on task, but in terms of the 'style' that the individual comes to adopt. As this 'style' is also not considered to be a simple reflection of basic dispositions (Ames 1986) the possibility of environmental influences is readily accepted, indeed assumed. Distinctions between intrinsic and extrinsic motivation are important. Deci and Ryan, in particular, are concerned with this and have produced substantial evidence to suggest that intrinsic motivation (engendering a sense of control over activities and outcomes on the part of the pupil) is educationally beneficial. Further, their research shows that the relative dominance of intrinsic or extrinsic processes within any one pupil can be influenced by the environment within which they work. Similar concerns are revealed in Dweck's (1985) work with mastery-oriented children.

Following on from the work of Weiner (1979; 1984) a substantial literature is now available examining the role that causal attributions play in motivational and expectancy processes. An individual's motivational style is held to be related to the typical pattern of attributions that he/she makes for instances of success and failure. Of particular concern is the use that the individual makes of attributions to ability and effort. Very simply, individuals who typically attribute failure to a lack of ability on their own part are likely to respond quite differently, and less favourably, to achievement-related tasks than individuals who typically attribute similar failure to lack of effort. Conversely, attributions to ability to account for success are more likely to prove to be enhancing as far as motivation is concerned. In recent years, attribution research has started to move out of the laboratory and into the classroom and as it has done so questions concerning the role of the school environment in determining attributional patterns, and the development of particular attributional styles by different pupils have acquired greater prominence.

Researchers concerned with intrinsic motivation have established that the experience of schooling is almost invariably associated with a decline in levels of intrinsic, as compared to extrinsic, motivation (e.g. Harter 1978; DeCharms 1980; Eccles *et al.* 1984; Nicholls 1984). Almost certainly such effects are associated with the greater degree of control that will be exerted over a young child's learning experiences in the school environment, with the much greater opportunity for comparison with peers and with the almost inevitable increase in competitive approaches to learning. All of these factors, control, comparison and competition, are known to be associated with relatively low levels of intrinsic motivation.

However, inasmuch as the decline seems to be a universal one it is not in itself especially relevant to expectancy processes. (It ought to be noted here that this assumes that concern is focused upon within-class expectancy effects. If between-class, or between-school, expectancy effects are of concern then differences between schools in respect to the amount of comparison, competition etc. that takes place may well be important). An understanding of the process involved is needed so that one might begin to assess the possible impact of differential expectations for pupils held by teachers. Deci and Ryan (1985) discuss the ways in which the environment created, in part, by the class teacher will have an effect on the development of intrinsic motivational levels by the pupil.

Central to Deci's and Ryan's analysis is the distinction between controlling and informational environments. A controlling environment leaves the pupil dependent upon the teacher for the determination of objectives and the assessment of progress made towards them. An informational environment is one that provides feedback to the pupil that has the effect of not only encouraging the pupil to define his/her own objectives and to assess progress but also of providing the information needed to be able to do this. Deci and Ryan (1985) provide evidence to show that individual adults differ in the degree to which they make these environments available.

In order to establish a link between these processes and the teacher expectancy effect it is necessary to demonstrate that the degree to which a teacher will attempt to control the pupils (in the sense meant by Deci and Ryan) will be related to the expectations that they have of the pupil. Such a link is tentatively provided by the work of Cooper (see Cooper 1985 for review).

Cooper *et al* (1980) find that there is a relationship between the degree to which the teacher feels able to control the pupil's learning-related activities and the number of private interactions that the teacher initiates with that pupil. Following from their detailed study of expectancy effects, Cooper and Good (1983) argue that the concerns of teachers of young children (third to fifth grades, 8 to 10 years old) with respect to control vary within a hierarchical framework. Initial concerns with the pattern of teacher–pupil interaction give way to a concern with academic outcomes which in turn develop into a concern with developing the pupil's autonomous learning abilities, reflected particularly in a concern with the effort expenditure of the pupil. Each progression along the way is preceded by a decision that concerns at the earlier stage have been met. Critically, Cooper is claiming that the level of control that a teacher will wish to exercise will be determined by his/her assessment of the level of progress made by and expected for that pupil. Pupils for whom teachers have low expectations will be held for longer at the lower levels of control than will pupils for whom teachers have high expectations.

Due then to the teacher's belief that a pupil is likely to perform at a relatively low level, and the associated belief that this will be best dealt with by keeping close control over interactions with the pupil, the teacher seeks to avoid public interactions (e.g. those held while the whole class is being addressed) and to concentrate instead on interactions in more private settings that can be more closely structured by the teacher. As mentioned above, several of the differences in teacher–pupil interaction identified by Good and Brophy (1987) as being related to the expectations held by the teacher for the pupil, are also associated with the exercise of teacher control. Low expectation pupils are, amongst other things, less likely to engage in public interactions with their teachers, less likely to receive lengthy and informative feedback and less likely to have their ideas taken up and used by the teacher. In each case, the actions of the teacher towards the low expectancy pupil will be seen, in Deci's and Ryan's terms, to be counter-productive as far as the maintenance of intrinsic motivation is concerned. Given the vulnerability of the intrinsic motivation of young pupils already referred to, it seems clear that the effect is likely to be heightened for the low expectancy pupil.

These findings suggest that the young pupil for whom the teacher has come to hold low expectations will be more likely to suffer motivational deficits as a result. The general susceptibility of the young to a loss of intrinsic motivation upon entering formal schooling compounds the effect. In addition to this, the expectations formed by the teacher of the young are more likely to have self-fulfilling properties (rather than being sustaining in nature) as the teachers themselves are more likely to form expectations that are inaccurate.

The above summary represents something of an over-simplification. There are some complicating factors that need to be examined. One of these is worthy of attention in the current context.

As was indicated above, attribution theorists have highlighted the role that attributions to ability and effort play, as causes of success and failure, in determining motivational style. An important difference is held to arise between individuals who typically attribute success to ability and failure to lack of effort, and those who attribute their failures to ability (or the lack of it) and successes to their effort, or more typically to some external factor over which they would be unlikely to see themselves being able to exercise any control. Attributions to ability for a failure are motivationally detrimental as they encourage the view that there is little, if anything, that the individual can do to improve the situation. An individual who repeatedly attributes failures to lack of ability is likely to develop severe motivational deficits, learned helplessness (Dweck and Reppucci 1973). This analysis is based on the assumption that ability is perceived, by the attributor, as a stable cause of success and failure. Evidence is available (Nicholls and Miller 1984) to show that this view of the nature of ability is not shared by young children.

Nicholls has demonstrated that young children, those in the first one or two years of regular schooling, tend to regard ability as a variable entity. Indeed, he claims that the young child essentially fails to distinguish between ability and effort at all. Those who do well are judged to be both able and industrious; those who do not do well lack both ability and effort. The important consequence of this, for present purposes, is that the young child is less likely to respond to failure by assuming that success is now impossible.

Other researchers have also investigated the relations of the young child to failure experiences. The general conclusion (see Stipeck 1984 for details) is that the young child remains optimistic for the future under circumstances where older children might begin to despair. In addition to the differences detailed by Nicholls in respect to the young child's beliefs about the nature of ability, Stipeck argues that young children are inclined to allow wishful thinking to over-rule a more rational assessment of their circumstances.

The negative effects of teacher expectations are held to occur when the low expectations held by a teacher are communicated to and then accepted in some way by the pupil. Through the intermediary effects of self-concept and/or motivational processes children come to accept the view that they are relatively unlikely to achieve success (relative perhaps to their peers in the class, certainly relative to the self-expectations that they would have held if it had not been for the communication of low expectations from the teacher) and are, therefore, less successful.

Stability of expectations is a central assumption of this process. The expectations of the teacher, if the expectancy effect is to take place, must remain constant and not be adapted in the light of contradictory feedback from the pupil. The pupil must also come to hold a similarly low set of expectations for the self and be equally unlikely to adapt these to other sources of information. The young child's conceptions of ability as a plastic entity, and the enduring optimism that seems to go along with it, would seem to militate against the expectancy effect taking place at this stage in a child's development and schooling. Yet the available evidence from research into expectancy effects seems to suggest that the opposite is in fact the case.

The apparent paradox is perhaps not that difficult to untangle. The claim that the young child is particularly susceptible to teacher expectancy effects, and especially those of a self-fulfilling rather than of a sustaining nature, does not necessarily imply that the effects of this susceptibility will be immediately apparent. As developmentally-orientated work into expectations and motivational processes gathers some momentum, it becomes increasingly clear that the young child is actively involved in the process of acquiring a motivational style. At least this will involve the child developing a relative orientation to intrinsic rather than extrinsic processes (Harter and Connell 1984; Deci and Ryan 1985), developing an understanding of the nature and range of different possible causes of success and failure (Nicholls 1984; Little 1985; Rogers 1986) together with an understanding of the ways in which these various causes might relate to each other (Weiner and Kun 1976; Nicholls 1984) and the development of an understanding of the meaning of success and failure itself in academic contexts (Frieze *et al.* 1983).

Some of these developmental processes are likely to be lifelong ones. The meaning of success and failure, for example, will vary across different situations and is also likely to be influenced by changes in societal values. Others are likely to be a feature of the early years and the ways in which these early developments take place will have a bearing upon the individual's future motivational style. At a later stage in life, motivational style, as understood through the making of attributions, can be altered (Andrews and Debus 1978; Dweck 1975; Maehr and Kleiber 1987) but perhaps only with careful and fairly intensive intervention programmes. A feature of the attributional model of motivation is that self-sustaining cycles are established that lock the various participants into rather predictable pathways. The feature of early teacher expectations most worthy of our future attention will be the effect of this on the pathway that the individual sets out on, rather than on the immediately identifiable consequences of the first few steps.

REFERENCES

Ames, C. (1986) 'Effective motivation: the contribution of the learning environment', in R.S. Feldman (ed.) *The Social Psychology of Education: Current Theory and Research*, Cambridge: Cambridge University Press.

Ames, C. and Ames, R. (eds) (1985) *Research on Motivation in Education: Vol. 2. The Classroom Milieu*, London: Academic Press.

Ames, R. and Ames, C. (eds) (1984) *Research on Motivation in Education: Vol. 1. Student Motivation*, London: Academic Press.

Andrews, G.R. and Debus, R.L. (1978) 'Persistence and the causal perception of failure: modifying cognitive attributions', *Journal of Educational Psychology* 70: 154–66.

Blease, D. (1983) 'Teacher expectations and the self-fulfilling prophecy', *Educational Studies* 9: 123–30.

Braun, C. (1976) 'Teacher expectation: socio-psychological dynamics', *Review of Educational Research* 46: 185–213.

Brophy, J. and Good, T. (1974) *Teacher–Student Relationships: Causes and Consequences*, New York: Holt, Rinehart & Winston.

Burns, R.B. (1979) *The Self-Concept: Theory, Measurement, Development and Behaviour*, London: Longman.

Burns, R.B. (1982) *Self-Concept: Development and Education*, London: Holt, Rinehart & Winston.

Cooper, H. (1979) 'Pygmalion grows up: a model for teacher expectation communication and performance influence', *Review of Educational Research*, 49: 389–410.

Cooper, H. (1985) 'Models of teacher expectation communication', in J.B.

Dusek (ed.) *Teacher Expectancies*, London: Erlbaum.

Cooper, H. and Good, T. (1983) *Pygmalion Grows Up: Studies in the Expectation Communication Process*, New York: Longman.

Cooper, H., Hinkel, G., and Good, T. (1980) 'Teachers' beliefs about interaction control and their observed behavioural correlates', *Journal of Educational Psychology* 72: 345–54.

Crano, W.D. and Mellon, P.M. (1978) 'Causal influence of teachers' expectations on children's academic performance: a cross-lagged panel analysis', *Journal of Educational Psychology* 70: 39–49.

DeCharms, R. (1980) 'The origins of competence and achievement motivation in personal causation', in L.J. Fyans (ed.) *Achievement Motivation: Recent Trends in Theory and Research*, London: Plenum Press.

Deci, E.L., and Ryan, R.M. (1985) *Intrinsic Motivation and Self-Determination in Human Behavior*, New York: Plenum Press.

DES (1988) Statistical Bulletin 4/88, London: HMSO.

Dusek, J. (ed.) (1985) *Teacher Expectancies*, London: Erlbaum.

Dusek, J. and Joseph, G. (1983) 'The bases of teacher expectancies: a meta-analysis', *Journal of Educational Psychology* 75: 327–46.

Dweck, C. (1975) 'The role of expectations and attributions in the alleviation of learned helplessness', *Journal of Personality and Social Psychology* 31: 674–85.

Dweck, C. (1985) 'Intrinsic motivation, perceived control and self-evaluation maintenance: an achievement goal analysis', in C. Ames and R. Ames (eds) *Research on Motivation in Education: Vol. 2. The Classroom Milieu*, London: Academic Press.

Dweck, C. and Reppucci, N.D. (1973) 'Learned helplessness and reinforcement responsibility in children', *Journal of Personality and Social Psychology* 25: 109–16.

Eccles, J., Midgley, C. and Adler, T. (1984) 'Grade-related changes in the school environment: effects on achievement motivation', in J. Nicholls (ed.) *Advances in Motivation and Achievement*: Vol. 3. *The Development of Achievement Motivation*, London: JAI Press.

Elashoff, J.D. and Snow, R.E. (eds) (1971) *Pygmalion Reconsidered*, Worthington, Ohio: Jones.

Frieze, I.H., Francis, W.D. and Hanusa, B.H. (1983) 'Defining success in classroom settings', in J.M. Levine and W.C. Wang (eds) *Teacher and Student Perceptions: Implications for Learning*, Hillsdale, NJ: Erlbaum.

Good, T.L. and Brophy, J.E. (1987) *Looking in Classrooms*, 4th edn, New York: Harper & Row.

Harris, M.J. and Rosenthal, R. (1985) 'Four factors in the mediation of teacher expectancy effects', in R.S. Feldman (ed.) *The Social Psychology of Education: Current Research and Theory*, Cambridge: Cambridge University Press.

Harter, S. (1978) 'Effectance motivation reconsidered: toward a developmental model', *Human Development* 1: 34–64.

Harter, S. and Connell, J.P. (1984) 'A model of children's achievement and related self-perceptions of competence, control, and motivational orientation', in J. Nicholls (ed.) *Advances in Motivation and Achievement*:

Vol. 3. *The Development of Achievement Motivation*, London: JAI Press.

Leigh, P.M. (1977) 'Great expectations: a reconsideration of the self-fulfilling prophecy in the context of educability', *Educational Review* 29: 317–24.

Little, A.W. (1985) 'The child's understanding of the causes of academic success and failure: a case study of British schoolchildren', *British Journal of Educational Psychology* 55: 11–23.

Maehr, M.L. and Kleiber, D.A. (1987) *Advances in Motivation and Achievement:* Vol. 5. *Enhancing Motivation*, Greenwich, Conn.: JAI Press.

Mitman, A.L. and Snow, R.E. (1985) 'Logical and methodological problems in teacher expectancy research', in J. Dusek (ed.) *Teacher Expectancies*, London: Erlbaum.

Murphy, J. (1974) 'Teacher expectations and working class under-achievement', *British Journal of Sociology* 25: 326–44.

Nicholls, J. (ed.) (1984) *Advances in Motivation and Achievement:* Vol. 3. *The Development of Achievement Motivation*, London: JAI Press.

Nicholls, J. and Miller, A.T. (1984) 'Development and its discontents: the differentiation of the concept of ability', in J. Nicholls (ed.) *Advances in Motivation and Achievement:* Vol. 3. *The Development of Achievement Motivation*, London: JAI Press.

Palardy, J.M. (1969) 'What teachers believe – what children achieve', *Elementary School Journal* 69: 370–4.

Peterson, P.L. and Barger, S.A. (1985) 'Attribution theory and teacher expectancy', in J. Dusek (ed.) *Teacher Expectancies*, London: Erlbaum.

Raudenbusch, S.W. (1984) 'Magnitude of teacher expectancy effects on pupil IQ as a function of the credibility of expectancy induction: a synthesis of findings from 18 experiments', *Journal of Educational Psychology* 76: 85–97.

Rist, R. (1970) 'Student social class and teacher expectations: the self-fulfilling prophecy in ghetto education', *Harvard Educational Review* 40: 411–51.

Rogers, C.G. (1982) *A Social Psychology of Schooling*, London: Routledge & Kegan Paul.

Rogers, C.G. (1986) Attributions for success and failure: the effects of classroom activity, BERA Annual Conference, Bristol, September.

Rosenthal, R. (1973) 'The mediation of Pygmalion effects: a four-factor "theory" ', *Papua New Guinea Journal of Education* 9: 1–12.

Rosenthal, R. (1985) 'From unconscious experimenter bias to teacher expectancy effects', in J. Dusek (ed.) *Teacher Expectancies*, London: Erlbaum.

Rosenthal, R. and Jacobson, L. (1968) *Pygmalion in the Classroom*, New York: Holt, Rinehart & Winston.

Stipek, D.J. (1984) 'Young children's performance expectations: logical analysis or wishful thinking', in J. Nicholls (ed.) *Advances in Motivation and Achievement*: Vol. 3. *The Development of Achievement Motivation*, London: JAI Press.

Weiner, B. (1979) 'A theory of motivation for some classroom experiences', *Journal of Educational Psychology* 71: 3–25.

Weiner, B. (1984) 'Principles for a theory of student motivation and their application within an attributional framework', in R. Ames and C. Ames (eds) *Research on Motivation in Education. Vol. 1. Student Motivation*, London: Academic Press.

Weiner, B. and Kun, A. (1976) 'The development of causal attributions and the growth of achievement and social motivation', in S. Feldman and B. Bush (eds) *Cognitive Development and Social Development*, Hillsdale, NJ: Erlbaum.

Weinstein, R.S. (1985) 'Student mediation of classroom expectancy effects', in J. Dusek (ed.) *Teacher Expectancies*, London: Erlbaum.

11 Transactional models of early education effectiveness: what is the message for policy?

Martin Woodhead
Source: *Early Child Care and Development* (1990) 58, pp. 129–41.

'A HEAD START PAYS OFF IN THE END'

This was the dramatic headline that confronted business commuters in the USA when they opened their copy of the *Wall Street Journal* on 29 November 1984. The feature article began:

> If ever there was a program for the 1980s, a program that addresses the needs for greater productivity and the needs of women and the problems of poverty, it is – are you ready? – pre-school education.
>
> (Crittenden 1984)

This is a very strong claim for early education, a powerful message for policy, and it was based largely on the evidence of systematic research. Most significant, it was not published in a specialist journal with a circulation restricted to committed advocates for early childhood, but a major national newspaper with a readership normally more preoccupied with business investment than child welfare issues. The article argued that it was time for that traditional divide to be bridged:

> One of the strangest anomalies in our economic thinking is our tendency to view investment in hardware terms; to see expenditure on plant and machinery as 'hard' and expenditure on people as somehow 'soft' and social – more akin to welfare than to capital spending.
>
> (Crittenden 1984)

It was a tantalizing argument, based on converting research data from a long-term follow-up of children who had experienced a pre-school programme into cost-benefit terms. It seemed to demonstrate quite conclusively that the modest expenditure required to run an early education programme would in the long run save money on remedial and special education services, save money on criminal proceedings, save money on social welfare provisions, and so on. Since the mid-1980s newspapers and television reports in the USA have included many similar proclamations about the pay-off from investing in the early years, with a ripple effect extending throughout Latin America, Europe and much of the rest of the globe.

In view of the widespread impact of recent research it seems important to look closely at the message in the data, especially the claims that have been made for policy. In this chapter I shall not be challenging the validity of the evidence as research data, which by general consent appears to be reasonably robust. My concern is with trying to understand and interpret the evidence. My conclusions do not alter the impressive evidence of the data, but they do modify the message for policy.

THE RESEARCH BACKGROUND

First let me sketch in a little of the background. Evaluations of early education are not a particularly new phenomenon. The first systematic study was carried out over seventy years ago (reviewed by Wellman 1945). But the main impetus for research came in the 1960s. In the USA it was associated with the 'War on Poverty', especially Project Headstart (Zigler and Valentine 1979). In Britain it was linked with the Urban Aid programme and the Educational Priority Area Projects (Halsey 1972). With these initiatives, research into early childhood education became for the first time closely linked to questions of public policy.

Developments in early education research were part of a more general trend. For example, twenty years ago Campbell proposed:

> an experimental approach to social reform, an approach in which we try out new programs . . . and in which we retain, imitate, modify or discard them on the basis of apparent effectiveness on the multiple imperfect criteria available.
>
> (Campbell 1969: 409).

This vision of research-led policy-making appealed to the values of scientific/technological societies. It offered the promise of efficient planning, tidying-up the public agenda, discarding worn-out methods that had been based on a combination of tradition, intuition and expediency, and replacing them with clearly defined, modern, empirically verified strategies.

Research and policy are more closely intertwined in the USA than in Britain (Sharpe 1978). But even in Britain research is the subject of increasing public attention, exemplified by the impact of the various school effectiveness studies that have been carried out during the last twenty years (e.g. in secondary education, Rutter *et al.* 1979; in primary education, Mortimore *et al.* 1988).

Preschool education has not been included in these evaluations. It has always been somewhat separated-off from the rest of schooling, the subject of repeated struggles to become established as an essential but distinctive component of the British education system (Woodhead 1989a). In this climate it is a great advance to be able to make a case for early education based not on faith and intuition, but on systematically collected scientific evidence, even if that evidence does come from the other side of the Atlantic. None of the British research initiated in the late 1960s was followed up sufficiently to permit conclusions about long-term effects (Smith and James 1975). There is one exception: Osborn and Millbank (1987) have worked on the database of a major longitudinal cohort study (Child Health and Education Study), and claim to have conclusive evidence on the positive effect of ordinary nursery schools and playgroups (Osborn and Millbank 1987: 216). But the methodological difficulties in controlling adequately for social background variables in their data are immense (see Woodhead 1989b) and their conclusions are at best only indicative of a possible effect.

Finally, in recent years there has been a welcome growth in the number of evaluations carried out in a wide range of contexts throughout the world (e.g. Turkey, in Kagitcibasi and Bekman 1987; Latin America, reviewed in Halpern and Myers 1985). But, for the time being at least, there is nothing to compare with the US research in terms of quality of design and length of follow-up. In addition to the various evaluations of Headstart itself over the years (Westinghouse Learning Corporation 1969; Hubbell 1983; Harrell 1983; McKey *et al.* 1985), numerous experimental and quasi-experimental projects were set up in the early 1960s and followed up their children through into school (e.g. Beller 1974; Deutsch *et al.* 1983; Gray *et al.* 1982; Karnes *et al.* 1974; Weikart *et al.* 1978).

THE RESEARCH EVIDENCE

Early results from the US projects were encouraging, but measured improvements in experimental-group children's abilities appeared to 'washout' during the early grades of elementary school, as reviewed by Bronfenbrenner (1974). I have discussed the relationship between these early findings and the changing fortunes of Headstart elsewhere

Table 11.1 The Perry Pre-School Project: major findings at 19 years of age

Category	Number[a] responding	Pre-school group	No-pre-school group	p[b]
Employed	121	59%	32%	0.032
High school graduation (or its equivalent)	121	67%	49%	0.034
College or vocational training	121	38%	21%	0.029
Ever detained or arrested	121	31%	51%	0.022
Females only: teen pregnancies, per 100	49	64	117	0.084
Functional competence (APL Survey: possible score 40)	109	24.6	21.8	0.025
% of years in special education	112	16%	28%	0.039

Notes: [a]Total N = 123.
        [b]Two-tailed p-values are presented if less than 0.100.
Source: Berrueta-Clement *et al.* 1984: 2

(Woodhead 1985a). Suffice it to note that the generally pessimistic mood at this time (echoed in Britain in Barbara Tizard's review to the Social Science Research Council (SSRC), Tizard 1974: 4) prompted collaboration and long-term follow-up by eleven of the best-designed US projects, as the Consortium for Longitudinal Studies (1977; 1978; 1983; Darlington *et al.* 1980; Lazar *et al.* 1982). Undoubtedly the single most widely publicized of theses studies is the Perry Pre-School Project, conducted by David Weikart and colleagues at the High/Scope Educational Research Foundation in Michigan (Weikart *et al.* 1978; Schweinhart and Weikart 1980; Berrueta-Clement *et al.* 1984). Summary findings from their follow-up when the sample was 19 years old will illustrate their impressive, not to say startling, evidence (see Table 11.1).

It was this research that prompted the headline with which this chapter began. One of the face of it, the early education programme appears to have been highly cost-effective, as the research team themselves stressed in their economic analysis, arguing that the initial outlay on the pre-school programme was recovered many times over, in terms of savings made on reduced welfare and juvenile court costs, etc. amongst the experimental group. A.H. Halsey (who had directed the British Educational Priority Area projects) was in no doubt about the message for policy:

> a pre-school programme, properly devised, can be a most economical investment for a government wishing to save money on schools. And for a government determined to relieve the handicaps of those who come from poor families, a preschool programme discriminating in their favour seems to be one of the crucial weapons in the armoury.
>
> (Halsey 1980: 342)

The data are certainly powerful ammunition for the advocates of better services for young children and their families. But they surely raise as many questions as they answer, especially one central question that will be the main focus of this chapter:

> How could a few hours of pre-school activities each day, plus a weekly home visit, make such a pervasive permanent impact on children's fortunes, right through into adult life?

Finding a satisfactory answer to this question is I believe of more than just theoretical significance.

The simplest and most attractive explanation for long-term effects would be that pre-school activities altered children's approach to learning, their skills and abilities, and this enhanced competence stayed with them right through their schooling. Linking intervention to a sensitive period in children's development was the rationale for Headstart envisaged by influential American developmental psychologists in the early 1960s (Hunt 1961; Bloom 1964).

As it turns out, the evidence offers little support for this linear model of long-term effects. As I have already noted above, early results from these projects showed that experimental-group children's abilities were significantly improved for up to two years after the end of the programme, but thereafter average intelligence scores rapidly converged with those of the control group. In other words, the facts of staying on longer at school, going to college, finding employment, and so on, were not due to enhanced abilities, at least as measured by IQ tests. The evidence of long-term effects comes from the very same group of projects that had been reviewed by Bronfenbrenner (1974).

If there is no evidence of direct effect on children's abilities, how do we explain the long-term results? When the researchers first encountered this problem there was much talk of 'sleeper effects' (reported by Lewin 1977). It seemed that initial effects had not washed

Table 11.2 Percent of students placed in special education classes, program versus control

Project	Programme (%)	Control (%)	χ^2	p
More nearly randomized designs				
Gordon ($N = 82$)	23.2	53.8	5.10	0.024
Gray ($N = 53$)	2.8	29.4	8.16	0.004
Weikart ($N = 123$)	13.8	27.7	3.55	0.060
Median	13.8	29.4	—	—
	Pooled $z = 4.04$; pooled $p < 0.001$			

Note: Data collected when most of the children were in the following grades: Gordon, grade 5; Gray, grade 12; Palmer, grade 7; Weikart, grade 4.
Source: Lazar *et al.* 1982: 32.

out at all. They were like overwintering hedgehogs, lying dormant, waiting to be re-awakened by some later environmental change or process of maturation. The appeal of a 'sleeper effect' was short-lived (Clarke and Clarke 1981; 1982; Seitz 1981), not least because it amounted to little more than a pseudo-scientific way for the researchers to say 'we don't understand'.

A TRANSACTIONAL MODEL OF LONG-TERM EFFECTS

Resolution of the apparent paradox of short-term washout but long-term effects demands thinking in terms of a quite different model of children's development and educational effects. It is essential to move away from thinking in terms of the pre-school programme influencing individual children in isolation and begin to recognize the respects in which effects on their development and educational progress are embedded in a series of social contexts. Long-term effects appear to be due not to a permanent change in children's psychological make-up, but to an altered relationship between children and their teachers as they progress (or fail to progress) through a particular school and community system. This idea can best be illustrated by looking more closely at Consortium data on one variable in particular, referral to special education.

Table 11.2 summarizes data for three of the best-designed projects in the Consortium follow-up. In each case, over twice as many control as experimental-group children had been referred to special classes during their school careers. This is one of the most impressive results in the Consortium follow-up, and is closely linked to effects on the related variable, retention in grade. Such results are clear evidence of early education affecting children's competence and approach to learning sufficiently in the short term that elementary school teachers and school psychologists judged many more of them fit to remain within the mainstream and progress alongside their age-mates. But are these findings merely 'results'? Aren't they more than just 'effects' of the pre-school programme? I want to argue that differential referral rates to special education classes play a much more important role in the story. They don't just have statistical significance as an 'effect'. They also have explanatory significance as a 'cause', mediating the process of long-term effects. Being referred to special education modified children's subsequent experience of schooling, their self-concepts as learners and their prospects for attainment. This is, I think, one of the clues that can help solve the mystery of how to explain long-term effects.

The authors of the Consortium follow-up recognized the explanatory significance of retention in grade and referral to special education, and suggested some of the processes that might be involved:

> Assignment to special classes in itself *affects* children. They are labelled in their own eyes and the eyes of others. Labels such as 'emotionally disturbed' or 'mildly retarded' have a life of their own, remaining on children's records for years and potentially affecting each new teacher's expectations for and treatment of a child.
> (Lazar *et al.* 1982; 58, emphasis added)

A similar interpretation was offered by the authors of the Perry Pre-School Project (Schweinhart and Weikart 1980: 12). Both groups of authors make explicit reference to the power of a transactional model (Sameroff and Chandler 1975; for more recent discussion, see Sameroff 1983; 1988). It seems that long-term effects were transmitted, at least in part, through complex social processes of expectancy and labelling, linked to procedures for assessment and referral of children judged to be incapable of making the grade. The pre-school programmes were effective because of their proximity to one of the most crucial transition points in children's educational careers, starting full-time school. Children who had been to a pre-school group projected short-term changes in ability and attitude at a point when the education system was highly sensitive to signs of competence and adjustment. These initial transactions with the school triggered a chain reaction. In other words, it appears that a characteristic of the school system into which children moved after they had participated in the pre-school programme played a critical role in mediating and perhaps even amplifying the initial effects of that programme. If this interpretation is correct, it means that the researchers were not just evaluating the effects of an early education programme on children. They were necessarily also evaluating the impact of the school, family and community system through which early education effects were transmitted. This transactional model has important implications for policy. For example, how effective would early education be in a gentler school system that muffled the initial effects of the programme by failing to interact with them? The answer to that question will become clear by drawing a parallel with the processes at work at a later transition point in children's educational career, when they are about to start secondary school.

A parallel example

During the post-war years the 11+ exam was widely used in Britain to select children for grammar versus secondary modern schools; in some local education authorities similar selective tests are still in use today. In view of the importance of the 11+ in shaping children's educational fortunes, it was common practice during the weeks and months leading up to the exam for teachers to coach children on questions similar to those they would meet in the actual papers. Now, imagine that the effects of this pre-exam coaching had been subject to a major piece of systematic research. An experimental design would randomly assign a sample of children of borderline ability to one of two groups: a 'pre-exam coaching' group (experimental) and a 'no preparation' group (control). All the children would then go on to take the exam, the successful candidates from both groups being accepted into grammar school and the rest referred to secondary modern or other schools. Let us suppose that the researchers were successful in securing a research grant to follow the progress of the two groups of children through to the end of schooling and into adult life. What results would we expect? I don't think we would be surprised if they reported finding significant differences between the two groups throughout their school careers, and beyond. Some of the most significant results favouring the experimental group (who had received the pre-11+ coaching) might include: later school leaving age; greater numbers of O and A level passes; higher entry-rate to university and college; and improved employment prospects.

This would be impressive evidence of long-term effects, but where would we look for an explanation? One line of argument that the researchers might offer would emphasize the weeks and months before the 11+ as a critical or sensitive period in children's cognitive development. The research would apparently show that there can be enormous pay-off from investing educational resources in this particular period of life, with implications for policy in the middle/ later primary years. The researchers might even employ an economist to make a cost-benefit analysis to quantify the pay-off of a few weeks' educational investment in low-cost coaching for a productive, high-income labour force.

Let us suppose that this line of argument is entirely consistent with the evidence. Even so, I doubt that many of us would be convinced by it. In this case it is obvious that the success of the coaching in enhancing children's cognitive competence is not in itself of enduring significance in either developmental or policy terms. It becomes significant only because of the proximity of the coaching to school selection procedures that do have a decisive influence on their educational future. The 11+ exam functioned like a gateway, sensitive to the short-term differences in competence produced by the coaching, but transforming these into another variable, namely type of schooling, through which those differences would be amplified. To reinforce the point, consider what message for policy would be appropriate following reforms to secondary education that abolished selection at 11 and introduced a comprehensive school system. If a replication of the coaching experiment were carried out in the absence of the 11+, I think we can safely assume that the results would be very different.

I hasten to add that I am not suggesting that the process of pre-school effects is anything like as straightforward as this 11+ example. The pre-school programmes were much more substantial than a few weeks' coaching, and the processes of referral were much less definitive than the process of school selection. Also bear in mind that referral to special education classes was only one of a number of transmission pathways for long-term effects, in the school, family and community (discussed in Woodhead 1988).

But I do want to argue that there are parallel features in the two situations. Just as coaching improved children's abilities and attitudes in the short-term sufficient for a higher proportion to pass through the 11+ gateway into the higher resources and expectations of a grammar school classroom, so a pre-school programme appears to have boosted children's abilities and motivation sufficiently in the short term that they were more likely to be retained in the mainstream of schooling and less likely than control groups to suffer the stigma of referral to special education classes, or retention in grade. Of course, low-ability former pre-school children were not sent to different schools as in the more extreme case of the 11+ example. But I would suggest that being required to sit in a class of younger children, or a class marked-off as being for children with learning difficulties, may have steered children onto a different educational track just as effectively as if they had been to a different school. Figure 11.1 is a summary of the causal model for the effects of the Perry Pre-School Programme (from Berrueta-Clement *et al.* 1984: 80). It well illustrates the function of special education in the long-term process. [An equivalent model for other projects is in Consortium 1983: 454].

In interpreting this model of early education effects it is essential to bear in mind the social and school context within which low-ability children from poor black families were growing up in the early 1960s in the USA. Their treatment within the school system was a source of deep frustration to many of those who initiated early education programmes. For example David Weikart wrote:

> Children unable to learn at the standard rate were seen simply as failures. The major remedy of choice was to require students to repeat grades until they learned the necessary skills. This practice produced, in Ypsilanti, the outlandish result of approximately 50 per cent of all ninth-graders being from one to five years behind in grade, and a 50 per cent drop out rate with legal school-leaving occurring for some youngsters as early as seventh grade.
>
> (Weikart *et al.* 1978: 2)

Critics of such an inefficient and divisive system were faced with several options. The pre-school researchers chose to try to increase children's chances of making the grade in the existing elementary school system. An alternative would have been to attempt to reform that school system to serve better the interests of such children.

If the organization of the elementary school system was one of the major factors contributing to the success of experimental pre-school programmes, it becomes important to ask whether referral processes in elementary schools still function in the same way in the USA now as they did in the early 1960s, and whether they would function in analogous ways in other education systems, such as Britain. In so far as they do not, which appears to be the case following major reforms in the mid-1970s (see Woodhead 1985b; 1988), then the message for policy becomes much less clear cut than the data suggest at first sight.

In order to highlight the argument, consider the following hypothetical, but, I hope, not too far-fetched scenario. Suppose that the experimental pre-school projects had been set up in a very different

Figure 11.1 A causal model for effects of the Perry Pre-School Program

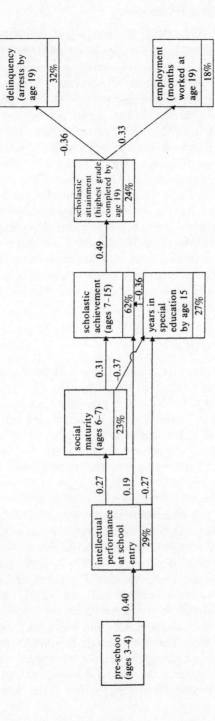

Note: Analyses are based on *N* = 112. Causal paths are indicated by arrows joining variables with direction of the arrows from cause to effect. Path coefficients are beta weights in ordinary-least-squares regressions; arrows connect variables only if paths are significant (at $p < 0.10$, two-tailed). The directions of paths between variables measured at the same time points are dependent on the model's theoretical framework and should be interpreted with caution. The percentage presented at the bottom of each variable is the percentage of variance in that variable accounted for by statistically significant predictors.

Source: Berrueta-Clement *et al.* 1984: 80.

social context from 1960s USA, in which it was also public policy to give a very high priority (and commensurate resources) to intensive, high-quality remedial and special education services for children referred during the early months of elementary school. This extra attention and resources would apply only to children judged by teachers to be below a threshold of ability and school readiness, and it would be sustained right through their schooling. All average and above average children would be taught in normal, modestly resourced classrooms. What would be the long-term effects of a pre-school intervention in this situation? I suspect that any benefits would be greatly attenuated. In fact it is conceivable that the experimental group who benefited from a pre-school programme would actually fare less well than the control group who received no preparation for school at all. Clearly the reason for this curious result would be that the short-term pre-school boost would make many borderline children appear more competent and they would thereby be denied extra positive attention and resources in the long term that would otherwise have been made available to them.

MESSAGES FOR POLICY

Let me try to draw together the implications of these speculations in terms of the messages of research for policy. The main point is that in trying to understand the effects of a pre-school programme (or any other educational intervention for that matter) we are dealing not only with a psychological and educational process, but also with a social process. For children, pre-school activities are one element in a complex network of interconnected experiences and relationships from birth to maturity, and beyond.

On this perspective, trying to make a definitive statement about the long-term effects of pre-school education becomes a little like trying to measure the importance of heredity. The pressure for policy is to give an absolute figure. But in social scientific terms this makes little sense. The effects of pre-school education are context specific. Account must be taken not only of the characteristics of children and content and design of programmes (reviewed in Woodhead 1985b). The extent and nature of pre-school effects also depends on the particular constellation of social practices and processes into which the programme and its effects are embedded. There is no single message for policy; hence the use of the plural in heading this section 'messages for policy'. The US projects have illustrated the powerful impact of early education within one particular school and social system at one particular point in time. What we need now, ideally, is for a series of equivalent projects to be carried out in diverse settings throughout the world. That would take at least fifteen years, always assuming resources could be spared for such a mammoth undertaking, which is unlikely. As second best, what we can do is take account of the lessons in the US research, launching smaller-scale investigations to explore the functions early education serves in relationship to school systems, as well as the relationship of any planned innovation to existing developmental pathways in family and community. In some settings early education might make a more profound impact even than in the US projects, while in other settings there may be much more effective strategies than a pre-school programme for improving educational prospects.

In future, it may be more profitable to work within a theoretical framework which sees pre-school not as an isolated educational strategy, but as one element in the transition process that children make into school. By focusing on the transition we are more likely to recognize variables in the school as well as the pre-school system as contributing to results, and as potential candidates for reform or innovation. In a review of pre-school evaluations worldwide, Robert Myers (1989) offers a neat characterization of the central issue, asking not only about the *readiness of children for schools*, but also about the *readiness of schools for children*. He notes that in sub-Saharan countries, where classes are large, instructional resources scanty, teachers minimally trained and prospects remote for anything beyond very basic teaching, any newly acquired skills that participants in a pre-school programme might bring to school are likely to be of little consequence in shaping the course of their school careers. And in some communities an effective nutrition programme may have a more decisive influence on children's prospects than either pre-school or school reform (Myers 1989).

A similar point has been made by Christine Liddell in her discussion of South African government plans to introduce a pre-school enrichment programme for black children, based on American and British models. Liddell notes that 58 per cent of black South African children failed to achieve the required standard during the first four years of schooling; amongst these 60 per cent had already been judged failures by the end of their first year. She concludes

failure rates might be lessened more effectively by modifications in the Grade One curriculum, rather than by implementation of preschool enrichment schemes.

(Liddell 1987: 129)

Finally, why is it that researchers, teachers, journalists and policy-makers have so widely overstated the message for policy in pre-school effectiveness research? One reason is of course that simple statements implying direct effects are politically persuasive in an area of policy not noted for generous funding. But there is another more subtle reason, which has to do with the experimental design on which the evidence is based. A well-designed experiment has many scientific virtues. But applied to the social world it has the disadvantage of encouraging disproportionate attention to be paid to the independent variable (in this case whether children attended an early education programme) as the cause of all subsequent differences between experimental and control groups, no matter how remote in time and nature the outcome measures are from the intervention. Expectations are in danger of becoming narrowly focused on the apparent single-handed power of one particular influence in children's lives. In reality, as we all know, growing-up is more complicated than that.

REFERENCES

Beller, E.K. (1974) 'Impact of early education on disadvantaged children', in S. Ryan (ed.) *A Report on Longitudinal Evaluations of Pre-school Programs*, Vol. 1, Washington, DC: Department of Health, Education and Welfare.

Berrueta-Clement, J.R., Schweinhart, L.J., Barnett, W.S., Epstein, A.S. and Weikart, D.P. (1984) 'Changed lives: the effects of the Perry pre-school program on youths through age 19', *Monograph 8*, Ypsilanti, Mich.: High/Scope Press.

Bloom, B.S. (1964) *Stability and Change in Human Characteristics*, New York: Wiley.

Bronfenbrenner, U. (1974) *Is Early Intervention Effective?* Washington, DC: Department of Health, Education and Welfare.

Campbell, D.T. (1969) 'Reforms as experiments', *American Psychologist* 25: 409-29.

Clarke, A.M. and Clarke, A.D.B. (1981) 'Sleeper effects in development: fact or artifact?', *Developmental Review* 1: 344-60.

Clarke, A.M. and Clarke, A.D.B. (1982) 'Intervention and sleeper effects: a reply to Victoria Seitz', *Developmental Review* 2: 76-8.

Consortium for Developmental Continuity (1977) *The Persistence of Pre-school Effects*, Washington, DC: Department of Health, Education and Welfare.

2Consortium for Longitudinal Studies (1978) *Lasting Effects after Pre-school*, Washington, DC: Department of Health, Education and Welfare.

2Consortium for Longitudinal Studies (1983) *As the Twig is Bent*, London: Erlbaum.

Crittenden, A. (1984) 'A Head Start pays off in the end', *Wall Street Journal*, 29 November.

Darlington, R.D., Royce, J.M., Snipper, A.S., Murray, H.W., and Lazar, I. (1980) 'Pre-school programs and later school competence of children from low-income families', *Science* 208: 202–4.

Deutsch, M., Deutsch, C., Jordan, T.J. and Grallo, R. (1983) 'The IDS Program: an experiment in early and sustained enrichment', in Consortium for Longitudinal Studies, *As the Twig is Bent*, London: Erlbaum.

Gray, S.W., Ramsey, B.K. and Klaus, R.A. (1982) *From 3 to 20: The Early Training Project*, Baltimore, MD: University Park Press.

Halpern, R. and Myers, R. (1985) 'Effects of early childhood intervention on primary school progress and performance in the developing countries', unpublished paper, Ypsilanti, Mich: High/Scope – USAID.

Halsey, A.H. (1972) *Educational Priority* Vol. 1, London: HMSO.

Halsey, A.H. (1980) 'Education can compensate', *New Society* 24 January.

Harrell, R. (1983) *The Effects of the Head Start Program on Children's Cognitive Development: Preliminary Report of the Head Start Evaluation, Synthesis and Utilization Project*, Washington, DC: US Department of Health and Human Services.

Hubbell, R. (1983) *A Review of Head Start since 1970*, Washington, DC: US Department of Health and Human Services.

Hunt, J. McV. (1961) *Intelligence and Experience*, New York: Ronald Press.

Kagiticibasi, D.S. and Bekman, S. (1987) *Comprehensive Preschool Education Report*, Istanbul: Bogazici University.

Karnes, M.B., Zehrbrach, R.R. and Teska, J.A. (1974) 'The Karnes preschool program: rationale, curricular offerings and follow-up data', in S. Ryan (ed.) *Report on Longitudinal Evaluations of Pre-School Programs*, Washington, DC: Department of Health, Education and Welfare.

Lazar, I., Darlington, R.B., Murray, H.W. and Snipper, A.S. (1982) 'Lasting effects of early education: a report from the Consortium for Longitudinal Studies', *Monograph of Society for Research in Child Development*, 47 (2–3).

Lewin, R. (1977) 'Head Start pays off', *New Scientist*, 3 March: 508–9.

Liddell, C (1987) 'Some issues regarding the introduction of pre-school enrichment programmes for black South African children', *International Journal of Educational Development* 7(2): 127–31.

McKey, R.H., Condelli, L., Ganson, H., Barrett, B., McConkey, C. and Plantz, M. (1985) *The Impact of Head Start on Children, Families and Communities* (Final report of Head Start Evaluation, Synthesis and Utilization Project) Washington, DC: CSR Inc.

Mortimore, P., Sammons, P., Stoll, L., Lewis, D. and Ecob, R. (1988) *School Matters: The Junior Years*, London: Open Books.

Myers, R. (1989) 'Preparing children for schools and schools for children', Chapter 8 of *The Twelve who Survive* (manuscript), New York: Consultative Group on Early Childhood Care and Development.

Osborn, A.F. and Millbank, J.E. (1987) *The Effects of Early Education*, Oxford: Clarendon Press.

Rutter, M., Maughan, B., Mortimore, P. and Ouston, J. (1979) *Fifteen Thousand Hours*, London: Open Books.

Sameroff, A.J. (1983) 'Developmental systems: contexts and evolution', in W. Kessen (ed.) *Handbook of Child Psychology. Vol. 1. History, Theories and Methods*, New York: Wiley.

Sameroff, A.J. (1988) 'The social context of development', in N. Eisenberg (ed.) *Contemporary Topics in Developmental Psychology*, New York: Wiley.

Sameroff, J. A. and Chandler, M. (1975) 'Reproductive risk and the continuum of caretaking casuality', in F. Horowitz (ed.) *Review of Child Development Research*, Vol. 4, Chicago: University of Chicago Press.

Schweinhart, L.J. and Weikart, D.P. (1980) 'Young children grow up', *Monograph 7*, Ypsilanti, Mich.: High/Scope Press.

Seitz, V. (1981) 'Intervention and sleeper effects: a reply to Clarke and Clarke', *Developmental Review* 1: 361–73.

Sharpe, L.J. (1978) 'The social scientist and policy-making in Britain and America: a comparison', in M. Bulmer (ed.) *Social Policy Research*, London: Macmillan.

Smith, G.A.N. and James, T. (1975) 'The effects of pre-school education: some American and British evidence', *Oxford Review of Education*, 1: 223–40.

Tizard, B. (1974) *Early Childhood Education: A Review and Discussion of Research in Britain*, London: SSRC.

Weikart, D.P., Bond, J.T. and McNeil, J.T. (1978) 'The Ypsilanti Perry Pre-school Project: Pre-school years and longitudinal results through fourth grade', *Monograph 3*, Ypsilanti, Mich.: High/Scope Press.

Wellman, B.L. (1945) 'IQ changes of pre-school and non-pre-school groups: a summary of the literature', *Journal of Psychology* 20: 347–68.

Westinghouse Learning Corporation (1969) *The Impact of Head Start: An Evaluation of the Effects of Head Start on Children's Cognitive and Affective Development*, Report to Office of Economic Opportunity, Washington, DC: Clearinghouse for Federal, Scientific and Technical Information.

Woodhead, M. (1985a) 'Early intervention', Unit 27 of course E206, *Personality, Development and Learning*, Milton Keynes: Open University Press.

Woodhead, M. (1985b) 'Pre-school education has long term effects: but can they be generalized?', *Oxford Review of Education* 11(2): 133–55.

Woodhead, M. (1988) 'When psychology informs public policy: the case of early childhood intervention', *American Psychologist* 43(6): 443–54.

Woodhead, M. (1989a) 'School starts at five . . . or four years old? The rationale for changing admission policies in England and Wales', *Journal of Education Policy* 4(1): 1–21.

Woodhead, M. (1989b) 'Is early education effective?', in C.W. Desforges (ed.) *Early Childhood Education*, British Journal of Educational Psychology Monograph Series 4, Edinburgh: Scottish Academic Press.

Zigler, E.F. and Valentine, J. (eds) (1979) *Project Head Start: A Legacy of the War on Poverty*, New York: Free Press.

Part four
Pupil perspectives on classrooms and playgrounds

Introduction

Children tend to feel vulnerable in school. They are aware of the power of teachers, of the personal assessment to which they are subject, of the control which is exercised over them and of the curriculum in terms of which they are expected to progress. . . . of course, children at school also have to cope with their peers and with the social world of other children. In this regard friendship and membership of a peer group seem to be particularly important.

(Pollard 1987: 4)

Children are at the heart of the educational process, so it is surprising how rarely they are asked about their understanding of school life. Chapters 12 to 14 illustrate several attempts to rectify this omission. Chapter 12 by Goodnow and Burns is an extract from a study of 2,000 Australian children's attitudes to school, family and friends. In this chapter the authors concentrate on what children think of their teachers. The concerns that they express seem to reflect a realistic appreciation of the need to learn under the guidance of an effective and friendly teacher. But the children's perceptions of their teachers are also strongly tempered by the inequality in their relationship. The teacher's omnipotence does not always appear in the children's eyes to be matched by equivalent wisdom and even-handedness. The issue of fairness is a major preoccupation.

In Chapter 13, Blatchford, Creeser and Mooney draw attention to another aspect of primary school life about which children hold strong opinions – playtime. Children spend as much time in the playground as they do on reading, writing and maths, but playtime has not received anything like commensurate attention from researchers. Two issues provide the starting-point for Blatchford *et al.*'s research. First, there is the question of whether traditional children's games are in decline in a children's culture increasingly dominated by manufactured toys and television. Second, there is the worry about whether the relative lack of supervision of playground activity puts children at risk of indiscipline and bullying. On both counts, Blatchford *et al.* argue that there is some cause for concern, at least in the particular social context of inner London. Elsewhere in the country there may be different patterns of playground play.

The chapters by Goodnow and Burns and by Blatchford *et al.* have the virtue of sampling a wide range of children's opinions. But they have the disadvantage of relying on what children say in relatively short interviews with a relatively unfamiliar adult. Arguably a full understanding of these issues is possible only if the researcher gives the time to establishing close relationships with children and observing their behaviour over a long period. Using small-scale, intensive 'ethnographic' research methods, Davies (Chapter 14) attempted to unravel the interpretative framework within which children understand their social world, and the social rules and priorities that govern their relationships. In this edited extract from her book, Davies illustrates the character of childhood friendships amongst a group of Australian children, including several Aboriginal girls and boys. The children were all attending a newly established (in the 1970s) open-plan school in a poor district of a large country town. Many more studies are needed to establish how far the principles of relationship described by Davies can be generalized beyond this social particular context.

REFERENCE

Pollard, A. (1987) Introduction to *Children and their Primary Schools: A New Perspective*, Lewes: Falmer Press.

12 Teachers: a child's eye view

Jacqueline Goodnow and Ailsa Burns
Source: J. Goodnow and A. Burns (1985) *Home and School: A Child's Eye View*, London: George Allen & Unwin.

School may seem a place where teachers evaluate children. The reverse is just as much the case. Children regularly compare notes about teachers. Like experienced travellers, they tell each other about schools and teachers they have encountered:

> This school is OK. I've been to some worse ones.
>
> (Grade 5)
>
> I had a teacher once in Mullingimbie and he was good.
>
> (Grade 4)

The evaluations start early and have many bases:

> Mr G. is a good teacher. He gives us sport.
>
> (Grade 2)
>
> They are good when they have time for you.
>
> (Grade 3)
>
> They have to understand the way that you think and be patient with us.
>
> (Grade 5)
>
> Someone with humour and someone with understanding. The kind of person who will understand you and doesn't get angry when you don't get it straight away.
>
> (Grade 6)
>
> I like a teacher that have feelings with their children.
>
> (Grade 6)
>
> I think the teacher should be able to get along with the children and should enjoy their work as much as the children who enjoy their work. And don't accuse until they find out what really happened.
>
> (Grade 6)

How does all this evaluation come about? What lies behind the qualities children look for, the features they note as 'good' and 'not-so-good'?

Part of the background is that children are indeed like travellers or voyagers. They make a major move from being 'at home' to being 'at school' and then continue to change regularly from one school grade to another. In this respect, they are like adults who regularly change jobs, houses or countries. With each change, they do not come to the new environment empty-handed. They bring the physical baggage of books, pencils, notes and bits and pieces from home, odd souvenirs from past years. More importantly, they bring – like every voyager – a set of *expectations*. These colour the experience of school and teachers. When the expectations are favourably met, everything is labelled 'good'. When the reality does not compare favourably, the response is one of disappointment, frustration and sometimes anger.

We shall be singling out three main hopes and expectations associated with school. First, there is the expectation that you are going to learn, and the teacher will make it possible: 'They give you education', to use a first-grader's comment. It is also hoped that the teacher will be human and friendly. He or she, in the words of a sixth-grader, should 'be a person, not a policeman'. Then, there is the expectation that you will be an accepted member of the class, and be respected at least as much as anyone else. Classrooms are large groups, and the problems of rivalry are even more complex than they are in families. A child generally wants to be noticed by the teacher and at the same time be an accepted member of your peer group, not a 'teacher's pet'. He or she usually hopes for at least 'equal' treatment.

A further part of the background to children's views is the special position of teachers in relation to children. In the children's eyes – and in reality – teachers have a great deal of power. They are score-keepers (and the score is often embarrassingly public). They are gatekeepers, controlling access to many of the good things one wants: knowledge, skills, good feelings about oneself, a reputation as competent, time 'outside'. Moreover, the relationship between children and their teacher is not like that between children and their parents. With parents, one may feel that there is an obligation to regard you as 'special' and to 'look after you all your life'. With parents, one may expect to be accepted, just 'because I'm me' or because 'I'm all they have'. Not so with teachers. Under these circumstances, a somewhat different set of expectations applies and a different bill of rights needs to be negotiated. As we shall see, one frequent reaction is to turn 'constitutional lawyer', proposing many a rule for fair and proper treatment.

Table 12.1 The main qualities mentioned by children from all grades in their definitions of a good teacher, parent and friend (shown as the percentage of all qualities mentioned)

	Teacher (%)	Parent (%)	Friend (%)
A caring attitude			
Loves, cares for, comforts you	14	27	23
Provides material things	—	6	—
Protects/looks after you	—	6	?
Does not hit/fight	4	4	4
Controls, but fairly	8	11	—
Total	26	54	27
Understanding and sharing			
Makes you feel special	5	8	22
Understands you	10	8	6
You understand them	8	2	6
Shares fun with you	6	3	19
Shares things with you	—	—	6
Total	29	21	59
Helping to open up the world			
Gives access to people and places	9	9	2
Teaches, explains, shows	28	4	1
Total	37	13	3

Note: We have omitted all qualities that account for 2 per cent or less of those mentioned.

Most of the material under discussion in this chapter comes from the question: 'What makes a good teacher?' Comments about teachers also appeared in answers to some other questions: 'If you could change one thing about school, what would you change?'; 'What do you like about school?'; 'Is there anything you don't like?' Among wishes for change, teachers are the subject of 9 per cent of the juniors' wishes (most wishes deal with activities: changes in what is learned and when). Teachers also appear briefly on the lists of what is liked about school (2 per cent and 3 per cent, respectively, of the juniors' and the seniors' remarks). However, they are more prominent on the lists of what is disliked (12 per cent of juniors' comments, 24 per cent of seniors'). Incidentally, the latter figures seem to suggest that children's feelings about teachers become increasingly negative as they proceed through school.

Suppose we ask first: *Are good teachers the same as good parents?* They are both adults, and perhaps children extend the same

Table 12.2 Changes by grade in the main qualities mentioned in definitions of a good teacher (shown as the percentage of all qualities mentioned)

	All grades	Grades 1 & 2	Grades 3 & 4	Grades 5 & 6
Loves, cares for, comforts you	14	17	19	11
Does not hit/fight	4	5	5	4
Controls, but fairly	8	4	7	9
Makes you feel special	5	5	4	6
Understands you	10	4	7	13
You understand them	8	10	8	8
Shares fun with you	6	5	5	7
Gives access to people and places	9	14	11	7
Teaches, explains, shows	28	28	31	27

expectations to one group as to the other. The answer to that question is: only partly. We have brought together in Table 12.1 the main features mentioned for good parents and good teachers (as well as good friends). [. . .] This table tells us that the main function of parents is to care for you, while the main function of teachers is to open up the world by teaching, explaining, showing you 'how'. The table tells us also that teachers are none the less not expected to be simply teaching machines. It is important to children that teachers care for them and understand them. The need for teachers to understand you (10 per cent of all comments on good teachers) is in fact higher than it is for parents (8 per cent). Teachers differ from parents, however, in the importance of your understanding them (8 per cent for teachers, 2 per cent for parents): a sign, perhaps, that children do not always regard teachers' behaviour as making sense.

Next we look at the question: *Do the children's opinions on the qualities of a good teacher change much from the early to the later grades?* That question is answered in Table 12.2.

Briefly the differences across grades are not striking. The children seem to have a fairly consistent picture of what the role of teacher should cover. At all grades, they agree that their primary task is to teach well. One difference that occurs is a decline in the importance of teachers looking after you, being comforting and sympathetic. This general need for caring drops from 17 per cent and 19 per cent among the younger children to 11 per cent among those in Grade 5 and 6, who presumably feel more able to stand on their own feet. The decline is offset by an increase over the grades in the importance given to the fair exercise of control and discipline (4 per cent, 7 per cent, 9 per cent) and to being understood (4 per cent, 7 per cent, 13 per cent). These are small differences, however. The most notable feature is the similarity of definition across grades. The children seem to come to school with expectations already in mind.

HOPES, EXPECTATIONS AND REALITY

We mentioned in the first section of the chapter three main hopes and expectations that children bring to their relationships with teachers.

We shall look at each of these expectations in turn, exploring the way children see them and give meaning to them.

The teacher will make learning possible

[. . .]

What exactly are teachers expected to do? Primarily they are expected to show you how or – to adopt a phrase used many times by children – to 'explain'. The flavour of the children's expectations is brought out for us by comments such as these, referring to 'good' and 'poor' methods:

If you don't understand something, she'll keep explaining it to you. She won't just say 'You haven't been listening'. She'll keep on explaining until you get it.

(Grade 6)

I'd like to have a teacher like we had last year . . . if you didn't understand something, she'd explain it very carefully.

(Grade 5)

I like how kind they are and how much they teach you, and it is really good when they go over it to make sure that we know it. And some teachers just put it on the board, like Mr N. in fourth grade.

(Grade 5)

She doesn't say 'Open the textbook to page 68' or something, and she doesn't read the book or something while you do it. She writes it up on the board and she goes round to people who don't understand.

(Grade 6)

They don't just say 'Right, it is on the board, and get it all right', and they make sure that everybody understands – and they help you if you don't.

(Grade 6)

So far we have talked about the expectation that learning will proceed in a successful fashion and that teachers will be able to 'explain' everything. Sooner or later, however, difficulties will be encountered. What is then likely to occur? One consequence is that children will simply cease to like school or to approve of teachers. Some children, however, look to themselves as the critical factor:

> I wish I could always be right at school.
>
> (Grade 2)
>
> I wish I was a good worker.
>
> (Grade 1)

More often, they look for causes in the teacher. The teacher has not explained things in the right way, or often enough. The teachers' views, of course, are likely to be in different terms and we shall have occasion to see that the children are well aware of these. We shall cite at this stage only one illustrative comment:

> When you stand up and ask questions, she says, 'You weren't listening; go back to your desk and figure it out'.
>
> (Grade 5)

The teacher will be human and friendly

The importance of this expectation is brought to light by the number of times that 'the good teacher' is defined in terms of feelings. Good teachers will understand you, be sympathetic, share a few jokes with you, make good sense to you.

What exactly do children expect? One component is patience and sympathy:

> They are good when they have time for you.
>
> (Grade 2)
>
> I like the way they are nice to you if you are hurt or anything and nobody will play with you.
>
> (Grade 4)
>
> I like a teacher that if somebody's crying, I reckon they should comfort you but they shouldn't butt in to other people's business.
>
> (Grade 5)
>
> I like a teacher that have feelings with their children. And sometimes, something's wrong, and wouldn't press on them if something's wrong because it will make them bad. Politeness, humour, understanding, and most inner feeling.
>
> (Grade 6)

There are other qualities which children appreciate:

> I like it when Ben H. makes fun of the teacher and the teacher smiles at him.
>
> (Grade 2)
>
> . . . gives a bit of a joke now and then.
>
> (Grade 6)
>
> Sometimes Mr K. is good because he is sort of funny. Like the other day. I am in our Christmas concert doing a tap dance and I was showing it to my friend, Elizabeth. And he comes over behind me and he sort of pulled faces and everything, and Elizabeth saw him and I didn't.
>
> (Grade 5)
>
> Good teachers, like Mr W. You can sit down and talk to him a lot. And sometimes he does things. Like yesterday afternoon, I was at the bus stop and he said 'Goodbye, Joanna'.
>
> (Grade 5)

Other comments show that children do not like being ignored or treated in a detached manner by their teacher:

> Like our teacher, outside he talks to the gardener, and like I said, he should stay with his class.
>
> (Grade 6)
>
> If you're playing outside in the garden, they should join in with you.
>
> (Grade 4)

Once again, these expectations are not always met. The children encounter teachers who are 'kind' and teachers who are 'crabby', who 'yell' or 'scream', 'get bad moods real quickly', 'throw chalk', 'hit' and 'act like policemen'. They also, inevitably, encounter penalties. They will not themselves always be 'good' and their departures from perfection will draw some kind of controlling reaction from teachers: from 'quiet talks' and writing lines to 'being told off', kept in, sent to the principal's office, or caned.

What is likely to occur under these circumstances? One consequence is that children come to like some teachers rather than others, and to judge some as better than others. Once again, they look for explanations. In addition, they show a strong interest in working out the rules and working out what is fair. The mental work is particularly pronounced when they need to reconcile the expectation that the teacher will be in charge ('They should be strict', 'They should not let kids do just anything') with the expectation that they will also be human and friendly. We shall soon be looking at this dilemma in more detail, concentrating on the rules children propose for how penalties should be administered. A few comments will give a brief foretaste of the children's proposals:

> A strict teacher makes a good one because then they can control the students, and they should have a good sense of humour with the kids and have fun with them.
>
> (Grade 6)
>
> Good teachers don't throw fits and chuck mentals and things.
>
> (Grade 5)
>
> A good teacher . . . If they are mad about something, they shouldn't take it out on you.
>
> (Grade 6)
>
> If one person is stupid, they shouldn't keep the whole class in.
>
> (Grade 5)

You will be an accepted member of the class

School, office, factory: these settings involve larger groups than encountered in the home. They present the individual with the possibility of not being known, even by name. To have someone say 'Goodbye, Joanna' is a sign that one is known. One may, especially at first in a large group, feel faceless, lost in the crowd. Small wonder that children sometimes have the types of feelings expressed by one fourth-grader:

> I wish I was the only person in the playground, and that the teachers thought I was the greatest person in the world.

Children may also wish that – if they cannot be special – at least their individual needs will be known:

> A good teacher is an understanding teacher, so she understands all your problems: why can't you do this, and can't do that.
>
> (Grade 4)
>
> A good teacher will not press on you when she knows you're having troubles at home.
>
> (Grade 6)

The reality is that teachers often do not know their children as individuals. Reasonable or not, the fact is that although teachers and pupils spend long days together, each child has to share a teacher's time, attention, affection, warmth and respect. You cannot be the only one in a class. Sharing must take place.

What is likely to occur under such circumstances? As with siblings –
but perhaps even more so – the children argue that if all cannot be
'special' then none should be. Everyone must be given 'fair' treatment.
In the forceful words of a sixth-grader:

> . . . a teacher should not show her likes and dislikes and press all
> her hate on one and shove them off where they can't see the board
> properly, and put her little pets in the front where they can see
> everything and give them all the nice jobs. A teacher should be able
> to give everybody a chance to try out their best and not to say which
> one looks the best.

Several fifth-graders echo the same theme:

> I don't like the teacher because when she gets stamps, she always
> gives it to the same person every time, and it's not fair.
> [Some teachers] tend to pick on people and they usually have one or
> two pets that they give things to and do things with more than the
> other kids.
> I wish we had more teachers that were fair to you, and to everyone
> else.

WORKING THINGS OUT: EXPLANATIONS FOR CLASSROOM EVENTS

How do people come to terms with hopes and expectations that are
not met? In all areas of daily life, one way of working things out is to
find causes: reasons for one's successes and problems, health or illness,
happy or unhappy interactions with others. In psychologists' terms, we
make attributions about behaviour or events.

What are the events or behaviour patterns that children work at
finding explanations for? Two stand out: situations where the children
are having trouble learning, and times when the teachers are angry,
'grumpy', 'moody' or 'unfriendly'.

Explanations for learning problems

The children's most frequent explanation is in terms of the teachers.
They 'don't explain'. They don't 'explain it properly', 'explain it so you
can do it', or 'explain it enough times'.

Why do teachers not explain'? Sometimes the children are aware
that their teachers place the blame on them:

He puts a new fraction on the board and we don't know how to do it. And when we put up our hand to ask, he says 'You should know that by now'.

(Grade 5)

I don't like Mr . . . He tells you 'Fold your arms' and when you're folding your arms, he says I'm dreaming, and I'm not dreaming. Well, maths I don't really like and he gives you hard divide.

(Grade 5)

Most times if you put up your hand to ask something – if you get stuck on a sum or something – when he says 'Yes', he ends up blowing you up and say 'You don't listen'.

(Grade 5)

And there's another thing I don't like about him. He said that if you ever want help, well you should put up your hand and ask the teacher. And one day I put up my hand and asked the teacher and he just said, 'Oh you never listen, do you'.

(Grade 5)

I wish that teachers wouldn't get quite so angry, and would help you out with your problems and not say 'Go back and use your brain'.

(Grade 4)

An occasional child accepts the teachers' refusal to explain – at least for a second time – and sees the refusal as for the child's own good:

A good teacher gets cranky if you keep getting it wrong, because she doesn't like to see you get it wrong. She likes to see you be able to do it, and be able to do it for high school, so that – you know – you are not just sitting around saying 'I can't do it, will you please help me?'

(Grade 5)

A kindly explanation is also offered by an interviewer at the end of a string of complaints, but not accepted by the children. The fourth fifth-grader in a row complains about teachers 'not showing you how':

I reckon they have to explain more things to you. And these days all the teachers hardly explain all the things to you.
Do you think they don't have enough time?
No, they've got time.

Most of the children are really indignant at the suggestion that they 'don't listen', 'dream', 'don't use their brains', or 'aren't trying'. They cling firmly to the belief that 'explaining' is the teacher's job:

I like the teachers if they understand. Like if maybe you can't do something and they will explain how to do it, and if you can't get it they don't go mad at you. 'Cause it is their fault really, 'cause they don't explain it properly.

(Grade 5)

What explanations are left then, for the teachers not explaining properly? A few children in the upper grades define a good teacher as someone who is 'brainy' and 'knows what they're talking about', implying that some teachers may explain poorly because of lack of ability. This type of explanation, however, is rare. These primary school children accept that teachers have the knowledge. The problem is that for some mysterious reason teachers 'won't explain'. In the words of a fifth-grader:

> I hate maths, because our teacher doesn't explain it to you. She says, 'Just try it'. And you just can't do it because you just don't know how to do it, and you just don't understand it. And the teachers *won't explain* it to you. And even when they do explain it, you get more confused.

All told, the children are describing a tug-of-war between teachers and children for the explanation of any difficulties in learning. Each side appears to choose the explanation that puts it in the best light, probably having more understanding of the other's position than is willingly admitted. What is maintained, on the one hand, is the right to have something explained one more time, and – on the other – the right to be listened to when one does explain.

Within the tug-of-war, there appears also to be a difference in the use of words. The children use the term 'explain' or 'explained properly' until they have understood it. Given this use of the word, it makes little sense for the teacher to say 'I have explained it', meaning 'to my satisfaction'. We suspect that not only children use words with such different shades of meaning. 'Why didn't you tell me?' 'I've told you several times'. That is a familiar exchange at many ages.

Explanations for teachers' negative behaviour

Teachers clearly are not always friendly. Even allowing for some exaggeration in the children's phrasing, teachers are often perceived as 'angry'. In the children's words, they 'yell', 'scream', 'throw fits', 'chuck mentals', 'blow you up', 'do their blocks', 'do their nanas', 'throw chalk', 'hit you', 'bash you'.

What are children to make of such behaviour? Part of working things out consists of drawing a distinction between angry behaviour when they have misbehaved (when they have done something 'really wrong'), and angry behaviour when they have simply not understood something. It is the second type of anger that the children find puzzling and object to.

Anger when you 'don't know something' or 'haven't understood' is a major issue. Again and again, one hears comments on this puzzling aspect of teachers:

> A good teacher . . . she likes to be around children. And she tries to understand what the children . . . Like when Adam did a '4' and did a back to front '4', she wouldn't scream.
>
> (Grade 3)
>
> I wish the teachers would help us when we get something wrong instead of scolding us.
>
> (Grade 4)
>
> I like a teacher who isn't cross when she doesn't understand you.
>
> (Grade 5)
>
> I don't like it when you don't understand something and they explain it to you, but you still don't understand it, and then they get really angry.
>
> (Grade 6)
>
> I wish the teachers wouldn't get quite so angry and would help you with your problems and not say 'Go back and use your brains'.
>
> (Grade 4)
>
> I like it when they don't yell at you all the time. They do things calmly and go through them slowly and if you don't know it, or couldn't hear properly, they don't blow your head off.
>
> (Grade 6)
>
> I like when teachers don't shout at you, and if you get a project and you get a bad mark they don't say 'Get out of here' or something like that. They say 'Try next time'.
>
> (Grade 6)

How do children account for such behaviour? Some of the accounts – as they were for teachers not 'explaining' – are in terms of it being for the children's own good:

> If you be naughty and the teacher has to growl at you, he doesn't want to, but he has to because he wants you to learn.
>
> (Grade 2)
>
> I reckon that it is good in a way that she gets cranky because you try harder to get it right.
>
> (Grade 5)

You might be cranky about something and the teacher yells and you might not want to do any more work and the teacher yells at you and you go back to doing your work.

(Grade 5)

If we didn't get told off, we'd probably be like those guys that go around who haven't learned anything. They kill people and things like that.

(Grade 6)

An occasional child sees the problem as lying in the children. In the words of a fourth-grader:

They are good when they have good students to make them happy.

Most of the explanations, however, have to do with the nature of teachers. The fault may lie in their dispositions, experiences or age:

They have no patience.

(Grade 4)

. . . has some children of her own so that they know how to teach them, and so they can teach us.

(Grade 5)

A good teacher is someone who is pretty young so they can remember what they went through at school. So they know how the kid feels.

(Grade 6)

It is only the seniors who expressed the notion that it is not part of human nature or daily life to be forever friendly and courteous. These kind of comments, like those that see angry behaviour as for the children's good, are again referring only to being 'told off' in words:

It is just that people are bossy sometimes, and sometimes something must be wrong with them, and they don't know they are really rousing on you, and they are pretending sometimes.

(Grade 5)

Sometimes they've had a bad night and are feeling crabby.

(Grade 6)

When you come to school, you're with friends most of the day. And teachers do get a bit bossy sometimes. But you have to give them sometimes to be in a bad mood.

(Grade 6)

Such tolerant ways of working things out are not offered for stronger forms of anger on the part of the teachers – which are not frequent.

Most of the children see teachers' anger as a teacher's problem, and account for it on the grounds that they are not 'good' teachers.

WORKING THINGS OUT: RULES FOR TEACHING

[...]

Proposals for reform or improvement are prominent in comments on teachers. More so than for parents, children sprinkle their comments on teachers with references to 'should' and 'ought'. These references are especially frequent in discussions of how teachers should teach, and how they should control a class or respond to misdeeds.

We have brought the many comments together in the form of 'rules' proposed by children. These rules serve several functions. They make it possible to judge teachers, sorting them into the 'good', the 'not so good', and the 'awful'. They also make possible conversations among children: conversations based on agreement or disagreement among themselves, adding to the store of gossip and information about the teachers' good and bad points, their foibles and their moods. Children clearly spend a great deal of time commenting on teachers and comparing them with one another. Finally, the 'rules' appear to serve as a basis for negotiations with teachers. To the extent that teachers and children agree on the rules that teachers should follow, children can argue that certain ways of proceeding are not 'fair' and may succeed in having a task or a penalty changed. They may also, it has been proposed, feel justified in being 'unruly' or 'disorderly' when they feel teachers are refusing to negotiate or to follow 'reasonable' unwritten rules.

In this section we shall consider the rules children propose for teachers assigning tasks. Overall, the children's comments amount to proposing that teachers should follow six rules. We might easily extend the same set to any work setting: home, office or factory.

They should make the work possible.

In the children's comments this appears particularly in the form of saying that teachers, when they set work, should also show you how to do it. They should, to repeat that much-used word, 'explain' it. In essence:

She tells you, makes you understand, doesn't just say 'Hey, do it'.
(Grade 5)

They should allow a reasonable amount of time for the job.

Three comments will serve as an example:

They should give you enough time. You really can't keep up at anything.

(Grade 3)

I like teachers that help you a lot and they give you time to finish your work. They don't kind of rush it and say 'Do this' and then you're on to the next thing. If they teach us like that, everyone will get their work done.

(Grade 3)

They give you one work and they give you so much time to do it and take out another book and you feel worried that you won't get it done.

(Grade 5)

They should pay some attention to your state and to the time of day.

Good teachers give you breaks when you are tired. They also do not give you the hardest job when you are least fresh.

Good teachers give you a break in your work and let your arms rest.

(Grade 6)

You come in after big lunch and you're really hot and sweaty and the teacher comes in and says 'Get out your social studies'. And she writes all that writing on the board and you don't want to do it, and if you don't do it you get into trouble, and you get very tired.

(Grade 4)

They should keep work within school hours.

This rule emerged in discussions about homework and about work taking over times considered as times for rest, play, sport or talk.

I don't like teachers who make you do things after the hooter has gone and you are supposed to be on free time.

(Grade 6)

And some teachers give you a lot of work, especially homework when that's the time for rest from school.

(Grade 6)

They should allow some choice and variety

This rule is prominent in comments on work that is 'boring' and in the wishes for activities and topics that are of the children's choice:

Why can't there be some time when we do what we want to do?

(Grade 6)

They should let us decide sometimes.

(Grade 5)

I wish teachers would let us set some of our own work.
I wish teachers would trust us.

(Grade 6)

They should keep track of work that is done, and recognize good work.

In the words of an aggrieved fifth-grader:

I hate it when you're told to do something and you've already done it. And then you get into trouble for not doing it and you get into trouble for not doing anything.

Keeping track also means keeping track for the class, in the form of not setting tests on work not covered (a grievance expressed strongly, but by only a few children).

Recognition of good work is a subtle issue. One suspects it is always an implicit rule, but the explicit references to it are mainly from juniors, perhaps because seniors have learned that an open interest in praise or reward is not acceptable behaviour. In the juniors' comments, teachers are 'good' when:

You do maths right and they tell you you're good.

(Grade 2)

You do good work sometimes and they give you stickers.

(Grade 3)

When this theme is mentioned by seniors, the phrasing is somewhat more subtle:

A good teacher should praise you when you are trying.

(Grade 5)

They should let the people go that are being good. Like Mr O., our new teacher. I cleaned up my desk and I was the first one standing and he let me go.

(Grade 5)

WORKING THINGS OUT: RULES FOR CONTROL AND DISCIPLINE

It is in this area that proposals for how things should be done are especially marked. The children's comments bring out three points. First, they see some form of control as necessary. Second, they seek some form of balance between control and harshness: 'strict but not too strict', 'soft but not too soft'. Third, they have in mind a specific set of rules that define proper forms of control. Let us take these points in order, giving most space to the rules themselves.

Children expect teachers to set limits on some activities, to establish rules, and to maintain a climate in which the activities of the day can proceed fairly efficiently and amicably. They may complain about 'too many rules' but they do not expect teachers to abdicate control. A teacher who is too 'soft' is not regarded with favour. 'If she was soft, you wouldn't learn anything', says a fifth-grader. 'A bad teacher will let you do anything', says another. Nor should a teacher yield too easily to the children's pressure. As some fourth-graders put it:

> I think that a teacher is maybe sometimes too soft on you so that you might want her to let you off and not do your work, and she gets upset at you because you have to learn, and people might think she is a nice teacher when she is just soft.
> A good teacher should not let you get away with things.

Further, a good teacher should not appear to plead ineffectively. In a sixth-grader's cutting description:

> If we talk, then she comes out and says: 'Now you must learn, children. You must be good and responsible – and don't talk. And your manners must be nice'. And we're getting sick of it and everything, and the boys, they get restless, and they get in more trouble, and they pretend they can't hear her.

The children argue for a balance, for a mixture of properties that may seem originally incompatible. 'Strict but not all that strict', 'stern but kind', 'reasonably strict but lets you have fun as well', 'strict but not too strict and she should be fair': these are phrases expressing the need for mixed qualities. 'Close but not buddy-buddy', 'soft and hard', are others. The search for the right mixture can tie one in verbal knots. Witness a fourth-grader:

I reckon half and half of everything. He should be strict sometimes but then again he should be a little bit not strict.

To help clarify what is meant by such statements we will look at some of the children's opinions on the types of rules good teachers should follow.

They should not punish the whole group

For example:

Some teachers . . . one person is stupid so they keep the whole class in as well.

(Grade 5)

If one person mucks up, he gets cranky at the whole class and then he sets us lots of homework.

(Grade 6)

Like someone talks when he wants silence, or while he is working out his estimates or something. And he punishes the whole class. And sometimes he knows who the person is who was talking but yet he punishes the whole class.

(Grade 6)

Such comments suggest that group punishment has some legal sub-clauses. It seems to become worse if most (or all but one) of the class is innocent and if the real culprit is known or suspected (that is the teacher does not make the effort to identify the one for the benefit of the rest). Interesting also is the scarcity of comment on group punishment being avoided by the children naming the guilty party. In all the comments on group penalties, we encountered only one suggestion of pressure on a child to 'admit it' so that a class would not be denied an excursion. Honour at this level seems to require suffering in silence, and one wonders when this type of unspoken rule might ever be broken.

They should not punish the wrong person

For example:

Well, some things I don't like about school is that if your friend starts talking to you, well the teacher says, 'Hey, were you talking?' and you get sent out and that's the part that's not really fair.

(Grade 6)

The innocent party, however, need not be oneself:

> Like Barry C. Sometimes some boys push him over and he gets into trouble instead of the other boys. They rumble him in the classroom and sometimes the teacher stands him in the corner instead of the other boys.
>
> (Grade 5)
>
> There is this boy and often he gets into trouble, but even when he doesn't, Mr W. jumps on him.

Punishing the wrong person meets special disapproval if the teacher is perceived as taking little effort to locate the culprit:

> When Mr C. is out in his storeroom, a lot of people talk. And he comes in. The first person he sees, he picks on.
>
> (Grade 5)
>
> I think teachers should have the right to belt people. But if he doesn't really have any proof of them doing the wrong thing, I think he usually blames it on the same person that did it before.
>
> (Grade 3)
>
> They're good when they don't jump to conclusions.
>
> (Grade 6)
>
> I think a good teacher should be able to understand and look into a person's point of view. Like some teachers just look at them and think that just because they've got a bad reputation, they've done something wrong. But they should look into their point of view and see what the person's thinking to see if she's guilty or not.
>
> (Grade 6)

They should give equal punishment for equal wrongs

This idea is expressed in remarks such as these:

> A guy in our class, he gets into trouble. But he *really* gets into trouble. The other boy, he does things just as bad but he doesn't. Our teacher doesn't really do much about it.
>
> (Grade 5)

They should not shame people

The sharpest comment comes from a group of fifth-graders discussing what they dislike about teachers (a long and lively discussion). The remark is in terms that seem to reflect first-hand experience:

I don't like when the teacher gives you a smack. And when you can't answer a question, they make you stand up and say it. Like Mr W., he makes you stand up and say 'I am a fool' five times.

(Grade 5)

Physical punishment also elicits concern about shaming. It is not only that children object to certain penalties when they are themselves the target. They also object to the public nature of the penalty, both when they are the watchers and the one being watched:

I don't like to see people getting into trouble.

(Grade 3)

I don't like seeing people get the strap.

(Grade 6)

I don't like it when the teacher gives you the ruler and all the kids are watching and you're not thinking of anything except that it hurts a lot.

(Grade 6)

They should not use physical punishment

This comment appears at many grade levels:

I wish people wouldn't get the cuts.

(Grade 3)

I don't like it when my friends get the strap or get into trouble.

(Grade 4)

I don't like getting smacked.

(Grade 3)

. . . getting into trouble and getting the strap.

(Grade 3)

When they punish you, it shouldn't be physical hurt. It should be something like staying after school.

(Grade 6)

They've even got a strap which is a piece of leather and it hurts you on your hand and it goes numb.

(Grade 6)

I'd rather get detention after school, then you don't cry.

(Grade 6)

When Mr J. gets angry, I think he's going to give me the cane, and you get all upset about it. Sometimes you get really angry and in a fighting mood.

(Grade 5)

As a disliked feature of school, physical punishment is singled out for specific mention by 3 per cent of juniors and 7 per cent of seniors, a fairly high rating when one considers the large number of possible topics that can be mentioned. But opinions can vary a little on physical punishment. An example is a group of sixth-graders in a coeducational school discussing the features of a 'good' teacher. They offered proposals for several kinds of penalty: picking up papers, doing extra work, or getting the cane. The last of these divided the group. 'Fair if you do something real bad', said one. 'Only for a big reason, not a little one', said another. 'Ineffective', said a third: 'Sometimes a person gets it too often and they get used to it and it doesn't hurt them' (an interesting argument in terms of effect rather than justice). A different note was sounded by one sixth-grader who disliked 'the way people get the cane' and added that 'they shouldn't be getting the cane because they [teachers] aren't responsible for the children, the parents are'. Overall, the comments on physical punishment are disapproving, and often heart-wrenching. One empathizes with the last child quoted. By what right do teachers act in this way?

Proposals for fair penalties

All forms of penalty attract some negative comments. Being caned or hit hurts physically. Being yelled at makes you upset. Being kept in means that you lose free time. Being sent out makes you 'feel lonely'. What do the children suggest? A number approve of being *'talked to quietly'*. Several point to the importance of being given *warnings* and *progressive penalties*, but not empty threats. Others point to the value of *individualizing* penalties:

Sometimes she doesn't smack you, and gives you a quiet talk if you've done something wrong.

(Grade 2)

She keeps you in at lunch and talks to you for a long minute.

(Grade 3)

A good teacher gives you a warning before you get in trouble.

(Grade 5)

Mr F. is good in a way because he gives you about five warnings, and he writes in his diary. As soon as you do anything, he doesn't go off his block.

(Grade 5)

I reckon the first time you should get told off, and if you do it again, you should maybe get 100 lines.

(Grade 5)

A good teacher is usually . . . You do it once and they say 'Don't do it again 'cause I will give you an imposition'. So you do it again and they give you another imposition of a hundred words. And do it again and she will double it and keep on doubling it until it gets to about 2,000 words. And then if you do it again, she won't double it. She will say, 'Come to the office', and get the stick. And then you deserve it anyway.

(Grade 5)

I think teachers, when they make a threat, they should carry it out. Don't just say it. Because this boy in our class, he's always getting warnings, but the warnings are never carried out on him.

(Grade 5)

Something you like to do – if you are naughty, he doesn't let you do it.

(Grade 2)

Not the cane. Some people prefer to go on excursions. And if they really like to go on excursions and they don't go: that's a really bad punishment for them.

(Grade 5)

Some children seemed to be proposing that the punishment should fit the crime:

I like the teacher if she doesn't throw a fit at you if you accidentally do something.

(Grade 5)

I don't like getting into trouble for nothing.

(Grade 3)

I think teachers should be considerate. I mean sort of not like our second class teacher . . . She kept slapping people on the bottom and things like that, and I don't think people should do that unless it's necessary.

(Grade 5)

We might say that the children are arguing for the need to temper power with justice, and justice with compassion and perhaps even a little humour.

Last year we had a teacher and he was really good. He understood us and he used to sort of play games with us. Like if someone was naughty he used to make us bend over and he used to pretend to smack us but he didn't. But we used to have talking time and we used to talk about things and that's what I think makes a good teacher.

(Grade 5)

A good teacher is someone who is pretty young so they know how the kid feels and to show power when it's needed, not when it's not.

(Grade 6)

[. . .]

Teachers should themselves obey the rules

In their close attention to the 'fairness' of teachers, children are quick to spot and to pass judgment on teachers who do not themselves observe the rules. These comments come from all grade levels:

They don't let us eat in class. They say 'You're gonna drop crumbs on the floor' and *they* eat in class.

(Grade 6)

I wish we could have a kind teacher who doesn't smoke in class and chew chewing gum in front of the class.

(Grade 5)

She smells. She's always smoking.

(Grade 2)

Smoking – it is a health hazard and could learn bad habits to the pupils.

(Grade 5)

They don't use their manners enough. Like if you were to go and get him something from the office like a glass of water, which he is really fussy about it. He can't go and get it himself so he has to get Tracey. And he says, 'Tracey, go and get me a glass of water'. And he doesn't say 'please' or anything, and when she comes back he doesn't say 'thank you' or anything.

(Grade 5)

In the children's eyes, 'do as I say', if not accompanied by 'do as I do', does not make a good teacher.

[. . .]

13 Playground games and playtime: the children's view

Peter Blatchford, Rosemary Creeser and Ann Mooney

Source: *Educational Research* (1990) 32(3).

[. . .]

INTRODUCTION

There are a number of reasons why playtime is an important but neglected aspect of education. One is that it takes up a significant part of the school day. In a longitudinal study of children's progress in London primary schools, based at Thomas Coram Research Unit (TCRU), observations of 7-year-old children showed that playtime and dinner took up 28 per cent of the school day, which was exactly as much time as was spent in the combined areas of reading, writing and maths (Tizard *et al.* 1988).

Events that take place at playtime can also create problems in school. In an earlier study of teachers' views on playtime (Blatchford 1989) it was found that time in classrooms could be spent by teachers sorting out problems that had arisen at playtime, particularly during the long dinner break. Teachers felt that the quality of relationships within the school could be undermined because of violence and conflicts between children at playtime.

A concern with disruptive behaviour within schools has recently taken on a new urgency and led to the setting up and reporting of the Elton Committee on discipline in schools (DES 1989). But it is often overlooked that unacceptable behaviour on school premises often takes place not within the school building itself, but in playgrounds. Indeed one main impetus behind the concern with school behaviour – the murder of the British Asian boy in a Manchester High School – took place in the playground, where adult presence and supervision were relatively thin. The same is true of bullying, about which there has also been growing concern recently (e.g. Tattum and Lane 1989);

by its nature, bullying tends to take place away from adults, and often in the playground (Stephenson and Smith 1989).

Playtime is also an important part of the school day for children. In the TCRU longitudinal study, children were interviewed individually when aged 7 years. Although they seemed to like playtime, two-thirds of the children were worried about teasing and name-calling and two-thirds of the children said they got into fights (Tizard *et al.* 1988). On a more positive note, Sluckin (1981) has argued that peer relationships in the school playground have an important role in the development of adult social skills, like knowing how far to go, and taking on roles. Gudgeon (1988) has argued that playground games are a powerful mechanism for the transmission of the social order and cultural information, particularly about gender.

Considering its likely significance for children, though, there is very little evidence on their views about playtime and on what takes place then. This is a significant omission when one considers that in a very real sense, children are the experts on what happens in the playground, and often the only witnesses.

It is widely believed by teachers that the quality of children's outside play is declining. There is a perception of increased aggression and desultory behaviour (Blatchford 1989). Certain groups of children, particularly girls, are seen to get a bad deal, losing out on space and equipment if any is available. In particular, traditional children's games of the kind described by the Opies (1969) and Gomme (1984), and experienced by older teachers in their own childhood, are seen to be in steep decline.

The school playground is one of the main settings for outside play, which is completely free from adult control. As play spaces of the kind described by the Opies (1969) are lost to development, and as parents become increasingly (and understandably) concerned about letting children play unsupervised in streets and parks, it may be that the school playground is one of the few places where children *do* play outside the home. It has increased importance, therefore, as a setting for children's games, and also for their study and documentation.

In earlier work at TCRU on playtime, the focus was on teachers' views on problems that arise at playtime, and ways that playtime could be improved (Blatchford 1989). A number of suggestions for improvement were put forward, including ways of dealing with unacceptable behaviour in the playground, ways of improving supervision during the long lunch break, and ways of improving the playground itself.

But there is a problem of evidence here. Teachers are often the first to admit that they can have only a limited idea of what takes place in the playground. If on duty they are often occupied with moment-to-moment concerns of supervision; if not on duty they are likely to be in the staffroom.

What then are the children's views on playtime? There are a number of questions to which we need to know their answers. Do they like playtime? If so, why? If they do not like playtime, why is that? More specifically how do they find the short mid-morning and mid-afternoon breaks, and the long dinner playtime? In what ways can playtime be improved? In particular, what do they say they do in the playground? What games do they play? What do they do in the playground when not playing? And are there differences between children in their perspectives, for example between girls and boys, and children from different ethnic groups?

It is important to ask children these questions, for two reasons. First, [. . .] they have a uniquely informed view of what goes on, and their 'evidence' is therefore crucial. Second, any improvements, to be effective, will have to take on board their views.

An opportunity to find answers to these questions came in the follow-up of the original TCRU longitudinal sample of children, when they were contacted again at 11 years, in their last year of junior school. When aged 7 the children were interviewed about a number of topics, including the playground (see Tizard *et al.* 1988). It was now possible to interview them again, four years on, and this time to extend questions on the playground and playtime.

These questions were designed to obtain their views on five areas:
1 The mid-morning, mid-afternoon, and dinner playtimes.
2 Staying in and going out.
3 Why they liked and disliked playtime.
4 How playtime could be improved.
5 What games they played and what else they did in the playground.

METHOD

Sample

The sample consisted of children who entered reception classes in September 1982 of thirty-three infant schools within the Inner London Education Authority (ILEA). These schools came from six divisions within the authority and in keeping with the aims of the study were in multi-racial areas. The majority of the schools were in working-class areas, and on most indices of disadvantage (for example proportion of children receiving free school meals, fathers in semi-skilled and unskilled occupations or unemployed) they were below the mean for the ILEA as a whole.

Each school, to be included, had to have two children entering whose parents were of Afro-Caribbean origin, and two whose parents were white indigenous. For the purpose of this paper these two groups will be called the 'black' and 'white' groups. Numbers of children in other ethnic groups were small. The bulk of the children in the study were from these two groups. Interviews were conducted only with children from these two groups. Children interviewed at 7 years (N = 133) and still in the study schools were re-interviewed, with the addition – to increase the sample size – of all black boys and girls who started school at the same time but who were not previously interviewed. In addition, to make sample sizes of the four groups more equal, in those schools with white children not previously interviewed, one white boy and one white girl, chosen at random, were added to the sample. Children who were interviewed at 7 but who had moved to other schools within the ILEA area were also re-interviewed.

A total of 175 children were interviewed at 11 years, made up of 41 black girls, 46 white girls, 38 black boys and 50 white boys. The children were interviewed by one of the three authors. Full details of the sample selection, and background to, and results from, the infant school stage of the research project can be found in Blatchford *et al.* (1985) and Tizard *et al.* (1988).

Interviews

Children were interviewed individually in their schools by a research officer. The interview had questions on four areas: playtime and playgrounds, teasing and fighting, attitudes to work and school, and out of school activities. Results for the last three areas are being written up separately.

Like the 7-year-old interviews (see Tizard *et al.* 1988), there was a mixture of closed and open-ended questions. The form taken by questions will be described below, as results are presented. The interviews took about 45 minutes per child on average.

RESULTS

Dinner, morning and afternoon playtime

How do you feel about dinner time playtime?

In order to find out how children felt about dinner playtime they were shown the same set of five faces they saw when aged 7. The face on the

Table 13.1 Views on dinner playtime (%)

	1 Love it	2 Like it	3 Neutral	4 Don't like it	5 Hate it
All (N = 174)	58	26	9	4	2
Boys	67	28	3	0	0
Girls	49	24	14	8	5

left of the page had a big smile and bubble over it with the words 'Great, I love it'. The next face had a less pronounced smile and the words 'OK. I quite like it' above it. The middle face had a straight line for a mouth and the words 'I don't feel one way or the other'. The fourth face had an upturned version of the mouth of the second face and the words 'I don't like it very much'. And the last face had an upturned version of the first mouth, i.e. a hugely unhappy face, with the words 'Ugh, I hate it' above it. The first two faces therefore expressed degrees of liking, the fourth and fifth faces degrees of disliking, and the middle face neither liking nor disliking.

As can be seen in Table 13.1, children were very positive about their feelings for the long dinner playtime: 84 per cent of children liked dinner playtime and 58 per cent of these said they loved it. Boys were most positive: 95 per cent *v.* 73 per cent for boys and girls respectively for 'love it' and 'like it' faces together (x 19.6, $p < 0.001$). Only 6 per cent of the children said they did not like dinner playtime: these were all girls (see Table 13.1).

How do you feel about morning play?

Again views were mostly positive, though less marked than for dinner playtime; 72 per cent said they liked or loved it, 15 per cent said they did not (i.e. chose the last two faces). There was no overall difference between boys and girls.

How do you feel about afternoon playtime?

A quarter of the children were in schools that did not have an afternoon break. Of the rest, 55 per cent liked or loved it and 9 per cent

Table 13.2 Views about staying in or going out at playtime (%)

	All (N = 174)	Boys	Girls
I really look forward to going out	32	41	23
I look forward to going out	38	44	33
I would prefer to stay in and get on with work	31	18	43
I would prefer to stay in and do something else	17	14	20

did not like it. Girls liked the afternoon break more than boys did (x 12.68, $p < 0.05$).

Views about staying in or going out at playtime

Despite a generally positive view about playtime we wanted to find out more directly whether children wanted to go out or would prefer to stay in. The children were shown and read four sentences and asked to say which sounded 'most like them'. The sentences are shown in Table 13.2. Children could choose more than one answer if they wanted to, though few did. Although many looked forward to going out (a total of 70 per cent of answers for the two 'look forward to going out' statements), 48 per cent of answers expressed a desire to stay in, either to work or do something else. So just under half of the 175 children would like the option of staying in, at least for some of the playtime. (Because of the possibility of double coding, numbers of children may be slightly – but not much – fewer than numbers of answers.)

There was a clear sex difference (see Table 13.2). Girls were much more likely to want to stay in; boys were more likely to look forward to going out. It is girls, therefore, who would particularly like the option of staying in.

Why children liked and disliked playtime

What do you like best about playtime?

Children were probed with 'Anything else?' in order to get three different answers to this question. What they liked best about playtime was that it was a break or rest from work, when they could have fun or relax (41 per cent of children). A third (33 per cent) of the children liked being able to play games, perhaps mentioning the particular game they liked playing. About the same number (32 per cent) liked being with and talking to friends, perhaps not in the same class. This was mentioned more often by girls than boys (43 per cent *v.* 20 per cent). A quarter of the children liked the idea of getting out into the fresh air; 16 per cent liked playing football (boys more than girls – 25 per cent *v.* 7 per cent); and 15 per cent mentioned exercise and running around. Eight children specifically said they liked getting a break from their teachers, for example from being told off. Three children liked talking to staff on duty.

What don't you like about playtime?

Children expressed a wider range of things that they did not like about playtime. There were twenty different categories used in coding the answers to this question. None was mentioned by more than a quarter of the children. The most frequent complaint was about the weather (26 per cent), usually the cold or wet, but also being too hot. This was much more likely to be expressed by girls than boys (41 per cent *v.* 11 per cent).

Slightly fewer children (21 per cent) were worried by disruptive behaviour, such as bullying, being 'beaten up', fights and people starting trouble. This did not seem to bother black girls (only 10 per cent mentioned it).

Fifteen per cent of children disliked playtime because they said they had nothing to do or no one to play with. This bothered girls (21 per cent) and in particular white girls (24 per cent) more than boys (10 per cent).

Twelve per cent of children said they did not like playtime because of frustrations that arose out of specific games or activities, for example trying to play football in a confined space, being knocked over when running, getting footballs in the face, losing balls over fences or when children messed about or cheated during games.

Other worries were never mentioned by more than 10 per cent of the children. They included getting hurt (4 per cent), being disciplined (8 per cent), restrictions, like not being allowed to play certain games, or not being allowed on the grass (5 per cent), and there being too many people in the playground or not enough space (3 per cent). Four children (2 per cent) said they did not like playtime because it interrupted their work.

Seventeen per cent of the children said there was nothing they disliked about playtime.

How children thought playtime could be improved

Again there was a wide range of answers to this question. The most frequently suggested improvement (35 per cent) was for permanent equipment to be installed, for example, a swing, an adventure playground, scramble nets and climbing frames. Another 18 per cent would have liked to take out portable equipment, e.g. bats and balls.

A quarter of the children identified a change of use of playground space, e.g. separate playgrounds for boys and girls, young and old, or for infants and juniors, or separate areas for football, for races or for skateboarding. One in ten wanted alterations to the playground surface, for example more or better game markings, e.g. hopscotch and stepping patterns, or proper games pitches. The same number wanted to see 'green' additions, such as gardens, wild life areas and the planting of flowers. Even more fundamentally, ten children wanted to see major structural changes such as the building of shelters and additional walls, taking down unwanted fences, and having toilets inside.

Thirteen per cent wanted to see more control of bad behaviour, for example by suspending bullies, not allowing people to play in toilets, stopping fighting, banning ex-pupils from school premises and stopping rudeness to adults. Seven children (4 per cent) wanted to see more staff on duty to deal with problems and three children wanted to see better supervision, for example not being bossed around, and teachers taking more notice. Eleven children (7 per cent) wanted to see certain activities or games changed or introduced, for example girls being allowed to play football, and big children playing games with small children.

There was not a general desire to reduce the amount of football, though, either amongst girls or boys. Only two children (both girls) said football should be banned.

Conversely 12 per cent wanted more freedom of behaviour to be allowed, e.g. listening to personal hi-fi, taking out sweets, bringing in skateboards and toys, and allowing banned games. Another eleven children (7 per cent) wanted to have a shop, or drink dispenser outside.

Activities at playtime

What games do you play in the playground?

The children were asked to name three games that they played in the playground. When the game was not known to the interviewer the child was asked to describe how it was played. The games were then classified under twenty-four different headings. This was not always easy because children's descriptions were not always complete or clear. The names given may have been inaccurate or may have been heard incorrectly. There are in fact enormous difficulties involved in documenting and categorizing children's games. Gomme (1984), for example, reports thirty different names for the game 'Three Dukes'. Games with the same name may have been played differently by different children or in different schools. There can also be overlap between games, for example 'Hide and Seek Had' can be classified as both a chasing game and a seeking game (priority in the present study was given to the 'Had' component). In sorting out the children's descriptions we found the Opies' (1969) work particularly helpful. Some of their categories were used and others added as appropriate.

Results are shown in Table 13.3. Two types of game were mentioned far more than the others. They were chasing games and ball games. *Chasing games* were defined in the same way as the Opies, that is games in which a player tries to touch others who are running freely in a prescribed area. The Opies' method of grouping different types of chasing games was then adapted. By far the most common type of chasing game was the basic game of 'It', 'Had' or 'He' (46 per cent of children). Other forms of chasing game were mentioned much less frequently. They were where the caught joined the chaser (e.g. 'Chainy', 'Runny Ally', 'Family Had' and 'Chain-He') (7 per cent), where the chased had to get to a base (e.g. 'Had round the Trees', 'Dungeons') (6 per cent), where touch was attained with a ball (e.g. 'Ball-He', 'Kingy', 'Stingball', 'Had with the Ball') (6 per cent), where the touch had a noxious effect (e.g. 'Stuck in the Mud', 'Sticky Toffee') (5 per cent), where the chased had immunity (e.g. 'Feet off the Ground', 'Feet off London') (3 per cent) and where the chaser was at a disadvantage (e.g. 'Blindman's Buff', 'Hide and Seek Had') (2 per cent).

Ball games were divided into three main groups – football, other ball games and ball games involving a wall. Football was the most common game of all: 60 per cent of children said they played it. Virtually every boy said he played (84 per cent). Other ball games included netball, basketball, cricket, rugby, American football, handtennis, 'Buzz Ball', just throwing a ball, and rounders. They were played by 32 per cent of children. Ball games involving a wall included 'squash', 'donkey', 'sevens', 'pathball' and 'packball'. They were played by a further 9 per cent of children.

In terms of frequency there was a third group of games. *Seeking*

Table 13.3 What games children say they play in the playground

Types of games	N	%
Chasing games		
Basic	80	46
Back to base	10	6
Touch with ball	11	6
Chased at disadvantage	11	6
Chased have immunity	5	3
Chaser at disadvantage	3	2
Caught join chaser	12	7
Touch has noxious effect	9	5
Catching games	27	16
Seeking games	30	17
Racing games	20	12
Daring games	1	1
Guessing games	2	1
Pretending games	10	6
Ball games		
Football	105	60
Other ball games	55	32
Ball games using wall	15	9
Skipping games		
With rope	15	9
With elastic	11	6
Games using playground markings	6	3
Marbles	0	0
Ring and clapping games and rhymes	3	2
Toy and pretend fights	2	1
Others	11	6

Note: Children were allowed up to three answers.

games were played by 17 per cent of the children. These were defined in the same way as the Opies, as games in which a player tries to find others, who obtain safety by remaining out of sight, or by getting back to base. Game included here were 'Hide and Seek', '4040', 'Tin Can Tommy', 'One Gypsy comes a Riding'.

Catching games were only slightly less frequent (16 per cent of children). These were defined, with the Opies, as games in which a player attempts to intercept other players who move from one designated place to another, and who, if caught, assist or take the catcher's place. They included 'Run Outs', and 'British Bulldog'.

Racing games (races and chases over set courses) were mentioned by 12 per cent of children.

Skipping games with a rope were done by 9 per cent of children, skipping with elastic ('French skipping', 'Chinese skipping', 'Jingle Jangle') by 6 per cent.

There were also several games that were mentioned by only a very few children. They were daring games (one child), guessing games (two children), pretending games (ten children), games using the playground markings (six children), ring games, rhymes and clapping games (only three children), and pretend fights (two children). No children said they played marbles. There were eleven games mentioned that could not be coded.

There were a number of differences between girls and boys. As described above, boys were more likely than girls to play football (84 per cent); even so, 36 per cent of the girls said they played. Girls were more likely to say they played seeking games (27 per cent *v.* 8 per cent), pretending games (9 per cent *v.* 2 per cent), and skipping games (26 per cent *v.* 5 per cent). Only girls said they played guessing games, daring games and ring games, rhymes and clapping games. Only boys mentioned toy fights. They were also more likely to play touch with a ball (11 per cent *v.* 1 per cent).

What else do you do in the playground?

This was a separate question to see what else children did in the playground, apart from playing. Only three activities occurred with any frequency. Just under half of the children (48 per cent) said they talked with friends, boys as much as girls, but black children less than white children (37 per cent *v.* 57 per cent). A third of the children (32 per cent) said they walked and wandered about and hung around, white girls the most (47 per cent) and white boys the least (18 per cent). And 28 per cent of the children said they just sat down.

What did you do in the playground this morning?

To give a more direct picture of playground activities, the children were also asked what they did in the playground on the morning of the interview. If the interview took place before playtime in the morning, they were asked to say what they did the previous morning

A very similar picture to that from the previous questions emerged. The single most frequent playground activity was football (played by 36 per cent of the children) and, as expected, boys played more than girls (48 per cent *v.* 11 per cent). Chasing games were mentioned by 20 per cent of the children, and one-half of these were the basic game of

'It' or 'Had'. Other activities were catching games (9 per cent of children), other ball games (7 per cent), and talking with friends (7 per cent). None of the other activities was mentioned by more than six children. Fifteen children (9 per cent) did not go out to play. This was more likely to be girls than boys (twelve girls, three boys) suggesting it was not entirely to do with wet play.

DISCUSSION

It is clear that the top junior children interviewed in this study liked playtime, and were particularly happy with the long dinner break. The main reasons for liking playtime were that it was a break or a rest from work, when they could relax or have fun, and it was a time when they could play games, and in particular football. They also liked it because they could meet and talk with their friends, perhaps not in the same class. There can be little doubt, therefore, that for these children playtime was an enjoyable part of their school day – probably the most enjoyable part – and its importance to them should not be under-estimated. It is difficult to think of good reasons why these results should not, in general at least, apply to children in other schools in other parts of the country.

If children do enjoy playtime, it is not because of any thought given to it by staff in schools, or other professionals in education. For the most part, playtime and playgrounds seem still to be taken for granted and, apart from minimal supervision, children are left to make of it what they will. Of course this may be one reason why it is so popular with them, that is just because it is an alternative to the largely teacher-controlled activities within the school. This would be consistent with the view of the Opies (1969), who made much of the impenetrability to adults of the outside play of children, within which games are passed on from older to younger child.

So any reservations about playtime, to be described below, and any strategies for improvement, must take this massive vote of confidence seriously. If there is room for improvement, and we believe there is, it must be built upon this already positive view.

But children did have worries about playtime. They could be miserable because of the weather, usually the wet and cold, but sometimes it was too sunny and hot for them. Some also complained about not knowing what to do in the playground. And some were worried about disruptive behaviour in the playground – about bullying, fighting and being beaten up.

There were differences between children. In particular girls were more bothered by the cold. They were more likely not to like playtime because they did not know what to do. Of the minority of children who did not like the long dinner playtime, all were girls. Girls were much more likely than boys to want to stay in at playtime.

So alongside the enjoyment there was also concern, from at least some of the children. It seems to be implicitly assumed within schools that both enjoyment and concern are the two inevitable outcomes of a situation within which children are given a good deal of freedom to do as they like, but in an environment that has little on which they can focus their attention. But must children take the pain with the pleasure? Are the squabbles and troubles that arise at playtime just a normal part of learning to play with peers? Is the concern expressed by some children inevitable and unavoidable?

We believe it is and should be avoidable, and that steps can be taken to improve playtime. One reason for children's worries is often overlooked. Although behaviour in the playground may be unconstrained, there is usually no choice at all about being there. In most schools, playtime is compulsory. Weather permitting, all children must take an enforced recreational break with other children in the playground. It seems inevitable that some children will not be as comfortable there as others. They can be made miserable by the cold and damp, and may not know what to do with themselves. The present results show they are likely to be girls. One humane solution, therefore, is to allow children choice about going out. Despite the general popularity of playtime, just under half of the children, girls far more than boys, would have liked the option of staying in and getting on with work or other activities.

Worries about giving children this option centre on the disruption that might be caused if children are allowed inside and how they can be adequately supervised. As described elsewhere (Blatchford 1989), these problems are not insoluble, with a willingness to take on a little extra supervision. Teachers' own needs for a break can still be satisfied.

What can be done about disruptive and desultory behaviour in the playground? One should be careful not to exaggerate the problem; only a minority of children in the present study mentioned bad behaviour (though some may have been reluctant to express their concerns during the interview). But are these consequences of playtime taken too much for granted? Is there acceptance of much higher levels of aggression and idleness than would ever be tolerated inside the school itself ? More seriously, are we allowing in the playground the creation of a confrontational moral code that runs counter to the spirit of co-operation and toleration many teachers strive to encourage in the classroom?

Some ways of combating unacceptable behaviour in the playground, suggested by heads and teachers, are detailed in Blatchford (1989), and will not be taken up here. In the present study children themselves suggested ways that bad behaviour should be dealt with, for example by suspending bullies, having more staff on duty to deal with problems, and introducing activities and games. A few specifically wanted better quality supervision, for example making sure teachers actually noticed bad behaviour when it occurred.

Children also detailed other possible improvements; some felt that the playground itself could be improved. They would like to see permanent equipment such as swings and climbing frames, which poses problems for school staff. First, large items of equipment are very expensive, and money would have to come from parents, sponsorship, and so on. Second, there are safety worries. But permanent large apparatus may not be the answer anyway: they do not inevitably lead to better quality play (Blatchford 1989). Another possible improvement mentioned by children was taking out equipment, for example balls and bats.

Children had other suggestions. Better use could be made of space and surfaces in the playground. For example the playground could be divided up into separate areas for certain groups of children or certain activities, like football and racing. Perhaps skipping, clapping and ring games could be encouraged by designating certain areas for them. Some children also wanted structural changes to the playground, such as the removal of fences and buildings.

All of this suggests that children are aware that the playground environment itself can be a negative influence on their playground behaviour and that they would be receptive to coherent and fair attempts to think about, and improve, the playground. It seems worth considering whether we could apply imagination and energy to the playground, in the same way as staff in good primary schools do as a matter of course to the classroom environment.

Children's games

Before conclusions are drawn from the present data on children's games it is important to be clear about their limitations. The present study has the virtue of getting the children's view – and this has obvious advantages over teachers' perceptions. But the analysis is based on what children say they do and, while there is little reason to think they were not telling the truth, and while their accounts can be helpful in interpreting their games, the exact equivalence to their behaviour in the playground cannot be assumed. Ideally one would need to combine observation and interviews with children.

Bearing this limitation in mind, what general picture emerges of children's playground games? Can we conclude, as many teachers have (Blatchford 1989), that children's outside play often consists of low-level and gratuitous squabbling, and that traditional games are in decline?

For the children interviewed in this study, there was a wide variety of games played but many were not frequently mentioned. The most common games are football, basic chasing games, and other ball games like netball and rounders. These seem to dominate. In particular, football seems to dominate boys' lives in the playground. They can't wait to play it, and no doubt thoroughly enjoy themselves when they do. To this extent, these 11-year-old boys seem involved, but limited, in their play. Girls seem to have a more varied repertoire of games. If any of the guessing, daring and presenting games occur they will be played only by girls. And girls are the only ones to say they play ring and clapping games and rhymes. Gudgeon (1988) has argued that oral playground games are almost entirely the province of girls, for whom they are a means of resistance and empowerment against boys and teachers.

However, this sex difference should not be exaggerated; these games are not mentioned often, and for the most part girls, too, are playing 'Had', chasing and seeking games, and other ball games. And football is the second most commonly mentioned game played by girls.

Should one conclude, therefore, that traditional games are in decline? One needs to be clear about what is meant by traditional games. Webb (1984) draws a distinction between two forms of games. The first is games without singing or dialogue – he mentions ball games, 'Tiggy', marbles and conkers – most of which he feels are associated with boys. These he feels have been unaffected by the passage of time. The second type is singing and dialogue games, which he feels are in decline. This distinction, when applied to results from the present study, is a useful one, and there does seem to be general support for Webb's conclusion: that is chasing and ball games were frequently played in the playground, but singing and dialogue games were not. However, we do not have data on the prevalence of games at previous points in time, and so cannot comment on trends over time.

There is a possibility that singing and dialogue games of the kind described by Gomme (1984) and the Opies (1969) were underestimated in the present study. The question asked of children was 'What games do you play in the playground?'; it may be that they did not feel singing and rhymes were being asked for. Rhymes and songs may also have accompanied other games, particularly skipping games, and children may not have felt an additional comment about them was necessary. In the course of the interview children were asked about any dips (rhymes that decide, for example, who is to be 'It') they knew, and a list of several pages in length was produced. They also volunteered other rhymes they knew. Recently Gudgeon (1988) and van Peer (1988) have described children's playground rhymes and dips.

On the other hand it is true that these were not mentioned at all in response to the follow-up question, 'What else do you do in the playground, other than games?', or in response to the request to say what they did in the playground on the morning of the interview. So a best estimate is likely to be that they are not common. It may be they are a part of a repertoire of songs, rhymes and dips that were once learnt and used but which have given way to other games like football, which, to boys especially, may well seem more appropriate to the image they have of some one nearing secondary school. Put concretely, their fathers and their older brothers may well be very interested in football, and they may well watch football on the television. But there is virtually no outlet in the popular media for traditional rhymes.

Although chasing and ball games were common, the two other games mentioned by Webb – marbles and conkers – certainly were not. The absence of the latter was because of the time of year (though we do not know whether the game of conkers occurs in these schools in the autumn). As for marbles, these were not used or mentioned by any child in any school. It is tempting to speculate whether games that make use of traditional materials, like marbles, are in decline, as much as singing and dialogue games. The only materials used by these children were balls, of course, and 15 per cent of the children mentioned skipping, either with ropes or elastic.

Another type of game was surprisingly rare: those that made use of game markings on the playground surface or walls. This is surprising because almost all school playgrounds no doubt have the obligatory hopscotch or other design on the asphalt; these seem to hold little interest for children, or perhaps the playground is too crowded for their use.

So traditional games in the form of chasing, catching and seeking games, but not singing games, do appear commonly in these inner city playgrounds. Many of these games also appear in the Opies' book, though names of games change and are subject to regional variations. None of the games described by the children was, to our knowledge, taught by teachers, so presumably the informal transference of knowledge about games is passed from child to child, as described by the Opies.

Perhaps the main conclusion to be drawn is that there is a need to think of ways of extending the variety of children's games, and in particular to encourage games that involve singing, rhyme and dialogue, games that use materials, like marbles, and games that make use of playground markings. Some ways this might be done are described in Blatchford (1989), and include having festivals involving, say, four schools within which children can present and discuss with each other games they know. Teachers, too, might seek to encourage games from their own childhood, though there is always the possibility that the involvement of adults can serve to lessen children's interest in games (Opies 1969; Gudgeon 1988). A recent book by Heseltine (1989) lists some co-operative games that might be introduced. Schools with children from different ethnic backgrounds have great potential for the sharing of a rich variety of games. One task is to find ways of tapping informally acquired games that can be rich in their form and use of language. Much more could also be done to encourage the use of playground markings and to make these more interesting – perhaps working with children to devise designs to their own specifications (see Blatchford 1989).

One word of caution though. As Webb says, 'One thing is certain: a game will flourish and spread only if it is fun NOW. Children have no sense of preserving a game because it is of historical interest' (1984: 14).

Football

Given the prevalence of football in this study, it seems appropriate to end with a closer look at it. It is quite extraordinary how much this one game dominates boys' playground games. Even this probably underestimates its true domination because, by its forceful nature, a game of football can affect, perhaps in an unwanted way, the activities of other children in the playground, who do not wish to play. Staff in many schools have agonized over football. Should it be banned? Should it be restricted to certain parts of the playground, or to certain days of the week? Should steps be taken to involve girls more (see Blatchford 1989)?

For the most part, football in the playground is at best taken for granted by staff, and its worst excesses of accidental knocking over and balls in the face dealt with as they arise, or else it is deliberately frowned on and barely tolerated. But given its central place in playground life, is this fair? Perhaps it needs to be taken more seriously by staff. One likely reason why it is not, in primary schools, is because many staff are women, who do not themselves play football and probably have little interest in it. Given its prevalence it is worth considering what the positive effects of football might be. One likely one is that it offers a constructive outlet for the energies of increasingly powerful 11-year-old boys. Indeed some said that they did not get into trouble or fights in the playground because they were too busy playing football. Moreover, football depends on agreement with at least a basic set of rules, and the cohesion of a team of children working together toward a common end. Within this context, there is room for, and appreciation of, individual skill and flair. For enthusiasts, it is also a very gripping game. It is not an historical accident that football, despite all its present troubles, is watched and enjoyed by so many.

Efforts might therefore be made to find out more about the football that is played so enthusiastically in the playground. Are matches played? Who plays whom? What rules are followed? It might also be possible to tap their enthusiasm and work with children on a coaching basis, for example on skills of passing, trapping and shooting.

REFERENCES

Blatchford, P. (1989) *Playtime in the Primary School: Problems and Improvements*, Windsor: NFER-Nelson.

Blatchford, P., Burke, J., Farquhar, C., Plewis, I. and Tizard, B. (1985) 'Educational achievement in the infant school: the influence of ethnic origin, gender and home on entry skills', *Educational Research* 27(1): 52–60.

DES (1989) *Discipline in Schools*, Report of the Committee, of Inquiry chaired by Lord Elton, London: HMSO.

Gomme, A.B. (1984) *The Traditional Games of England, Scotland and Ireland*, (first published in two volumes in 1894–98) London: Thames & Hudson.

Gudgeon, E. (1988) 'Children's oral culture: a transitional experience', in M. MacLure, T. Phillips and A. Wilkinson (eds) *Oracy Matters*, Milton Keynes: Open University.

Heseltine, P. (1989) *Games for All Children*, Oxford: Basil Blackwell.

Opie, I. and Opie, P. (1969) *Children's Games in Street and Playground*, London: Oxford University Press.

Sluckin, A. (1981) *Growing up in the Playground*, London: Routledge & Kegan Paul.

Stephenson, P. and Smith, D. (1989) 'Bullying in the junior school', in D.P. Tattum, and O.A. Lane (eds) *Bullying in Schools*, Stoke-on-Trent: Trentham.

Tattum D.P. and Lane O.A. (eds) (1989) *Bullying in Schools*, Stoke-on-Trent: Trentham.

Tizard, B., Blatchford, P., Burke, J., Farquhar, C. and Plewis, I. (1988) *Young Children At School in the Inner City*, Hove: Erlbaum.

Van Peer, W. (1988) 'Counting out: form and function of children's counting-out rhymes', in M. MacLure, T. Phillips and A. Wilkinson (eds) *Oracy Matters*, Milton Keynes: Open University.

Webb, F.D. (1984) Introduction to Alice B. Gomme, *The Traditional Games of England, Scotland and Ireland*, London: Thames & Hudson.

14 Friends and fights

Bronwyn Davies
Source: B. Davies (1982) *Life in the Classroom and Playground*, London: Routledge & Kegan Paul, ch. 4.

INTRODUCTION

[. . .] There are critical ways in which adults do not want children to share their world. Parents and teachers encourage children to play with each other in order to have time to get on with their adult pursuits. Children's culture can be seen partially as a response to this separateness. When children first arrive at school they may be traumatized at the situation they find themselves in if they have no contacts amongst their peers. Until they make friends they cannot participate in children's culture. [. . .] Once they have made friends, and gained access to childhood culture, they must be careful not to annoy or offend their friends, or they may find themselves alone again. The fearfulness of this aloneness, the possibility of being outside children's culture, should not be underestimated when seeking to comprehend the children's understanding of the world of friendship. [. . .]

ADULTS' VIEWS CONTRASTED WITH CHILDREN'S VIEWS ON FRIENDSHIP

Adults and children, each from the perspective of their own culture, can be seen to have very different views on what friendship is. Beliefs about friendship from the perspective of adult culture are linked with the notions of liking (or love), affection and loyalty. Children appear to have a rather fickle attitude towards friendship, and to engage in an unnecessary amount of fighting and bickering. In fact it would seem to adults that children do not 'really understand' what friendship is. Speier claims that adults have difficulty in seeing children's culture. Along with Speier, I would see children's culture as existing in its own right, though intimately related to and developing partly in response to adult culture:

> If there is any scepticism about the existence of children's culture, it is a reflection of our own adult ideological commitment which has all but obscured the fact of its existence. The work of parenthood consists mainly of the practical 'science' of child management in the family household. Likewise the work of a teacher is devoted largely to the practical 'science' of child management in the classroom and around the school establishment. Yet the Opies, for example, have documented the existence of children's culture among schoolchildren in Great Britain by accumulating a vast amount of data on children's traditional lore and games which do not originate out of the practical activity of child management. Likewise my own research on children's play activity at home, and my filming of children's interactions associated with school activity outside the classroom, indicates the existence of children's culture. It would appear to essentially be neither a miniaturized or a half-baked adult culture, nor an imitated version of it – but a culture in its own right.
>
> (Speier 1976: 99)

During the earlier part of the year of my study, I had a great deal of difficulty understanding the ups and downs of the children's relationships with each other. The following field notes were made after several days taken out from interviewing to observe friendship patterns. I was able to describe what I saw and what I had heard and yet was unable to find a satisfactory interpretation of what was going on. Despite the fact that the children seemed to know quite clearly what they were doing, I felt (quite incorrectly) that because I could not understand *why* they were doing what they were doing that *they* did not really understand what friendship was:

> Some insight perhaps into the extent and intensity of girls' fights. They seem to be experimenting with interactions to see how much power they have over each other and the boys, e.g. I witnessed Mandy ask Roddie for her pen back. Roddie had lost it. Mandy told him he would have to buy her a new one, Roddie then found that Warwick had it and called out to Mandy several times but was ignored and told again that he would have to buy a new one. She was deliberately being difficult and perhaps even stirring trouble. Later on she was playing with Roddie and Warwick and was turfed out by the other girls. She was deeply hurt and tearful because she felt no one liked her. Her power games had backfired, and she was a

lost and unhappy little girl. Suzie and Linda were busy comforting her in the library at lunch time. She stopped crying when I suggested that she didn't really have a problem as long as Suzie remained her friend, which she very obviously was. The need to know that you are a likeable person is evident in this sort of situation. Two troublesome problems for children of this age:

how to be likeable

how to show others your liking.

Roddie's solution is to hate everyone else but his friend so that the contrast can be seen. Warwick and Jane have been described as nice because they 'give things'. Mandy and Suzie have developed little rituals of hand hitting and twisting which are symbolic or affirmative of friendship. But since, in general, they have difficulty in defining what a friend is, they also have difficulty in *being* a friend because they are not quite sure what it is to be one. Thus they are offensive and hurtful without intending it, and so the conflicts flare up all the time, i.e., in this case it seems that lack of theory really does screw up the action. To further complicate the picture, the behaviour which they display in the library which appears to *me* to be friendly (supportive comments during traumatic personal discussion) are not counted as signs of friendship amongst the children.

The Opies, too, find childhood friendships chaotic and unpredictable, and acknowledge that it is from the adult perspective that they seem so:

> Children's friendships are far from placid. Perhaps because of the gregariousness of school life they make and break friends with a rapidity disconcerting to the adult spectator. Two girls will swear eternal friendship, arrange signs and passwords, exchange necklaces, walk home together from school, invite each other to tea, and have just settled down together, so it would seem, when suddenly they are very 'black' with one another and do not speak any more. They seek a new friend, and have no sooner found one than they are with their old pal again.
>
> (Opie and Opie 1959: 324)

The central argument put forward in this chapter is that, from the perspective of the children's culture, these makings and breakings serve two important functions, first in terms of the *maintenance of the orderliness* of the children's world and, second, in terms of *satisfying their need for exploration and discovery* of the dynamics of interpersonal relationships.

Adults assume that the reason friendships develop is that people like one another. They construe their own friendships as developing from reciprocated feelings of attraction. Children, in contrast, while they do not negate liking as having some considerable importance, see proximity, or being with someone, as the first and basic element of friendships. Homans, in contrast with many social psychologists, would tend to agree with the children, that the nature of the other is no more (and perhaps less) important than the fact of being with the other. He says, 'an increase of interaction between persons is accompanied by an increase of sentiments of friendliness between them.' In other words, we come to like the people we associate with because we associate with them, rather than because they are intrinsically likeable. He goes on to say, 'You can get to like some pretty queer customers if you go around with them long enough. Their queerness becomes irrelevant' (Homans 1951: 115). An apparently simple proposition and yet one which seems contrary to what friendship should be. From our adult perspective, liking should come first. Children often mention liking as part of friendship. However, they are clearer about the pragmatic nature of the liking than most adults. One of the children of my study wrote, in an essay on friendship:

> Why have I got a friend. Because if I didn't have a friend, I would have nobody to play with. I think it is good to have a friend don't you. If I had a soccer ball I would give him a game of soccer.

Another wrote:

> My friend is my friend because she looks after me and plays with me and its good to have a friend. A friend is a girl or boy that plays with you.

[. .] Other children have placed being with your friend high on the list of the defining features of friendship:

> My best friend is John Corbett and the reason why I like him is that he is so nice to me and we both draw space ships, and what's more he plays with me nearly every time in the playground.
>
> (Opie and Opie 1959: 323)

And the following conversation with 11-year-old Paul is reported by Damon (who, however, maintains his own adult views on friendship):

> Who's your best friend? *Don.* Why? *We hang around together.* How did you meet him? *At school; he's the first one I met.* Is that why he's your best friend? *Yeah, he showed me around the school.* Why do

you like Don? *'Cause we play football together and we like to bike ride around.* Do best friends have to like the same things? *Not always.*

(Damon 1977: 159)

Damon claims that friendship as we have thus far described it, based on proximity, characterizes *low-level* friendship. Children who, in contrast, have achieved a higher level, he says,

> realise that friendship is subjective, in the sense that one person may like or dislike another because of certain dispositions and traits of the other. In other words, the bestowal of affection (and consequent establishment of friendship) no longer is automatically associated with frequent play contact but, rather, hinges upon subjectively determined personal characteristics of the other ('niceness', kindness, trustworthiness, and so on).

(Damon 1977: 157–8)

Damon's analysis of 'higher level' friendship perfectly typifies the *adult* position in which the liking is perceived as causal. He assumes a higher quality inheres in the adult model, i.e. the model with which children gradually learn to construe their friendships. Damon's model implies that children have achieved a 'higher order' of friendship when they cease seeing what is actually occurring within their friendships, and see rather what they have learned from adults about what 'ought' to be the case in friendship.

Certainly when pushed, Paul went on to talk about these characteristics of his friend Don. He none the less mentioned being with Don and his happenstance meeting with Don as the first part of the equation. Along with Damon and the adult population in general, Paul will eventually learn to perceive the second half of the equation, the intrinsic likeableness of the other, as the essence of friendship. He will learn as well to feel some revulsion for the 'lower level' notion, that proximity leads to friendship. And thus the children's theories about friendship are difficult to understand because our own assumptions about what friendship is or should be cloud our vision. We apply the wrong mental set or template and do not understand what we see.

When children first arrive at school they are thrown on their own resources to a considerable extent. Making sense of this strange new world is a task they engage in with each other. The teachers may spell out the rules for classroom behaviour, but the sense to be made of it all is something adults cannot really provide. Friends are the source of meaning-making in this new situation. They are the source of meaning and therefore the source of identity. They can, by their presence and shared meaning world, render the world a sensible and manageable place. Their particular mode of viewing the world, with its accompanying language, taboos, rituals and sanctions which function to maintain this meaning world, is developed in interaction with each other.

In Bruner's terms (e.g. Bruner 1974) the children develop their own templates for viewing the world. If Homans's propositions on friendship hold, the children's template may actually be closer to what happens in friendship both for adults and for children than the adult template. Be that as it may, the playing, the fighting, the making and breaking of friendships are necessary ingredients for the development and maintenance of the children's shared world.

CONTINGENCY FRIENDS

Friends not only alleviate the uncertainty which stems from being alone, but also via companionship and co-operativeness go on providing the means for warding off the vulnerability which attends being alone. *Being with* your friend, then, is important. Moreover, the more advantaged children have *contingency friends* ready for emergency situations where their friend is absent or where their friend offends them in some way. If they withdraw to their contingency friends their bargaining power over their 'best friend' is quite high.

In the following transcript Vanessa relates a tale of misery. Inadvertently she failed to be with her friend Pat when Pat thought she should be. Unfortunately for Vanessa, Pat had contingency friends to turn to and she is now left alone in turn. The conversation takes place amidst, and parallel with, a noisy conversation with some of the boys, but with minimal prompting from me Vanessa tells her tale:

Transcript 14.1 Vanessa, Sally and Betty

1 **B.D.:** OK, I want to ask Vanessa how it turned into a horrible day.	1 Vanessa had earlier claimed that the day had started out well but it was now horrible.
2 **Vanessa:** Oh we were playing up in the bike shed I came down because, um, I wanted to come down just to sit on the bike (*unclear*) and when I came down and the bell rang while I was putting my bike away and I was saying,	2 Vanessa left Pat simply to do something she wanted to do and Pat took offence.

and I was talking to Pat, I
was saying something to Pat
and she went (*makes a rude
sign with her thumb*) and
ever since then, ever since
the bell she won't talk to me.

3 *B.D.:* And you don't know
why she did that Vanessa?

3 I ask Vanessa for a causal
explanation of the event.

4 *Vanessa:* I haven't had an
answer.

. . .

4 Her reply is in the terms that
matter to her. She has sent a
message to Pat, and not had
a reply.

5 *Vanessa:* If I go away and do
something and I don't stay
up with her she gets the
cranks.

. . .

5 She then replies to my earlier
question.

6 *Vanessa:* And she goes off to
Linda or Mandy and then
we're not friends.

. . .

6 She explains the contingency
friendship plan.

7 *Vanessa:* I do everything she
wants and I can't do any-
thing I want, has to be all
her way.
(*20 minutes of other conversation*)

7 There is an imbalance in the
relationship as to who calls
the tune.

8 *Sally:* Pat is your friend.

8 Sympathetic reassurance
from Sally

9 *Vanessa:* No she's not.

9 Clearly Pat's actions are stra-
tegic moves within the friendship. Until she reaffirms the
friendship (which she probably will do when full reciprocation for offence is carried
through) Vanessa will be
alone and uncertain.

10 *B.D.:* You mean she's cranky
with you? And who have you
got for your friend if Pat is
not your friend?

10 This indicates I have just
cottoned on to the fact
that Vanessa and Pat have
fallen out. The surrounding
conversation had been dis-

11 *Vanessa:* Nobody.

12 *B.D.:* Betty. Betty just said she's your friend.

tracting me from paying attention to Vanessa. I now ask who her contingency friends are.

12 Betty is 'friends' with whoever happens to be around. She explained in a separate conversation with me that her friend is whoever is doing anything interesting. She had noted Vanessa as her friend at the beginning of the conversation simply because Vanessa was there and doing something interesting (talking to me).

13 *Vanessa:* Yeah, I know, but I got no one to talk, no one, 'cos Betty's with Mandy mostly or/

13 Vanessa knows Betty will not do as a best friend because Betty is a drifter, not having the same wish or ability to establish bonds as the others do and thus forever breaking friendships by simply not being there with her friend, when they expect she should be

14 *Betty:* You gotta be kiddin'!

15 *Vanessa:* But I'm with no/I just gotta sit around and do things myself.

. . .

16 *Vanessa:* Pat was good you know, good, and I, I've got really nobody in, ah, this school because the teachers are all against me. Mr Hunt especially.

16 In the event of no friends, the adult world is still obviously a possibility for contact. For Vanessa this possibility does not seem to be available.

Note here that an offer of friendship from Betty does not solve the problem. Betty is notorious for not allying herself with anyone for long, the others constantly criticize her for her behaviour and according to her account she hates sitting around talking anyway.

(Her learning of the teachers' ideas of acceptable behaviour has apparently been more successful since she is well liked by the teachers.) Certainly she is no substitute for Pat, and Vanessa's misery at losing her friend makes life look very bleak indeed. Physical removal of oneself from one friend to another is one way of letting your friend know that her behaviour was inappropriate. For this technique to work, however, one must know who one's contingency friends are. The distress that Vanessa experienced when Pat left her need not have been so acute if she had had a contingency friend ready for the emergency. [. . .]

The centrality of *being with your friend* for friendship is illustrated through the effects that leaving your friend can have. Children do not like to be left alone but will leave their friend alone if it seems appropriate to do so. The contingency friendship plan is vital for the success of this strategy. Moreover, contingency friends increase the bargaining power of those children who know they will not be left alone if their friend chooses to leave them in the event of a disagreement or fight.

Finally, children [. . .] who consider they have quite high bargaining power will play out the contingency friendship plan until all suitable apologies and appeals have been made. Adrienne, for example, in discussing a bout of fisticuffs she had just had indicates that however fearful she may feel, she expects the other to take the first initiative in restoring the friendship:

> Because if you punch up your friends you feel, you feel that they won't ever like you again. But they do make up with me. I'm not the one that turns back and says 'Will you be my friend?' They come back and say 'Will you be friends with me?'

THE RULES OF CHILDHOOD CULTURE

The advantage of the squabbles the children had among themselves was that they created in natural form the sort of situation Garfinkel (1967) was after, when he had his students disrupt the order of things to find out what was being taken for granted about the social order before the disruption occurred. The disruptions described by the children of my study were different in a significant way from Garfinkel's, however, in that they were considered to be part of the normal order of things, rather than as abnormal events. [. . .] In case this is taken to indicate an unusual lack of stability amongst the group studied, I should remind the reader that there were several steady friendships and friendship groups.

Even though these disruptions are considered normal by the children ('It's always normal, every year we have about three or four fights through the year, but we always come back together'), they nevertheless prompt an examination or restatement of the taken-for-granted rules attending friendship. Vanessa, for example, in wondering why Pat has deserted her (Transcript 14.1), with little or no prompting, works through the conditions of friendship as they operate amongst the children. The ideas she produces were possibly not ideas she could have produced before the incident. Only when she reflects on what has gone wrong does she begin to make clear some of the basic rules of friendship, that you should be with your friend, and that isolation or reciprocation rapidly follows the breaching of this rule.

I have isolated three critical constructs within children's culture which related to acceptable and unacceptable ways of behaving within that culture.

Reciprocity

I am a mirror to you which provides you with my perception of your behaviour towards me.

This is a different proposition from the looking-glass self put forward by Cooley: 'In imagination we perceive in another's mind some thought of our appearance, manners, aims, deeds, character, friends and so on, and are variously affected by it' (1972: 231). Cooley proposed the *imaginative* construction of self whereas the children's proposition involves *active reflecting back* to the other of the other's self.

Related rule: I should behave to you as you behave to me. I should reciprocate any wrongdoing which you do towards me, and, less importantly, I should reciprocate correct behaviour as well. Behaviours which were defined as wrong from one's friends (though not necessarily wrong from others) were: getting the snobs, getting the cranks, teasing, lying, showing off, getting too full of yourself, posing, bashing people up, being piss weak, wanting everything your way, being spoilt, being stupid, dobbing (i.e. telling tales). On the other hand, you should be with your friend, play properly, share, be tough, stick up for your friends and know each other's feelings.

(Dobbing was the only behaviour on the list which took cognizance of the adult world. In so far as it involved calling in extra and unhandleable adult forces it was regarded as totally unacceptable behaviour. For children who were unable to reciprocate bad behaviour, dobbing was a surrogate form of reciprocity.)

Events have a discoverable facticity

Children's constant quarrels about 'what happened' illustrate their belief in a single truth. Relativist philosophies were not relevant in their dealings with each other. Though over *time* what was true changed as a result of new perceptions and insights, and though they recognized a multiplicity of ways of explaining any event, they adhered steadfastly to the ideal of the facticity of events at any single point in time.

Related rule: the facticity of the phenomenal world should be maintained by challenges to inadequate approximations in others' talk. The behaviours which were unacceptable in relation to this rule were lying, posing, showing off, and getting too big for yourself (i.e. making yourself out to be better than you really are).

People have an existential or plastic quality

What is so about people today may be demonstrably untrue tomorrow. One's *character* is not assumed to have absolute continuity through time or across situations.

Related rule: one's actions towards others should be appropriate to the present. Thus behaviours which are unacceptable towards one's friend (such as leaving them) can become appropriate in the present if one's friend is behaving badly. Similarly with bashing up, getting the snobs and teasing.

These three constructs emerged in the children's talk, not directly, but indirectly. For instance, in the following transcript Jane expresses puzzlement at Mandy's failure to reciprocate apparently aggressive behaviour from Betty:

Transcript 14.2 Jane

---

1 *Jane:* It's funny, I'm not saying anything against anyone. We were having a game with Betty's ball, Mandy got bashed in the eye by Betty

1 Jane is being very cautious here. She doesn't want the word around that she is criticizing anyone. Nevertheless, reciprocity of action is

and then she's back sitting next to her. It's a wonder that she didn't get the huffs!

both natural and important, even where the original offence was not intended.

It might be worth noting here that Mandy can't afford to get the 'huffs' since she and Suzie are still estranged and Betty is her contingency friend. To get the huffs with Betty would be to force the reconciliation with Suzie. Mandy's failure to get the huffs with Betty indicates that the groundwork for reconciliation with Suzie is not yet complete.

Except where such limiting conditions exist, reciprocation follows fairly rapidly. The following transcripts illustrate in a variety of ways transgressions against the rules, and the attitudes and responses brought to these transgressions. The importance of these transgressions, it must be remembered, is that it is through the breaking of rules that people discover or rediscover precisely what the rules are. That is, they discover the dimensions and limits of their taken-for-granted world.

Transcript 14.3 Anne and Adrienne

---

1 *B.D.:* Tell me about the fight you two had.

2 *Anne:* When?

3 *B.D.:* Didn't you say earlier that you two had had a fight?

4 *Adrienne:* Oh yea, that one. (*Anne giggles*)

5 *B.D.:* Tell me about it.

6 *Adrienne:* Anne said come and do something and I had to do my number facts.

7 *Anne:* Yeah, Adrienne said 'I ca–ant, I have to do me wo–ork'.

8 *Adrienne:* And Anne said 'All right then!' (*Anne giggles*) and then she walked out of the classroom.

1 Referring to an earlier point in the conversation.

2–4 Fights are sufficiently frequent to need clarification as to which fight I am talking about, though the children may not find them memorable, nor regard them as frequent.

6 Anne suggested the two of them do something together.

7 Adrienne replied in a wingeing voice that she couldn't come (i.e. she was piss weak).

8 Anne in response speaks huffily to her and then *walks away from her*.

9 *B.D.:* So you felt Anne should have come with you instead of doing her work?

10 *Anne:* I didn't know she had to do her number facts again! Just the way she said it!

11 *B.D.* So it was just the tone of her voice she had that put you off. (*Anne nods agreement*)

9–11 It was not the fact that Anne refused to come with her that constituted a breach of rules. It was the *manner* of her refusal. By walking away Anne signals that she is temporarily withdrawing her friendship and spending her time with someone else.

Tone of voice has been noted as important to children, in some cases more important than actual words. They know if offence is intended through the manner of the delivery rather than the insult itself. In this case no offence was intended, but Adrienne discovered that her tone of voice had unwittingly delivered an unacceptable message.

The delicate balance between fun and serious fighting is illustrated in the following conversation with Vanessa and Jane. Mostly for these two it is fun but there is an air of exploration and challenge, of trying each other out, which leads on occasion to behaviour which causes genuine offence.

This friendship is a new one: negotiations are still in progress as to how they will ultimately relate to each other, so the emphasis is on exploration, or trying out. Yet this exploration follows an orderly, rule-bound sequence of action and reciprocation. In what follows, the girls both talk about and display the reciprocity inherent in their relationship:

Transcript 14.4 Jane and Vanessa

---

1 *B.D.:* What sort of person are you at school?

2 *Jane: (laughs)* Aw, sometimes I get real low, and other times I am real happy.

3 *B.D.:* How would you describe her, Vanessa?

4 *Vanessa: (laughs)* I dunno (*unclear*) squabbling.

5 *Jane:* Yeah, Vanessa and me/

6 *Vanessa:* She's a good friend when we are not squabbling, but when we are squabbling, ugh!

7 *B.D.:* What sort of things do you squabble about?

8 *Vanessa:* I dunno, just like/ (*giggles*)

9 *Jane:* She might leave a letter out in a word and I'd say, 'Oh yeah, you've left out a letter in that', and she says 'All right!' and I say 'OK I won't talk then!' Then she gets mad and then I get mad and we don't talk to each other.

    9 Jane describes a pattern of criticism causing offence, then counter-offence, followed by withdrawal of friendship. This is told in a dramatic style which recreates (displays) the incident for my benefit.

10 *B.D.:* How long do you stay mad for?

11 *Jane:* Aw, about ten minutes until we've said our pieces to each other and then we'll go back to good friends, won't we?

    11 The pattern of mutual offence is typically followed by mutual reaffirmation of friendship after a period of no interaction. (Neither of them has 'contingency' friends to withdraw to at the time of this conversation.)

12 *Vanessa:* Yeah, we are trying to stop our squabbling but we haven't succeeded.

    12 The taken-for-granted rule of reciprocity is more powerful than the wish that either of them has to put an end to it.

13 *B.D.:* Why are you trying to stop?

14 *Jane:* Aw, we don't like it much.

15 *Vanessa:* But we always do it.

16 *Jane:* Every morning. (*Both are giggling*)

| 17 | *B.D.:* You're like an old married couple aren't you? Squabbling with each other. (*Both giggle*) | 17 | In so far as they seem to have no clear alternative to their friendship with each other my joking analogy is quite apt. |

[. . .]

The unquestioning way in which reciprocal acts are engaged in clearly involves a controlling element, though the children do not necessarily accept 'control' as their motivation. Their actions, rather than having retribution as their major purpose, seem to relate more closely to equilibrating and maintaining the social world. This point was brought home to me in a discussion with Paul.

When Daniel (aged 8) was irritating Paul (aged 11) and Paul was handing out reciprocal irritation, I tried to persuade Paul that if he desisted, Daniel would grow to like him better, and therefore spend less time finding ways to irritate him. Paul considered that a failure on his part to 'pay him back' would clearly mean that Daniel would repeat his irritating ways without cease. My response was, 'Well, if you want to control him to stop him from doing what he is doing, you are going to have to find more subtle ways of going about it. Simply paying him back each time isn't working.' With some anger and indignation Paul declared that he did *not* want to control him. Any approach I took to the argument, and I tried several, arrived at exactly the same point. If Paul didn't pay him back he would do it again and yet he definitely considered that he did not want to control him. Reciprocation is common sense; control is unacceptable. (Perhaps 'controlling' is what adults do.)

The rule of negative reciprocation seems to be a very basic law within childhood culture. [. . .] The children of my study, and of Rosser's and Harré's study (1976), spoke most often of *negative* reciprocity. Perhaps this is because 'social rules seem to operate . . . more "in the breach than in the observance". We are not aware of breaking one until after the act' (Cook-Gumperz 1975: 142). In other words, negative reciprocation will be more consciously engaged in, in the construction and maintenance of the world-taken-for-granted, i.e. in the creation and maintenance of a coherent world.

In the following description by Simon of the relationship between him and Roddie, the reciprocation takes a considerable amount of time, and offence (often apparently unintended) occurs regularly, so they are rarely in a state of friendship. They both want to be friends with Warwick, and they both wish that Warwick would cease being friends with the other:

Transcript 14.5 Simon

1 *B.D.:* You and Roddie don't get on do you?	1–6 Simon takes fighting as an indication of enmity (in partial contrast to Vanessa and Jane).
2 *Simon:* No, not much.	
3 *B.D.:* Why is that?	
4 *Simon:* 'Cos we keep on fighting.,	Again, as with Vanessa and Jane, the fighting seems to be an unexplained fact.
5 *B.D.:* Why do you fight?	
6 *Simon:* Dunno.	
7 *B.D.:* Roddie said that when he first went to the last school that the teacher asked who wanted to look after him and you and Warwick said you would.	7 The friendship between Roddie and Warwick (and sometimes Simon) commenced on a happenstance proximity when Roddie first arrived at the previous school.
8 *Simon:* Yeah.	
9 *B.D.:* But then Warwick got on with Roddie and you didn't.	
10 *Simon:* Yeah.	
11 *B.D.:* What was it you didn't like about him?	
12 *Simon:* Oh, you know, he keeps on, you know, walkin' past goin' (*demonstrates*) hit me on the back of the head for a joke, and I don't like it, keeps on bumpin' me when I'm workin'.	12 These punches, as with Jane's, are intended as a joking challenge and yet are not acceptable to Simon. After all, Roddie is not Simon's only or even best friend.
13 *B.D.:* He just does little things to irritate you, does he?	
14 *Simon:* Yeah.	
15 *B.D.:* Have you ever tried to be his friend?	15–20 Despite the annoyance Simon feels at Roddie's challenge, Simon will be his
16 *Simon:* Yeah.	

17 *B.D.:* When was that?

18 *Simon:* Oh, when the show was on and the times after that.

19 *B.D.:* And what happened? What went wrong when you tried to be friends with him?

20 *Simon:* Oh, he done the same thing.

21 *B.D.:* Just sort of hitting you and pushing you and that? (*nods*)

22 *B.D.:* How come he and Warwick get on so well?

23 *Simon:* 'Cos, um, he isn't game to hit Warwick.

24 *B.D.:* Why isn't he game to hit Warwick?

25 *Simon:* 'Cos Warwick can beat him in a fight.

friend as long as he refrains from challenging him. But Roddie cannot resist challenging him. (The 'show' is the local fair.)

22–25 Simon reads Roddie's challenges as deliberate insults (though Roddie may intend them as jokes) since he does not behave in the same way to a respected person.

[. . .]

To sum up so far, the children have quite clear strategies for coping with unacceptable behaviour from each other. They can walk away from each other, either with the intention of being followed, or to seek out a contingency friend. Putting an end to reciprocal bouts of unacceptable behaviour is almost impossible if the freedom to walk away does not exist, as the case of Vanessa and Jane illustrates. An alternative to walking away, not used by Vanessa and Jane, is an all-out fight, though this is not always possible. These strategies do not spell the end of friendships: they are manoeuvres within friendships. A friend can walk away or fight with you and you can still count him as your best friend (after certain additional manoeuvres have been completed). To fight someone when it is not called for, however, is unthinkable.

[. . .]

POSING, TEASING AND FIGHTING

Friends not only save you from being alone, but also help you to build up a working knowledge of who you are. This may be indirectly through facilitating certain ways of being or it may be directly through praise or censure. Friends are not enough, however, since non-friends seem necessary to provide the Garfinkelian element which clarifies or crystallizes even more clearly who you are. One of the behaviours counted as inappropriate for friends was 'posing' or showing off, yet the children admitted that posing was something everyone did sometimes. Posing is seen as big-noting yourself or making out that you are better than you are. Even though everyone does it, posing is read by others as offensive, since it involves inaccurate presentation of self and also the possibility that by contrast to the posers one will be made to feel weak or inferior. There is a certain ambivalence, then, towards posing.

Transcript 14.6 Sally, Henry and Roy

---

1 *Sally:* Everyone 'ates Mr
  Droop 'cos, you know,
  everyone talks behind his
  back. 'Specially Mandy.
2 *Henry:* Yeah, she's a freckle
  face! I'm going to shoot her
  too.
3 *Sally:* She sticks her thumb
  up at Mr Droop. She do's all
  that stuff. (*unclear*)
4 *B.D.:* Why don't you like
  Mandy, Henry?
5 *Henry:* She shows off.
6 *Roy:* Yeah, she shows off.
7 *Sally:* She follows Roddie
  around.
8 *Roy:* And Warwick.
9 *Henry:* And Roddie don't
  want 'er/
10 *Sally:* And Roddie likes,
  um,/
11 *Henry:* Anne.

12 *Sally:* Yeah, Anne.
13 *B.D.:* But Anne doesn't like
    him.
14 *Sally:* Sometimes.
15 *B.D.:* But you don't like
    Mandy because she shows
    off?
16 *Sally:* Yeah.
17 *Henry:* Yeah.
18 *Roy:* What's the use of say-
    ing that because we show off
    too sometimes.

Teasing is closely related to posing. It can be a pose if you tease (i.e. making out that the other's style is inferior or wrong and therefore to be teased) or teasing can be a response to posing (you are teased for making out that you are superior). Teasing is generally taken to be offensive, and not many children can receive teasing with cool. In fact rarely is it seen as appropriate to receive it with cool, since such cool may be interpreted as weakness, or inability to reciprocate the offence. Friends generally place a taboo on teasing each other (except where it is agreed to classify the teasing as a joke, and even then it might run the risk of being taken as a serious challenge). They reserve most of their teasing for others. Another way of looking at this would be to say that friends have usually negotiated and agreed upon the details of acceptable behaviour and therefore have no need to tease, though teasing may well have played some part in the negotiations.

In the following transcript Linda explains that she has modified her school behaviour as a result of teasing.

Transcript 14.7 Linda, Suzie and Terry

---

1 *B.D.:* You are more responsible at school?

2 *Linda:* Yes, at home I sort of
  do everything, I sorta show
  off a bit at home.

1 Linda has claimed she is
  quite different at home from
  at school. She is having trouble formulating the difference so I make a suggestion.

2 She agrees, but subsequent
  conversation indicates I am
  off beam.

3 *Suzie:* Yes!

4 *Linda:* I don't show off at school 'cos, you get called/

5 *Terry:* 'Poser! Poser!'

6 *Linda:* Yeah, 'Poser! Poser!' Or if you are a flirt they call you/

7 *Suzie:* Yeah and they call ya, they say/

8 *Linda:* 'Flirt! Flirt! Flirt!' something like that.

9 *Suzie:* And if you're goin' round with a boy or somethin', talkin' to him or somethin' like that and somebody says somethin' about you or somethin', and your family's going around with a boy and you also those people would say/

10 *Linda:* 'Oh now you've got a boyfriend.'

11 *Suzie:* And the people who are going around with a boy will just say, 'You're jealous.'

---

3 Suzie has witnessed this behaviour at home.

4 The reason she is different at school is that she would be teased if she didn't modify her behaviour.

5 Said in a sing-song teasing voice.

6-8 Chanted in a teasing voice. Being teased for flirting is a response to people who are thought to be setting themselves up as more attractive than anyone else.

9 Suzie explains you can even be teased however for aspects of your home life which are unavoidable, i.e. if your family goes out with another family who has a boy of your age.

10 Sing-song teasing voice.

11 But there are words you can use to defend yourself which deliver a reciprocal offence.

[. . .]

Sometimes physical violence itself is the pose. Fist fights were not uncommon among the boys and the girls. If your friend is tough and bashes others up then you are all the safer since he will most likely defend you when necessary, so to be tough is admirable. On the other hand you may be on the receiving end of the toughness in which case it is no longer perceived as admirable. The tough guy from the point of view of the loser and perhaps one of the loser's supporters is seen as a poser – someone who is fighting to big-note himself. To be seen as a poser does not feel very good – the word in itself can act as a form of social control to prevent someone from posing. Paradoxically then, the tough guy in a fight can find himself either admired or despised or even both.

Transcript 14.8 Garry, Vanessa and Suzie

1 *Garry:* Ian Wilkins, he's a poser because he can beat me in a fight.	1 To win a fight is to be a poser (or to run the risk of being called one) i.e. Garry may mean that he poses because he wins or the very fact that he wins makes him a poser by definition.
2 *B.D.:* Mm, hm.	
3 *Vanessa:* So's Mandy because she beats me.	3 This applies to the girls as well.
4 *Garry:* And Terry! God he's a pose. Ian Wilkins, when everybody's around he gets in and fights me and beats me just so everybody'll get around 'im and be his friend and that.	4 Winning fights and posing call for admiration and friendship – at least so it seems from the loser's point of view.
5 *Vanessa:* 'n, have a look.	5 Everyone will look at you being beaten.
6 *B.D.:* So if you're tough, everybody likes you?	
7 *Garry and Vanessa:* Yeah.	
8 *B.D.:* What happens if you're not tough?	
9 *Vanessa:* Nobody likes you.	
10 *Garry:* Yeah, they call you chicken.	10 Moreover you will be teased about it.

[. . .]

Fighting is a *natural* response to irritation and it protects you and your friends from outside attack. It is a useful skill to be developed and therefore requires practice. Most importantly, it gives you a reputation as someone to be respected and taken into account. It is the most direct form of negotiation engaged in by the children in establishing *who* they are, but it takes place within carefully defined situations.

The complex strategies that the children develop to maintain the friendship are not necessarily for love of the particular friend, but because of the functions friendship fulfils. Children may 'make and break friends with a rapidity disconcerting to the adult spectator' (Opie and Opie 1959: 324), but that is perhaps because the adult spectator does not actually understand what is going on. The friendships are in fact quite stable as I have indicated. What appear to be breakages are, rather, manoeuvres within the friendship. The children have developed words and related concepts which describe or explain what it is they are doing. These words and concepts are alien to adults. They belong to the social world of childhood [. . .]

REFERENCES

Bruner, J.S. (1974) *The Relevance of Education*, Harmondsworth: Penguin (first published by George Allen & Unwin 1972).

Cook-Gumperz, J. (1975) 'The child as practical reasoner', in M. Sanches and B.C. Blount (eds) *Socio-Cultural Dimensions of Language Use*, New York: Academic Press.

Cooley, C.H. (1972) 'Looking-glass self', in J.C. Manis and B.N. Meltzer (eds) *Symbolic Interaction*, Boston, Mass.: Allyn & Bacon.

Damon, W. (1977) *The Social World of the Child*, San Francisco, Calif.: Jossey Bass.

Garfinkel, H. (1967) *Studies in Ethnomethodology*, New York: Prentice-Hall.

Homans, G.C. (1951) *The Human Group*, London: Routledge & Kegan Paul.

Opie, I. and Opie, P. (1959) *The Lore and Language of Schoolchildren*, Oxford: Oxford University Press.

Rosser, E. and Harré, R. (1976) 'The meaning of trouble', in M. Hammersley and P. Woods (eds) *The Process of Schooling*, London: Routledge & Kegan Paul.

Speier, M. (1976) 'The child as conversationalist: some culture contact features of conversational interactions between adults and children', in M. Hammersley and P. Woods (eds) *The Process of Schooling*, London: Routledge & Kegan Paul.

Part five
Gender, 'race' and the experience of schooling

Introduction

I would argue that childhood innocence has a special status in the ideology of infants' teachers. . . . The state of innocence . . . required young children to be protected from what were thought to be unpleasant aspects of the outside world – an attempt to preserve a world of childhood in the face of adult reality.

(King 1988: 87–8)

King was one of the first sociologists to draw attention to the sense in which the image of childhood conveyed by 'child-centred' theories of primary education (notably as in the Plowden Report of 1967) is a cultural construction masquerading as natural law. The argument is that developmental psychology (especially Piagetian theory) has legitimized primary teachers' belief in 'childhood innocence' along with such other key features of child-centred ideology as 'individualism', 'developmentalism' and 'play as learning'. But the reality of classroom life is very different. For example in one study of London infant schools, children were observed to spend most of their time on task-work; there was a heavy emphasis on teaching the 3 R's and relationships with teachers were mostly passive and rarely one-to-one (Blatchford *et al.* 1988). In this final part we concentrate on the significance for classroom life and children's learning of two social issues of particular contemporary significance, gender and 'race'.

The starting-point for Croll and Moses (Chapter 15) is the claim that primary schools reinforce and even amplify the gender inequalities in society. Reviewing systematic observation and evaluation studies in Britain and the USA they claim that while schools are certainly gender differentiated, there is no consistent pattern of evidence that girls are at a disadvantage. They are generally reported to have more positive attitudes to school; their achievement is broadly similar to boys and in some areas better, and their teachers view them in a favourable light in terms of behaviour and achievement. They do receive less teacher attention than boys, but Croll and Moses argue that this is more a management than a sex bias problem, due in many cases to the problematic behaviour of small numbers of boys who engage a disproportionate amount of teachers' attention.

Skelton (Chapter 16) rejects this line of argument, claiming that gender discrimination operates at a much more subtle level, in terms of the ideas, values and confidence conveyed to children through, for example, reading schemes, curriculum content and power-relationships in school. Skelton argues that providing superficial equal opportunities is not enough. Children are daily exposed to role models in school that delineate adult-males as dominant and females as subordinate (e.g. head teachers versus class teachers; caretakers versus cleaning staff). The difficulties Skelton experienced trying to work with children to construct an anti-sexist classroom environment echo the frustrations reported by pioneering parents who endeavour to do the same at home (Statham 1986).

In Chapter 17 we turn to the issue of 'race' and pupil identity. Woods and Grugeon summarize their ethnographic study of pupil transitions, friendship patterns and curriculum experiences in six primary schools. The social context of the schools was very varied, ranging from 'progressive' urban multi-ethnic to 'traditionalist' rural all-white. Yet all had expressed eagerness to respond to the recommendations of the Swann Report on multi-racial education (DES 1985). In this sense it is important to note that these schools were by no means typical.

Even so, Woods and Grugeon describe the problems faced by a 5-year-old Asian boy making the transition into school, and the processes through which another child was 'ruled out' of mainstream education through the process of statementing. Points of transition later in the school system were also a source of anxiety to pupils and their parents as school rules about uniform, timekeeping and use of playgrounds were more strictly applied, also there were a greater number of teachers to establish relationships with new expectations about attending school meetings.

Finally, in Chapter 18, Short examines the implications of our conceptions of young children's development for the way we approach anti-racist and anti-sexist education. He argues that the dominant belief in 'sequential developmentalism' has prevented teachers from recognizing the possibility and appropriateness of curriculum development in these areas. Piaget's theory was developed in respect mainly of logical and mathematical thinking, but it has been applied right across the curriculum. Adoption of a social constructivist perspective, on the other hand, opens up the possibility of working with young children on controversial social issues in a sensitive way, appropriate to their level of understanding and interests.

REFERENCES

Blatchford, P., Burke, J., Farquhar, C., Plewis, I., and Tizard, B. (1988) 'A systematic observation study of children's behaviour at infant school', in M. Woodhead and A. McGrath (eds) *Family, School and Society*, London: Hodder & Stoughton.

DES (1985) *Education for All: Report of the Committee of Inquiry into the Education of Children from Ethnic Minority Groups* (Swann Report), Cmnd 9543, London: HMSO.

King, R. (1988) 'Informality, ideology and infants' schooling', in A. Blyth (ed.) *Informal Primary Education Today*, Lewes: Falmer Press.

Statham, J. (1986) *Daughters and Sons*, Oxford: Basil Blackwell.

15 Sex roles in the primary classroom

Paul Croll and Diana Moses

Source: C. Rogers and P. Kutnick (eds) (1990) *The Social Psychology of the Primary School*, London: Routledge, ch. 11.

[. . .]

INTRODUCTION

The focus of attention of this chapter is an exploration of the differences between the educational experiences of boys and girls in their primary schools. Are girls and boys treated differently from one another and do they have different educational experiences in the early years of schooling? If so, what significance and consequences does such differentiation have? Do boys and girls develop different skills and attitudes, for example, and do any differences between classroom experiences and educational attitudes and achievements which emerge in the primary school years have implications for later educational performance and in the adult world of work?

As we shall see later in this chapter, there is evidence that girls flourish in the primary school. They at least hold their own on measures of academic attainment compared with boys and they are much less likely to experience problems, either in connection with their academic performance or with their behavioural and emotional adjustment to school. On the other hand we know that, later in life, females are most unlikely to enjoy the same degree of occupational success and financial rewards as their male peers. In Britain in the 1980s women still do not enjoy the same occupational opportunities as men. They earn considerably less on average and, even within the same occupational groups, tend to have lower incomes. Much of the work done exclusively or virtually exclusively by women is particularly poorly paid. Women are under-represented at the top of all occupations, even those such as nursing and primary school teaching, which have traditionally been the preserve of women and in which they still predominate numerically (see Equal Opportunities Commission 1987, for a summary of some of the relevant statistical information on the economic situation of women).

The question naturally arises of whether, despite apparently satisfactory performance of girls at primary level, they are, nevertheless, in some way being prepared to be second best to boys. A number of writers have suggested that the educational system is, in various ways, implicated in the disadvantages females appear to suffer in later life (for example Acker 1984; 1988). Related to such arguments is the suggestion put forward by Sara Delamont that schools do not simply reflect the different sex roles and gender differentiation of the wider society but exaggerate and amplify such distinctions (Delamont 1980; 1983). Delamont argues that schools operate as a conservative force in which traditional female roles are emphasized and exaggerated and in which females suffer discrimination greater than that prevailing elsewhere.

In this chapter we shall attempt to summarize the available information on various aspects of the different school experiences, attainments and responses of girls and boys in British primary schools. First we shall consider the extent of gender differentiation in the everyday experience of the primary classroom. This analysis will be extended to look at possible disadvantaging features of classroom life, especially those related to teacher–pupil interaction. We shall then examine the learning outcomes for pupils, comparing the attainments in academic subjects and the extent of academic and related difficulties experienced by girls and boys. Finally we shall consider evidence on differences between female and male pupils' attitudes to and perceptions of school and differences in the ways that teachers perceive male and female pupils. Following the presentation of the empirical evidence on gender differences in the experience of primary education, we shall return to the question of the link between early educational experience and later occupational and financial disadvantage, and also consider whether schools exaggerate gender differentiation compared with that existing in the wider society.

GENDER DIFFERENTIATION IN THE CLASSROOM

Gender differentiation is a prominent feature of this and other societies and it is not surprising that differentiation between boys and girls should be a feature of schools. Schools cannot exist in a vacuum and by the time they come to school, and then alongside their school experience, children have learnt and continue to learn a great deal about the world from their parents, their peers, books, comics, television and other sources. When they come to school at the age of 4 or 5 the child will have a clear image of her/himself as a boy or girl. The great majority of given names are specific to males or females; similarly the clothes children wear are often gender specific. Boys and girls are likely to have been treated rather differently from the time they were born and, for instance, given different toys to play with. Evidence on sex differences in pre-school play is given by Serbin (1983).

Studies such as those of King (1978) have documented the routine pattern of gender differentiation in a variety of school routines and activities. Teachers automatically used gender as an organizing category within the classrooms in his study. Boys' and girls' names were listed separately on the register, coats were hung up separately, record cards were in different colours for boys and for girls, histograms containing data from the children were done separately for girls and boys, and so on. King notes that a significant feature of these practices was that they were 'taken for granted' and not regarded as in any way problematic by the teachers, who did not think they needed explaining, still less justifying. In a study of a Scottish primary school Hartley (1985) describes the predominance of organizational practices based on gender and also notes that children's friendships tend to be same-sex specific. Another feature of the classrooms described by King was the use of competition between boys and girls both as a strategy for control and as an organizational feature of the classroom. Contrasts between the behaviour of the groups were made by teachers and 'gender-inappropriate' behaviour commented on. Tasks were sometimes divided between boys and girls with a competitive element introduced.

However, gender differentiation is not always a feature of descriptions of classrooms. As Delamont (1980) points out, the British observational studies of classrooms conducted before that of King made no reference at all to gender. Later studies have not generally seen gender as central although studies such as those of Hartley (1985) consider gender differences. Pollard (1985) considers gender as an issue but concludes that other differentiating characteristics of children are more relevant for his analysis of the social experience of schooling. He writes, 'the close similarity in the perspectives of boys' and girls' friendship groups regarding school which led me to focus primarily on the goody, joker and gang distinction as having more analytic power than that of gender' (Pollard 1985: 195). King, who is one of the researchers to put most emphasis on gender differentiation, also stresses that this is only one of the differentiating factors in the classroom and not the most important of these (King 1978).

What emerges from these studies is that primary classrooms are, in a common-sense fashion, heavily gender differentiated. Primary classes are made up of little boys and little girls rather than little children and reference to this and the use of it for organization, control and class management is a routine feature of teaching in primary school. Such a differential is probably the most obvious single feature of primary classrooms and the lack of reference to it in many discussions of teaching is an indication of its 'taken-for-granted' nature. This is different, however, from saying that gender differentiation is the most important feature of primary classrooms or, in particular, that it operates in a way that disadvantages one or other of the sexes. Some possible ways in which the different experiences of the primary classrooms may in fact be disadvantaging, in particular girls, will be considered below.

TEACHER–PUPIL INTERACTION IN THE CLASSROOM

One possible difference in the classroom experience of boys and girls which has received recent attention is that girls may be disadvantaged in the classroom by receiving less attention from the teacher than is given to boys. Some fairly extreme claims about this gender imbalance have been made, especially by writers approaching the issue from a feminist perspective. Perhaps the best known work in this tradition is that of Spender who writes of boys receiving 'so much more attention from teachers than do girls' (Spender 1982: 54). Spender also claims that gender imbalances are so routinized and expected in classrooms that even when teachers are trying to equalize attention girls get only just over a third of the teacher's time (Spender 1982). However, no details are given of the basis of these assertions.

Similarly Stanworth (1981), reporting on a study of pupil perceptions of classroom interactions, shows pupils reporting boys as twice as likely to seek teacher attention and four times as likely to offer contributions to discussion. Buswell (1981: 196) writes of lessons in which female pupils took no part at all and that there were 'many more classes [in which] girls received only minimal attention compared with boys'.

Some of these assertions come from studies of classrooms using a qualitative observational methodology. Other studies of classrooms using such an approach do not report such differences. As was shown above, Pollard (1985), in an extensive observational study of primary schools, made little use of gender as an explanatory category. Similarly gender differences do not emerge from the observations in infant classrooms reported by Sharp and Green (1975). King (1978) and Hartley (1985) both focus on gender differences in their studies of primary classrooms but do not report differences in levels of teacher interaction.

The obvious way to establish whether boys get more attention than girls in the primary classroom is to observe in a substantial sample of classrooms and to count or time in a systematic fashion the number of teacher interactions which are directed to boys and girls to see if they differ. If we wish to go beyond statements about the relative number of interactions and say something about the type of interaction it will also be necessary to distinguish between different types of interactions in the counting or timing procedure. Data relevant to this issue come from the many studies which have conducted systematic observation in classrooms.

Systematic observation provides a method of getting precise quantitative data on aspects of interaction and behaviour in classrooms. Observations are made by using a predetermined set of categories and a precise timing system. For example, a very simple system relevant to the present discussion would be one where an observer focused observation on a teacher and every ten seconds noted whether or not the teacher was involved in a one-to-one interaction with a pupil and, if so, whether this was with a boy or a girl. Such an observation system allows a precise estimate to be given of the amount of teacher interaction with male and female pupils. Clearly such a system could be made more sophisticated and could also allow the categorization of type of interaction such as curriculum-related or non-curriculum-related, or whether the teacher or the pupil had initiated the interaction. A full account of this kind of classroom research can be found in Croll (1986).

A large number of studies using systematic observation have been conducted in school classrooms, most of them in the United States, but also in British classrooms. Although the issue of differential attention to boys and girls has not usually been the main focus of these studies, many of them provide data on such differences. Alison Kelly has recently published a meta-analysis of eighty-one research studies which provide quantitative data on the relative amount of teacher interaction received by boys and girls in classrooms (Kelly 1988). Meta-analysis is a technique for summarizing the results of different studies to give an overall estimate of an effect (Kelly 1986). In addition to data on overall differences in teacher interactions with boys and girls, Kelly also retrieves information about different aspects of the interactions from many of the studies.

The analysis of overall differences in the amount of teacher interaction with boys and with girls derived from the meta-analysis shows that girls receive 44 per cent of all classroom interactions and boys receive 56 per cent. The types of interactions in which girls were least well represented were those involving criticism by the teacher. Girls received only 35 per cent of criticisms and only 32 per cent of criticisms directed at behaviour. However, the under-representation of girls cannot be accounted for simply by the boys being more heavily criticized: girls received 44 per cent of questions, 44 per cent of response opportunities, and 48 per cent of praise. The analysis also shows that the under-representation of girls in classroom interactions does not arise from an unwillingness to participate, as girls were more likely than boys to volunteer or put their hands up (52 per cent). They were, however, less likely than boys to call out answers (41 per cent). Another result to emerge from the study was that when children were divided into those having desirable characteristics (high ability, good behaviour, and so on) and those having undesirable characteristics (low ability, poor behaviour), the sex bias was more pronounced among the 'desirable' group than among the 'undesirable' group.

The studies analysed by Kelly covered a variety of age ranges and not just the primary years. Relatively few of the studies were conducted in Britain and over 80 per cent of them were American. A breakdown of the estimates from different groups of studies shows that in those conducted by British authors the sex bias was very slightly less (45 per cent). Studies conducted on 6- to 11-year-olds also show a slightly lower sex bias (46 per cent) although the sex bias in studies of children under 6 is much greater (41 per cent).

This sort of meta-analysis provides a very valuable overall estimate from a wide range of studies, but it is not possible to derive from it specific estimates for British primary schools. Moreover, a number of recent major studies of British primary schools were not included in the analysis. For these reasons, and also because it is interesting to locate estimates of interaction differences in specific identifiable studies, a number of researchers using systematic observation in British primary school classrooms will be discussed below. There are five studies published within the last ten years which give quantifiable data on teacher–pupil interactions in a large sample of English primary school classrooms, and which allow distinctions to be made between interactions with male and female pupils. These are the

ORACLE research, which provides observational data on 120 classrooms across the junior age range (Galton *et al.* 1980), the *One in Five* study (Croll and Moses 1985) which provides data on 34 second-year junior classes, the NFER study (National Foundation for Educational Research 1987) giving data on 59 third- and fourth-year junior classrooms, the Inner London Education Authority (ILEA) study (Mortimore *et al.* 1988) giving data on 50 Inner London junior classrooms, and the Thomas Coram study (Tizard *et al.* 1988) based on observation on 30 infants' classrooms. Of these studies only the ORACLE research was included in the meta-analysis described above (Kelly 1988: Appendix 1), probably because the others were published too recently for the information to be available.

The ORACLE research (Galton *et al.* 1980) was the first large-scale observational study to be conducted in British classrooms. Gender differences were not a feature of the main analysis which concentrated on the impact of different teaching approaches and the consequences for classroom interaction of a predominantly individualized approach to teaching. It showed how, even when teachers interacted mainly with individual pupils, the main contact with the teacher of pupils in the class was as a member of the whole class audience. This clearly has implications for differences between boys and girls in the amount of teacher attention they received. In the data derived from observations of individual pupils and describing the amount of teacher interaction they received, boys were observed to receive more individual attention than girls. In the terms used by Kelly, boys received 54 per cent of the teachers' attention to individuals while the girls received 46 per cent. But when all interactions, including whole class interactions, are included in the analysis, girls are involved in over 49 per cent of interactions compared with 46 per cent of individual interactions.

The research reported in *One in Five* (Croll and Moses 1985), and in a subsequent analysis of these data (Croll 1986), was mainly concerned with children with special educational needs, but also included observational data on the classroom interactions of a control sample of other children in second-year junior classrooms. These data provide a very similar picture of sex differences in pupil–teacher interaction to those of the ORACLE study. Girls receive 46 per cent of individual teacher interactions and boys 54 per cent. As in the ORACLE study, the great majority of teacher–pupil interactions were whole class interactions where there were no sex differences.

The ILEA junior school project followed the progress and school experiences of 2,000 children as they went through 50 Inner London junior schools and observed children in second- and third-year junior classes. This research found that 'Teachers contributed more at an individual level with boys than with girls' (Mortimore *et al.* 1988: 167). Expressed in terms comparable with those used in the Kelly analysis, girls received 46 per cent of the teachers' individual attention in the second-year classroom and 42 per cent in the third-year classrooms. The major difference between boys and girls was that boys received more comments, both critical and neutral, about their behaviour, but this did not completely account for the gender imbalance.

These three projects all found sex differences in levels of teacher interaction with boys and girls. The final two studies, however, found no such differences. A project conducted by the National Foundation for Educational Research used the ORACLE observation system to observe language and mathematics lessons in 59 third- and fourth-year junior classes (NFER 1987). This study found no differences in the amount of teacher attention to boys and to girls in either mathematics lessons or language lessons.

Finally, research conducted by the Thomas Coram Research Centre observed pupils in thirty classes in ethnically mixed Inner London infant schools (Tizard *et al.* 1988). This study also reported no differences in overall levels of teacher interactions with boys and girls.

A consideration of Kelly's meta-analysis and of the five British studies discussed above shows that there is a consistent tendency for girls, on average, to receive slightly less individual teacher attention than boys, although this is not invariably so in either individual classrooms or in all studies. The studies reviewed by Kelly range from those which show no differences in interaction to those showing girls receiving fewer than 40 per cent of interactions. Averaged across all the studies girls received 44 per cent of interactions. Of the five recent large-scale British studies, three showed lower levels of interaction with girls of an extent broadly comparable to Kelly's results while two showed no differences. No study has shown girls receiving more individual teacher attention than boys. The studies which show boys getting more attention almost invariably show that this is in part due to boys receiving substantially more behavioural criticism, but the studies also show that this does not account for the overall differences in levels of interaction. Compared with the claims reported above about the discrepancies in teacher attention across the sexes, the differences reported here are not large but, as Kelly (1988) points out, over a school career they amount to a considerably lower level of direct contact with the teacher for individual girls.

Various explanations have been put forward for this pattern of inequality in teacher interaction. Some authors have suggested that sexist bias is so prevalent in society that male dominance is 'natural' and effectively invisible (for example Megarry 1981; Spender 1982). Kelly (1988) suggests that the emphasis that teachers put on working with children as individuals and responding to their individual needs may mean that lack of equality between groups such as males and females is not apparent or not important to them. An observation originally made by French and French (1984) is that there is not a general pattern of higher levels of interaction with all boys but rather a tendency for a few boys to get more attention than other pupils generally. This explanation was tested by Croll (1986) in an analysis of classroom interaction in thirty-four second-year junior classes. The hypothesis that the increased attention to boys occurs because teachers regard a much higher proportion of boys than girls as having special educational needs was also investigated. The results of this analysis suggest that to some extent the increased attention to boys is a result of a higher proportion of boys having special educational needs. Both boys and girls identified as having special needs received very much above average levels of teacher attention which were equal across the sexes. This matches the result reported in Kelly's meta-analysis that sex imbalances were greatest among pupils having 'desirable' characteristics and least among pupils having 'undesirable' characteristics. However, these differences did not entirely account for the imbalance of attention to boys and girls and the suggestion put forward by French and French was also supported. In these classrooms a few boys, who were not identified as having special needs, nevertheless were involved in very high levels of teacher interaction in a way that was not true of girls.

If it is the case that there is not a general pattern whereby all or most boys get slightly more attention than all or most girls, but rather a pattern whereby a few boys get very much more attention than all other pupils, then the gender imbalance is best seen as a problem of classroom management rather than necessarily a problem of sexist bias. Such a pattern would also explain both the overall similarity between studies and the pattern of variation in results whereby in some classrooms there is no sex bias and in others there is a bias towards boys, but no studies report a bias towards girls. If the imbalance reflects poor classroom management strategies or poor class control then this is something which we should expect to vary considerably between teachers and possibly between schools and types of schools. Such a view also offers an explanation of the way that some qualitatively-based studies claim very much greater levels of inequality than are reported in any of the systematic observation studies. The qualitative studies by their nature are focused on very few classrooms and may chance upon classrooms where problems of management are greatest. It is also likely that a few incidents involving very high levels of attention to certain boys can come to dominate the researcher's perception of the classroom and disguise the similar levels of attention given to most boys and most girls.

OTHER ASPECTS OF CLASSROOM BEHAVIOUR

Teacher interaction is one of the most contentious areas for looking at differences in the classroom experiences of boys and girls, but there are other areas where differences may arise. The ORACLE study gives the most detailed account of classroom behaviour and interactions of primary-aged pupils and, as in the case of teacher interaction, differences in other types of behaviour are small, although girls have slightly higher total work involvement than boys (Galton *et al.* 1980). The study of infant classrooms by Tizard *et al.* (1988) found very similar patterns of classroom experience and, for example, the same level of time-on-task for boys and girls. One difference which did emerge in this study was that white boys in the sample spent more time engaged on mathematics tasks and this seemed to reflect teacher allocation rather than pupil choice (Tizard *et al.* 1988).

One aspect of classroom interaction which is apparent from the ORACLE research and from other studies is the marked tendency for girls to interact with other girls and boys to interact with other boys. In the ORACLE study same-sex seating pairs were observed to interact twice as frequently as opposite sex pairs. In mixed sex groups interaction is twice as likely to be with a pupil of the same sex and the grouping pattern with the highest levels of pupil–pupil interaction were same sex groups. In all, over 80 per cent of pupil–pupil interactions were with members of the same sex and this clearly arose, for the most part, from pupil choice rather than from teacher grouping arrangements (Galton *et al.* 1980). In respect of pupil interactions, gender differentiation in the primary classroom is imposed by the pupils themselves through their social behaviour. These results are in accord with those of researchers such as Hartley (1985) who reports a strong tendency to same-sex friendship choices in the primary school.

SEX DIFFERENCES IN ACADEMIC ACHIEVEMENT

Perhaps the central issue in any consideration of the consequences of sex differences and gender differentiation in the primary school is in the area of educational achievement. Academic achievement, especially in the areas of reading, language and mathematics, is central to the aims of primary school teachers (Ashton *et al.* 1975) and predominates in the content of the primary curriculum (Galton *et al.* 1980). If there are sex role differences in primary schools and, in particular, if differentiation works to the disadvantage of girls, differences in patterns of achievement, if they occur, would be the most serious manifestation of these differences.

An important source of evidence for levels of achievement in the primary school is the work of the Assessment Performance Unit (APU). Surveys of achievement among 11-year-olds in language, mathematics and science were conducted by the APU in the late 1970s and early 1980s. The 1979 survey of language (APU 1981a) showed no significant differences between the performance in reading of boys and girls but found that girls were ahead in writing skills. A survey a year later found that girls were ahead in both reading and writing. These differences were statistically significant but in absolute terms were small (APU 1982a). Surveys of mathematics achievement were made in 1978, 1979 and 1980 (APU 1980; 1981b; 1982b). In all of these studies there were sex differences between the various subcategories of mathematics achievement tested, with girls scoring higher in some and boys in others. However, in all three surveys boys received higher scores in the majority of the subcategories. The survey of achievement in science made in 1981 showed no overall differences in performance between girls and boys. However, boys performed better at measures of science concepts while girls performed better at measures concerned with representing information. The report suggests that boys were performing better at the specifically scientific aspects of the assessments (APU 1981c).

The research conducted in infant classrooms in London by Professor Tizard and her colleagues at the Thomas Coram Research Centre provides evidence on the achievements of a group of children at an early stage in their primary school careers (Tizard *et al.* 1988). At the end of the children's time at nursery school, through the infant school, and in the first year of the juniors, a variety of tests measuring reading, writing and number skills were administered. The results at the end of the nursery school show that at this stage there were few sex differences in performance although the girls had better writing skills. In reading girls and boys made about the same progress up to the middle infants but girls made slightly more progress in their year in the top infants. In the first-year juniors, girls were ahead on reading. In writing girls maintained but did not increase their lead over boys through the infant school. Writing was not tested in the junior schools. In mathematics boys had made more progress than girls by the top infants and were ahead in the first-year juniors.

Recent studies of the attainments of junior-aged children include the ORACLE research (Galton and Croll 1980), the ILEA study (Mortimore *et al.* 1988), and the *One in Five* study (Croll and Moses 1985). The ORACLE research showed an overall identical level of performance by girls and boys. Within this overall figure was a slight advantage to boys in the mathematics test and a slight advantage to girls in the language test. Performance on the reading test was identical for boys and girls (Galton and Croll 1980). The ILEA study followed 2,000 children through their four years in the junior school. The test results showed a general pattern of somewhat higher attainments for girls. Girls had higher levels of attainment at each of the assessment points for both reading and writing. However, the higher attainments in each of these subjects at the end of the junior school years were no more than would have been predicted from the girls' higher level of attainments at the beginning of junior school: progress, as opposed to level of attainment, was the same for boys and girls. In the case of mathematics there was little difference in attainment or progress between boys and girls although girls made more progress during the third year of the junior school. No sex differences were found in performance on tests of oral skills (Mortimore *et al.* 1988). The *One in Five* study assessed both second-year and fourth-year juniors on tests of reading and non-verbal reasoning. Girls were found to be slightly ahead on both these measures (Croll and Moses 1988).

The APU surveys and the primary school research projects described above have broadly comparable results to those of a much earlier study of children's attainments, the Medical Research Council longitudinal study reported in *The Home and the School* (Douglas 1964). This research replicated earlier results in indicating that girls are more successful than boys at primary school. In this study girls performed better on tests of verbal and non-verbal intelligence, tests of sentence completion and tests of arithmetic than boys. The girls' advantage was noticeably greater in the sentence completion tests than in the arithmetic tests. The study conducted during the time of selection for secondary education at 11+ also showed that girls were more likely than boys to be selected for grammar school education (Douglas 1964).

All of these studies are in broad agreement that girls perform at least as well and generally slightly better than boys during the primary school years. They also agree that the relative performance of girls and boys differs across subjects and, to some extent, across different aspects of a subject. Girls consistently do better on language-related aspects and relatively less well on mathematical aspects of assessments, although in some of the studies they still do as well or better than boys at mathematics.

At the time of Douglas's research, although girls were outperforming boys at primary school and were more likely to be selected for grammar school, far fewer girls than boys were successfully completing 16+ and 18+ examinations and continuing to higher education. The possibility needs to be considered that even though the recent studies show girls doing as well or better than boys at primary school they are, nevertheless, in some way being prepared for failure later in their school careers and their equality or advantage will disappear in the secondary school. The most recent data relevant to secondary school performance of boys and girls come from the 1987 edition of the Department of Education and Science statistics (DES 1987). The figures given here relate, for the most part, to the academic year 1985–6 when children in the ORACLE study and in some of the APU surveys were entering post-compulsory education.

These figures suggest that there is no longer an increasing under-achievement of girls as they pass through the school system. As an indication of performance at 16+ the DES statistics gave the proportion of boys and girls leaving school with O levels at grade C or above or Grade 1 in GSE (irrespective of any A levels obtained). Of the girls, 58 per cent had at least one such grade compared with 52 per cent of boys. This performance is also reflected in the way that a higher proportion of girls than boys in the 16–18 age group remain in post-compulsory education, 34.9 per cent compared with 30.5 per cent of boys. Of those remaining in the school sector of post-compulsory education there was again a slightly higher proportion of girls, 18.1 per cent, compared with 17.2 per cent of boys (DES 1987).

A comparison of the A level performances of boys and girls for the 1985–6 school year shows a very similar pattern in overall performance. An identical proportion of girls and boys, 18.5 per cent, left school with at least one A level. Fractionally more boys than girls, 14.9 per cent compared with 14.3 per cent, left school with two or more A levels. This equality is not sustained into higher education, however. Among the 19- to 20-year-old age group, for example, 13.3 per cent of males were in higher education compared with 11.8 per cent of females. And in 1985, 56 per cent of those receiving first degrees were male (DES 1987).

Although the overall level of secondary school achievement is similar for boys and girls, the achievements in different subjects differ considerably. The direction of this difference reflects in an exaggerated form differences which had begun to be apparent at primary school. At 16+, 46 per cent of girls received an O level pass or CSE Grade 1 in English compared with 35 per cent of boys. In contrast, 35 per cent of boys achieved this result in mathematics compared with 30 per cent of girls. In post-compulsory education this tendency has become much stronger: 55 per cent of boys with two or more A levels included mathematics in their results compared with 32 per cent of girls, while 51 per cent of girls with two or more A levels passed A level English compared with 27 per cent of boys (DES 1987).

As has been apparent from the measures of academic achievement presented above, there is no straightforward way in which girls can be regarded as academically disadvantaged in the primary school. Their overall performance is at least as high as that of boys and in most studies is rather higher. Measures of achievement and participation rates in secondary school also show that girls achieve equally with boys. It is not until entry into higher education that the disadvantages women suffer in occupations and in the wider society appear in their educational experience. This makes it unlikely that the primary school can be regarded as in some way preparing females to fail despite their apparent equal or higher achievement compared with males.

The question of subject bias in achievement is more complex. It is plain that girls' higher levels of achievement manifest themselves most clearly in aspects of achievement related to language and reading. In mathematics and science girls are generally either not ahead of boys or performing slightly less well. This polarization of achievement is only very marginal at primary level, especially with regard to girls' under-achievement. At secondary school, however, the polarization of achievement and subject choice between linguistic/humanities-orientated subjects and mathematical/scientific subjects is very apparent. The consequences of this polarization are more difficult to establish. At primary level reading achievement is the single most important academic aim for teachers (Ashton *et al.* 1975). Reading is central to primary classrooms as a medium for instruction and a criterion for assessment, and dominates the judgements teachers make of children's academic ability (Croll and Moses 1985). At this level it is certainly not a less highly valued skill than scientific and mathematical achievements.

SPECIAL EDUCATIONAL NEEDS

Although the difference between the average attainment of boys and girls in the primary school is relatively small, it is boys who are far more likely than girls to have special educational needs. Several studies have found that, over the whole range of special needs, boys outnumber girls by approximately two to one. This was the conclusion reached by the epidemiological studies of Rutter *et al.* (1970) and Pringle *et al.* (1966).

More recently, in a study of teachers' views of special educational needs, Croll and Moses (1985) found that twice as many boys as girls were regarded as having special educational needs by their class teachers. The research showed that, overall, teachers of junior-aged pupils thought that 24.4 per cent of boys in their classes had special educational needs but only 13.2 per cent of the girls. When various kinds of educational needs are considered, interesting differences emerge. Learning difficulties were attributed to 19.5 per cent of the boys and 11.1 per cent of the girls and behavioural problems to 10.9 per cent of boys and 4.5 per cent of girls. Although, in total, relatively few children were regarded as being discipline problems, boys outnumbered the girls by nearly four to one (boys 6.4 per cent and girls 1.7 per cent). These boys were not simply indulging in boisterous 'boylike' behaviour that was a nuisance to the teacher but expected and accepted. Virtually all the boys who were regarded as discipline problems were also thought to have emotional and behavioural difficulties which were creating problems for the child as well as being a nuisance to the teacher. Behaviour problems were also associated with learning difficulties, and many more boys than girls experienced this complex of special needs.

As we have seen, there are only small differences between the average scores of boys and girls on reading tests but there are many more boys than girls who experience problems with reading in the primary school. Croll and Moses (1985) compared the reading ages of boys and girls in thirty-four second-year junior classrooms and found that nearly twice as many boys as girls had a reading age of two years or more behind their chronological age (6.7 per cent of boys and 3.6 per cent of girls). The proportion of boys scoring between one and two years behind their real ages was half as great again as the proportion of girls (17.6 per cent of boys and 11.8 per cent of girls). These figures are a clear indication that more boys have reading difficulties, and it is not surprising that the 428 junior class teachers interviewed by Croll and Moses described 9.5 per cent of the girls in their classes as 'poor readers' compared with 17.5 per cent of the boys. However, a comparison of test scores with teacher assessments suggested that, when performance is taken into account, teachers tended to under-estimate the extent to which girls had reading difficulties compared with their estimation of the reading difficulties of boys.

Previous discussions of the relationship between teachers' views of their pupils and the pupils' actual performance have tended to concentrate on the possible advantages accruing to children who are favourably regarded by their teachers and the disadvantages of being less well regarded. Concern with the effect of teacher expectations and with 'self-fulfilling prophecies' has led researchers to concentrate on the positive aspects of being favourably regarded by teachers and the possible unfairness this involves to the other children in the class. If we take this view then the advantage is overwhelmingly in favour of the girls. Nevertheless, there is little solid evidence for such processes (see Boydell 1978 and Croll 1981 for a review of some of the relevant evidence). It is, at least on the face of it, at least as plausible that a child may be disadvantaged by not having her or his difficulties recognized as that such a recognition will become self-fulfilling.

ATTITUDES TO SCHOOL AMONG GIRLS AND BOYS

There is evidence that girls express more positive attitudes towards school than do boys. The ORACLE study found that girls scored higher than boys on a measure of contentment at school and on intrinsic motivation to do well at school (Croll and Willcocks 1980) and the ILEA research reported that girls had higher scores on a scale of attitude towards school and also had more positive self-concepts in relation to school (Mortimore *et al.* 1988). However, there is also evidence that girls have higher levels of anxiety (Croll and Willcocks 1980). Tizard *et al.* (1988) report that among infant school children boys are more likely than girls to rate themselves as above average on academic tasks although their performance did not justify this. Evidence on aspects of pupil attitudes with regard to particular curriculum areas can be found in the Assessment of Performance Unit (APU) surveys. In mathematics there was no difference in expressed levels of enjoyment between boys and girls, a result also reported in the ILEA study (ILEA 1988). There were also no differences in their perceptions of the usefulness of mathematics. However, boys had more confidence in their own mathematical ability than did girls (APU 1980). In the case of science boys were more positive than girls about the experimental aspects of science and rated these more highly than the non-experimental aspects in a way that was not true of girls (APU 1981c).

It seems that in their overall view of school girls are rather more positive and motivated than boys. However, there is some tendency for girls to be more anxious and for boys to be more self-confident about school work.

TEACHER PERCEPTIONS OF GIRLS AND OF BOYS

There is ample evidence that teachers perceive boys' classroom behaviour as being more problematic than that of girls. When considering special educational needs we saw that teachers were much more likely to describe boys as having behaviour problems and as posing discipline problems in the classroom. Earlier studies such as that of Douglas (1964) also report teachers as being much more critical of boys than of girls. The ILEA research and the London infant school survey also showed that boys were more likely than girls to be described as having behavioural difficulties (Mortimore *et al.* 1988; Tizard *et al.* 1988). In his detailed case study of a primary school Hartley (1985) reports that teachers have more positive views of girls and regard boys as noisy and disruptive. A similar study in infant classrooms by King (1978) reports that boys were reproved more and that teachers had more favourable assessments of girls' behaviour.

It is less clear if these perceptions have any wider consequences for the classroom experiences of boys and girls. Boys are more likely to be seen by teachers as having learning difficulties than girls (see p. 285), but this still applies to only a minority of boys. However, Douglas shows that at the time of the 11+ examination teachers were more likely to think that girls rather than boys should be given grammar school places, even though there was little difference in their test scores (Douglas 1964). The ILEA research reports that primary records are more favourable to girls than to boys (Mortimore *et al.* 1988), and King (1978) found that in the infant classrooms he studied boys were typified by teachers as making less progress than girls.

For the most part these differences in teacher perceptions almost certainly reflect real differences in pupil behaviour and attainment. The poorer behaviour of boys and their greater likelihood of having learning difficulties are mirrored in their teachers' views. It should also be noted that, as King (1978) points out, the most important typification teachers make of pupils is as individuals. Although King describes the different perceptions teachers had of boys and of girls, he emphasizes that such generalizations were of limited importance compared with the teachers' stress on each child's individuality.

DISCUSSION

The studies discussed above have pointed to aspects of both difference and similarity in the educational experiences of girls and boys at primary level. In many respects sex roles are highly differentiated in the primary classroom. Children are differentiated by their names, their clothes and some of the activities they engage in. Gender groupings are also an important aspect of the way classrooms are managed and most of the children's own social and work interactions are with pupils of the same sex. However, in other respects boys' and girls' educational experiences are very similar: they have broadly similar levels of academic achievement, broadly similar attitudes towards school and broadly similar levels of interaction with the teacher. Where differences emerge in these areas the extent to which they can be regarded as disadvantaging either girls or boys varies. Boys get rather more individual attention from the teacher, are slightly more confident and sometimes perform better at mathematics; girls like school more and are more motivated, perform slightly better, especially in the area of language, and are considerably more favourably regarded by their teachers. However, in all these respects differences within gender groups are very much more important than differences between them.

The research reviewed here cannot be regarded as supporting the thesis that gender differentiation in the primary school contributes in any substantial fashion to the disadvantages females suffer in the outside world and, in particular, in the world of employment. Not only do girls succeed in the primary school, but also they continue to perform equally with boys throughout secondary schooling. If the primary school is preparing them for failure, it takes a long time for this effect to make itself felt. It has sometimes been argued that it is the failure of girls to choose and to do well in mathematical and scientific subjects which in part accounts for their disadvantaged occupational position (for example Deem 1978). The beginnings of this process can be identified in some of the studies of primary schools although the underachievement of girls, even where it occurs, is small. What is ignored in this argument, however, is that boys who study the subjects in which girls excel are not disadvantaged in employment. [. . .]

A further issue to be considered is whether schools go beyond gender differentiation in society as a whole and impose a more rigid division into traditional sex roles. Sara Delamont argues that schools are essentially conservative institutions in which prevailing sex stereotypes not only are not challenged but also are exaggerated (Delamont 1980; 1983). This is an important and carefully stated argument, but while we accept that schools do not in general challenge prevailing societal assumptions about sex roles and gender divisions (Acker 1988), the extent to which they can be seen as exaggerating them is far less clear. Examples of exaggerated gender divisions include rules about clothing, separate registers, separate games, and so on. Other examples, however, could include equal levels of achievement, equal (or higher) representation in high achieving streams, equal access at the primary level to virtually all of the curriculum and all its central aspects, and equal regard for their achievements by teachers. Although these features seem so obviously right that they are not worth commenting on, it should be noted that such equality does not generally prevail in society. These are also the aspects of school which are central to their purpose. It is in these areas where schools are most distinctive that they are also more equal than society at large. Although girls are differentiated at primary school the evidence suggests that they are not disadvantaged. [. . .]

REFERENCES

Acker, S. (1984) 'Sociology, gender and education', in S. Acker *et al.* (eds) *World Yearbook of Education: Women and Education*, London: Kogan Page.

Acker, S. (1988) 'Teachers, gender and resistance', *British Journal of Sociology of Education* 9(3): 307–22.

Ashton, P., Kneen, P., Davis, F. and Holley, B.J. (1975) *The Aims of Primary Education*, London: Macmillan.

Assessment of Performance Unit (APU) (1980) *Mathematical Development: Primary Survey Report 1*, London: HMSO.

Assessment of Performance Unit (APU) (1981a) *Language Performance in Schools: Primary Survey Report 1*, London: HMSO.

Assessment of Performance Unit (APU) (1981b) *Mathematical Development: Primary Survey Report 2*, London: HMSO.

Assessment of Performance Unit (APU) (1981c) *Science in School Age 11*, London: HMSO.

Assessment of Performance Unit (APU) (1982a) *Language Performance in School: Primary Survey Report 2*, London: HMSO.

Assessment of Performance Unit (APU) (1982b) *Mathematical Development: Primary Survey Report 3*, London: HMSO.

Boydell, D. (1978) *The Primary Teacher in Action*, London: Open Books.

Buswell, C. (1981) 'Sexism in school routines and classroom practices', *Durham and Newcastle Research Review* 9: 195–200.

Croll, P. (1981) 'Social class, pupil achievement and classroom interaction', in B. Simon and J. Willcocks (eds) *Research and Practice in the Primary Classroom*, London: Routledge & Kegan Paul.

Croll, P. (1986) *Systematic Classroom Observation*, Lewes: Falmer Press.

Croll, P. and Moses, D. (1985) *One in Five: The Assessment and Incidence of Special Educational Needs*, London: Routledge & Kegan Paul.

Croll, P. and Willcocks, J. (1980) 'Personality and classroom behaviour', in M. Galton and B. Simon (eds) *Progress and Performance in the Primary Classroom*, London: Routledge & Kegan Paul.

Deem, R. (1978) *Women and Schooling*, London: Routledge & Kegan Paul.

Delamont, S. (1980) *Sex Roles and the School*, London: Methuen.

Delamont, S. (1983) 'The conservative school? Sex roles at home, at work, and at school', in S. Walker and L. Barton (eds) *Gender, Class and Education*, Lewes: Falmer Press.

DES (1987) *Statistics of Education 1987*, London: HMSO.

Douglas, J.W.B. (1964) *The Home and the School*, London: MacGibbon & Kee.

Equal Opportunities Commission (1987) *Women and Men in Britain: A Statistical Profile*, London: HMSO.

French, J. and French, P. (1984) 'Gender imbalances in the primary classroom: an interactional account', *Educational Research* 26(2): 127–36.

Galton, M. and Croll, P. (1980) 'Pupil achievement and progress', in M. Galton and B. Simon (eds) *Progress and Performance in the Primary Classroom*, London: Routledge & Kegan Paul.

Galton, M., Simon, B. and Croll, P. (1980) *Inside the Primary Classroom*, London: Routledge & Kegan Paul.

Hartley, D. (1985) *Understanding the Primary School*, London: Croom Helm.

Inner London Education Authority (ILEA) (1988) *The Junior School Project*, vols 1–3, London: ILEA.

Kelly, A. (1986) 'A method to the madness? Quantitative research reviewing', *Research in Education*, 35: 25–41.

Kelly, A. (1988) 'Gender differences in teacher–pupil interactions: a meta-analytic review', *Research in Education* 39: 1–23.

King, R. (1978) *All Things Bright and Beautiful?* Chichester: Wiley.

Megarry, J. (1981) *Sex, Gender and Education*, Glasgow: Jordanhill College of Education.

Mortimore, P., Sammons, P., Stoll, L., Lewis, D. and Ecob, R. (1988) *School Matters: The Junior Years*, Wells: Open Books.

National Foundation for Educational Research (NFER) (1987) *Teaching Styles and Pupil Performance at the Primary Level*, Windsor: NFER mimeo.

Pollard, A. (1985) *The Social World of the Primary School*, London: Holt, Rinehart & Winston.

Pringle, M.L.K., Butler, N. and Davie, R. (1966) *Eleven Thousand Seven Year Olds*, London: Longman.

Rutter, M., Tizard, J. and Whitmore, K. (1970) *Education, Health and Behaviour*, London: Longman.

Serbin, L. (1983) 'The hidden curriculum: academic consequences of teacher expectations', in M. Marland (ed.) *Sex Differentiation and Schooling*, London: Heinemann.

Sharp, R. and Green, A. (1975) *Education and Social Control*, London: Routledge & Kegan Paul.

Spender, D. (1982) *Invisible Women: The Schooling Scandal*, London: Writers and Readers Publishing Co-operative.

Stanworth, M. (1981) *Gender and Schooling: A Study of Sexual Divisions in the Classroom*, London: Women's Research and Resources Centre.

Tizard, B., Blatchford, P., Burke, J., Farquhar, C. and Plewis, I. (1988) *Young Children at School in the Inner City*, Hove and London: Erlbaum.

16 Demolishing 'The House that Jack Built': anti-sexist initiatives in the primary school

Christine Skelton
Source: B. Carrington and B. Troyna (eds) (1988) *Children and Controversial Issues*, Lewes: Falmer Press, ch. 10.

Where primary education is universal and free, girls tend to do as well as boys and sometimes better.

(Megarry 1984: 15)

The view that primary schooling does not discriminate against girls is one held by many people including teachers. However, substantial evidence is available which demonstrates that such a belief is misconceived (Clarricoates 1980; Hough 1985; French and French 1986). Gender discrimination is as prevalent in the primary school as in secondary education yet operates at a subtler level. For example, while it is a relatively easy task to identify the imbalance in numbers of girls and boys opting for science subjects, it is not so easy to assess the influence that gender-stereotyped reading schemes have on girls' self-confidence. As it stands, then, schooling affects girls' and boys' life chances in two ways: first, *selection* provides situations in which children either succeed or fail, and this in turn affects what job opportunities are available to males and females; second, the type of schooling children receive influences their *learning* specifically with regard to the ideas, values and confidence girls and boys develop through their educational experiences (Yates 1987). The intention here is not to rehearse the arguments adequately represented elsewhere (Whyte 1983; Marland 1983; Holly 1985) illustrating how and where gender discrimination occurs in primary schooling; rather it is to indicate *why* gender stereotyping is regarded as a non-issue in primary education and *what* action has been taken to redress the gender inequalities which exist (Skelton 1985). At the same time, it should be noted that although the principles which underpin anti-sexist and anti-racist education share many commonalities, the studies referred to in this chapter have focused upon predominantly white, if not all-white, school populations. It is clear that work has to be done which examines the relationship between the effects of sexism on white girls and the so-called double oppression of sexism and racism experienced by black girls within primary education. As such information is not yet available, the suggestions given in this chapter may have to be modified or changed in the light of future research into this area.

So, what is it about primary education that has resulted in gender issues being given so little attention? Most primary teachers pay lip-service to the idea that girls and boys should be given equal educational opportunities, but only a minority of teachers are aware of the implications the use of this term has for girls' experiences of schooling. The concept of equal educational opportunities as applied to gender was given increasing prominence by policy-makers in the 1970s, and was defined in terms of equalizing school resources and educational benefits; the idea was that if girls and boys were provided with equal access to the current educational system any imbalances in examination achievement and subsequent career opportunities would be resolved. The problem of gender inequalities in education was seen simply as relating to male and female examination achievement. However, by 1980 the question was being asked whether girls had gained anything from this interpretation of equal opportunities as the strategies developed to resolve gender differences did not tackle fundamental aspects of girls' education (see Weiner 1986). As Lyn Yates (1987) has pointed out, the question as to why girls' equal access to education has failed to make any significant advances in widening career choices and further studies may be related to the content of what girls learn and the attitudes they form about their capabilities. The argument has moved from one which assumed that equal access to education is sufficient to ensure equality between the sexes (Byrne 1978) to one which emphasizes the process of schooling on girls' attitudes and expectations. This has meant an examination of the male–female power relations within educational institutions, specifically the structure, organization and content of present-day schooling (Mahony 1985; Lees 1986).

Therefore, when any discussion of 'equal opportunities' takes place we need to be aware of where the emphasis is being placed; that is on *access* or *outcome*. Madeleine Arnot and Gaby Weiner (1987) have neatly summarized the distinction between the approaches. When there is a concern for girls' access to education (known as an 'equal opportunities' or libertarian approach) the strategies adopted include providing a common core of subjects for all pupils, analysing classroom texts and resources for stereotyping, and devising policy guidelines and courses promoting gender 'awareness'. If the concern is for the outcome of girls' schooling experiences then strategies are adopted which place girls and women at the centre of the classroom, so challenging the dominance of male experience (known as a radical or anti-sexist approach). At the same time, although adopting an equal opportunities approach to girls' education fails to recognize male power, many teachers have introduced anti-sexist initiatives by using some of the equal opportunities strategies as a 'way-in'. To refer to Weiner (1986) again, the two approaches are not discrete, rather anti-sexist or

> girl-centred education [is] not necessarily an alternative to egalitarian strategies but [is] a much more powerful dimension and extension to their work.

> (Weiner 1986: 273)

There are indications that primary teachers, especially at infant level, attach much importance to the notion of individual children developing in their own way and at their own pace (King 1978; Alexander 1984). So, when primary teachers state that gender inequalities are not a problem in their classrooms because 'all children are treated the same', they are most likely to be referring to girls and boys having access to the same schooling rather than to measures which confront structural inequalities. To develop and implement anti-sexist initiatives requires an awareness of how and where gender discriminatory practices occur, together with an understanding of the principles of anti-sexism. By focusing upon two specific areas, namely school hierarchy and organizational practices, and teaching approaches and resources, I shall illustrate my own and others' attempts to develop anti-sexist education in primary schools.

SCHOOL HIERARCHY AND ORGANIZATIONAL PRACTICES

By considering the staffing structure of a 'typical' primary school the differences in male/female teaching status can be easily identified. At the beginning of the 1980s I was employed as a teacher at Andover Wynn, a large primary school situated on a new housing estate. The teaching staff of twenty included four males who held the posts of head teacher, senior master and third- and fourth-year junior team leaders. This imbalance in both number of male teachers in primary education and positions of responsibility is a common feature of schools (Whyld 1983). In addition, the sexual division of labour amongst the ancillary staff reinforced the children's awareness of male dominance. That is, there was a male caretaker in charge of an all-female cleaning staff. Now, quite clearly, when there is such an obvious sexual division both in function and seniority, a powerful message is being daily enacted for the pupils. The reasons for these differences and the implications they have for the careers of women teachers have been discussed elsewhere (e.g. Marland 1983; Evetts 1987). It is enough to say that from the moment they enter school children are exposed to role models which clearly delineate adult males as the rule-enforcers, decision-makers and 'controllers' while adult females 'look after' the younger children and carry out the instructions given by the predominantly male hierarchy.

Although schools can do little to alter the ratio of male to female members of staff, steps have been taken to redress the current sexual division of labour within primary schools. 'Equal opportunity' local education authorities (LEAs) are aware of the need to encourage women not only to apply for promotion, but also to undertake management courses specifically designed to develop women's confidence. As yet these courses are few and far between, but it is not simply a matter of women teachers being seen to hold positions of authority within schools that is the sole concern. The appointment of more women to posts of responsibility is useful only if these women use their position to challenge the staff hierarchies of which they have become a part. At the same time, there is value in providing children with alternative role models, and schools aware of the influence of gender role models have recognized the need to restructure the teaching staff's areas of responsibility to reflect females in a more positive light. Consequently female teachers may co-ordinate the 'high status' areas of the primary curriculum, such as maths and science, and supervise extra-curricular computer clubs rather than needlework/handicraft clubs. It is equally important to have male teachers working with the younger primary-age children but there is often a reluctance to do so. The men on the staff of Andover Wynn would be quite happy to take the odd storytime session, yet were horrified at any suggestion that they take a class of infants for a year.

Part of the hidden agenda of teacher socialization is that the teaching of younger children should be undertaken by females. Male teachers are often dissuaded from teaching younger children either actively, in that 'it wouldn't benefit chances of career promotion', or by more subtle insinuations that there is something suspicious about a man who wants to work with young children (Skelton 1985). Teachers of nursery/infant children are seen by many people as being of lower status than teachers of junior age children. It is not uncommon for a teacher who has taught a reception class one year and a junior class the next to be asked if they have been 'promoted'. And how many times have teachers of younger children challenged the expression 'going down to the infants' ? Supposedly the idea that one goes 'down' to the infants has little to do with the actual location in the school of the nursery/infant departments but rather more to do with an all-too-common perception of the teaching of young children as being equivalent to child-minding. The aim of anti-sexist education is to raise the status of women's characteristics, skills and achievements; so, as a 'woman's job', teaching the nursery/infant age range has first and foremost to be valued for its own sake. Some of the problems associated with achieving this aim have been noted by Acker (1983) in her assessment of the underlying assumptions that exist about the influence of gender on teachers' careers. She notes how female teachers are often blamed by researchers for their subordinate position in schools, and their apparent lack of ambition is often attributed to their orientation towards the family rather than a career. Radical changes in attitudes have to occur towards 'infant' and 'junior' teaching as well as what are 'appropriate' age bands for males and females to teach. Peter Gordon's (1986) study of the way men teachers view themselves suggests that the first step is for a school staff to examine their own attitudes and expectations of the teaching role through discussion and in-service courses.

Developing an awareness of gender discriminatory practices and implementing anti-sexist strategies requires the involvement of all the members of a school, children as well as adults. A problem immediately arises when there is no firm understanding of, or genuine commitment to, gender equality. In 1982 the LEA I worked for designated itself an 'equal opportunities' employer. Up until this time there had been no mention of equal educational opportunities by the staff of Andover Wynn and the day-to-day organization and routines of the school reflected all the gender discriminatory practices found in primary schools (see Clarricoates 1978; Delamont 1980). The LEA asked each school to nominate one of its teaching staff as equal opportunities representative. In the initial stages there was a notable absence of organized in-service courses for either the nominated representatives or the whole school staff. The only contact the representatives from each school had with each other was through an unofficial working party which was formed to establish a communication network. The working party of twenty teachers included only two members of staff from primary schools and, perhaps not surprisingly, resulted in the issues specific to primary education never reaching the agenda. The lack of a supportive network and appropriate guidance as to what primary schools could do to resolve gender discriminatory practices meant that only overt forms of discrimination were tackled. The staff of Andover Wynn, like so many other primary schools in the LEA, believed they had dealt with gender discrimination simply by amending the way in which registers were called and ceasing to 'line up' the children in rows of girls and boys.

Obviously these superficial measures could not make any real changes in girls' option choices at 13+ nor were they going to encourage girls to develop greater self-confidence. This does not mean to say that these school practices should be allowed to pass, but there has to be a recognition of what children are learning when exposed to these taken-for-granted forms of organization. For example, children are selected as 'monitors' to facilitate the smoother running of school and classroom organization, but the question is: who is asked to do what jobs and what are the children learning about their role in the school? Some monitoring jobs are seen as more suitable for one gender than another: so girls wash up the art pots, look after infants during wet playtimes and take messages around the school (missing out on lesson time), while boys set out the PE apparatus and have responsibility for moving computer equipment and 'problem-shooting'. There are clear implications here for girls' and boys' perceptions of their importance to the functioning of the school which cannot be resolved merely by switching roles. Similarly it is not uncommon for primary schools to have two playgrounds, one for infants and one for juniors, although some schools designate the infant playground as available to junior girls (Whyte 1983). Even where this 'official' gender separation does not occur, segregation still takes place with the boys dominating the space by kicking balls and running about, ensuring that girls are pushed to the periphery of the playground (Wolpe 1977; Mahony 1985).

Several primary schools (in the ILEA) have taken up the challenge of devising schemes which place value on girls' playtime activities and confront boys' displays of aggression. These ideas range from demarcating playground space, allocating various areas for specific functions, using the hall at lunchtime for quiet activities such as reading and board games, and using PE lessons to provide children with alternative playground activities, placing the emphasis on collaborative rather than competitive games. Whatever approach has been adopted the aim has been to move towards creating an ethos and atmosphere where girls can walk and talk without intimidation, ensuring that girls are given space inside and outside the building. The importance of collaborative work in establishing anti-sexist principles in the primary classroom has been noted by Hilary Claire (1986). She records how children, when left to themselves, gravitate into single sex groups, from the reception class upwards. Approaches should be adopted whereby teachers deliberately encourage mixed sex collective groups, as this form of organization helps children to see the other sex as partners and not rivals, and provides opportunities for girls and boys to get to know each other in both a work and play context.

The principles of co-operation, democracy and egalitarianism which are central to anti-sexism can also form the basis of the learning experiences provided for children in the primary classroom. There is a steady increase in the literature on collaborative learning (Sharan 1980; Yeomans 1983; Biott 1987), and it is the use of this approach and teaching resources which will be taken up and developed in the next section.

TEACHING APPROACHES AND RESOURCES

The concern of strategies for reform has been that what is taught, the way things are taught and the way schools are organized should draw on what women have done and do in society as well as from men, and should value what girls bring to schooling and the ways they want to learn.

(Yates 1987: 19)

By the time children reach secondary school it is too late to expect girls and boys to develop an interest in particular subjects when the skills required have not featured in the primary phase of a child's education. The question is, 'What happens in primary schools which enables children to maintain traditional stereotypical "interests"?' As Alexander's (1984) work has suggested, the ideology of child-centredness may act as a constraint upon the implementation of an equal opportunities policy in primary schools. In theory, child-centred approaches involve children learning through discovery and choosing the activities they undertake. However, the 'free choice' element does not result in equal experiences as children tend to 'choose' traditional stereotyped materials. Thomas (1986) observed the free play of nursery age children and noted how the girls frequently played in the home corner and were reluctant to use the large toys in the outside area, while the boys preferred to undertake activities using big bricks and constructional toys. She also discovered very little evidence of cross-sex play, either in the classroom or out of doors. Even when children are directed by the teacher towards specific activities, the experiences they receive are very different and stereotyped images continue. Hough (1983) gives the following example of what happened when a teacher directed children to the 'choosing equipment':

> different roles [were] played out in the play house, the girls being mum, baby, or big girl, the boys would be daddy, a dog, a monster or playing out an adventure game. When using the large blocks the girls would construct a house, or a spaceship to play house in, the boys would construct motorways and spaceships for adventures.
>
> (Hough 1983: 3)

In addition, girls and boys do not get equal shares in the teachers' time. Recent research by the Equal Opportunities Commission in Belfast (1987) has shown that the informal teaching studies found in most primary schools help boys to be more assertive at the expense of girls. The open and less direct methods of teaching acted in favour of the 'visible' children in the class who interacted more with the other children. They also gained more of the teacher's time and attention. The 'visible' children in each class proved to be predominantly boys. We know that boys and girls have different learning styles, with boys being active, participatory and demanding while girls are more passive, less participatory and lacking in assertive skills (Whyte 1983). In most classrooms, it is the teacher who does most of the talking and any discussion takes place through the teacher. For example a common format for discussion in a classroom is for the teacher to choose a topic, ask a question and remind children of the rules (e.g. 'Put your hand up', 'Don't shout out the answers'). But, as French and French (1986) have shown, small groups of boys (rather than boys as a whole) tend to dominate the 'discussion' and circumvent these rules by interrupting and passing more comments. Furthermore, the study in question suggests that teachers often select boys to answer questions as a way of controlling them.

The idea, then, that primary classrooms provide equal educational experiences because, on the surface, teachers attempt to provide the same opportunities, is totally misconceived. On the one hand, any whole-class teaching approach cannot cater for the differences in learning styles of girls and boys, although the evidence given above suggests that boys are more likely to be able to deal with this situation. On the other hand, Hough's (1983) study has shown that the influence of the media, parents and peer group on girls' and boys' gender stereotyping cannot be overcome simply by forcing children to undertake specific activities in the vague hope they will develop 'all-round' skills. My first attempts at remedying gender inequalities with a class of first-year junior children were concentrated upon balancing the amount of time and attention given to girls and boys. Like many other feminist teachers, I discovered that, while it was a difficult enough task to convince male colleagues they have to relinquish their hold on practices which sustain and reinforce their dominant status, it was an even more complex task convincing primary age boys. As Spender (1982) realized, even when teachers make a determined effort to equalize their time, the actions of boys prevent it taking place. The types of requests girls and boys make differ, with the boys demanding more of the teacher's time. For example, girls would ask 'Is this work right?', and 'What should I do now?', whereas boys would ask 'Can you help me/show me what to do?' It rapidly became clear that the approach I was adopting, a mixture of whole-class teaching and group work (with children sharing resources but completing individual tasks), did not alter the ability of the boys to dominate the classroom proceedings.

Classrooms can be microcosms of the power/control systems of wider society and, whether knowingly or unknowingly, generally reflect a patriarchal authority structure. Any attempts to challenge this situation demand a shift in the power balance away from relying on authority figures, at the same time making this explicit to the children. In practice, this means replacing competitive or individualistic modes of working, whereby a child succeeds only at the expense of others' failure, with collaborative forms of working. The intention here is not to argue a case for collaborative groups (see Brunger 1986) but to point out the aims and one or two of the problems of using this approach for anti-sexist purposes. As experience proved to me, collaborative group work is not simply a matter of sitting a group of children together, giving them a task and telling them to get on with it. One of the aims of anti-sexist education is to help children to develop respect for themselves and others, and this may be achieved by creating situations in which girls and boys must work together in order to complete a task.

In practical terms, this means setting up situations in which children learn to listen to each other. But they often have difficulty in listening to each others' ideas and in assimilating or assessing them when their ideas interrupt their own train of thought (Tann 1981). When the intention is for girls to learn to value themselves and boys to learn to value girls' experiences, then group composition is of fundamental importance. Unfortunately there are no simple solutions.

The research by Tann (1981) showed that when children are placed in mixed groups, boys tend to take risks and are more dynamic, and 'low ability' boys respond well. In contrast, girls are more consensus orientated and avoid challenging each other: their main concern, even in all-girl groups, is to seek agreement and reduce tension, thereby failing to probe or challenge each other. I found that deciding upon groups likely to be able to work together depended to a great extent on simply knowing the children and keeping the size of the groups to three or four. Once the composition of the groups had been decided, exercises and activities were devised which encouraged children to listen to each other, talk and eventually report back to other groups (Horton *et al.* 1982; Biott 1984; Claire 1986 are a source of practical suggestions).

What needs to be stressed here is that, although it is not *necessary* for girls to participate in discussion in order to secure educational advancement, it is important for the social aspect of girls' development. That is in the context of discussion, girls learn to see themselves as less significant than boys and, unless appropriate steps are taken by the teacher, assumptions regarding boys' confidence and girls' reticence are continued and reinforced. The results of failing to challenge these assumptions are that stereotyped attitudes are reinforced, and manifestations in behaviour become more evident as children move through the educational system (Mahony 1985; French and French 1986).

Changing one's teaching approach from one which is based upon authoritarianism and competition to one which promotes democracy and co-operation is but one factor in developing a classroom environment underpinned by anti-sexist principles. The materials used in schools are often biased in that they show females in marginal roles or render them invisible. As such, textbooks, literature, posters, science kits and project packs tend to reinforce traditional gender stereotypes (see Lobban 1975; Kelly 1981; Northam 1982). When I first began to use collaborative techniques with my class it seemed that the choice was either to refuse to use any of the resources in my classroom or to develop strategies which would allow the children to question their gender bias. As it is impossible, or at least very difficult, to 'manage' a class of more than twenty-five children without resources, I set about devising several courses of action so that the materials could be used in a more appropriate way. An initial step was to change all the packaging of science kits, project packs and toys (e.g. Lego, table-top games) with an apparent gender bias. I also managed to obtain some non-traditional posters from the ILEA Resources Centre and the

EOC, also realizing that the children's preconceived ideas about appropriate careers for men and women would not allow them to relate, for example, to illustrations of female carpenters. Julia Hodgeon's (1985) work in nursery schools showed that female teachers would become involved with activities in the home corner or table-top games, such as jigsaws or lotto, but they would stand back from the 'messier' or mechanical activities and offer only verbal encouragement. Now, in the same way that sitting children in front of computers does not provide them with programming skills, giving children non-traditional role models does not overcome prejudice and discrimination. However, positive real-life' models may go some way towards creating alternative perspectives for girls and boys. So, a policy was adopted whereby the female ancillary staff and female parents became actively involved with the children using the woodwork bench or tasks involving sand and water, and, whenever possible, male colleagues would be asked to take cookery sessions or bandage cut knees at playtimes. With regard to textbooks and literature, the children were asked to rewrite popular fairy tales, changing the gender of the main characters, and a great deal of time was spent compiling class books on women scientists, women in history and women's achievements in the local community.

Teachers who are committed to providing equal educational opportunities, whether as supporters of 'liberal' or 'radical' ideas, usually welcome suggestions as to how the lot of girls can be improved. If changes are required in their teaching approach then, generally, alternative teaching strategies will be adopted. However, attempts by individual teachers to underpin classroom life with anti-sexist principles are likely to fail as, unless there is an effort by the whole school, individual teachers and their classes become isolated. After struggling for two terms with a first-year junior class, certain events took place which highlighted the 'gap' an anti-sexist curriculum had created between my class and the rest of the school. For example, on the occasions when the children had to go to another teacher there was great consternation as to whether they should 'line up' as boys and girls, because the games teacher liked the boys to do football and the girls netball, and the music teacher preferred to have girls and boys sitting on opposite sides of the classroom to 'harmonize'. In effect the children were having to come to terms with two different school expectations and as one girl said, 'Sometimes I wish we could be like the other classes outside the hut [our mobile classroom] but I like being just people in the classroom'. In a similar way, as I was the token equal opportunities representative, my attitudes singled me out from colleagues and, although there was never overt aggression towards the anti-sexist initiatives I practised, it was often the subject of staffroom jokes. This kind of reaction is not uncommon, as Ord and Quigley (1985) discovered when they attempted to introduce anti-sexist initiatives in their school:

> It is frightening how quickly we run into hostility or dismissive amusement when even quite small changes are suggested . . . it is well to be aware . . . that power is not given away, that there will be conflict and that we need to be prepared for it. Opposition takes various forms: aggressive personal attacks, the raised eyebrows of 'oh no, not this again', the stereotyping of one or two members of staff as 'the equal opportunities people'.
>
> (Ord and Quigley 1985: 106)

The reasons for this hostility are concerned with a deep-seated reluctance to challenge dominant ideological assumptions (Arnot and Weiner 1987). Teachers would appear to be generally unwilling to broach in discussion so-called 'controversial issues' such as sexism (Alexander 1984; Harwood 1985), and often hide behind the notion of childhood innocence as a justification for not tackling these issues. Anti-sexist education involves developing a policy of positive discrimination for girls and many teachers believe that this move would marginalize boys, thereby undermining the essence of child-centred education. As Kate Myers has pointed out: 'The fact that girls have not had their fair share of attention for some years now, does not seem to inspire the same feelings of guilt' (1981: 28). Support networks for teachers committed to both equal opportunities and anti-sexist education are of fundamental importance, both to promote a feeling of optimism that change can come about and to present a united front in a climate in which it is becoming increasingly difficult even to keep these issues on the agenda.

CONCLUSION

The extent to which any real change can be brought about in girls' educational experiences in the current political climate is highly debatable. The history of feminists' struggle to ensure girls and women get an equal share of the cake has succeeded in obtaining what Acker (1986) has called the 'vague support' of the Department of Education and Science (DES). Searching for a policy on gender in DES reports and publications is akin to looking for a needle in a haystack. In the past few years committees of inquiry have been set up to investigate racial disadvantage in education (DES 1985a) and special needs children (DES 1978). Yet no similar empirical investigation has been undertaken in respect of gender inequalities in education since the HMI reported on curricular differences in 1975, nor has the DES considered gender as a priority for in-service funding. Recent influential reports, such as *Better Schools* (DES 1985b), Curriculum Matters 5–16 series, and *Quality in Schools: The Initial Training of Teachers* (DES 1987), make little or no reference to the question of gender discrimination. Similarly with the exception of a few DES regional in-service training courses on aspects of gender stereotyping in education and short courses on promoting equal opportunities in schools (Orr 1985), there have been no attempts by the DES to develop a consistent interventionist programme. The DES has neatly side-stepped its responsibility for ensuring that the measures laid down in the Sex Discrimination Act 1975 are complied with by placing the onus on LEAs, with the DES itself occupying only an 'advisory' role. More importantly, the guidance given in Circular 2/76 (DES 1976) to LEAs suggested strongly that any interpretation of the Sex Discrimination Act should be related specifically to *curriculum* inequalities:

9 . . . Responsibility for evaluating curriculum to provide equal access to experience, information and guidance rests with local education authorities, managers and governors, and, most important of all, the teachers. While the Secretary of State will not hesitate to use his powers to stop any particular act of discrimination, he does not control the curriculum and it is important for teachers, with the support of local authorities, to take a hard look at the organization of the curriculum and to consider whether the materials and techniques they use, and the guidance they give, especially in the early years, inhibit free choice later.

(DES 1976: 5)

The results of this have been that, while many LEAs have equal opportunity policy statements, they remain at the level of being nothing more than pieces of paper sitting in advisers' filing cabinets and head teachers' desk drawers. These policy statements enable LEAs to be able to be seen to facilitate change without actually implementing change.

Also, however worthless these policies are when there is no intention to implement them, it should be realized that many equal opportunity statements fail to recognize that girls experience a specific form of oppression. As it stands, policies of equal opportunities have attempted to resolve current inequalities by trying to 'educate' girls, different cultural groups, working-class and handicapped pupils to aspire to, and achieve, in the same way as a white, middle-class, able-bodied male. Girls do not 'underachieve' at school, yet they still lose out because of the discriminatory structure of school life. As Yates (1987) has said:

> Saying that school and society do not sufficiently take account of girls and women might be a better way of seeing the problem than saying that girls lack things or are 'disadvantaged'.

> (Yates 1987: 10)

Academic success is obviously important today when there is greater competition for fewer jobs, and, increasingly, those jobs which are available demand technological skills, traditionally a male sphere. Equally important is what we are teaching and how we are teaching. There is a clear need for teachers to reflect upon the structural constraints placed on the approaches they use in the classroom. Too often it is a case of 'Do as I say, not as I do'. Teachers may put up Equal Opportunities Commission posters on the wall or tell children they have to respect themselves and each other, but because of the pressures placed upon them, recourse is made to authoritarian, undemocratic techniques which serve only to reinforce the power/control systems operating in the wider society. At the same time, the possibility that 'real change' will occur in a political climate which celebrates and instigates policies on teacher appraisal, account-ability, a national curriculum, and testing, is, to say the least, a remote one.

REFERENCES

Acker, S. (1983) 'Women and teaching: a semi-detached sociology of a semi-profession', in S. Walker and L. Barton (eds) *Gender, Class and Education*, Lewes: Falmer Press.

Acker, S. (1986) 'What feminists want from education', in A. Hartnett and M. Naish (eds) *Education and Society Today*, Lewes: Falmer Press.

Alexander, R. (1984) *Primary Teaching*, Eastbourne: Holt, Rinehart & Winston.

Arnot, M. and Weiner, G. (eds) (1987) *Gender and the Politics of Schooling*, London: Hutchinson.

Biott, C. (1984) *Getting on Without the Teacher*, Sunderland Polytechnic/

Schools Council.

Biott, C. (1987) 'Co-operative group work: pupils' and teachers' membership and participation', *Curriculum* 8(2): 5–14.

Brunger, A. (1986) 'Collaborative learning – theory and practice', unpublished DAES dissertation, School of Education, University of Newcastle upon Tyne.

Byrne, E. (1978) *Women and Education*, London: Tavistock.

Claire, H. (1986) 'Collaborative work as an anti-sexist process', *Primary Matters*, ILEA, Centre for Learning Resources, 43–5.

Clarricoates, K. (1978) 'Dinosaurs in the classroom – a re-examination of some aspects of the "hidden curriculum" in primary schools', *Women's Studies International Quarterly* 1(4): 353–64.

Clarricoates, K. (1980) 'The importance of being Ernest, Emma, Tom, Jane: the perception and categorisation of gender conformity and gender deviation in primary schools', in R. Deem (ed), *Schooling for Women's Work*, London: Routledge & Kegan Paul.

Delamont, S. (1980) *Sex Roles and the School*, London: Methuen.

DES (1976) *Sex Discrimination Act*, Circular 2/76, London: HMSO.

DES (1978) *Special Education Needs, Report of the Committee of Inquiry into the Education of Handicapped Children and Young People*, Cmnd 7212, London: HMSO.

DES (1985a) *Education for All: Report of the Committee of Inquiry into the Education of Children from Ethnic Minority Groups*, (Swann Report), Cmnd 9453, London: HMSO.

DES (1985b) *Better Schools*, Cmnd 9469, London: HMSO.

DES (1987) *Quality in Schools: The Initial Training of Teachers*, London: HMSO.

Equal Opportunities Commission (1987) *Gender Differentiation in Infant Classes*, Belfast: Equal Opportunities Commission.

Evetts, J. (1987) 'Becoming career ambitious: the career strategies of married women who became primary headteachers in the 1960s and 1970s', *Educational Review* 39 (1): 15–29.

French, J. and French, P. (1986) *Gender Imbalances in Infant School Classroom Interaction* (Final report to the EOC), Manchester: Equal Opportunities Commission.

Gordon, P. (1986) 'Examining our own attitudes – a male perspective', *Primary Matters*, ILEA, Centre for Learning Resources, 14–16.

Harwood, D. (1985) 'We need political not Political education for 5–13 year olds', *Education 3–13* 13(1): 12–17.

Hodgeon, J. (1985) *A Woman's World: Report on a Project in Cleveland Nurseries on Sex Differentiation in the Early Years*, Cleveland Education Committee.

Holly, L. (1985) 'Mary, Jane and Virginia Woolf: ten-year-old girls talking', in G. Weiner (ed.) *Just a Bunch of Girls*, Milton Keynes: Open University Press.

Horton, N., Turner, S. and Whitton, S. (1982) *Anti-Sexist Teaching Strategies in the Primary School*, London, Centre for Urban Educational Studies.

Hough, J. (1983) *Deprivation of Necessary Skills*, Manchester: Equal Opportunities Commission.

Hough, J. (1985) 'Developing individuals rather than boys and girls', *School Organization* 5(1): 17–25.

Kelly, E. (1981) 'Socialisation in patriarchal society', in A. Kelly (ed.) *The Missing Half*, Manchester: Manchester University Press.

King, R. (1978) *All Things Bright and Beautiful*, Chichester: Wiley.

Lees, S. (1986) *Losing Out*, London: Hutchinson.

Lobban, G. (1975) 'Sex roles in reading schemes', *Educational Review* 27(3): 202–10.

Mahony, P. (1985) *Schools for the Boys?* London: Hutchinson.

Marland, M. (ed.) (1983) *Sex Differentiation and Schooling*, London: Heinemann.

Megarry, J. (1984) 'Sex, gender and education', in S. Acker *et al.* (eds) *World Yearbook of Education 1984: Women and Education*, London: Kogan Page.

Myers, K. (1981) 'Beware of the backlash', *School Organization* 5(1): 27–40.

Northam, J. (1982) 'Girls and boys in primary maths books', *Education 3–13* 10(1): 11–14.

Ord, F. and Quigley, J. (1985) 'Anti-sexism as good educational practice: what can feminists realistically achieve?', in G. Weiner (ed.) *Just a Bunch of Girls*, Milton Keynes: Open University Press.

Orr, P. (1985) 'Sex bias in schools: national perspectives', in J. Whyte *et al.* (eds) *Girl Friendly Schooling*, London: Methuen.

Sharan, S. (1980) 'Co-operative learning in small groups: recent methods and effects on achievement, attitudes and ethnic relations', *Review of Educational Research* 5(2): 241–71.

Skelton, C. (1985) 'Gender issues in a PGCE teacher training programme', unpublished MA thesis, Education Department, University of York.

Spender, D. (1982) *Invisible Women*, London: Writers and Readers Publishing Cooperative.

Tann, S. (1981) 'Grouping and groupwork', in B. Simon and J. Willcocks (eds) *Research and Practice in the Primary Classroom*, London: Routledge & Kegan Paul.

Thomas, G. (1986) "Hallo, Miss Scatterbrain. Hallo, Mr. Strong": assessing nursery attitudes and behaviour', in N. Browne and P. France (eds) *Untying the Apron Strings*, Milton Keynes: Open University Press.

Weiner, G. (1986) 'Feminist education and equal opportunities: unity or discord?', *British Journal of Sociology of Education* 7(3): 265–74.

Whyld, J. (ed.) (1983) *Sexism in the Secondary Curriculum*, London: Harper & Row.

Whyte, J. (1983) *Beyond the Wendy House: Sex Role Stereotyping in Primary Schools*, York: Longman for Schools Council.

Wolpe, A. (1977) *Some Processes in Sexist Education*, London: Women's Research and Resources Centre.

Yates, L. (1987) *Girls and Democratic Schooling*, Sydney: New South Wales Education Department and Curriculum Development Centre.

Yeomans, A. (1983) 'Collaborative group work in primary and secondary schools', *Durham and Newcastle Review* 10(51): 99–105.

17 Pupils, 'race' and education in primary schools

Peter Woods and Elizabeth Grugeon
Source: British Journal of Sociology of Education
(forthcoming)

THE PREPS RESEARCH

The research reported here was formulated and carried out in the wake of the Swann Report (DES 1985). Swann advocated *Education for All*, which involves giving all pupils the 'knowledge and skills needed not only to contribute positively to shaping the future nature of British society but also to determine their own individual identities, free from preconceived or imposed stereotypes of their "place" in that society' (DES 1985: 316). Education also has 'a major role to play in countering the racism which still persists in Britain today', and should work to remove discriminatory practices and procedures, to help students 'understand the social and economic origins of prejudice', and to promote the principles of 'equality and justice' (1985: 320). Such an approach was thought to be 'even more necessary in all-white areas and schools'. The Swann Committee, however, were unable to offer any examples of 'good practice' based on the principles they enunciated. Following publication of the report there was a flurry of activity among LEAs issuing policy documents and *aides-mémoires*, though some previous research showed that such earlier attempts had little influence on practice (Troyna and Ball 1985).

However, though 'top-down' approaches may not have had much success, some teacher-initiated, school-based work of that kind almost certainly existed (Antonouris 1985) even if it might be difficult to find in some 'white hinterlands' (Verma 1989). Our plans, therefore, involved locating, identifying, documenting and evaluating such practice. It was seen as less of a category and more of a process. Some practice might aspire closer to the Swann principles on some occasions and under some conditions than others, and we were interested to discover what influenced such variation. In conjunction with this teacher-centred work, we adopted a pupil-centred approach which sought to monitor their responses to these attempts, and to school experience more generally as they passed through some key processes and stages. It could be argued that pupil beliefs, attitudes and values are largely shaped in the formative years of primary school. It could equally be argued that it is at this stage that the type and direction of their school career and their ways of coping are formed. What part does 'race' play in the establishment of these unfolding careers and developing identities?

In pursuing these aims, we judged it essential to work collaboratively with teachers. This is becoming more popular among sociologists as they seek to address theoretical gains to policy and practice (Connell *et al.* 1982; Burgess 1985; Whyte 1986; Hustler *et al.* 1986; Woods and Pollard 1988). It has been shown that teachers have a sound basis for theorizing about their work (Elbaz 1983; Tripp 1987), for reflectivity and for research. Above all, however, the very principles that Swann advocated for schools with respect to teaching seemed essential for the research in the interests of ethical consistency (see also Troyna and Carrington 1989). If some might argue that this would unduly condition and constrain the research, there is a further, very practical, point: that is, if educational change is the end product, this can hardly take place without the whole-hearted co-operation of teachers (McLaughlin and Marsh 1978). External demands for radical change are threatening and alienating (Nixon 1985). This is how much of the 'anti-racist' drive has been seen. Foster (1988: 505–6) argues that despite the correctness of some of their arguments, anti-racists have 'failed to map out how they see their particular ideology being practically applied in schools', and have regarded teachers 'as, at best, cultural dopes naively reproducing the social structure, at worst, as racist monsters ensuring the failure of every black student they teach'. They have, however, exposed some of the more tokenist forms of 'multiculturalism' (Troyna 1987; Finn 1987). Perhaps we have reached a stage where we might try to 'find ways of combining the positive elements in both approaches while avoiding their negative features' (Cohen 1987: 4). Certainly some forms of multiculturalism seem to have done something in raising awareness of racism (Arora and Duncan 1986; B. Taylor 1987); and moves to include anti-racist strategies within a multicultural education context appear to have had an influence on teacher perspectives (Antonouris and Richards 1985).

It is time for this debate to move to the field of action, the classroom. As Cohen (1987: 4) notes, 'it is at the level of teaching methods that both anti-racist and multicultural education are at their weakest; there is, for example, no detailed ethnographic study of the *process* of such work'. Demaine and Kadodwala (1988: 199) agree that 'it is much more constructive for teachers and their pupils to examine specific forms of practice within the institutions in which they live, work and play'. Such an approach would be in line with the recommendations of the Swann Report. Ethnography seems most appropriate for the study of cultures which should be 'empathetically described in their own terms' (DES 1985: 329); and for the study of the 'detailed texture of school life', of 'what teachers actually do', and for the 'detailed classroom observation' demanded by Marland (1987: 119–21).

Consultation among educational advisers, teachers' centres, multicultural centres and educational institutions in the three counties concerned produced a number of schools keen to work with us on this project. They ranged from 'progressive' urban multi-ethnic to 'traditionalist' rural, all-white, but all were eager to respond to the new multicultural imperative. They were, inevitably, at different starting positions. We spent one or two days a week for periods ranging from a term to eighteen months in six main schools. The main research techniques used included observation, naturalistic interviews, diaries, and study of documents. Pupils and teachers were seen and conversed with in many contexts and on many occasions. Field notes were taken, a research diary kept, lessons tape recorded (where agreed), and a radio microphone used for tuning in to pupils' conversations and work in groups. The collaboration took two main forms: (1) where teachers and researchers worked together in assembling material on a particular issue, and in analysing; and (2) where the researcher prepared a report for teachers. In all instances, the particular objectives were worked out collaboratively. In this chapter we reflect on some of the features of the main issues examined bringing out some of the more successful and unsuccessful aspects and the conditions attached to them in each case. A full account of the research is given in Grugeon and Woods (1990).

We discovered a number of contrasting experiences. First, in the crucial area of adjusting to school, on the one hand a young Muslim boy who could speak very little English succeeded in 'becoming a pupil'; on the other, another boy was 'ruled out' of mainstream education through the process of 'statementing'. Second, a school transfer at age 7 leads to a quantum leap in pupil development; elsewhere, a transfer at age 9 appears, in some respects at least and to some pupils, retrogressive. A third area of contrast is in inter-ethnic relationships, where we found a high degree of integration in some areas, in contrast to marked differentiation in others. Fourth, pupils' experience of the multicultural curriculum differed considerably in terms of effectiveness. The contrasts enable certain conclusions to be drawn.

ACQUIRING CULTURAL COMPETENCE

Starting school is a difficult time for many children (Ghaye and Pascal 1988). The problems are heightened for ethnic minority children who speak little or no English. We monitored the progress of one such child through his first term at school. We wanted to gain some appreciation of his difficulties, and how he, and others, tackled them. Abbas was a 5-year-old Asian boy, of rather large build, whose sole visit to a pre-school playground had him 'screaming and clinging' to his mother. When he started school, he was clearly not happy, and for the first week experienced 'exclusion'. He seemed reluctant to take part in activities with others, found 'playtime' and routine procedures like 'going to the toilet' difficult, had problems in moving, 'appearing inconspicuous', and finding things to fit him because of his size, and above all, in communicating. There was a certain amount of baiting and bullying from others. But already, by the end of the first week, Abbas had made great strides, learning such things as the pattern of the school day, some basic procedural rules, developing some skills such as drawing, and relating to others. He had to rely chiefly on gesture, facial expression and very emphatic use of a few English words. Though the difficulty of communicating had considerable frustrations for him, his limited success laid the basis for a 'coming out' period beginning in the second week. He was observed organizing and carrying out tasks on his own, talking more, relating more positively to other children, venturing into a number of areas with more confidence. By the end of the third week there were more indications that he was 'becoming a member'. He had now gained a friend, developed more strategies for communicating, learned more ground rules, and how to avoid being bullied, had mastered basic survival tasks like going to the toilet, and enjoyed the satisfaction of doing a relatively difficult task well and of participating with others in group activities.

From then on, Abbas continued to grow in confidence, to be more active, less passive. He developed a repertoire of coping strategies, like employing delaying tactics so that he could see what other people were doing, withdrawal from difficult tasks using his limited resources in a versatile and creative way, such as 'Dunno' to indicate switching-off from a difficult task, or 'Ers doing, I dunno' to tell the teacher he did not understand something. He continued to acquire skills such as using a saw, deriving pleasure from the praise his efforts brought, and to become 'grooved in' (Smith and Geoffrey 1968; Edwards and Westgate 1987) to the 'hidden' rules that facilitate the smooth progression of social life, so that he identified the merest signal that brought them into play. However, celebrating his new-found powers led to over-reaching at times, and being 'quite a nuisance', but this was recognized as an inevitable part of the process of adaptation. Above all, he continued to pick up and experiment with the English language, finding a range of uses to suit his purposes, such as asking and responding to questions, giving information, demonstrating, describing, instructing, commenting, reasoning, negotiating. Invariably these were first used in an 'incorrect' idiosyncratic way, but are to be seen as 'transitional constructions' (Dulay *et al.* 1982), which show that the second language learner is engaged in an active process of deciphering and producing a new system.

What are the factors conducive to acquiring cultural competence? Abbas could have done with a chance to use his mother tongue in the classroom, more opportunity for extended talk in English with an adult, perhaps some structured language teaching and an immersion in books and stories. Since he had to make quite profound cultural adjustments, there might have been more for him to relate to in the school environment. He had variable parental support, strong and perhaps too strong at times, weak or absent at others. He certainly had a sensitive teacher, alive to his quietest murmur or gesture though he was often swamped by more competent, voluble English speakers. Above all, he showed remarkable persistence and creativity himself in coming to terms with his new situation.

By contrast, 6-year-old Balbinder Singh did not make sufficient progress to ensure his continuance in mainstream education, and after three terms was 'statemented' and sent to a special school. We monitored this process also, trying to view it from Balbinder's and his family's point of view. Ethnicity played a very large part in the process. The family spoke Punjabi exclusively at home, and had strong views about their children not losing touch with their language and culture. Balbinder was slower to talk than his two elder brothers, and reluctant to speak English. This, together with poor concentration and behavioural difficulties, led to his eventual statementing. Arguably, however, these difficulties were a product of cultural distance rather than educational special needs. His mother was mystified by much of the advice given to her. For example, the educational psychologist had suggested, among other things, that Mrs Singh could help improve one of her sons' English by reading to him at bedtime, and could help to improve his numeracy by encouraging him to spend and account for his pocket money. Both ideas were culturally alien to Mrs Singh. There were no English children's books in the house, and the boys did not shop on their own or have regular pocket money. Besides, she saw progress in these fields as the responsibility of the school.

So much of school was mystifying to her. The list of clothing for a school trip included 'night dress' and 'sponge bag'. The Singh children slept in their underpants, and Mrs Singh asked one of the authors (Elizabeth) if she could lend her some of these things. Letters from school inviting parents to join the 'Parent–Teacher Association', visit the 'Spring Fair', or attend 'Maths Workshop' were put in the bin uncomprehended. She was concerned that one of her sons was not making progress but was met with the worst kind of judgemental labelling: 'He is in the bottom set, you must accept that. You can't put it there if it's not there'. When Elizabeth tried to console her by reminding her of the teacher's comment about what a nice boy he was, she said pointedly 'Nice is in every child'.

The Education Act 1981 defines a child with special needs as one who has 'significantly greater difficulty in learning than the majority of children his age'. Since the Act, children are assessed in order to discover their individual special educational needs. The Act also gave parents the right to be involved in the process of assessing and preparing a statement, and in the decision-making. However, Balbinder's parents had difficulty understanding the school's 'normal' operations, let alone the intricacies of special needs and provision. For them, the statementing process was part of the mystifying apparatus of British education. Though the head teacher and the educational psychologist tried to explain the situation and the procedures, Mrs Singh had difficulty comprehending at various levels. In the first place, she found it hard to understand why Balbinder was not progressing. At times, she thought it was her fault, at times the school's for not making him try hard enough. Much of the discussion went over her head, few concessions being made for her ill-acquaintance with terms like 'special', 'learning difficulties', 'becoming anxious', 'experienced', 'look and say', and 'phonics'. The legal side of statementing is complex enough for anyone. For Mrs Singh, it was so much more mystification. Throughout the inexorable progress of the procedures, which seemed to have a life of their own, she clung to aspects she could understand, such as 'They learn – that is nice', and the prospect of an early return to mainstream education. This, however remote in reality, helped to modify her sense of deviance and abnormality.

Parental involvement specifies a particular role for them. The schools, for example, declared that 'Parents are helped to understand the nature of learning difficulties of their child and are encouraged to visit the school frequently to develop that understanding and to continue that approach at home'. Neither Mr nor Mrs Singh had the confidence to take on such a role, lacking the resources – knowledge of the system, command of English, time, transport – both to understand fully its requirements and to carry it out. In fact, Mrs Singh, far from being a co-arbiter in the case, was firmly linked to the role of her son. In a sense, she was also being statemented. There were times when she clearly felt that Balbinder's 'failure' was her fault. The process also would not only separate out her son, but also severely affect her own role as a young mother. She would lose all her social contacts in the community once she did not have to take him to school. Once Balbinder had started at his new school some distance away, she became effectively cut off from his education. The problem then, a not inconsiderable one at times, was seeing him on to and meeting him off his coach every day, and there were no other positive home/school links available. Further, the process has to be seen as one of a number of problems that assailed them during this period: a serious illness for which Mrs Singh required surgery, her husband's unemployment and some local racist harassment. At times, Balbinder seemed the least of her problems.

At his new school, his language, behaviour and attitude appeared to improve. He was no longer a 'problem', and his class teacher felt that he was 'pretty borderline for special school', though the prospect of his return, after nearly two years, to mainstream education was not being considered, and possibly was off the agenda for the rest of his school career. How much of this, one wonders, was Balbinder's and Mrs Singh's 'problem' and how much that of the system? Certainly there seemed some confusion between learning and language difficulty, and little account was taken of the disjuncture between the cultural norms of his home and community and the school. Too late for Balbinder came appropriate recommendations that assessment should be conducted in the pupil's first language (DES 1988), that a number of bilingual liaison officers should be employed, and that there should be more research to promote culturally unbiased tests (ACE 1989). Even without these, one wonders whether less marginalization of ethnic minority pupils and more sensitivity to their adaptational needs on the part of schools and teachers such as were shown with the other pupil, Abbas, would not have yielded a different result.

DEVELOPMENT AND RETROGRESSION ON TRANSFER

The range of schools under study revealed contrasting experiences at other key junctures in the pupil's career, especially transfer between schools. In one system, this took place at age 7, as infants became junior. In another system, pupils transferred from lower to middle school at age 9.

The former case involved a 7–11 primary school of some 200 pupils, composed of 44 per cent white children, and 56 per cent ethnic minority, consisting mainly of Hindus, but with some Muslims, and a few Afro-Caribbean, Italian and Chinese. One day a week was spent with a class of 7-year-olds during their first year at the school. After some initial concerns about what the teacher would be like, bigger pupils, and the size of the school, pupils began to make strides in all aspects of development. Capacities increased almost from the first day of term. Thus when Dipak wrote his news, he 'almost filled up the whole page'. James said he could 'remember when I would not read when I came to this school. But I can read and write now with a pencil or pen'. Hemang's handwriting had improved beyond measure. Looking back, Rajesh could see that they had been 'infants' in the other school 'doing baby work [but] at this school we do some hard work'. They learned 'joined-up writing', vastly increased their vocabulary and developed their sense of structure in writing. P.H. Taylor (1986) argues that

> literacy should become the stock in trade of primary education [and] must increasingly be recognized as essential to the development of thresholds of thought, feeling and action in many subject areas, not only of intellectual endeavour but also of social and moral insight in children.
>
> (P.H. Taylor 1986: 120–1)

The skills acquired, among other things, help the child to 'decentre' and to appreciate the perspectives of others – an essential element in multicultural/anti-racist education.

New skills and knowledge were accompanied by a sense of higher status as they passed from infants to juniors, with new appropriate behaviours, such as going to school on your own. More mature attitudes and finer appreciation of the need for joint contributions to social regulation were induced ('Go away! Go away! That's infant behaviour again!'). Personal identities developed apace as pupils 'came out'. Warish, withdrawn at first, was asking his teacher for words by the middle of the year, and 'even being a bit naughty'. Sarah had been tearful and very dependent, but by the first half-term 'was working well on her own'. Sanita, very quiet and retiring, found relief in drama, as an aid to self-expression. A few of the Asian children, especially girls, seemed to want an exclusively English cultural identity. Others seemed to adapt to dual cultures more readily, taking a pride and delight in their linguistic abilities, cultural activities and sense of history.

The first year of junior school is an important year also for social development, in learning to relate to others in ways beyond the immediate, physical, rather egocentric manner of early childhood. Psychologists argue that there are two critical stages of children's friendships, one at age 3–5 when the focus is on momentary specific physical actions and physical accessibility, and the other at age 11–12 when friendships involve more psychological compatibility and longevity (Rubin 1980). The first year of junior school appears crucial in the progress from one stage to the other. Again, our group appeared to take a quantum leap in movement toward the second stage. Boys very soon established their membership of the 'male club' (Lever 1976), showing none of the apprehensions of loss of friends and bullying typical of later transitions (Measor and Woods 1984). Girls, too, had more resources. Amina, for example, had 'more friends in this school and like it here the best'. A more sophisticated approach to friendship appeared evident involving reciprocation in kind, more investment of self in the friendship and more consideration of others. Others were being seen in psychological as well as physical terms, and social relationships were seen as more enduring systems (Rubin 1980). 'Caring' featured strongly within the school ethos, and in their own personal relationships, though it was not always easy to sustain in practice. There were some isolates, and the year was not without its problems, but on the whole, this seemed a period of considerable advance along a broad front for most pupils.

This was not the case with a group of pupils undergoing transfer in another authority. The two instances are not directly comparable, since transition took place at a later age, but the examples show how the process can be productive or counter-productive. The problems of transfer at 11+ or 12+ are well known: fear of losing friends, of older and bigger pupils, of unknown teachers, of new forms of work, of a large and strange school (Measor and Woods 1984). These problems are compounded at age 9 for some pupils. We studied the transition of twenty girls from lower to middle school, interviewing them before and after the event, and at the end of the first year in middle school.

Twelve of the girls were black, nine from families of Asian origin and two Afro-Caribbean; these had more difficulty than the white girls. These were to do mostly with language and culture.

There was a very different grasp of what was happening between children with English as their mother tongue and children, although they may have been born in this country, who still had difficulty with English as a second language. Many apparently confident bilingual speakers may simply not have acquired the vocabulary and experience to cope with ideas about the way the education system works. Many of the black girls feared the 'big people' and 'harder work' which they thought transfer would entail, whereas native speakers of English seemed able to contemplate change in a more informed way. Thus Parminder was worried about 'harder maths books' and 'having to write more', but Suzanne more confidently did not 'think they're going to be harder, they're going to have to bring us up a bit'. The more confident white girls reasoned that you 'had to be more sensible' at middle school, and that efforts were made to smooth the transition. They were less likely to express fears of bullying, getting lost and harder work. They explored these ideas but could propose an alternative version, looking forward positively to their new school. We suspected that these mainly middle-class white girls would have considerable discussion with parents about what to expect. Older siblings also helped them with some of the mystifying aspects, such as 'rough books', 'CS', 'SES', and 'humanities block'.

For the Asian girls, the prospect of showers after games lessons was alarming, as was the fact that 'There's a lot more man teachers' – for many their first encounter with male teachers. School rules affecting attendance and punctuality were also a worry, for these are often beyond such children's control. For cultural and social reasons ethnic minority children may be poor timekeepers and school attenders, but at lower and middle school decisions about attendance are largely in the hands of their parents. Reasons for absence may involve family commitments, weddings, funerals, and visits to relatives or to their country of origin. Religious observation, such as Ramadan, may keep children at home, and for girls there are often domestic responsibilities. There were similar cultural concerns about uniform. One girl was worried about having to exchange her traditional salwar and kameez for the unfamiliar skirt, blouse and tie demanded by her middle school. Others were acutely aware of the extra expenditure this would incur.

These children had a choice of middle school. Several of the ethnic minority pupils chose schools that took them away from the one most of their peers would be attending. From one lower school, for example, a number of Sikh and Muslim girls were going on to the Catholic school, despite the religious difference. Their reasons were social. It was nearer to their homes, and 'When it's dark nights and when I walk home it's going to be too dark for me because I've got to walk past that big park'. Another Sikh family from another part of the town chose to send their daughter on a particularly hazardous route to this school because their local school had children who 'made trouble', and who had mocked her appearance and performance in a ceremonial dance at the school. At this Catholic school, however, Kamla's culture and identity as a Sikh would probably have to go underground. Rather ironically, the school that she and her parents had rejected was committed to encouraging and developing pupils' awareness of their own culture and religion, reinforcing and continuing the multi-faith, multicultural policies of their lower school.

At the new school, their anxieties were largely confirmed in the early weeks. There were difficult rules, the work was hard, the subjects and timetable were bewildering, and the uniform was uncomfortable. Assemblies were comparatively dull affairs. In their lower schools these had been lively, participatory and personal, often the focal point of the day when the whole school came together to enjoy each other's company and share different experiences. They often set the tone for the day in particular ways, celebrating children's cultural diversity and emphasizing shared values. In the larger school, too, separate playgrounds for each year group cut across family relationships, a very important consideration for the ethnic minority girls. Boys dominated these play areas. In place of the strong relationship with one class teacher in their lower school, they now had uncertain relationships with a number of teachers, some of whom could 'come too eggy'. There were problems for some, too, in coping with homework and interpreting reports. As the system left the homely world of the lower school and became more complicated, so the difficulties of some ethnic minority children seemed to increase and to lock them into particular career routes.

The crucial difference between the two systems considered here appears to be one of 'integration'. In the former, transfer at 7+ system, pupils transfer from one infant school to one junior school. Both schools are situated in a quite strongly integrated community, where different ethnic groups have resided for some time, and live and work together harmoniously. Pupils pass from one class teacher to another, and continue to experience an integrated curriculum. There was strong liaison between the schools concerned, with several pre-transfer interschool visits by teachers and pupils; the school emphasized harmony and 'one-ness' with its assemblies, ceremonies, openness and general ethos. By contrast, 'differentiation' appeared to be the keynote in the three-tiered system. If, as some recent ILEA (1988) research suggests, first-year *secondary* school classes should become more like primary classes and move towards 'a greater integration of curriculum areas in the first year', it would seem even more important for middle schools who receive children two years earlier to do so. That they do not do so at present is claimed by the head teachers to be the consequence of continuous under-resourcing, falling rolls, and the failure of local authorities to see that positive strategies should be adopted to ease transfer, particularly for the 'vulnerable minority'. Integration applies also to home–school links. Tizard *et al.* (1988) stress the importance of these, finding that children's progress in reading and writing was related to the amount of parental knowledge of and contact with school. The parents of the ethnic minority pupils in our study had often not visited their children's new school. Lack of transport, shift work, and large families made attendance difficult for many parents. Differentiation was therefore the chief feature of the process in the three-tiered system. This, however, did not apply to perceptions of the cohort undergoing transfer which was seen as a homogeneous group in cultural and educational terms. Under such circumstances, groups with particular needs are bound to experience greater difficulty.

INTEGRATION AND DIFFERENTIATION IN PUPIL RELATIONSHIPS

Such experiences would encourage the separation of ethnic groups, and fuel the strong tendency for them to differentiate and polarize to some degree on their journey through secondary school (Troyna, 1978; Furlong, 1984; Mac an Ghaill, 1988). At Willis's (1977) comprehensive school, each of the three groups of Caucasian, Asian and Afro-Caribbean pupils had their own classrooms in the fifth year for 'friendship groups'. 'So much for integration!' declared the Head of Upper School (1977: 47). Several studies point to this process being well in train long before secondary school, as early, in fact, as four years of age. Most research in Britain since the 1970s suggests that pupils prefer to mix with others in their own ethnic group (Jelinek and Brittan 1975; Davey 1983; Davey and Mullin 1982; Kitwood and Borrill 1980). Tomlinson (1983) concluded that

> pupils in multi-ethnic schools do not appear to form inter-ethnic friendships to any great extent, being 'racially aware' and preferring

their own groups from an early age, becoming even more ethnocentric at secondary level.

(Tomlinson 1983: 129)

However, there are some exceptions to the general argument. Denscombe *et al.* (1986), for example, criticized the predominant use of sociometric tests in much of the earlier work. Using a range of methods, including extended fieldwork observation of free association in classroom and playground of two multi-ethnic classes, they found a high degree of racial integration, supporting teachers' own observations.

Our research supports this view and, indeed, in one multi-ethnic primary school classroom of 7-year-olds (the same class discussed in the previous section), pupils freely nominated friends from other ethnic groups, this actually counting as a desirable qualification in some instances. From their comments in writing and in discussion, and from observation, the chief things they felt about friends was that they spent time with each other, helped and cared about each other, were 'kind', shared and gave each other things, found each other attractive, played and had fun together. They provide physical, intellectual, emotional and moral support for each other. Friendships were for the most part gender specific and multiracial. Malcolm's friends, Surdip and Rajesh, were 'both helpful, we all liked playing football. I know that if I fell over they would fetch the teacher'. Warish liked Darren 'because he does not fight with me. I give Darren lollipops and he comes to my house'. Mary likes Rashan because 'she is pretty and she is Indian. She is kind and helps people. We share sweets and time together. We play with my ball, we play tickie as well. Rashan has got black curly hair and brown eyes. I like her. I like her because she is Indian and I have never had an Indian friend before.' Here ethnic difference is proving an attraction. These associations were long-lasting, most of them surviving our eighteen-month period at the school, despite occasional tiffs here and there. In their general interaction in class, there also seemed a high degree of racial interrelatedness. Michelle 'needed to know how to spell everything' and Rajesh always helped her, spelling the easier words himself and pointing out others on the board. One day when Winston was reading out an account he had written and began to struggle, Surdip came to his assistance, interpreting his untidy writing and making suggestions. Jonathan (white) and Daniel (Afro-Caribbean) held hands on an outing to the park, and so on; there were many such examples. This also illustrates the considerable resource pupils were to each other in learning. As Karen claims when she was sitting next to James, 'I give him words and nudge him if he's not listening'.

Ethnic difference proved an attraction also among the pupils of another class of 7-year-olds in the same school, and those of an all-white rural school, with whom their teachers arranged an 'exchange', with visits to each other's schools. From the very first exchange of letters, these two groups of children developed a strong sense of friendship. This included those pupils considered 'difficult' by their teachers, including one who had been known to use racial abuse to an Asian teacher. His teachers worried about what he might say to a child. His friend was Larry, an Afro-Caribbean, and they were very wary of each other at first. But, in fact, when they got back from the other school it was he who said 'Can I write to Larry?' Larry himself could be 'a most difficult child, and yet when he went over there he was super'. Sheila and Gita were perhaps the best example of making friends. They exchanged gifts, held hands and arms, gave each other piggy backs, and talked incessantly. They phoned each other between visits and arranged for other, independent meetings in a blossoming relationship which spread to their families. Gita's mother accompanied them on the trip to the other school. Sheila's mother said she would like to see Gita's Hindu Temple, and they were trying to arrange it. The effects thus spread at certain points into another generation.

Cultural integration was all part of the mixing. The white children took a delight in their friends' names. The black children who spoke English as a second language signed their names in English and in their first language. Some taught their white friends how to write *their* names in their first language. Amina Begum sent a song in Bengali 'to the children of the other school'. The children toured together, completed worksheets together, played together and shared food. The excitement caused by these liaisons acted as a catalyst for the curriculum work done around the project, as well as giving a boost to personal and social development. In a very real sense, therefore, this was 'learning through friendship'.

Others have found that some primary school children have fairly sophisticated ideas about 'race', as opposed to the more general view that they are too young to handle such concepts and that childhood is, and should remain, an age of 'innocence' (on the latter, see King 1978; Ross 1984; Alexander 1984). Carrrington and Short (1989) illustrate this (see also Donaldson 1978; Lee and Lee 1987; Blenkin 1988). Testing the children's racial preferences they found a high degree of in-group preference. However, like Denscombe they considered this not a straightforward matter as a majority of children said they were 'not bothered', and those expressing a preference usually gave it a context, preferring, for example, to be white in 'England' or 'Brixton' because that was the majority colour, but 'If most of my friends were black and I went to a black school, then I wouldn't really mind [what colour I was]'.

(Carrington and Short 1989)

As for secondary school, at least one study has shown that ethnic separation is not inevitable (Foster 1988).

This is not to say that differentiation does not exist, nor racism in quite extreme forms in some primary schools. Cohen (1987), for example, reports a London all-white primary school where the 'children exhibited a high level of colour prejudice . . . sometimes articulated with great emotional intensity, and often backed up by quite sophisticated arguments . . . and "rich" repertoires of racist images, jokes, stories and ritual insults'. Other current researches in other areas yet to be reported suggest that this is not untypical (e.g. Troyna and Hatcher, forthcoming).

What conditions, then, attend integration? As with the more successful transitions, so the closer interracial relationships seem promoted in areas that are strongly integrational in other respects. Foster (1988) identified three reasons for pupil harmony in his school. First, the area had been multi-ethnic for a long time, and there was a long history of fairly co-operative and tolerant relationships between two main ethnic groups. Second, some white students who were racist kept their views quiet as they were vastly outnumbered by pupils, both black and white, who were anti-racist. Third, the teachers had 'succeeded in conveying the importance of anti-racism'. These factors also applied to the primary school where we made this particular study. In particular, the values of 'caring' and 'togetherness' were central features of the school ethos. However, we also share another, less integrational, characteristic with Foster's school. He found that the only two Asians in the school were subject to abuse and name-calling from both Afro-Caribbean and white pupils. Were these, therefore, the *real* minority in the school and area, and persecuted for that reason? Similarly at our school of mainly whites and Hindus, despite the general unity, there were some isolates. Kamlesh, a Muslim, when asked to write about her friend, wrote about her teacher. Winston, an Afro-Caribbean, went through a period of what he and his mother thought was persecution. Kulmeet, a Sikh, was also excluded, even from the list of Gita's friends which included the whole of the rest of the class. The most prominent thing that distinguished them from their peers was the ethnic/religious factor. 'Minorities among minorities' would appear to be an important area for further research.

ENGAGING WITH AND DISTANCING FROM THE CURRICULUM

The final area of contrasts is to do with pupils' experience of the curriculum. Here again we found variable involvement and variable application and operationalization of multicultural/anti-racist principles. At its best this seemed to reflect the kind of 'good education' envisaged in *Education for All* (DES 1985). With regard to mathematics, this involves utilizing pupils' own interests, mathematics reflecting the real world, making use of the local environment, striking a balance between application in everyday life and more abstract ideas, employing different modes of learning, giving thought to communication, and seeking opportunities for cross-curricular work (National Curriculum Council 1989). All of these figured in the 'multicultural mathematics' project that took place in one multi-ethnic, strongly integrated lower school. This whole-school project, gradually built up over half a term, developed a 'street' that the children could actually walk down, with houses, pubs, shops, dentists, church, a trailer site for the traveller children – in short a representation of the neighbourhood with which all ethnic groups could identify. Authentic figures, complete with turbans where appropriate, populated the street. Things could be added, handled and moved, and a dice game with numbered squares was devised for moving. The fact that they could stand and move in the street helped develop pupils' sense of progression and of probability, as well as their conceptualization of number. This seemed to be not just an example of effective multicultural teaching, but effective teaching in general.

The same applies to the 'exchange' project mentioned earlier, predicated on the affective relationships established between the two sets of children and the teachers involved. They spent a day at each other's school. On their day out, the rural children visited the Hindu temple, played on the 'apparatus' in the larger school (they had none in theirs), and met and played with their friends. For the urban children, the outstanding features of their day were the bus ride, a walk round the village and over the fields, a visit to the church, and meeting, with increased excitement, their now established friends. The visits were the high point of the project, but there was much activity inspired by them before and after. The project had a marked effect on the enrichment of vocabulary, ability to discuss, motivation in writing (for example, letters to friends, poems), mathematics (bus fares, clocks, distances), environmental studies, physical education, religious education (the exchange provided an excellent basis for a comparative study at the children's own level of thinking), and social and personal development. The exchange thus provided a great educational boost to these children, and to their teachers, across the curriculum.

Both these projects contain the ingredients of an 'opportunities to teach and learn model' (Woods 1989; 1990). There is cognitive, social and affective matching. Teacher and pupil interests and intentions coincide. The aims do not outreach the available resources. There is stimulation, enjoyment, fairness and learning. There is a measure of pupil control over their learning. They tackle the potential constraint of race, and the influence of gender and social class do not appear to have acted as impediments in these instances. They were both pupil- and teacher-centred. In the exchange, for instance, apart from the initiation of the project, which arose from a creative 'spark' between the two main teachers, and the planning, there was a strong sense of teacher participation in learning, for example in the new environments.

However, circumstances do not always permit this mix of ingredients. The difficulties for teachers are illustrated in another project involving a well-intentioned attempt by an all-white Church of England primary school, in response to the Swann Report (DES 1985), to incorporate a multicultural perspective into its curriculum. The term-long project on 'Living and Growing' involved a vast amount of work for both teachers and pupils, 'research', reading and reporting. However, we concluded that this was largely a traditional programme which acquainted children with a number of facts but gave them no real understanding of other cultures. Indeed the 'facts' and their manner of presentation and report simply reinforced traditional stereotypes. Lists of facts, set up by teachers' questions on work-cards, use of the present tense and the generalizing pronoun 'they' produced statements that could lay the basis for the sort of oversimplified points of view which give rise to prejudice – 'They do not have houses like we have', 'The people of the Sahara desert live on water and meat'.

At times the knowledge gained was more clearly the *pupils'*. However, under the traditional model in operation, this was invariably ruled out of order. One example of this was the visit to the Commonwealth Institute, where a Nigerian teacher excited the pupils' interest in his country and culture. They talked at length and with enthusiasm among themselves and with the researcher about this visit, but it was not followed up by the teachers. The head teacher, in fact, had been more concerned about their *behaviour* on the visit. On another occasion, they were aroused by an evening television programme some had happened to see about the Kalahari Bushmen. They had learned certain facts about these nomadic hunters, but the programme brought home to the children their real plight.

> In the morning they were queuing up to express real feelings of outrage to their teacher. The school secretary, fired by their enthusiasm to do something, telephoned the BBC and was given an address which the children could write to. Their teacher thought that they might do this if there were time. The relentless pace of the project meant that they did not. There was no time for unscheduled events in the programme.
>
> (Grugeon and Woods 1990: 198).

Some might consider such a project a 'superficial irrelevance' as far as multicultural/anti-racist education is concerned (Mullard 1983). We would have to agree if the school failed to learn from the experience, and persisted in the same style. But it was clear from the study as a whole that the various schools were at different stages of development with regard to implementing such a policy, differently situated and differently resourced. For this school – traditional, middle-class, white, very successful in its own terms – this project was a beginning. Much discussion, reflection and self-examination lay ahead of them, and in this exercise they would require support from the local authority, and from other schools and educational institutions. The key test, perhaps, was whether they could sustain the will and commitment to the cause. The sheer exhaustion all the teachers experienced at the end of the term of the project raised doubts about its being sustained to any meaningful extent in the light of such constraints. This is where continuing collaborative work with external agencies which give assistance in terms of curriculum resource and independent evaluation might be helpful.

CONCLUSIONS

The research revealed both positive and negative elements to attempts to implement multicultural education. The negative aspects were associated with differentiation – of community, institutions and curriculum – and traditional and Anglocentric methods of teaching and views of content and process. There was also a lack of resource and of assistance to hard-pressed schools and teachers, desiring the ends of multicultural education as defined by the Swann Report, but lacking the means to put it into effect. The considerable impetus of a system in motion easily outweighed some attempts.

The more positive aspects were associated with more settled communities, stronger liaison and co-ordination within and between schools, an integrated curriculum, and a model of teaching distinguished by a basic principle of person-centredness in a structured framework. This approach is underpinned by constructivist learning theory which emphasizes the pupils' ownership and control of their learning and knowledge, and their progressive construction of cognitive representations through experience and action in the world (Donaldson 1978; Richardson 1985). It is not, however, a simple Plowdenesque child-centredness, but one that recognizes children as members of different social groups, who will have different experiences and who have much to learn through co-operation and collaboration through talk (Lee and Lee 1987). Such teaching, therefore, would employ both discovery techniques, and collaborative learning. It would have a view on information that needed to be 'appropriated' by the pupil and values – such as personal dignity, respect for others, fairness, individual and collective responsibility, and social justice – that needed to be learned and appreciated. But 'democratic processes underpinned by a progressive pedagogy' rather than 'instruction into correct perspectives' seemed to be more effective (Lee and Lee 1987: 219). There appears to be a broad measure of agreement on the efficacy of pupil collaboration in promoting multicultural education (Francis 1984; Brandt 1986; Carrington and Short 1989), mirrored by collaboration among the staff (Troyna 1988; Nixon 1985; Myers 1985; Tomlinson and Coulson 1988; Lynch 1987). This can clearly be extended to other schools (Stillman and Maychell 1984), and to parents (Arora 1986; Vassen 1986; Campbell 1986; Lynch 1987; Carrington and Short 1989).

In fact, parents were particularly important in our study. It revealed how closely parents were involved with the young children starting school and being statemented; their potential in smoothing transitions, and contributing to the education of their and other children in general. It showed, too, how much they themselves needed to learn about the educational system and processes. Failure to involve parents can have dire results (MacDonald 1988). Anderson (1988: 35) feels that, with the new powers given parents and governors 'without their co-operation equal opportunities policies may well flounder if indeed they are not strangled at birth'.

Collaboration reflects and keeps faith with the underlying values of multicultural education. These need to be reflected also in the decision-making structures within the school. A democratic regime emphasizing co-operation, collaboration and participation is more suited to their advancement than an authoritarian one featuring didacticism, hierarchy, competition and individualism (Carrington and Short 1989; Lynch 1987). This does not mean that strong leadership is not required, a factor that figures prominently in the 'school effectiveness' literature in general (Reynolds 1985; Mortimore *et al.* 1988). This certainly figured in our research, but the most successful was democratic leadership aimed at whole-school policies derived and implemented by consensus (Grugeon 1989). This resulted in decisions and activities that teachers could feel were 'theirs', in the same sense as pupils identified with their own learning. Person-centredness thus applies to teachers as well as pupils. Those who were more effective appeared strongly committed to multicultural principles, and to improving their professional skills. They were reflective about their practice (Schön 1983), open to new ideas, and keen to innovate. They appreciated opportunities to be creative. Rather than starting with a set of principles and seeing how a number of teachers selected on some other basis measured up to them, it would seem more logical and consistent to identify such teachers, observe them in action and discuss their views, teaching and results with them. We might then help to contribute to the small archive of teacher practice in the area (ALTARF 1984; B. Taylor 1987; McLean and Young 1988; Epstein and Sealey 1990) and develop the study of theory into practice through collaborative research.

REFERENCES

ACE (1989) ACE Conference: *Asian Children and Special Education*, ACE, *Bulletin* 28, March–April.
Alexander, R.J. (1984) *Primary Teaching*, London: Holt, Rinehart & Winston.
ALTARF (All London Teachers Against Racism and Fascism) (1984) *Challenging Racism*, London: ALTARF.
Anderson, B. (1988) 'Equal opportunities and the National Curriculum – a challenge to educators', in H. Simons (ed.) *The National Curriculum*, London: British Educational Research Association.
Antonouris, G. (1985) 'Developing multicultural education in all primary schools: some suggestions', Nottingham: Trent Polytechnic (mimeo).
Antonouris, G. and Richards, K. (1985) 'Race in education', *Trent Papers in Education* 85/4, Nottingham: Trent Polytechnic.
Arora, R.K. (1986) 'Towards a multicultural curriculum – primary', in R.K.

Arora and C.G. Duncan, *Multicultural Education: Towards Good Practice*, London: Routledge & Kegan Paul.

Arora, R.K. and Duncan, C.G. (1986) *Multicultural Education: Towards Good Practice*, London: Routledge & Kegan Paul.

Blenkin, G. (1988) 'Education and development: some implications for the curriculum in the early years', in A. Blyth (ed.) *Informal Primary Education Today*, Lewes: Falmer Press.

Brandt, G. (1986) *The Realization of Anti-Racist Teaching*, Lewes: Falmer Press.

Burgess, R.G. (1985) *Issues in Educational Research*, Lewes: Falmer Press.

Campbell, J. (1986) 'Involving parents in equal opportunities: one school's attempt', in *Primary Matters: Some Approaches to Equal Opportunities in Primary Schools*, London: ILEA.

Carrington, B. and Short, G. (1989) *'Race' and the Primary School*, Windsor: NFER-Nelson.

Cohen, P. (1987) 'Racism and popular culture: a cultural studies approach', *CME Working Paper No. 9*, Institute of Education, University of London.

Connell, R.W., Ashenden, D.J., Kessler, S. and Dowsett, G.W. (1982) *Making the Difference: Schools, Families and Social Division*, Sydney, George Allen & Unwin.

Davey, A.G. (1983) *Learning to be Prejudiced: Growing Up in Multi-Ethnic Britain*, London: Edward Arnold.

Davey, A.G. and Mullin, P.N. (1982) 'Inter-ethnic friendship in British primary schools', *Educational Research* 24: 83–92.

Demaine, J. and Kadodwala, D. (1988) 'Multicultural and anti-racist education: the unnecessary divide', *Curriculum* 9(2): 99–102.

Denscombe, M., Szule, H., Patrick, C. and Wood, A. (1986) 'Ethnicity and friendship: the contrast between sociometric research and fieldwork observation in primary school classrooms', *British Educational Research Journal*, 12(3): 221–35.

DES (1985) *Education for All: Report of the Committee of Inquiry into the Education of Children from Ethnic Minority Groups*, (Swann Report), Cmnd 9543, London: HMSO.

DES (1988) *Report of the Task Group on Assessment and Testing* (TGAT Report), London: HMSO.

Donaldson, M. (1978) *Children's Minds*, London: Fontana.

Dulay, H., Burt, M. and Krashen, S. (1982) *Language Two*, Oxford: Oxford University Press.

Edwards, A.D. and Webster, D. (1987) *Investigating Classroom Talk*, Lewes: Falmer Press.

Elbaz, F. (1983) *Teacher Thinking: A Study of Practical Knowledge*, London: Croom Helm.

Epstein, D. and Sealey, A. (1990) *Where It Really Matters: Anti-Racist Education in Predominantly White Primary Schools*, Birmingham: Development Education Centre, Selly Oak Colleges.

Finn, G.P.T. (1987) 'Multicultural anti-racism and Scottish education', *Scottish Educational Review* 19(1): 39–49.

330   *Gender, race and the experience of schooling*

Foster, P.M. (1988) 'Policy and practice in multicultural and anti-racist education: a case study of a multi-ethnic comprehensive school', PhD thesis, Milton Keynes: Open University.

Francis, M. (1984) 'Antiracist teaching in the primary school', in M. Straker-Welds (ed.) *Education for a Multicultural Society: Case Studies in ILEA Schools*, London: Bell & Hyman.

Furlong, V.J. (1984) 'Black resistance in the liberal comprehensive', in S. Delamont (ed.) *Readings and Interaction in the Classrooms*, London: Methuen.

Ghaye, A. and Pascal, C. (1988) 'Four-year-old children in reception classrooms: participant perceptions and practice', *Educational Studies* 14(2): 187–208.

Grugeon, E. (1989) 'Teacher development through collaborative research', in P. Woods (ed.) *Working for Teacher Development*, Cambridge: Peter Francis.

Grugeon, E. and Woods, P. (1990) *Educating All: Multicultural Perspectives in the Primary School*, London: Routledge.

Hustler, D., Cassidy, A., and Cuff, E.C. (eds) (1986) *Action Research in Classroom and Schools*, London: George Allen & Unwin.

ILEA (1988) 'Secondary Transfer Project, Final Report', *Bulletin 17*, London: ILEA Research and Statistics Branch.

Jelinek, M. and Brittan, E. (1975) 'Multiracial education: (1) inter-ethnic friendship patterns', *Educational Research*, 18: 44–53.

King, R.A. (1978) *All Things Bright and Beautiful*, Chichester: Wiley.

Kitwood, T. and Borrill, C. (1980) 'The significance of schooling for an ethnic minority', *Oxford Review of Education* 6(3): 241–52.

Lee, V. and Lee, J. (1987) 'Stories children tell', in A. Pollard (ed.) *Children and Their Primary Schools*, Lewes: Falmer Press.

Lever, J. (1976) 'Sex differences in the games children play', *Social Problems* 23: 478–87.

Lynch, J. (1987) *Prejudice Reduction and the Schools*, London: Cassell.

Mac an Ghaill, M. (1988) *Young, Gifted and Black*, Milton Keynes: Open University Press.

MacDonald, I. (1988) *Burnage High School Inquiry*, Manchester: Manchester City Council.

McLaughlin, M. and Marsh, D. (1978) 'Staff development and school change', *Teachers College Record* 80(1): 69–94.

McLean, B. and Young, J. (1988) *Multicultural Anti-Racist Education: A Manual for Primary Schools*, London: Longman.

Marland, M. (1987) 'The education of and for a multi-racial and multi-lingual society: research needs post-Swann', *Educational Research* 29(2): 116–29.

Measor, L. and Woods, P. (1984) *Changing Schools: Pupil Perspectives on Transfer to a Comprehensive*, Milton Keynes: Open University Press.

Mortimore, P., Sammons, P., Lewis, L. and Ecob, R. (1988) *The Junior School Project*, London: ILEA Research and Statistics Branch.

Mullard, C. (1983) 'Anti-racist education: a theoretical basis', Race Relations Unit, Institute of Education, University of London (mimeo).

Myers, K. (1985) 'Beware of the backlash', *School Organization* 5(1): 27–40.

National Curriculum Council (1989) *Mathematics: Non-Statutory Guidance*, York: NCC.

Nixon, J. (1985) 'Education for a multicultural society: reviews and reconstructions', *Curriculum* 6(2): 29–36.

Reynolds, D. (1985) *Studying School Effectiveness*, Lewes: Falmer Press.

Richardson, K. (1985) *Learning Theories*, Units 8/9 of *Course E206 Personality, Development and Learning*, Milton Keynes: Open University Press.

Ross, A. (1984) 'Developing political concepts and skills in the primary school', *Educational Review* 36(2): 133–9.

Rubin, Z. (1980) *Children's Friendships*, London: Fontana.

Schön, D.A. (1983) *The Reflective Practitioner: How Professionals Think in Action*, London: Temple Smith.

Smith, L.H. and Geoffrey, W. (1968) *The Complexities of an Urban Classroom*, New York: Holt, Rinehart & Winston.

Stillman, A. and Maychell, K. (1984) *School to School*, Windsor: NFER-Nelson.

Taylor, B. (ed.) (1987) *Ethnicity and Prejudice in 'White Highlands' Schools*, Perspectives 35, School of Education, University of Exeter.

Taylor, P.H. (1986) *Expertise and the Primary School Teacher*, Windsor: NFER-Nelson.

Tizard, B., Blatchford, P., Burke, J., Farquhar, C., and Plewis, I. (1988) *Young Children at School in the Inner City*, Hove: Erlbaum.

Tomlinson, S. (1983) *Ethnic Minorities in British Schools*, London: Heinemann.

Tomlinson, S. and Coulson, P. (1988) *Education for a Multi-Ethnic Society: A Descriptive Analysis of a Sample of Projects Funded by Education Support Grants in Mainly White Areas*, Lancaster: University of Lancaster.

Tripp, D.H. (1987) 'Teachers, journals and collaborative research', in J. Smyth (ed.) *Educating Teachers: Changing the Nature of Pedagogical Knowledge*, Lewes: Falmer Press.

Troyna, B. (1978) 'Race and streaming: a case study', *Educational Review* 30(1): 59–65.

Troyna, B. (1987) 'Beyond multiculturalism: towards the enactment of anti-racist education in policy, provision and pedagogy', *Oxford Review of Education* 13(3): 307–20.

Troyna, B. (1988) 'The career of an anti-racist school policy: some observations on the mismanagement of change', in A.G. Green and S.J. Ball (eds) *Progress and Inequality in Comprehensive Education*, London: Routledge.

Troyna, B. and Ball, W. (1985) 'Styles of LEA policy intervention in multicultural/anti-racist education', *Educational Review* 37(2): 165–76.

Troyna, B. and Carrington, B. (1989) 'Whose side are we on? Ethical dilemmas in research on "race" and education', in R. Burgess (ed.) *The Ethics of Educational Research*, Lewes: Falmer Press.

Troyna, B. and Hatcher, R. (forthcoming) *Racial Incidents in Primary*

332 *Gender, race and the experience of schooling*

Schools, London: Routledge.

Vassen, T. (1986) 'Curriculum considerations in the primary school', in J. Gundara, J. Jones, and K. Kimberley (eds) *Racism, Diversity and Education*, London: Hodder & Stoughton.

Verma, G. (ed.) (1989) *Education for All: A Landmark in Pluralism*, Lewes: Falmer Press.

Whyte, J. (1986) *Girls Into Science and Technology*, London: Routledge & Kegan Paul.

Willis, P. (1977) *Learning to Labour*, Farnborough, Saxon House.

Woods, P. (1989) 'Opportunities to learn and teach: an interdisciplinary model', *International Journal of Educational Research* 13(6): 597–606.

Woods, P. (1990) *Teacher Skills and Strategies*, Lewes: Falmer Press.

Woods, P. and Pollard, A. (eds) (1988) *Sociology and Teaching*, London: Croom Helm.

18 Children's grasp of controversial issues

Geoffrey Short
Source: B. Carrington and B. Troyna (eds) 1988 *Children and Controversial Issues*, Lewes: Falmer Press, ch. 2.

'PRIMARY IDEOLOGY' AND THE CURRICULUM

Various commentators in recent years have drawn attention to the neglect of controversial issues in the primary curriculum. Ross (1984: 131), for instance, believes 'it would be fair to say that most primary teachers have never considered politically educating their children' and adds that 'politics is something that teachers [of young children] wish to avoid'. Harwood (1985: 12) apparently concurs with this view, for when reflecting on his experience of in-service courses he also noted 'a fairly general resistance to the idea of political education amongst primary [and] middle school teachers'.

There are, no doubt, a number of reasons for staff in the primary sector steering clear of contentious material. According to Harwood (1985: 12) the resistance stems partly from 'teachers' [lack of] confidence in their ability to handle political education and [their uncertainty] about the nature of its objectives'. Explanations have also been sought in the *alleged* prevalence among teachers in infant and junior schools of what Robin Alexander (1984) has dubbed 'the primary ideology'. This is a form of pedagogic folklore which, *inter alia*, views childhood as an age of innocence and recognizes that infants in particular, while capable of unacceptable behaviour, remain free from malicious intent. In marked contrast to the doctrine of original sin, evil is assumed to reside in a world beyond childhood and thus teachers (together presumably with other adults) have a responsibility to protect the young from a harsh and corrupt reality. The acceptance by infant teachers of children's moral purity was commented upon by King (1978) in his observational study of three schools. Among the incidents he reported was that of a class teacher who had reinforced a 6-year-old's faith in fairies offering financial compensation for lost teeth. The teacher later remarked to King (1978: 13): 'it's not up to me to destroy his innocence'. On another occasion staff were found removing infirm guinea pigs from the classroom, partly 'to prevent their deaths being witnessed by the children (1978: 14). Now if observations such as these are typical of infant teachers it is hardly surprising that they eschew any form of political education in which conflict and controversy are the principal elements. Junior school teachers might be expected to show rather less concern with protecting the naive innocence of their pupils, but they too appear to draw the line at controversial issues (Ross 1984).

Despite the paucity of empirical evidence (Desforges 1986), Alexander may well be correct in pointing to a second facet of primary ideology as a major constraint on the teaching of contentious subject matter to young children. I refer to the notion of 'sequential developmentalism' defined by Alexander as

> the idea that the child passes through a naturally ordered sequence of physiological, psychological and social development where . . . the rate of development will vary from child to child [but] the sequence and stages will be the same. Linked with developmentalism [is] the notion of 'readiness' particularly in relation to reading – the idea that children's capacity to cope with specific sorts of learning is determined by the developmental stage they have reached.
>
> (Alexander 1984: 22)

The theoretical roots of both developmentalism and readiness are, of course, linked most often with the name of Jean Piaget. It is he who has provided the best known (though certainly not the only) description of cognitive development as a series of discrete stages, each defined in terms of a specific cognitive structure (or unique way of understanding the world), and associated with an approximate age range. According to his account, most children under the age of 7 or so are incapable of logical thought, for they tend to be seduced by appearances and thus cannot conserve; nor can they regard experience from any point of view except their own – clearly an obstacle to the reversibility of thought required for logical reasoning. During the junior school years, however, Piaget believes that the average child develops an ability to reverse actions mentally, though only in so far as they refer to 'concrete' situations. At this juncture too, most children manage to focus their thought on more than one aspect of a situation simultaneously and are thus in a position to relate ideas to one another. Finally, Piaget claimed that it is not until the secondary stage of schooling that children can normally think in the abstract and so discuss political and other concepts without having recourse to their own experience.

While our understanding of children's progression towards logical thought has obvious relevance for the teaching of mathematics and the natural sciences, our understanding of how children of different ages think about morality has particular relevance for the teaching of controversial issues. Here too Piaget has been active and in 1932 published a monograph mapping the developmental milestones *en route* to adult conceptions of morality. He claimed that children below the age of 6 or 7 tend to subscribe to a heteronomous way of thinking in which rules are regarded as sacrosanct and punishment is thought to follow inevitably upon their contravention. In addition, ethical judgements are generally based on consequences rather than intentions. Children at junior school, in contrast, are more likely to adhere to an autonomous morality where rules are seen as arbitrary, the acceptance of immanent justice is less in evidence and intention assumes a more prominent role in moral judgement.

If primary teachers accept Piaget's views on children's cognitive limitations, it follows, *ceteris paribus*, that they will oppose all exhortations to stretch, or test the limits of, their pupils' intellectual competence. Circumstantial evidence in support of this speculation focuses on the extent of under-expectation alleged to exist in primary schools (e.g. Nash 1976; Sharp and Green 1975); a charge which has prompted Alexander (1984: 24) to link under-expectation with an exaggerated commitment to sequential developmentalism. By way of illustration, he cites the following extract from the NUT's response to HMI's (1978) Primary Survey:

> The Union would not agree with [HMI's] analysis of what is suitable in the teaching of history to young children; the passage of time is a very difficult concept for children of this age to grasp.
>
> (NUT 1979: 25)

In so far as political education is thought to demand a high level of abstract thought, teachers influenced by Piaget are unlikely to consider it a suitable subject for the primary curriculum. Probing the young child's grasp of controversial issues might be expected to prove particularly unremunerative since the skills required to appreciate a range of arguments and to evaluate conflicting evidence are normally assumed within Piagetian theory to be unavailable prior to adolescence.

LEARNING ABOUT SOCIETY: THE CASE FOR SEQUENTIAL DEVELOPMENT

Regardless of whether primary ideology is as widespread as Alexander believes, it would appear that until comparatively recently, developmental psychologists and educationists have offered primary teachers little encouragement to challenge the fundamental validity of Piaget's conclusions. On the contrary, the stress that Piaget placed on the young child's limited intellectual grasp has been extended (in the form of various stage analyses) to areas that Piaget himself never considered. Selman (1980), for instance, has proposed five stages, or levels, in children's social-perspective taking, an intellectual function with obvious implications for political education. He maintains that children below the age of approximately 6 adopt an egocentric viewpoint in that they fail to distinguish their own interpretation of an event from what they consider to be true. Between the ages of 6 and 8 they become aware that others may have a different perspective and over the next two years learn that individuals can know about other people's thoughts and feelings. These early stages are then followed by a period of 'mutual role-taking' when children, usually aged between 10 and 12, develop the ability to view an interaction from the standpoint of a third person such as a parent or mutual friend. It is only when children are at secondary school that they finally come to terms with the full complexity of human behaviour and acknowledge, for example, the impact of genetics, social class and other forces over which the individual has no control.

Other theorists whose work reflects Piaget's ideas on the growth of understanding include Damon (1977), who studied children's changing notions of authority, and Livesley and Bromley (1973), who did likewise in respect of person perception. The best known extension of Piaget's own work has been provided by Kohlberg (1958 *et seq.*). He charted the course of moral development well beyond childhood but retained Piaget's emphasis on the core concepts of stage and sequence.

Researchers with a more direct interest in children's political literacy have sometimes nailed their theoretical colours to Piaget's mast (in the sense of prospecting for stages) and, in the process, may unwittingly have reinforced conventional beliefs concerning the 'right' age to teach politics. Leahy's (1983) study of how children understand social class is a case in point. In anticipating the nature of his data, he wrote:

Cognitive-developmental theory suggests that the ordering of societal conceptions will be similar to the ordering of other kinds of social cognition, such as moral judgment, person descriptions and attributions for achievement. This is based on the idea that intelligence is *organised* – that is, common structures will be applied to a variety of contents.

(Leahy 1983)

Essentially the same point is made by Furth (1979). He asserts that

Piagetian research and theory has been severely limited by an almost exclusive emphasis on strictly logical-mathematical thinking. If the theory is to be maximally useful, it is necessary to apply it to other areas.

(Furth 1979: 233)

In a manner fully consonant with Piagetian theory, Furth examined the way that children aged between 5 and 11 understand money, societal roles and the concepts of community and government. In reviewing the cognate literature, he highlighted studies of national and ethnic identity (Jahoda 1963; Hartley *et al.* 1948) which, *prima facie*, confirm the young child's lack of political sophistication. Jahoda's subjects were aged between 6 and 11 and came from both working- and middle-class schools in Glasgow. They were initially asked questions such as 'Where is Glasgow?' 'Where is Scotland?' 'What is Scotland?' and 'What is Britain?' Jahoda analysed and classified the children's responses in terms of a four-stage sequence. The first (and least mature) is characterized by a notion of Glasgow as 'some kind of vague entity' close to the children's actual geographical location. According to one 6-year-old: 'It's up by the park there – you go round the corner'. At this stage, the children's concept of Scotland is also somewhat nebulous. A 7-year-old said it was a street and when asked if there was a place called Scotland, added: 'Yes, Scotland the Brave, it's up in the Highlands'. Another 7-year-old claimed that 'Scotland is the capital of Edinburgh. It's in Glasgow'.

The majority of children at this point could say nothing at all about Britain, and although Jahoda's second stage is distinguished principally by the realization that Glasgow refers in some way to the immediate vicinity, the idea of a country remains ill-defined. One 7-year-old said of Britain: 'It's a city in England' and a 9-year-old thought it 'a city in Scotland'. Superficially children begin to understand the concept of a country during stage three. They possess the appropriate vocabulary but Jahoda believes it amounts to little more than empty rhetoric. He cites an 11-year-old as saying: 'Britain is a lot of different countries ... Glasgow, London, France'. The most advanced level of comprehension (stage four) is marked by an awareness of Britain as a composite unity. In the words of a 6-year-old: 'Glasgow is in Scotland. Scotland is a country in Great Britain. Britain is some countries joined together'. (This final stage was reached by the vast majority of children from middle-class schools but by less than half of those from working-class schools.) When asked if it was possible to be both Scottish and British, a number of children who replied affirmatively could not provide an adequate justification. Those who denied the possibility often confused language with nationality, a 9-year-old saying 'You can't talk Scottish and British at the same time'.

The struggle that many primary children apparently face in grasping the concept of nationality has also been observed in respect of ethnicity. In one of the earliest studies in the area, Hartley *et al.* (1948) examined children's perceptions of ethnic group membership and were particularly interested in 'the role of being Jewish in America'. Once the children (aged between 3½ and 10½) had identified themselves as either Jewish or American in response to the question 'What are you?' they were asked, 'What does Jewish mean?' and 'What does American mean?' Responses to the definition of Jewishness included the following: 'It means Jewish people. God makes them. The whole world is Jewish' (age 6:6). 'Jewish is people who don't go to church' (7:11). 'Jewish is a religion just like Christian. You go to Hebrew [school] . . . It means to believe in these things, to respect your parents. You shouldn't steal' (10:5). With reference to their understanding of the term 'American': 'I was an American when I had my gun, but when they took my gun away, I wasn't any more' (4:0). 'God makes us Jewish or American which is both the same, just that some people talk American instead of Jewish' (7:1). 'A nationality. A nation you come from. If you are a citizen born in America, you are American' (9:10). Hartley *et al.* summarize their data by suggesting that

> Younger children, who characteristically define their life-space concretely in terms of activities, describe ethnic terms comparably. Older children are mentally mature enough to attempt the use of abstractions.
>
> (Harley *et al.* 1948: 389)

Thus far, I have tried to show how Piaget and some of his apostles have *indirectly* bolstered, or at least done nothing to undermine, primary teachers' reluctance to broach controversial issues with their pupils. Other researchers, in contrast, have quite openly related their findings to the classroom and, in particular, to the teaching of social studies. Hallam (1969), for example, has discussed the secondary school history syllabus from the standpoint of Piaget's theory. He seems chiefly concerned to demonstrate that if 'material is too advanced for the children they will either assimilate it without understanding, or will reject it with possible damage to their whole attitude to the subject' (1969: 6). To obviate this possibility, he recommends that

> history taught in the early years of secondary school should not be over-abstract in form, nor should it contain too many variables . . . Used wisely, topics . . . can be arranged so that the younger children learn the less detailed history of early times, while the history of recent years, which contains important yet complex topics, can then be taught when the pupils are able to reason at a more mature level.
>
> (Hallam 1969: 4)

While the research of Jahoda and Hartley *et al.* and the evidence adduced by Hallam in support of his prescriptions may be perfectly valid, the inferences drawn from these and related studies have been both misleading and damaging. For, if children are unable to cope with a given task administered under specific conditions, it cannot, *a priori*, be assumed that they will encounter similar difficulties in an experimental or pedagogic setting that departs, however slightly, from the original. It is the failure to appreciate the extent to which data generated in one context *cannot* generalize to others that has been responsible, at least to some degree, for the persistent belief in children's limited grasp of controversial issues. I turn now to consider the legitimacy of this belief in the light of recent critiques of Piaget's work.

DETHRONING PIAGET

Although criticism of Piaget's ideas stretch back more than half a century (e.g. Isaacs 1930), it is only during the last couple of decades or so that his continued pre-eminence as an authority on cognitive development has been seriously threatened. Essentially he stands indicted for reading too much into his own experiments and hence failing to realize that alternative procedures could yield very different results. Donaldson (1978) points out that some of Piaget's studies made no human sense to the children involved, for they dealt with subject matter which was unfamiliar and largely meaningless. In relation to egocentricity, her own work has indicated that, contrary to Piaget's conclusions, young children, *under certain circumstances*, can envisage situations from a point of view other than their own. Thus, as

Gelman (1978: 319) states: 'It no longer seems appropriate to characterise the thought of pre-schoolers as egocentric'. Some researchers such as Bryant (1974) have also claimed that particular intellectual skills may be present at an earlier age than Piaget suggested. They reached this decision having shown that Piaget devised experiments which either tested memory rather than logic or led the child to assume that logical reasoning was not required.

Although other major criticisms can be levelled at Piaget's work (such as whether or not stages of development actually exist), it is his underestimation of children's cognitive abilities that is critical as far as the introduction of controversial issues to the primary classroom is concerned. As a result of recent research focusing on a range of issues previously unexplored, or treated very differently, the reigning orthodoxy now recognizes young children as less naive politically than has traditionally been assumed. An example of this recent research is provided by Stevens (1982) who studied the political consciousness of eight hundred 7- to 11-year-olds in the South of England. She interviewed some of the children directly and administered a questionnaire to the rest. Of her discussion with a couple of 7-year-olds she wrote

> the little girls found no difficulty in joining in a political discussion. At ease and interested, they were able to show some awareness of highly complex issues, for example, of the limitations of power, of government by consent of the governed and the . . . notion of accountability.
>
> (Stevens 1982: 32)

She concluded that

> Seven year olds can be seen to have some cognitive contact with the political world [encompassing] political information, awareness and not least, interest. What comes across most strongly is the sense the children seemed to have of political power being limited, consented to and conditional upon results.
>
> (Stevens 1982: 38)

Stevens found that concepts of democracy, leadership and accountability of government were accessible to 9-year-olds. She also found that some children of this age were able to consider alternative social and political arrangements and to justify them in terms of principles. As this ability is usually associated with the stage of formal operations, Stevens asks whether, in relation to social or political understanding, the stages either contract to some degree or overlap more than in other areas. Piaget, of course, attached far greater importance to the invariant sequence of development than to the average age of children at particular stages within the sequence and, to this extent, Stevens's findings cannot be seen as contradictory. Her work does, however, add further weight to the view that children may generally be more *au fait* with their socio-political environment than has traditionally been acknowledged. To emphasize the point, she noted that by the age of 11 children were able to

[link] politics not only with roles, structures and policies, but with topics such as conservation, women's rights and an economic re-organisation of the country.

(Stevens 1982: 150)

When one considers the content of popular children's fiction, the evidence of political consciousness amongst 7- to 11-year-olds becomes all the more convincing. Juvenile comics, for example, not only deal regularly with questions of authority, hierarchy, social class and wealth, but as Dixon (1977) and others (e.g. Carrington and Short 1984) have revealed, they promote racism, sexism and xenophobia as both natural and acceptable. Dixon (1977: 50) asserts that 'name-calling . . . national stereotyping [and] hatred of foreigners . . . is found nowhere so much as in comics published in the United States and Britain'. While not suggesting that this form of literature is the sole, or even the most potent, source of aggressive nationalism in children, it is worth noting that Johnson (1966) has uncovered a positive correlation between the reading of certain comics and feelings of antagonism towards some of Britain's erstwhile enemies.

The socio-economic attitudes that comics purvey have also come in for critical scrutiny. Referring to stories where 'myths and illusions . . . blur the real issues', Dixon notes the prevalence of

charity, which oils the wheels of the system and . . . alleviates . . . the distress of the poor and the guilt of the rich; the 'ladder' concept of society, which holds out the hope that . . . anyone can succeed [and] moral virtue which the unfortunate and the unsuccessful usually have.

(Dixon 1977: 32)

Although Stevens has shown clearly that children at primary schools are politically informed, the full significance of her study will not be appreciated unless it is considered in conjunction with recent criticisms of Piaget's research. In this respect, the likely impact of McNaugh-ton's (1982) contribution to the debate surrounding the place of controversial issues in the primary curriculum is to be regretted. For while recognizing the constraints implicit in the notion of stage, he seems either to be unfamiliar with the findings that now contradict much of Piaget's work, or has chosen to ignore them. He argues that

> If the teacher . . . believe[s] that no student should be involved in formal political studies until s/he is able to cope with abstract ideas and with arguments that cohere on principles then they would be well advised . . . to put formal political studies off until the fourth year [of secondary education]. Whereas if they are prepared to be satisfied with sensible discussions about political . . . matters that concern and involve students in . . . institutions to which they belong . . . then they could probably start them on political studies during primary schooling.
>
> (McNaughton 1982: 273)

While McNaughton should be commended for stressing the young child's political awareness, and for advising teachers to capitalize on it, his recommendation surely has negative implications for the teaching of controversial issues. For the latter may well *not* be categorized as 'political and social matters that concern and involve students in the groups and institutions to which they belong'. Racism and sexism are cases in point. Would McNaughton argue that children who attend an 'all-white' or single sex primary school are incapable of benefiting from teaching about race and gender respectively? The evidence, in the form of children's knowledge of these issues, suggests otherwise.

CHILDREN AND RACE

That very young children are racially aware in the sense of being able to distinguish black people from white will clearly surprise no one (Laishley 1971; Marsh 1970). However, the fact that 3- and 4-year-olds can express genuinely hostile racial attitudes is, perhaps, rather less obvious, certainly as far as infant teachers committed to childhood innocence are concerned. The earliest reported indications of racism in pre-schoolers were noted by Horowitz (1936). He found

> The development of prejudice against Negroes begins very, very early in the life of the ordinary child . . . boys, barely over five years of age, demonstrated a preference for whites. . . . Some few attempts at testing special cases at three and four years of age elicited such comments as (from a three year old) 'I don't like black boys' and (from a four year old) 'I don't like coloured boys'.
>
> (Horowitz 1936: 117–18)

The British study that arguably offers the closest parallel to Horowitz's findings was conducted by Jeffcoate (1977) in a Bradford
nursery school. It was undertaken in order to draw teachers' attention
to the specious nature of the widespread and 'commonsensical' view
that, during their time at primary school, children are incapable of
displaying animosity towards individuals *qua* members of a racial or
ethnic group. Jeffcoate exploded the myth by showing that 4-year-olds
not only can discriminate racial differences but also can express
racially abusive remarks. When the children were initially asked by
their teacher to discuss pictures portraying black people in a 'variety of
situations and in a respectful and unstereotyped way', the children's
responses could not possibly be construed as racially offensive.
However, when the same set of pictures were left 'casually' around the
room (but in locations close to concealed tape recorders), the
comments made by the children, in the assumed absence of an adult
audience, were undeniably racist in tenor. Although this study confirmed the results of previous research into the early onset of anti-
black sentiment in white children, it is, perhaps, more important in
showing that, even at the nursery stage, children are cognizant of the
socially unacceptable nature of these feelings and of the need to
conceal them in the presence of adult authority.

At this very young age, children's knowledge of race is probably
restricted to a vague intuition that some racial groups should be
disparaged. As Allport puts it (1954: 307), the child 'is stumbling at the
threshold of some abstraction, aware that a particular group is
somehow hateworthy but unable to associate the emotion with the
referent'. Children of junior school age have no such problem. In
Trager and Yarrow's (1952) research with 7- to 9-year-olds, it was
found that

> concepts and feelings about race frequently include adult distinc-
> tions of status, ability, character, occupation and economic
> circumstances. . . . Among the older children stereotyping and
> expressions of hostility are more frequent.
>
> (Quoted in Milner 1983: 111)

In the doll and picture tests used by Trager and Yarrow, the children
allocated poor housing and menial employment to black people and
generally superior environments to whites.

Not only do children at the upper end of the primary age range
possess a sophisticated understanding of individual and structural
racism but also, as Bruce Carrington and I have recently demonstrated

(Short and Carrington 1987), this understanding is available to children living in an 'all-white' environment who, under normal circumstances, may not construe the world in racial terms. Our case study of anti-racist teaching with a class of top juniors was partly concerned with the children's untutored knowledge of racism. Among the tasks we set the class was to imagine that they had recently entered Britain from either the West Indies or the Indian sub-continent and were writing a letter home to a close relative or good friend who was planning to join them. The class discussion that preceded the writing was intended to excavate the ideas which the children already possessed, no attempt at this stage being made either to refine them or to suggest more plausible alternatives. In their 'letters' the children referred to manifestations of racial violence, racist name-calling and discriminatory practices in housing and work. The following extracts are typical of the children's response:

John: . . . us Black people get beat up as soon as we get off the ship. Would you fancy having to take your luggage everywhere by yourself while people just look and laugh at you as you go from house to house trying to get a place to spend the night? Just guess what their reply was after me begging for a bed. It was 'Sorry, it's been took' or just a simple 'No, get lost. We don't give rooms to niggers like you'. In the end, when you get a house, they throw you out just because you were not used to their terrible food that they call pasties. And what about the jobs you said were very good for someone like me? Oh, I got a job alright. It was a dishwasher in a rotten old fish and chip shop where the dishes must have been at least twenty years old. Then I got kicked out for dropping an old chipped plate by accident.

Clare: . . . I never thought it would be like this as we all get on so well back in India. I advise you to stay at home and forget about Britain. The other day I decided to start looking for a job. As you know, I have plenty of skills. I thought even if nobody likes me I'll be sure to get a good decent job but I was wrong. Instead, I got an awful job cleaning toilets. Over here, that's all they seem to think we're good for. Anyway, I started this job today. It was horrible, people pushing you around. One person even flushed my head down the toilet. I wish I never brought Julian, our son, to school. All he ever does is get picked on. He came home the other day covered with bruises and cuts. I am having second thoughts about staying here. Most people are prejudiced.

(Short and Carrington 1987: 227)

Despite occasional strains on the credulity ('get beat up as soon as we get off the ship') these imaginative accounts provide unequivocal evidence of the children's awareness of racism in its various guises. John's allusion to food is of particular interest in that it shows how some children of this age are able to grasp the relationship of racism to ethnocentrism. Clare's 'letter' is noteworthy in that it demonstrates some cognizance of stereotyping ('that's all they seem to think we're good for'), a concept which had not been mentioned in the previous class discussion. It is also of interest because it refers directly to the gulf between the expectation and the reality of immigrant life in Britain.

CHILDREN'S UNDERSTANDING OF GENDER AND SEX ROLE STEREOTYPES

Among the many similarities in the development of children's understanding of race and gender is the age at which identification of self and others is made in terms of the two categories (i.e. male or female, black or white). For the majority of children this milestone is reached by the age of 3 although the foundations of racial awareness and concepts probably develop somewhat later and are more variable (Katz 1983).

A further similarity concerns the acquisition of stereotypes. Those relating to sex roles have been studied in a variety of ways including direct questioning. Kuhn *et al.* (1978), for instance, read statements such as 'I'm strong' and 'When I grow up I'll fly an airplane', to a group of 2- to 3-year-olds. The children were then required to select the doll (Lisa or Michael) most likely to have made the statement. The results not only revealed a high level of agreement with adult stereotypes, but also showed that the children thought positively about their own sex and negatively about the other.

There seems to be little doubt that by the age of 5 most children make few 'errors' in assigning sex stereotyped labels to activities, occupations and playthings (Katz 1983). The learning of sex-typed traits, however, appears to develop rather later. Best and his colleagues (1977) illustrated this developmental progression by asking 5-, 8- and 11-year-olds whether particular attributes were more often associated with a male or female silhouette. They found that less than a quarter of their 5-year-olds responded above a chance level as compared with nearly three-quarters of the 8-year-olds and virtually all the 11-year-olds. The traits that children found easiest to differentiate by sex (such as aggression) were those having a relatively familiar concrete referent.

Studies which permit a 'both' or 'neither' response to stereotyped statements (e.g. Marantz and Mansfield 1977) generally show an increase in flexibility with age. Damon's (1977) research, though, suggests that the relationship may, in fact, be curvilinear. His sample comprised children aged between 4 and 9. After reading them a story about a little boy (George) who wished to play with dolls despite his parents' protestations, he asked the children a number of questions. These included 'Why do people tell George not to play with dolls? Are they right? Is there a rule that boys shouldn't play with dolls?' The 4-year-olds in this study thought it quite legitimate for George to play with dolls if he wanted. In contrast, the 6-year-olds thought it quite wrong. At this stage, what boys and girls *tend* to do is synonymous with what they *ought* to do. The oldest children were able to recognize sex roles as a social convention and could distinguish the latter from both laws and social values. One of the 9-year-olds said: 'Breaking windows you're not supposed to do. And if you [boys] play with dolls, well you can, but boys usually don't' (Damon 1977: 263).

This brief and selective review of the literature on children's understanding of race and gender lends powerful support to the Swann Committee's (DES 1985) recommendations on political education.

> Some educationists have argued that school pupils are insufficiently mature and responsible to be able to comprehend politically sensitive issues . . and to cope with them in a balanced and rational manner. Even primary-aged pupils however have views and opinions on various 'political' issues. . . . We believe that schools have a clear responsibility to provide accurate factual information and opportunities for balanced and sensitive consideration of political issues in order to enable pupils to reflect upon and sometimes reconsider their political opinions within a broader context.
>
> (DES 1985: 336–7)

PIAGET, THE TEACHER AND CONTROVERSIAL ISSUES

It seems to be generally agreed that Piaget had relatively little interest in formal education. Bryant (1984: 252), for instance, contends that 'Piaget . . . thought teachers played an insignificant role in children's cognitive development'. In particular, he seemed to lack interest in what he disparagingly referred to as the 'American question', that is the extent to which a child's progression through the stages can be accelerated. Piaget thought that the rate of progress could be hastened but only within narrows limits and some research findings support this conclusion. Evaluating the literature on the stage of concrete operations, Gardner (1982) has written:

> In Piaget's view, concrete operations must develop naturally, over time, as a consequence of direct actions on objects. Attempts to train a child in an operation cannot succeed until the child is just about ready to develop that capacity and by that time training is hardly necessary.
>
> (Gardner 1982: 403)

The same point has been made rather more pithily by Phillips (1975) in the form of the following syllogism: 'If a child is not ready to change, no teacher can help him; if he is ready, the change will occur without intervention; therefore, intervention is superfluous'.

If primary teachers accept Piaget's explicit reservations regarding the value of formal instruction, the likelihood of them exploring their pupils' capacity to understand controversial issues is bound to diminish. However, other psychologists, most notably Vygotsky (1956) and Bruner (1960), have argued forcefully, and contrary to Piaget, that the teacher's role in fostering cognitive development is crucial. Vygotsky views intellectual potential, not as some innate physiological property, but rather as a quality created in the process of upbringing and education. He distinguishes between children's existing and potential levels of development, the former defined by what they can do without adult assistance, the latter by what they can do with it. Vygotsky refers to the gap between these two levels as the zone of next development. In Sutton's words (1983: 196), it 'indicates what the child is ready to master next on the basis of present achievements, given the best possible adult attention'.

The optimistic implications of Vygotsky's work reinforce Bruner's (1960: 33) well-known dictum that 'any subject can be taught to any child of any age in an honest way'. He explains

> Research on the intellectual development of the child highlights the fact that at each stage of development the child has a characteristic way of viewing the world and explaining it to himself. The task of teaching a subject to a child at any particular age is one of

representing the structure of that subject in terms of the child's way of viewing things.

(Bruner 1960: 33)

Exactly the same argument had, in fact, been advanced some years earlier by Allport (1954). In advocating what we would describe as an anti-racist initiative, he stated

> The age at which these lessons should be taught need not worry us. If taught in a simple fashion all the points can be made intelligible to younger children and, in a more fully developed way, they can be presented to older students. . . . In fact . . . through 'graded lessons' the same content can, and should, be offered year after year.
>
> (Allport 1954: 511)

Although Bruner has argued convincingly for this sort of spiral curriculum, the proof of his theoretical pudding, so far as teaching controversial issues is concerned, will, of course, lie in the eating. From the standpoint of anti-racist education, the prospects are encouraging (e.g. Short and Carrington 1987), for children at opposite ends of the primary age range seem able to cope, in their own way, with its demands. However, the full extent to which young children at school can understand and benefit from a study of controversial issues will be known only when their teachers acquire an immunity to ideological and other constraints and begin to find out for themselves.

REFERENCES

Alexander, R.J. (1984) *Primary Teaching*, London: Holt, Rinehart & Winston.

Allport, G.W. (1954) *The Nature of Prejudice*, Reading, Mass.: Addison-Wesley.

Best, D.L., Williams, J.E., Cloud, J.M., Davis, S.W., Robertson, L.S., Edwards, J.R., Giles, H. and Fowles, J. (1977) 'Development of sex-trait stereotypes among young children in the United States, England and Ireland', *Child Development* 48: 1375–84.

Bruner, J. (1960) *The Process of Education*, New York: Vintage Books.

Bryant, P. (1974) *Perception and Understanding in Young Children*, London: Methuen.

Bryant, P. (1984) 'Piaget, teachers and psychologists', *Oxford Review of Education* 10(3): 251–9.

Carrington, B. and Short, G. (1984) 'Comics – a medium for racism', *English in Education* 18(2): 10–14.

Damon, W. (1977) *The Social World of the Child*, San Francisco, Calif.: Jossey-Bass.

DES (1985) *Education for All: Report of the Committee of Inquiry into the*

Education of Children from Ethnic Minority Groups (Swann Report) Cmnd 9453, London: HMSO.

Desforges, C. (1986) 'Developmental psychology applied to teacher training', in *Child Psychology in Action*, London: Croom Helm.

Dixon, B. (1977) *Catching Them Young 2: Political Ideas in Children's Fiction*, London: Pluto Press.

Donaldson, M. (1978) *Children's Minds*, Glasgow: Fontana/Collins.

Furth, H.G. (1979) 'Young children's understanding of society', in H. McGurk (ed.) *Issues in Childhood Social Development*, London: Methuen.

Gardner, H. (1982) *Developmental Psychology*, Boston, Mass.: Little, Brown.

Gelman, R. (1978) Cognitive development', *Annual Review of Psychology* 29: 297–332.

Hallam, R. (1969) 'Piaget and the teaching of history', *Educational Research* 12: 3–12.

Hartley, E.L., Rosenbaum, M. and Schwartz, S. (1948) 'Children's perception of ethnic group membership', *Journal of Psychology* 26: 387–97.

Harwood, D. (1985) 'We need political not Political education for 5–13 year olds', *Education 3–13*, 13(1): 12–17.

HMI (DES) (1978) *Primary Education in England: A Survey by HM Inspectors of Schools*, London: HMSO.

Horowitz, E.L. (1936) 'Development of attitudes towards negroes,' in H. Proschansky and B. Seidenberg (eds) (1965) *Basic Studies in Social Psychology*, New York: Holt, Rinehart & Winston.

Isaacs, S. (1930) *Intellectual Growth in Young Children*, London: Routledge & Kegan Paul.

Jahoda, G. (1963) 'The development of children's ideas about country and nationality. Part 1: The conceptual framework', *British Journal of Educational Psychology* 33: 47–60.

Jeffcoate, R. (1977) 'Children's racial ideas and feelings', *English in Education* 11(1): 32–46.

Johnson, N. (1966) 'What do children learn from war comics?', *New Society* 7 July: 7–12.

Katz, P.A. (1983) 'Developmental foundations of gender and racial attitudes', in R.L. Leahy (ed.) *The Child's Construction of Social Inequality*, New York: Academic Press.

King, R. (1978) *All Things Bright and Beautiful? A Sociological Study of Infants' Classrooms*, Chichester: Wiley.

Kohlberg, L. (1958) 'The development of modes of moral thinking and choice in the years ten to sixteen', unpublished PhD thesis, University of Chicago.

Kuhn, D., Nash, S.C. and Brucken, L. (1978) 'Sex role concepts of two- and three-year-olds', *Child Development* 49: 445–51.

Laishley, J. (1971) 'Skin colour awareness and preference in London nursery-school children', *Race* 13(1): 47–64.

Leahy, R.L. (1983) 'The development of the conception of social class', in R.L. Leahy (ed.) *The Child's Construction of Social Inequality*, New

York: Academic Press.

Livesley, W. and Bromley, D. (1973) *Person Perception in Childhood and Adolescence*, London: Wiley.

McNaughton, A.H. (1982) 'Cognitive development, political understanding and political literacy', *British Journal of Educational Studies* 30(3): 264–79.

Marantz, S.A. and Mansfield, A.F. (1977) 'Maternal employment and the development of sex-role stereotyping in five- to eleven-year-old girls', *Child Development* 48: 668–73.

Marsh, A. (1970) 'Awareness of racial differences in West African and British children', *Race* 11: 289–302.

Milner, D. (1983) *Children and Race: Ten Years On*, London: Ward Lock.

Nash, R. (1976) *Teacher Expectations and Pupil Learning*, London: Routledge & Kegan Paul.

NUT (National Union of Teachers) (1979) *Primary Questions: The NUT Response to the Primary Survey*, London: NUT.

Phillips, J. (1975) *The Origins of Intellect: Piaget's Theory*, New York: W.H. Freeman.

Piaget, J. (1932) *The Moral Judgement of the Child*, London: Routledge & Kegan Paul.

Ross, A. (1984) 'Developing political concepts and skills in the primary school', *Educational Review* 36(2): 131–9.

Selman, R.L. (1980) *The Growth of Interpersonal Understanding*, New York: Academic Press.

Sharp, R. and Green, A. (1975) *Education and Social Control: A Study in Progressive Primary Education*, London: Routledge & Kegan Paul.

Short, G. and Carrington, B. (1987) 'Towards an anti-racist initiative in the all white primary school', in A. Pollard (ed.) *Children and their Primary Schools: A New Perspective*, Lewes: Falmer Press.

Stevens, O. (1982) *Children Talking Politics: Political Learning in Childhood*, Oxford: Martin Robertson.

Sutton, A. (1983) 'An introduction to Soviet developmental psychology', in S. Meadows (ed.) *Developing Thinking*, London: Methuen.

Trager, H. and Yarrow, M. (1952) *They Learn What They Live*, New York: Harper & Row.

Vygotsky, L. (1956) *Selected Psychological Research*, Moscow: Academy of Pedagogic Sciences of USSR.

Name index

Subject index